THE FOURTH WORLD

Rhodesia

Camera Press

The Fourth World

Victims of Group Oppression

EIGHT REPORTS FROM THE FIELD WORK OF
THE MINORITY RIGHTS GROUP

edited by
Ben Whitaker

One law for the lion and the ox is oppression
William Blake

SCHOCKEN BOOKS · NEW YORK

From the Universal Declaration of Human Rights, adopted by the General Assembly of the United Nations on 10 December 1948:

Article 1
All human beings are born free and equal in dignity and rights. They are endowed with reason and conscience and should act towards one another in a spirit of brotherhood.

Article 2
Everyone is entitled to all the rights and freedoms set forth in this Declaration, without distinction of any kind, such as race, colour, sex, language, religion, political or other opinion, national or social origin, property, birth or other status . . .

CONTENTS

Preface by Ben Whitaker

The Measure of Humanity by Milovan Djilas

What Do We Mean By Rights? by Philip Mason

56250

PREFACE

by Ben Whitaker

Gandhi declared that civilization is to be judged by its treatment of minorities. Prejudiced behaviour in the world today against groups who are vulnerable by reason of their numbers or status, of which this book describes various examples, can result in threats to peace as well as large-scale suffering. And anti-semitism, apartheid and Northern Ireland's trauma remind us that such denials of human dignity and rights are just as capable of occurring in allegedly developed societies.

The Minority Rights Group was recently formed to try to fill the need – particularly since minorities as yet have no forum at the United Nations – for an independent and international non-governmental body to work in this field. Although registered as a Trust in London where it has its headquarters, its scope is world wide. M.R.G. has two main objects. First, by investigating and publishing facts such as are contained in its reports in this book, it aims to help the position of persecuted or disadvantaged ethnic, religious or cultural minorities (or majorities) in any country. Secondly, by its work it hopes to develop an international conscience with regard to minorities' treatment and human rights, and – as and when funds permit – by its research to increase knowledge about the factors which create such tensions and prejudices.

It is a pre-requisite for the success of any such effort that it should remain accurate and politically neutral. Although M.R.G. has no formal membership, its supporters include people of almost every nationality, race, religion and political view. M.R.G.

9

is concerned with the problems, not the politics. In its investigations and reports, M.R.G. attempts to keep a world balance,
and also to include and draw attention to some of the less well
known groups' predicaments. (Not many other minorities have
the effective lobby that Soviet Jewry has.) We try to avoid the
embrace of the C.I.A., M.I.5 or the K.G.B.; several of the
great powers infiltrate dissident minorities within the territories
of governments they dislike – though their support, most often,
is the kiss of death.

M.R.G.'s work operates on the theory that an informed world
opinion forms the only real safeguard for human rights. However
idealistically one may draft international charters or laws, in
the long term their effectiveness is going to depend on the concern
of the public and the press to see that they are implemented. The
first crime of Northern Ireland was that it was not until the
violence began that people outside paid any attention to the
discrimination there. It is encouraging that – as Amnesty International has found – even some recalcitrant dictatorships,
prompted perhaps by the spread of television and tourism, show
themselves increasingly sensitive to criticism. In fact, the oppression by a majority in a democracy can be a more intractable
problem than persecution by a tyrant, since at least the death
of the latter can hold out a hope of relief.

Some minorities are far from faultless (liberals tend to forget
that people do not become virtuous merely by reason of their
predicament); and of course majorities too have their rights as
well as their responsibilities. One of the most interesting questions
raised by group stigmatization is why some minorities are seen as
a threat or a scapegoat while others are tolerated. Psychologists at
Bristol University have found evidence that people, as soon as they
are divided into groups, automatically begin to discriminate
against outsiders. Many species besides humans fear and attack
non-conformity; indeed it has been argued that all people need a
pecking-order and a group to look down upon – until in turn they
are united by a new enemy. Perhaps it is in order to avoid
facing up to the less pleasant parts of ourselves, or through failure
to realize the real roots of our frustration, that we project our
aggression and fear on to other safer targets – of whom visibly
distinct groups, such as immigrants, women or policemen, are
often the most easily available. This anti-social re-direction of
violence and anger is likely to continue until we are able to
recognize and come to terms with the aggressive emotions that are
in all of us, and learn to channel them into some constructive
and relevant outlets. Even in the field of human rights, it is

easy to be aroused by cruelties, as long as they are not our own: but only when we stop blaming other people for what we are, can we hope to begin to attain maturity. At times one may think our own generation is beyond hope, and we should concentrate our efforts on our successors. Psychologists suggest that a tolerant attitude is encouraged by the security of a person's early upbringing, together with an education that tries to give people insight into their own weaknesses.

Each and all of us, as an individual, is a minority. The really unforgivable inhumanity, I believe, is our habit of viewing a person not as himself, but distorted by a group judgement generated by often tribal emotions. As a defence against the complexities of life, we all categorize people – generally on very inadequate evidence. Few are the communicators in any country who do not at least unconsciously glorify their own race, sex and nationality. Ethnocentrism – the belief in the extraordinary value of one's own group, coupled with a suspicion of anything different – permeates homes, schools, books and newspapers throughout the world. Prejudices, which are often used as pretexts for denigrating political, social or economic opponents, provide men with excuses to exploit other classes, races or women. Leaders use them as calculated weapons; the led, from their need for security, shelter behind such blinkers and thereby are diverted from focussing upon the real causes of the injustices they are suffering. This is no modern political demagogue's trick. 'Of all the vulgar modes of escaping from the consideration of the effect of social and moral influences upon the human mind,' wrote Mill, 'the most vulgar is that of attributing the diversities of conduct and character to inherent natural differences.' Minorities often reveal wider social problems. Much inter-ethnic conflict is due not to pluralism but to societies' imbalances of power. Prejudice, which is also capable of being self-fulfilling, can be reinforced by competition in jobs, sex or housing; and less well-off people are obviously those who are most vulnerable to a threat to their basic existence. Hence it is generally only the comfortably-off who can afford to indulge in 'Afghanistanism' – the interesting characteristic of parlour Panthers that finds it much easier to show righteous concern over far-away and generalized causes, than to do any work about issues nearer home (particularly if this might demand a personal relationship or sacrifice).

Recently several areas have shown a resurgence of interest in ideas of autonomy, perhaps as part of a wish to decentralize society and break down its impersonality. Ralf Dahrendorf has argued: 'For freedom in society means, above all, that we recog-

11

nize the justice and the creativity of diversity, difference, and conflict.' In some of the United States, ethnicity programmes have been started which attempt to educate children to accept and respect their own origins and to learn that others' differences do not imply inferiority. Previously, many immigrants had been under pressure to shed their roots and to be fused into an all-American identity – often in reality a euphemism for WASP values. (The status and economic reward offered by the melting-pot for those who succeeded in jettisoning the background of their parents' culture was a frequent cause of inter-generational tension.) Many, but not all, minority groups prefer mutual tolerance to synthesis in a society: integration – defined by Roy Jenkins as 'equal opportunity accompanied by cultural diversity in an atmosphere of tolerance' – rather than assimilation. I would suggest that the decision whether to integrate or assimilate should be one for the individual; but any such choice requires that both options are made available to him. As Tagore stated, 'The wide-world problem today is not how to unite with all differences, but how to unite with all differences intact . . . when natural differences find their harmony, then it is true unity.'

In the task of tackling urgent social problems, however, one must be wary of the paralysis of mere analysis. Attempting to avoid the Scylla of repressive tolerance and the Charybdis of liberal paternalism, people must press for the establishment of an international ombudsman – preferably an effective United Nations Commission for Human Rights. Almost every member government has several minorities inside its borders, and a consequent interest in preventing human rights machinery from operating. Nevertheless we should remember that the U.N. charter begins with the words, 'We, the peoples . . . ', not 'We, the governments.' For who can know whether they in turn will not be a minority in need tomorrow?

THE MEASURE OF HUMANITY

by Milovan Djilas

Milovan Djilas was born in Montenegro in 1911. At Belgrade University he was a Communist organizer, and this led to his torture and three years' imprisonment by the royalist government. By 1940 he was a member of the Politburo of the Yugoslavian Communist Party, and was a partisan leader against the German invasion. After the war, he was successively Minister, Head of Parliament, and Vice-President of Yugoslavia. He published The New Class *in 1957. He was imprisoned from 1956–61 and from 1962–66.*

As far as work and ideas are concerned, the Minority Rights Group has its defects. However, they appear to me nowadays to be the least that can be imagined in this sphere.

I do not emphasize this because I am also one of the sponsors and supporters of the Group. My work within the Minority Rights Group was purely representative and does not deserve any particular consideration. I have examined the published reports and that is why I can unreservedly find its activity worthy of praise.

This I do mainly because the ideas and the work of the Minority Rights Group do not pretend to change the world, not even concerning the rights of minorities, for which the Group was founded. Nor has it any final or unique vision of the world. It may even be said that the Minority Rights Group has no final unmistakable

13

aim as to what ought to be done in the world today as regards the rights of the minorities. Its aims and means – at least the way I understand them – refer to stating the facts, and to acquainting officialdom with the legal and social situation of the minorities in various parts of the world. In this way the Minority Rights Group undoubtedly affects the conscience without asking for anything in return, and, to a lesser degree, without imposing solutions on anybody.

The only cohesive approach, which also reinforces the work of the Minority Rights Group, is to indicate that minorities should be assured clear and indestructible legal rights. This approach however, has an element of 'craftiness' implied in it, since, once the legal rights of the minorities have been secured, this may mean the beginning of equal rights between the minorities and the majorities, the latter being those who lay down the law. It will only be racialists, chauvinists, dogmatists and oppressors who will feel the destructive power of legal rights, even if these are ones which they themselves prescribe. This problem can form an abyss of the darkest rooted human evil.

I said, 'the darkest rooted human evil'. Yet in fact nobody can say with certainty which human evil is the greatest or of the oldest origin, since all evils, as far as we know, made their appearance with the creation of human life. And in various countries and periods in history, different evils prevail at successive times. Perhaps evils do not lessen, they only change form or adapt themselves to circumstances. It is certain that subjugation, contempt and even persecution have resulted from differences of race and all the tribes from time immemorial. Because men do not learn, they do not improve on their predecessors, neither do they form part of a community dissimilar to all others. They are born and develop as different beings, even as members of different communities. We can add that their conscience and their experience inevitably lead to their co-existence as different beings even when opposed to other communities – social, ethnic, racial and spiritual.

The circle of wrong seems to be complete; evil is increasing in the human mind. But it is not just that: human beings and human communities do not only vary, and oppose each other; they are also identical, and no doubt are under pressure to combine and to fraternize. In so far as this happens through their own free will, the circle of evil is defeated. This is the measure of humanity that people do not know or recognize a value greater than human liberties.

However, for every person, particularly in the removal of

contempt and hatred towards other communities, a conscious effort is required, and the risks are inevitable: it is essential to free oneself from inherited conformist customs and surroundings. The easiest way out – the most comfortable one – is love for one's own community, and hatred and contempt towards a foreign community. This 'love' often is – always is, except when we fight for equality for the liberation of our own community – a hidden contempt for that community, including everything it stands for.

The most civilized regions have gone through a process of opposing other different communities, racialist or ethnic or highly ideological foreign or social groups. It appears that the racial barrier in Europe has been broken and has lost ground in most of the world. Oppression and loss of rights due to one's religion, race or nationality have been reduced throughout the world and could be abolished. However, this may require long and strenuous efforts, since no evil disappears of its own accord, particularly when it concerns the difference between a Serb or a Croat, an Irishman or an Englishman, a Jew or a Moslem, a black or a white man.

As is the case with any other evil, that regarding minorities everywhere always appears as a concrete evil – by the deprivation of rights and oppression of certain groups by specific rules and in a particular manner . . . Today, however, this evil is outdated when compared with slavery at the beginning of the nineteenth century. In a world which recognizes the special peculiarities of all races, religions and ethnic groups, dispossession of minorities is repulsive, irrational and non-productive. It becomes unhealthy and offensive because in reality majorities do not deprive minorities of their rights. Even where minorities are numerically majorities, this deprivation of rights is being done by privileged minorities for selfish, materialistic reasons and to preserve out-moded forms and inherited prejudices.

There is nowhere on the earth's surface where free men could not demonstrate their desire to promote neighbourly relations and respect for humane conditions. This is the simplest, the least pretentious and the most realistic way of fighting for the rights of the minorities – because there are minorities everywhere, of one kind or another.

And in my country, for as long as I can remember, there have been religious, national and political minorities . . . My conscience bleeds. I came into a world in which the powerful surrounding empires have in fact treated my people as a minority, and I gave my youth and adult life to fighting against the subjugation and dismemberment of my fatherland. But these were times when the

15

whole of Europe and a great part of the world found themselves in the same position. My father could not be happy in such conditions when, for my people, the right to a religion equalled the right to live. But he considered that all men should have equal human rights, although his own nation – the Serbian nation – was the best in the world. I have considered people and nations as equals and have not compared them with my nation. My son thinks the same way, adding that even if races and nations were not equally valuable, still nobody should be deprived of his rights.

Is this the evolution of a conscience of society, or of the human community? And who is whose teacher or judge? In my father's time, my nation has undergone uprisings and wars to prove its right to independence, even to its existence. I wish my son may never have to be forced to do this! This would be his most valuable inheritance – to him and to the generations who follow him: that he should start his life not necessarily in an easier way than myself, but without being persecuted by prejudices, dogmas, injustices because of different colour, different speech or different ideas.

This is the highest, the most eternal way in which humanity could glorify the present time.

Belgrade
February 1972

WHAT DO WE MEAN BY RIGHTS?

by Philip Mason

After a distinguished career in the Indian Civil Service, which he joined in 1928, *Philip Mason retired at independence in* 1947. *Between* 1952 *and* 1958 *he was Director of Studies in Race Relations at Chatham House, and then became Director of the Institute of Race Relations from* 1958–69. *He has written many books, including* The Founders *(as Philip Woodruff),* Year of Decision *in* 1960, *and* Patterns of Dominance *in* 1970. *He is an honorary fellow of the School of Oriental and African Studies, and holds an honorary doctorate of Bristol University.*

In the discussions about peace treaties after the First World War, President Wilson's principle of self-determination was no doubt often cynically used as a cover for national interest – as 'legitimacy' had been a century earlier. Nonetheless, the principle – over-simple and indeed naive though it now seems – was, in the broadest sense, put into practice; it profoundly changed the map of Europe. It meant, in terms simply of numbers, that far fewer people than before found themselves under the rule of aliens. But there was a new crop of problems which were no less intense than the old. There were still many minorities; their awareness of their grievances was increased, still more their expectations.

Is it better to belong to a small minority – too small to be a threat, with no hope of liberation and therefore treated with tolerance, like the Protestants in Southern Ireland – or to a group big enough to make itself felt, and therefore an object of hostility? The treatment a minority receives is affected by its numbers, and also by an awareness of its own grievances and strength, an expectation of relief, and a degree of militancy. There is thus a qualitative as well as a quantitative aspect to each problem. Looked at quantitatively, there are many areas – for example in northern and eastern Nigeria – where it is impossible to draw a map that would satisfy every distinguishable group and produce areas of a size that makes sense administratively; as you free minority group B from the domination of majority group A, you turn B into a majority and expose group C to its tyranny. And there is a strong probability that C will resent B's tyranny more than A's. 'We would rather be ruled by the Fulani than by the Tiv; the Fulani are further away,' said the representative of a small people in northern Nigeria in 1957, opposing a separate state in which the Tiv would have been the majority. Further, in the old days, when B and C were alike under the yoke of A, C had no prospect of anything better; if not exactly contented, they were at least quiescent. But that B's hopes have been fulfilled arouses C's expectations; independence is in the air. So you solve one problem only to create another. The fact remains that some maps are better than others.

In an essay of this length, it would be absurd to attempt an exhaustive classification of the different kinds of minority. Nonetheless, it does seem worth listing some of the main groups. One is an aftermath of Empire and arises from the tenderness of British colonial officers for people at a primitive stage of social organization. This game-warden attitude kept the Nagas and the peoples of the Southern Sudan naked and apparently happy much longer than they would have been otherwise. No one had told them that they were naked or that they were a minority. At the time, it seemed a kindness to prevent their way of life from being destroyed; it is not easy now to be sure that it was not cruel. They were shut off in their paradise, isolated from the main tradition of their principal neighbours – Hindu in one case, Arab and Islamic in the other. The discovery that they were both naked and a minority was harsh.

Very different is the ideological minority, which is a problem because the majority believes that there is one 'correct' view of the state and of society, and that any other view, particularly if it is shared by any body of opinion outside, involves a second allegiance and is anti-social. Here of course the religious minorities in the Soviet Union are a complete example, but other minorities are affected to a lesser extent by this kind of attitude. Another group arises from an ancient stratification now formally repudiated but still operating – the former untouchables of India, the out-castes of Japan, the blacks of America and Brazil. Then there are the problems arising from the combination of increased mobility and economic pressures; here Indians provide examples in British Columbia and Britain, in Fiji, Mauritius and Malaya. Perhaps it is under this head that one should put also the overflows from former tribal territories, which arise because one group has gone ahead in Western education faster than another, or because their land is insufficient, or their old organization breaking down; the Ibos in northern Nigeria were once an example. There is another great group of the conquered and unassimilated – American Indians, Australian aborigines and Maoris. And there is a final class of gypsies and other odd cases whom it is not easy to put under any general description.

Here in this volume are eight reports published by the Minority Rights Group. One in fact concerns not a minority but an 'op-pressed majority', which also comes within the Group's terms of reference. The reports are clear, informative, fairly and objectively expressed. The Group has performed one service in publishing them, another in putting them between two covers. The eight reports discuss at least a dozen communities, and, to anyone who looks at them together, parallels and patterns are bound to spring to mind. For example, the same British tenderness for an ancient way of life protected the negro peoples of the Southern Sudan from the better educated Arabs of Khartoum and – neatly reversing the pattern – the Islamic northern peoples of Nigeria from better educated southern negroes. Again, it is impossible to read of the Japanese 'outcastes' – note the spelling – without thinking of India's former 'untouchables'. Both are occupational groups, excluded from the main society because their work was polluting or degrading. Both include skinners, leather-workers, basket-makers, scavengers. In both cases, the main society cherishes the belief – wholly myth in one case, partly in the other – that they are racially distinct, aboriginal peoples, conquered before history began. In both cases, discrimination has been outlawed, but prejudice remains. Indeed, more than prejudice, for it is impossible in the twinkling of an eye to provide self-confidence for a people who for centuries have known that they were outside the social system, despised and rejected. No one has yet found a way out of the vicious spiral; despise a man and he will despise himself and will in fact become what he is being despised for being.

And this brings us to the heart of a modern difficulty which

19

arises from a greater awareness of other people's lives, from greater expectations. A minority may for a long period lie enclosed in a larger political group, quiescent on the whole because not actively interfered with. But as awareness of the larger national life begins to grow, ambitions and wants arise. Two stages seem to follow. First, individuals from the minority, struggling for wealth and power and satisfaction, see their road to the top as lying within the majority culture. They have to master the techniques, the speech, the habits of thought, of the majority, and beat them at their own game. And at this stage, the minority are proud of the native son, their famous and successful representative. But suddenly it comes home to them that he is no longer one of themselves; he has become one of the majority. 'He is not really a Moslem, only a Hindu with a beard,' I heard said forty years ago. And today, wherever there is a minority, you will hear the same point made of some leader; he is a white man with a black face; he is no longer an Indian, he has turned Spanish; he is only Welsh when it suits him. The minority has discovered that it can win material success only at the expense of its special separate identity. And it indignantly refuses to pay the price.

But the material wants are not abandoned, and they are international; they do not speak Basque or Creole. Everybody wants schools, doctors, hospitals, roads, jobs – and isolation will not provide these things. Only large-scale economic and political combinations can pay for them. And yet there is something that chills the spirit about vast continental agglomerations. Men need a society small enough to feel at home in. It is only in the last fifty years that the Nagas have learnt that they were Nagas; before that they were conscious only of much smaller tribal units covering a few hill-tops and valleys. Yet now they are expected to regard themselves as part of a sub-continent – from where else than the sub-continent will the hospitals come? It seems likely therefore that minority problems will become worse rather than better. Economic wants increase, and with them the need for large markets, while on the other hand peoples first become aware of an identity of culture, language and feeling they had ignored – and then suddenly perceive that it is in danger of extinction, liable to be swamped by the pressure of radio, television and the press, of swift communications, of international business. So they set about defining and asserting their national identity and demanding the fullest expression for it. And so eager are they to eliminate any trace of subservience to any other culture that they repudiate the leaders who have most experience of a wider sphere, and who are the most likely to win them the material goods as well as the cultural freedom they want. This dialectic seems likely, during the next few years, to be more rapid and powerful than the development of a sense of international citizenship.

This is not to ignore the growth of what might loosely be called an international conscience; there *is* today a body of international opinion to which most states find it convenient to bow the knee, except when their own most intimate interests are threatened. But one of its first effects is to arouse the expectations of minorities everywhere, and in the short run this may in some cases lead to increased repression. It is unfortunate that we use the same word for a legal *right* which can be enforced in the law courts and for the 'rights' which men ought ideally to have in a just state. The U.N. declaration asserts that everyone has these ideal 'rights', which I show within quotation marks only to distinguish them from legal *rights*. The two senses seem to share one word in most languages; it is not a confusion that occurs only in English. South Africa illustrates the difference most clearly; a list of the U.N.'s ideal 'rights' corresponds very neatly with what an African has *not* got. He has virtually no legal *rights* in six-sevenths of the sovereign territory of which he is a subject. Legal *rights* are won by force or bargaining or persuasion and in Britain have been won gradually, piecemeal, one at a time. To distinguish them from ideal 'rights' might possibly help minority leaders to think of them as attainable step by step, while to say that everyone has 'rights' (which are taken to mean *rights*) when they patently have not is surely to encourage intransigence.

This is not to question the aims of the Minority Rights Group. Their purpose is clearly ameliorative and gradualist. They hope, by directing international opinion to the position of a minority, to awaken the majority to a sense of its shortcomings, and they further hope that the response will be to lighten the minority's burden. In many cases, this may be so, particularly – to take two examples only – in the case of Japan and India, both countries who have repudiated an ancient injustice but are inclined to forget that it still exists. Both countries are extremely sensitive in this respect. Let us hope for more reports, including the untouchables, gypsies, and black Australians. And what about the Moslems of India and Indians in the mountains of Ecuador? It is always good to strike a blow at the myth that there is no consciousness of colour and no discrimination in Brazil; the report on this subject is an admirable summary. Further, the Minority Rights Group are right in believing that there is some

sensitivity to world opinion even in the most hardened states –
though it may not always produce the reaction that liberals would
wish. Even if – and I believe there is a real danger here – focusing
an international search-light on it may sometimes increase a
minority's expectations and therefore its intransigence and thus
in the short run sharpen the conflict, it may well be that, in the
long run, speeding up a painful process may lead to an earlier
solution. Each case must be judged on its merits: to draw Stalin's
attention to a minority might have led to its extermination, or at
least to its dispersal. No solution is likely to be easy, and none is
likely to be complete. But it is better that what is wrong should
be seen than that it should be hidden.

1 THE ASIAN MINORITIES OF EAST AND CENTRAL AFRICA

by Yash Ghai and Dharam Ghai

Professor Dharam P. Ghai is the Director of Economic Research at the University of Nairobi. Professor Yash Ghai is his brother, and the Professor in the Faculty of Law at the University of Dar es Salaam.

THE ASIAN MINORITIES
OF EAST AND CENTRAL AFRICA

INTRODUCTION

One of the most striking problems following in the wake of decolonization in East and Central Africa has been the situation and fate of its minorities. Of these minorities, the Asians*, for reasons of colour and economic position, are the most clearly distinguishable.

The problem of Asian and other minorities did not, of course, arise only after independence. Most European colonies were plural societies, composed of various tribes and races, and the colonial period was by no means free from rivalries and tensions among these groups. European overrule, however, tended to contain these tensions within tolerable limits. This is not to say that conditions were ideal, and certainly the European colonial authority was seldom a passive and impartial umpire, particularly where immigrant minorities were involved. These were usually more favoured than the indigenous people, though not all immigrant groups were equally favoured.

The coming of independence changed the situation of the minorities in significant ways. There is always a struggle for the control of a new state. The forces involved draw their support from tribal or regional bases and the goal for which they contend is the establishment of a state with highly centralized powers. There is little of the 'federal' sharing of power, and though alliances may be struck among groups to participate in the government, there is a strong flavour of winner-takes-all about the spoils system which characterizes these new states. To be a politically weak minority is therefore an unfortunate circumstance.

In many respects the consequences are similar whether the minority is indigenous or immigrant. But there are also several important distinctions. First, an immigrant minority is regarded as alien – a view which is reinforced after independence when it is seen that large numbers of them are not and do not wish to become citizens of the new state. Second, they tend to be more

*For all practical purposes, the designation Asian refers to people of Indian or Pakistani origin, and indeed until the partition of the Indian sub-continent, the usual designation was Indian.

prosperous and privileged than the rest. These two factors often combine to mark them out for hostility and resentment. Indeed, many of the indigenous people wish to be rid of them altogether.

Unlike even small indigenous minorities, they have little political power. On the other hand, they have greater support from the outside. Their countries of origin may take a special interest in their welfare, and the former colonial power may be ascribed certain residual obligations in regard to them. Instances of racial discrimination attract more world attention than discrimination between tribes, and to some extent the problems of immigrant minorities tend to become 'internationalized'.

Immigrant minorities are assumed to have the option of emigration and so their future is not regarded as irrevocably tied to the host country, as that of indigenous minorities might be, though with the latter, examples are not lacking of emigration, if only across the border. Hence the refugee problem in Africa.

Nowhere yet in independent Africa has there been enough time to make it possible to suggest any ultimate solution to the problem of immigrant minorities. But in recent years certain trends have become apparent which have fairly clear implications for the future. This paper seeks to examine the situation of the Asian communities in East and Central Africa, specifically in the countries of Kenya, Uganda, Tanzania, Zambia and Malawi.

PART ONE:

HISTORICAL BACKGROUND

For all practical purposes, the main immigration of the Asian communities is a recent phenomenon. At no time have these immigrants been significant numerically, although their economic importance has been quite out of proportion to their numbers. On the other hand, they have seldom exercised much political influence.

Never a dominant power in East or Central Africa, their ability to influence historical factors has been limited. They have had no strong support from the governments of their countries of origin. They have had no ambitions of aggression and annexation. At the same time they have displayed a poor sense of history and limited vision. It is not surprising therefore if they are seen as merely responding to the forces around them rather than influencing them. Though they have not lacked initiative and have resisted pressures, the history of the Asian communities is largely one of accommodation to the prevailing historical situation.

25

Asian contacts with Eastern Africa date back many centuries. There is impressive documentary and archaeological evidence that trade between India and the coast of Africa flourished centuries before the advent of the Europeans. For over a thousand years people from India were at the centre of the economic activity which brought the influences of a wider world to the east coast of Africa, not only as merchants and sailors, but also as financiers and administrators. Some Asian settlements were already established in the early 19th century, and by the middle of that century the Asian population in Zanzibar alone was estimated at five or six thousand. Coastal settlements were also found at Kilwa Baganoyo, Pangani, Malindi and Mombasa.

There was less inland penetration in pre-colonial times, although one Musa Mzuri went as far inland as Tabora in 1825 and Allidina Visram was in Uganda in 1896, before the Uganda railway was built. By 1895 there were already over thirteen thousand Asians in Kenya, most of them labourers recruited for the work of railway construction then just beginning.

The colonization process gave an impetus to Asian immigration, both the immigration promoted by the European powers and private immigration designed to exploit the opportunities opened up by colonization. The former was relatively unimportant in East and Central Africa*.

The main recruitment of people from India was connected with the building of the Uganda railway. They were recruited on terms of indenture not only as construction workers, but also as clerks, surveyors and accountants. Contrary to popular belief, however, the present Asian population cannot be regarded as descendants of these workers. Of the 32,000 indentured, 16,312 returned to India at the expiry of their contract, 2,493 died, 6,454 were invalided home, and only 6,724 stayed on.

There was no indentured labour in Central Africa. Some 500 labourers were imported to construct the railway between Beira and Southern Rhodesia, but hardly any survived the ravages of heat, animals and insects. Railway workers were also imported into Nyasaland, where railway construction began in 1908. While some of them returned to India at the end of their contract, others stayed on. But even they constitute only a small proportion of the present Asian population.

As in East Africa, troops from India were relied upon to

*The Germans, who had controlled Tanganyika until the First World War, had tried to recruit labourers, clerks and other personnel from India, but their overtures met with resolute resistance from the British who then ruled India.

establish 'law and order', but here again, these Indian units were withdrawn as soon as African troops had been trained.

The majority of Asians, therefore, were those who came on their own initiative. In many ways they were different from those who came on indenture and who tended to be extremely poor, of very limited education and with little subsequent mobility. The 'free' immigrant had more ambition and enterprise. The majority came for the purposes of trade – typically, early on, in the form of the small general store known to this day as the *duka*, from the Indian word, *dukan*, meaning a shop. These storekeepers, known as *dukawalla*, were instrumental in opening shops even in remote parts of the country, buying local African produce, creating a demand for imported goods and helping to spread the use of money.

Many came as shop assistants, initially to work for their kinsmen but with hopes of starting their own shops. Others came as clerks and artisans, also harbouring ambitions of moving into commerce.

The great majority of the immigrants into East Africa came from Gujarat and the Punjab, with a substantial sprinkling of Goans. Most were of peasant background. In the Rhodesias and Nyasaland, on the other hand, the majority came from Gujarat. Thus there is greater cultural and linguistic homogeneity among the Asians in Central Africa than is the case in East Africa.

These forms of immigration were not a result of official inducement. In East Africa and Nyasaland clerks and artisans were indeed encouraged to come. But the initial situation, when Asian technicians and artisans had been actively sought by the early administrators, quickly changed as the prospects for white settlement of the region became clear. The European settlers soon perceived the threat to their own interests posed by the Asians, both economically and politically.

Even in Nyasaland, where no serious consideration was given to white settlement in the early days, there was opposition to Asian immigration. Commerce was then controlled by a large Scottish company, the African Lake Corporation, which complained of competition from the Asian shopkeeper. And in Kenya too, where the Europeans have never been interested in small-scale trading, the settlers opposed Asian commercial activity. It was essentially the colony of aristocrats and big landowners, but experience in Central Africa showed that the absence of the Asian trader and clerk provided additional opportunities for Europeans. In the Rhodesias hostility to the Asian traders was even more pronounced, and on occasion took the form of victimization and physical beatings.

27

The political factor was even more important. From the earliest times the settlers had hoped to gain control and looked to the big white dominions as models for their own future. The presence of Asians complicated matters. They claimed rights, occasionally on the basis of equality with the settlers; but worse, it was feared they might contaminate the Africans with political ideas. The activities of the nationalists in India, the experience of the Indian agitation in South Africa, as well as the initial militancy in Kenya of the people of Indian origin, made the Europeans wary.

The European settlers sought to express their opposition to Asian immigration through legal enactments. An essential part of the settlers' political platform in Kenya as well as in the Rhodesias has always been the banning of Asian immigration. Presented at first as a move to ensure the supremacy of the white settlers, it was later represented as a necessary protection for the Africans. It was alleged that the Asians exploited the illiterate Africans and prevented their progress by occupying the jobs to which Africans aspired. It was also said that the social and religious influence of Asians was undesirable; that their culture and religion were backward, obscurantist and unwholesome.

The settlers, however, came up against the imperial principle of common citizenship and therefore free immigration, and for a long time the political power to enact legislation restricting immigration eluded them. The exception was Southern Rhodesia, where as early as 1904 an ordinance was passed directing that no person should be admitted who was unable 'by reason of deficient education to write out and sign within his own hand in the character of any European language an application to the satisfaction of the Administrator'. This provision effected the exclusion of all but a few Asians. A complete ban was imposed in 1924 as one of the first measures taken by the settlers on their attaining self-government.

In Northern Rhodesia (later to become Zambia) the 1904 principle of literacy testing in a European language was introduced administratively. At first this had the effect of reducing immigration, but after 1939 the test requirements ceased to operate as any real obstacle. In 1954, however, with the formation of the Federation, Southern Rhodesia's 1924 legislation was extended to the other two territories also.

In East Africa the white settlers had to wait till the pressure of the war brought them into important positions in the executive before they could introduce the restrictions – as part of the war regulations. Subsequently these were reintroduced and enacted as ordinances in all of the East African countries. Thereafter immigration was small, being contingent upon possession of capital or special skills.

Turning to the pattern of Asian immigration, we find there was steady but slow growth from the turn of the century until the early 1930s. After that there was a virtual cessation of immigration, due in part to economic depression and the Second World War. After the war immigration picked up dramatically and continued at a rapid rate until enactment of the legislative bans just discussed.

In Central Africa there were relatively few Asians in the pre-war period. Most came after the war, in contrast to the experience in East Africa where a considerable Asian settlement had already taken place prior to the 1939–45 war.

The following table shows the growth of Asian population in the five countries:

YEAR	KENYA	UGANDA	TANGANYIKA	N. RHODESIA	NYASALAND
1917	11,787	—	—	39	481
1921	25,253	5,604	—	56	563
1931	43,623	14,150	—	176	1,591
1945	—	—	—	1,117	2,804
1948	97,687	35,215	46,254	—	—
1956	149,000	62,900	74,300	5,450	8,504
1961/62	176,613	77,400	88,700	7,790	10,630

The latest available figures are:

	KENYA	UGANDA	TANZANIA	ZAMBIA	MALAWI
	182,000*	80,000*	130,000*	10,705	11,299
	(1969)	(1968)	(1967)	(1970)	(1966)

*Estimates (unfortunately statistical sources tend
to be not always reliable and estimates can vary widely).*

SOME CHARACTERISTICS OF COLONIAL SOCIETY

Many of the problems with which the newly independent African governments were concerned were inherited as a legacy of colonial times. This is true also of the problems and dilemmas of the Asians. It would be misleading, of course, to say that the present predicament of the Asians is due entirely to the colonialists; they have themselves contributed to it in an important way. But the fundamental characteristics of colonial society and their administrations were determined by the colonial rulers. What we single out here are the characteristics which have a bearing on the Asian situation.

The key feature was the form of race relations, colonial society being organized on the basis of racial communities and *de facto*, if not always *de jure*, on the principles of segregation and discrimination. Racial tensions and communal rivalries were therefore stimulated at an early stage, although it is only fair to point

29

c

out that the Asians too showed a tendency towards social exclusiveness.

The categorization of people along racial lines strengthened prejudice, and this resulted not only in segregation and exclusiveness but also encouraged a belief in stereotypes, some deliberately cultivated, so that the behaviour of a few offending members served to condemn the entire community. Hence the Asian was thought of as a dukawalla who cheated and insulted his African customers and was mean and secretive. The African was said to be dull, unintelligent, lazy and dishonest. The European was seen as tough and aggressive, but as someone who has done much for the country. Racial attitudes in East and Central Africa have been strongly influenced by these stereotypes, and it is noteworthy that some of the anti-Asian speeches made today by African politicians in Kenya, Uganda and Zambia employ phrases identical with those which the early European settlers habitually used in their anti-Asian harangues.

British policy did little to promote racial harmony. When members of the different races were forced to attend different schools and live in separate localities and were not permitted to share social and cultural amenities, it is not surprising that they remained ignorant of one another's customs, needs and aspirations. The legacy of British imperialism was thus one of racial suspicion and misunderstanding, of antagonism rather than co-operation.

More specifically, the Asians were affected by official policy in their social and political activities, and in their economic roles. The colonial authorities not only supplied separate facilities for the different races, but did so on a discriminatory basis so that the facilities for Asians and Africans were not only grossly inferior to those provided for the Europeans, but were completely inadequate.

The response of the Asians was to supplement these facilities for themselves when they were able to do so. The Asian communities in Zambia and Nyasaland felt themselves to be the most deprived. There was no Asian secondary school in Nyasaland until 1959, for example. Unfortunately it was also in these two territories that the Asians were least able to help themselves, being few in number and rather widely dispersed. Furthermore, there were greater restrictions on their economic activities than in the north, and their financial means were correspondingly smaller.

The nature of politics in these countries likewise did little to break down communal barriers. Until the last phase of colonial rule there was explicit Asian political representation in the legislative institutions at the national and local levels only in East Africa. And in Kenya Asians were allowed the franchise only on their own communal roll. This meant that except in East Africa the Asians were seldom drawn into national politics on a regular basis and when they were tended to be preoccupied by communal matters. It was only towards the end of colonial rule that Asian politicians began to take stands on crucial national issues.

Perhaps the most important consequence of colonial policy was the allocation of economic roles to the various communities. There was need in the early years for artisans, clerks and traders, and the Asians were welcomed in most of the territories for these purposes. In any event they tended to enter occupations in which they could rely on their own initiative, and this was just as well since the colonial authorities sometimes effectively excluded them from certain occupations. In Kenya, for example, the best agricultural land was reserved for Europeans, while the rest was set aside for Africans.

In Tanganyika and Uganda the land was deemed to be held in trust for the Africans, and whatever little alienation of land there was to immigrants went to Europeans. Restrictive practices in land policy vis-à-vis Asians were pursued to similar effect in Nyasaland and Northern Rhodesia. An outlet for Asians in agriculture was therefore impossible.

However, it is not obvious that Asians would have taken to farming even if land had been available. In Zanzibar, where Asians did have some arable land, they preferred to be landlords rather than farmers. But the Zanzibar example is an early one, and it is possible that as the Asians perceived the narrowing of opportunities in commerce some might have turned to the land.

Equally remote to Asians were the upper reaches of the civil and other public services. In the East African territories the need for skilled and educated persons early on resulted in Asians occupying most of the lower and middle grades of the public services, like the railways. Next to commerce, public employment constituted the most important sector of Asian activity. Subsequently Asians filled similar positions in the bigger commercial and industrial enterprises, which were often owned by large European companies. Here Asians worked as clerks, accountants, sales assistants and in various technical capacities.

In the Central African territories, however, even these avenues were closed to them. Up to the time of the Federation there were barely ten Asians in the civil service, while the European enterprises preferred to employ whites for their top as well as middle grade of personnel. Here, therefore, even more so than in East Africa, Asians were forced to engage almost exclusively in commercial activities.

Even in commerce, though, there were ordinances preventing Asian traders in the East African territories from conducting business outside specified cities and townships. They tended therefore to concentrate in the urban areas, a factor responsible for the 'Indian look' of almost all the major towns and cities. Similar restrictions applied in Southern Rhodesia and to a lesser extent in Northern, but Asian trade there, as well as in Nyasaland, was restricted pretty well to African customers; for here, unlike in East Africa, the Europeans also had trading aspirations – and their own shops.

In the absence of any government encouragement for Asians to move into other areas of activity, the way out of the straitjacket of commercial and clerical employment lay through education. By and large the colonial authorities in East Africa had accepted certain, if minimal, responsibilities in regard to education for Asians. The first to do so was Kenya, where in 1912 the government undertook the operation of a public school which the railways had established by the turn of the century. Elsewhere the first initiatives came from the Asian communities themselves. By 1920 a number of private Asian schools had come into existence; it was not until 1925 that the governments made small grants to these schools.

The first Asian schools in Tanganyika were also established privately by the Asians, the government having decided that non-African education was to be provided primarily by the communities concerned. After 1929, however, the government assumed some financial responsibility. Much later it also took over the administration of schools.

Over the years the contribution of the governments to Asian education increased steadily, though it never kept pace with expenditure on education for Europeans. Private, communal Asian schools continued to play a key part in education right up to and after independence, particularly with regard to the education of girls.

Secondary school education was slow to develop, but gradually the importance of higher forms of education came to be appreciated. It was seen as providing a gateway to the professions, and in the years after the war a large number of young Asians went overseas to further their education and came back with qualifications in law, medicine, engineering, accountancy, nursing and teaching. This big investment in skills rapidly changed the character of the Asian work force and was in large part responsible for its significant contribution to the pool of skilled manpower in East Africa.

The situation in Central Africa was quite different. There the governments failed to provide anything like adequate educational facilities and the ability of the Asians to run their own schools was considerably less than in East Africa. Asian schools were first established in Southern Rhodesia, and children from the northern territories had to be sent there. Later some primary schools were set up in the north, although until 1959 there was no secondary school outside Southern Rhodesia. Even then there were but two Asian secondary schools (compared with thirty-eight for Europeans), and for many the only hope of acquiring secondary education was to attend schools in Britain or India, if their parents could afford it. Consequently the Asians in Central Africa have remained more dependent on commerce, few among them being professionally qualified, and therefore they have little economic mobility.

Thus at the time these countries became independent, the Asians in East Africa were dominant in commerce and shared in public employment, while those in Central Africa were almost entirely dependent on trade. The East African Asians had begun to move into industry, while those in Central Africa were still predominantly small traders, more important in the smaller than the bigger centres. Considering the East African situation it was inevitable that there would be a clash, for the Asians occupied most of the positions to which Africans were likely to aspire. Added to this growing economic rivalry was a long history of Asian-African relations in the social and political fields which must be understood in order to appreciate the situation of the Asians at independence. To this we now turn.

ASIAN-AFRICAN RELATIONS

While Asian-African relations have developed in context of the racial society which colonialism fostered, and while it is true that this discouraged inter-racial contacts, there were autonomous areas in which the two communities did interact.

Unfortunately relations were mostly at the shopkeeper-customer or master-servant level, neither calculated to inspire good feelings. Moreover, the Asians' treatment of their African servants has been generally scandalous, often involving abuse and indignity and the denial of basic rights. As clients of Asian traders, Africans have long felt themselves victims of exploitation. Accusations are made against shopkeepers everywhere, especially if they happen to be of a different race, but they are more liable to arise within a system of trading where there is little price control, prices are not displayed and the practice of bargaining is common.

Few incentives existed for closer social relationships between Asians and Africans, and there were enormous disparities between them in religious and cultural backgrounds. Partly owing to the caste system long prevalent in India, Asians had been used to living in more or less exclusive communities in their home societies, even within the compass of a village. The practice of social exclusiveness within a framework of commercial and administrative relations thus came naturally to them.

Furthermore the Asians' reasons for immigration were largely economic: they did not leave India for reasons of persecution or out of a missionary zeal. Once in East Africa their behaviour was largely determined by this factor. It did nothing to encourage a meaningful involvement with the indigenous people. If the newcomers had been fired with missionary zeal, they might have endeavoured to provide education for the Africans and introduce them to their own way of living and thinking. If they had had more overt political ambitions, they would have tended to cultivate people and leaders of the other races, particularly the Africans. Lacking these motives for seeking greater contact, Asian ways and religions remained mysterious to the Africans.

In the political field, the Asians have been accused of not having helped the cause of African nationalism or even of having collaborated with the colonists in frustrating African aspirations. This viewpoint ignores some early brave efforts by Asians and does scant justice to the achievements of a small group of them who helped African leaders at considerable personal sacrifice.

Asian political activity was greater in East than in Central Africa, due partly to the relative numerical strength of Asians there as well as to their higher standards of education.

One of the most significant contributions made by the Asians was in Kenya, but this had repercussions elsewhere. Their efforts undoubtedly helped to stem the tide towards a South African or Southern Rhodesian system. The Asians' prolonged struggle in the twenties for equality of treatment with the Europeans in Kenya was something of a turning point in the history of that country, for it was then that the interests of the indigenous population were officially accepted as being of paramount importance.

Although this was perhaps their best-known political activity, the Asians had also at other times offered resistance to the unfair practices of the settlers or the Colonial Office. In one sense the progenitor of African nationalism in East Africa was the early political consciousness of the Asians. Nor was it merely by example that African political activity was stimulated. Some of the earliest African presses and pamphleteering owed their existence to Asian support, while some Asian papers gave publicity and encouragement to African demands. Several African leaders were helped by Asian politicians. M. A. Desai aided and advised Harry Thuku, sometimes referred to as the father of African nationalism in Kenya. There was also a handful of radical Asian nationalists having a political sophistication beyond that of any African politicians at the time, who significantly influenced developing African nationalism in the early days.

In the period preceding independence, when African political parties were being formed and an active programme of agitation and negotiation was under way, the Asians were once again drawn into national politics. The traditional Asian political party in Kenya, the Indian Congress, was at first ambivalent and concerned to ensure that the Asian community would retain some special privileges after independence. But it was pushed into a greater commitment to the Africans by its younger, more radical members, who wanted complete support for the Africans and a form of government based on one man one vote, without any special provisions for minorities. In the crucial independence negotiations with the British government from 1960 to 1963, the Asians sided with the Africans.

In Tanzania the Asians had already adopted a similar position. The Asian Association, after an initial period of hesitation, had allied itself with TANU*, and given it what support it could. In Uganda, the Central Councils of India and Moslem Associations were driven to full support of the African nationalists under the influence of a ginger group, the Uganda Action Group.

In Nyasaland organized Asian politics began late, and then as a response to the debate about proposed federation in the early fifties. The Nyasaland Asian Convention opposed federation, and thus allied itself with the African nationalists. At the Lancaster House constitutional conference all the Asian delegates came out in support of self-government, one man one vote, and no safeguards for minorities. In Nyasaland itself, joint meetings with the Nyasaland Congress Party were organized in support of independence.

In Northern Rhodesia, while there was little organized political activity among the Asians, there was considerable support for

* Tanzania African National Union.

the African cause. The finances of UNIP* were largely supplied by Asian traders, and individual African leaders were helped in various ways by certain Asians.

It is necessary, however, to keep the Asians' political role in perspective. The official posture of their political parties was generally one of support for African demands, but it is doubtful if the community as such was enthusiastic about the prospect of independence. The Asian leaders who pressed for commitment to the African cause were seldom popular in their own community.

By the early sixties Asian support had become relatively unimportant in terms of its impact. In retrospect the Asian contribution may seem less in terms of support given to Africans than in the willingness to forego special minority provisions.

There was seldom close working collaboration with the African politicians and the day-to-day strategies were not planned together. On the other hand, the failure of early African-Asian collaboration to reach a state of sustained joint activity was partly a consequence of African reluctance to accept Asian guidance or support.

There is evidence that Harry Thuku encountered considerable opposition from other African politicians because of his links with the Asians, and the failure of African-Asian parties in East Africa in the immediate pre-independence period was due to the fact that African leaders alienated support by associating with Asians. The decision of the major African parties in all three countries to exclude non-Africans from membership till just before or after independence, whatever its justification, must also have affected the potential contribution of the Asians.

INDEPENDENCE

Independence in these countries found the Asians in the position of an unpopular minority. In East Africa they numbered about 360,000, with about half living in Kenya, 10,000 in Nyasaland and 8,000 in Zambia. Their numbers were too small to be politically significant, and yet too large to permit an easy solution of their problems. They themselves were deeply divided into various sub-groups, which made united action impossible. The Asian community was still regarded by the indigenous people as alien and thus potentially disloyal; nor did it have many friends outside Africa. While the British government was greatly concerned to secure protective provisions for the white settlers and civil servants, it displayed scant regard for the plight of the

* United National Independence Party.

Asians, even though in terms of legal status they were just as much the responsibility of the British.

The Indian government, which some might have expected to come to their support, kept aloof; its official advice was that the Asians should identify themselves with their new countries and should manifest this identification by taking on citizenship.

The strictly neutral position of the Indian government at this time was in contrast to its earlier stance. Before India became independent, the India Office in Britain and the Indian government had consistently championed the cause of the Indians overseas.

It was as a result of pressure from the Indian government that the grievances of the Kenya Indians were brought up at the Imperial Conferences, and in 1921 a resolution was passed at the Conference stating that it was incompatible with India's status as an equal member of the Empire that disabilities should be imposed upon the British Indians lawfully domiciled in other parts of the Empire.

But after India's independence the Indian government, anxious to lead the Third World, encouraged nationalist activity in Africa, and once the African countries had gained independence, showed itself even less inclined to become involved in the problems of Asians living there.

The achievement of independence in these countries brought about a radical transformation of the situation. It meant the transfer of power to the indigenous people, who hitherto had been the most under-privileged group and had most lacked opportunities for economic and social advance. So there arose a new group who now wielded political power but remained economically deprived. The old regime had been established primarily for the benefit of the immigrants, though it is possible to argue that the Asians were merely the indirect and unintended beneficiaries. It was obvious that the new political élite would replace that government with one more responsive to needs of their own community.

As the more vulnerable of the previously privileged minorities, this change had tremendous implications for the Asians, who were ill-prepared to meet them. The constitutional arrangements for independence had done little to protect or help them. The Europeans were well taken care of. For the civil servants a scheme was introduced whereby they could either retire prematurely and obtain special compensation, plus accelerated pensions, or stay on until they were asked to retire, and obtain these benefits then. The white farmers, really significant only in Kenya, were offered a comparable scheme: about £50 million was contributed by the British government to a land purchase fund so that any farmer who wanted to sell his farm could do so at the high 1959 market prices.

A campaign to extend the civil service arrangements to Asian employees was rejected, while a proposal for some compensatory scheme to buy out the Asian traders who wanted to sell never even received consideration. The Asians were, however, covered by the provisions for the protection of human rights, particularly those of personal liberty and property, which Britain wrote into each of the independence constitutions, except in Tanganyika.

In one way, the independence constitutions offered a fair deal to the Asians. This was in regard to citizenship. Many of those involved in the Indian diaspora in other parts of the world have suffered from being denied citizenship in the countries of their residence, and have agitated for it.

In East and Central Africa citizenship has now become the crucial issue for members of the Asian community. Before independence, most of the residents of these countries, including Asians, were British citizens or British protected persons. It was only with independence that national citizenship was established.

While there were some differences among them, all the constitutions introduced a similar scheme for citizenship. According to its provisions a person would become a local citizen automatically on independence, or would have an option to become so within a specified time at his request, or his pre-independence status would remain unchanged.

In East Africa and Malawi the ones who became local citizens automatically were those British citizens or protected persons who had been born in the country and who had one parent also born in the country.

In Zambia it was enough if the person was himself born there. Automatic citizenship was also conferred on those who had been born abroad if their father had been entitled to citizenship or but for his death would have become a citizen.

A second category, which involved an option, covered certain groups of people who had a close connection with the country but failed to qualify for automatic citizenship. Such persons were allowed to register as citizens; indeed they had a constitutional right to be so registered, provided they applied within a prescribed period – in each case two years from independence – but the categories of people entitled to registration varied from country to country.

In East Africa and Malawi also included in this category were persons who would have automatically become citizens by virtue of birth in the country but for the fact that neither of their parents was born there; such persons in Zambia, as we have seen, would have become citizens automatically.

Another category common to all countries related to persons who on the date of independence were British citizens (citizens of the U.K. and colonies) who had acquired that status by naturalization or registration in the country whose citizenship they were seeking.

In Kenya, but not in the other countries, there was an additional category: all persons who were citizens of the U.K. and colonies and the Republic of Ireland on the day of independence and were lawfully and ordinarily resident in Kenya. Malawi also had an additional category: persons who were citizens of the former Federation and who could prove a 'substantial Malawi connection' by his (or his father's) birth, registration, naturalization, residence, adoption, or voting rights. In Kenya and Zambia there was also an entrenched right to naturalization. Citizens of Commonwealth or certain African countries who had satisfied certain residential requirements (four years in the case of Zambia) had a right to citizenship.

Finally, all the constitutions provided that anyone born in the country after independence, unless the offspring of diplomats or enemy aliens, would automatically become a citizen. So in most cases would children born abroad of a local citizen father. Those who did not become local citizens automatically or by option were allowed to retain their earlier citizenship, which in most cases happened to be British.

A considerable number of Asians, especially in East Africa and Malawi, would have become automatic citizens but the exact number is difficult to determine. At the beginning the governments were anxious that the Asians should apply in significant numbers to become citizens. They were inspired both by their vision of a non-racial society and by a wish to demonstrate to the outside world the confidence with which their new regimes were regarded internally.

The Asian response, unfortunately, was a poor one, and particularly in the early months few applications were made. The reluctance was in part a result of their confusion about the implications of citizenship. The decision taken by many Asians to retain British or Indian citizenship arose primarily from their fear that to give this up would be to give up the right to any kind of protection in the event of confiscation of property or persecution.

This was a time of some anxiety, not so much on account of what was happening in East and Central Africa but because of disturbances in neighbouring countries. Also rumours were current that once a person gave up his foreign passport he would not be allowed to travel abroad, or at least not without the payment of a substantial sum of money. For many not taking up local citizenship was seen as a way of keeping open an option to settle elsewhere. These Asians expected redundancy and victimization and felt they might eventually have to build a home in some other country. Furthermore, and this factor was particularly strong in Central Africa, there was fear for their culture – sometimes seen as the forced marriage of their daughters to outsiders – and if the preservation of their culture required it, they would emigrate.

The slowness of the Asian response no doubt irritated the new governments and their leaders. The rush of applications as the two-year period of grace drew to a close added to the irritation. Africans felt the Asians had been an unconscionable time weighing the pros and cons. Moreover, the governments were beginning to be embarrassed about the Asians who had become citizens. Policies were being formulated to bring Africans into commerce, to advance their educational and other progress, and in order to realize these aims discrimination in favour of the Africans was deemed essential. The more Asians who became citizens and therefore entitled to the same rights as the Africans, the less effective would this discriminatory policy be. Also a feeling developed that many Asians were becoming citizens merely in order to avoid the adverse effects of discriminatory policy and legislation; they were seen as opportunists and 'paper citizens'. In consequence the governments became much less enthusiastic about granting citizenship. A number of applications filed within the prescribed period were not processed, and some still remain so to this day – seven or eight years later.

Moreover, some of the governments proceeded to amend their laws so as to prevent or restrict the acquisition of citizenship. Kenya amended the section in its constitution which had conferred a right to citizenship on Commonwealth residents of prescribed length so that they lost this right and merely became 'eligible'.

Malawi introduced new legislation in 1966 under which children born there after 5 July 1966 no longer became citizens automatically. Such children could become citizens only if one of their parents were both a citzen of Malawi *and* a person of African race. Others could apply to become citizens, but whether their application was granted or not depended entirely on the discretion of the government. As a result children of non-African citizens could become stateless. Similarly, children born of Malawian citizens abroad could become Malawians only if one of the parents were a citizen by birth *and* of African race.

In Uganda, when the government announced its proposals for the new constitution in June 1967, racial provisions similar to Malawi's were put forth, but these were finally abandoned as a result of the opposition they encountered. Nevertheless the new constitutional provisions were more restrictive than they had been at independence: children born in Uganda were citizens only if one of their parents or grand-parents were a citizen of Uganda.

In Tanzania, as a result of the union of Tanganyika and Zanzibar, new citizenship regulations were promulgated, which in practice affected the Zanzibaris only. The result was to intro-duce an important new category among the East African Asians. Under these regulations, all who were citzens of Tanganyika and Zanzibar on 25 April 1964 became citizens of the Union – with some exceptions. Excluded from Union citizenship were three major categories: (a) those who had been deprived of their Zanzibar citizenship by the Revolutionary Council, or deported or exiled from Zanzibar; (b) Zanzibar citizens who had become so solely by virtue of their naturalization or registration in Zanzibar under the 1948 British Nationality Act; and (c) Zanzibar citizens by virtue of birth or father's birth in a part of the domin-ions of the Sultan other than that included in the State of Zanzibar. While many in the last category might have some other nationality as well (e.g. the Asians in Kenya's coastal strip), others in this group and almost all in the first two categories, became stateless. It is estimated there are something like 7,000 Asians in this cate-gory, most of whom are either in Zanzibar or have fled to Dar es Salaam.

Another group of stateless persons – or at least whose status is unclear – comprises certain Uganda Asians. Many who had acquired Uganda citizenship suddenly found themselves deprived of it because apparently they had not renounced their British citizenship. The status of such persons is still unclear and at least some of them could become stateless. Before the over-throw of Dr Obote, discussions had started between officials of the Uganda and British governments to determine the status of these persons. Likewise the Zambia President announced, in December 1970, that he had decided to establish a ministerial committee to process applications for Zambian citizenship, some of which have been pending for many years and others which have been rejected on arbitrary grounds.

PART TWO

THE PRESENT SITUATION

THE NATIONALITY PROBLEM

To summarize the tangled nationality position of the Asians in East and Central Africa, they can be divided into four broad categories.

First there are those who are citizens of a country in East or Central Africa, referred to here as local citizens. It is very difficult to obtain precise figures but our own estimates are as follows – in Tanzania about 20,000 opted to become citizens, while another 60,000 are citizens by automatic operation of the law. The comparable figures for Kenya and Uganda are 20,000 and 50,000, and 13,000 and 30,000 respectively. Far fewer opted for citizenship in Central Africa: in Malawi not more than twenty; in Zambia about 100. Of those who became citizens automatically, there must be about 2,000 in each country, in most cases minors.

Secondly, there are those who hold some form of British nationality, either as citizens of the U.K. and colonies, or as British protected persons. In Kenya, at independence, there were just over 100,000 British citizens and 3,000 protected persons among them. There has been considerable emigration since, and now there are probably just over 50,000. In Tanzania there are probably not more than 25,000 British Asians, a considerable number of whom are protected persons. In Uganda there are about 40,000 British Asians, of whom again a sizeable number are protected persons. In Zambia there are about 8,000, and in Malawi about 10,000 to 11,000.

In the third category are citizens of India or Pakistan. Excluding the 'expatriate Indians' who have come largely since independence on short contract terms to work as technical staff, there are about 15,000 in East Africa, and fewer than 1,000 in Central Africa.

The final category concerns stateless persons or those of doubtful status. There are about 7,000 in Tanzania; the number in Uganda is not known.

POST-INDEPENDENCE

The future of the Asian community – whether or not it stays in Eastern Africa, and if so on what terms and under what conditions

– depends in large measure on the policies of the new governments. After an initial period of some vagueness, these policies
are becoming increasingly clear, at least in their implications for
the future of the Asian community. Discussion here will focus
on those aspects of the policies which have a bearing on the
situation of the Asians.

It is important at the outset to make two distinctions. While
it was possible to talk in a general way of the whole region during
the colonial period, each of the independent countries has adopted
different policies, even though it is possible to trace the influence
of one country on another. Secondly, the laws and the practices
of these nations distinguish between Asians who are citizens of the
country and those who are not. Therefore it is no longer possible
to speak of the whole Asian community as if it shared a common
fate, at least in the immediate future.

RESTRICTIONS ON NON-CITIZEN ASIANS

It is unlikely that significant numbers of non-citizen Asians will
remain in East and Central Africa for many more years. Each
of the countries has embarked on a programme described as
localization or Africanization, whereby the key areas of economic
and governmental activity will be in the hands of citizens.

Starting with the civil service, this policy has been extended
to private commerce and to a lesser extent, industry. Legislation
has been enacted in all the countries to give the authorities the
necessary powers to implement this plan. Africanization of the
civil service was relatively easy, as the government concerned
could determine its own recruitment policies. Non-citizens who
were already in governmental employment could be asked to
leave under legislative provisions especially enacted for this
purpose. These measures have been important in East Africa;
in Central Africa, as we have seen, few Asians were employed
in the civil service. The results of this policy can be seen in the
table below which shows the number (in thousands) of Asian
employees in the public services in Kenya and Uganda in recent
years:

YEARS	KENYA	UGANDA
1961	12·2	2·0
1962	12·0	1·8
1963	11·9	1·7
1964	8·8	1·8
1965	9·5	1·6
1966	10·6	1·6
1967	8·5	1·6
1968	8·0	1·3

43

It should be noted that these years brought a rapid expansion in the number of public employees in all three countries. Thus the relative fall in the number of Asian employees has been even greater than is brought out by this table. Secondly, a substantial but unknown proportion of the present Asian employees are citizens of these countries. Thus the fall in the number of non-citizen employees has been quite considerable.

Comparable figures for Tanzania are not available, but there is no reason to doubt a similar trend there. Most of the Asians displaced from the public services would fall into the category of clerical, executive and skilled manual grades, though a few in the higher reaches of the civil services have also been affected.

The other legislation which specifically affects non-citizens concerns immigration and trade. At the time of independence a majority of the Asians had acquired the status of 'permanent residents'. Everywhere, except in Malawi, this status was converted to a residence permit for a maximum of two years. In Tanzania it is provided that no non-citizen (except an African from any of a few neighbouring countries) can remain in the country without an entry permit. The permits are issued subject to conditions relating to the area within which the holder may reside, the occupation or business (if any) in which he may engage, and the restrictions, prohibitions, or limitations subject to which he may engage therein; the permits also specify the duration of his residence in the country.

Over and above all this, the permits are liable to be cancelled at the discretion of the immigration authorities, after confirmation by the appropriate minister. This legislation enables the government to exercise effective control over the numbers, location and occupation of non-citizens. It also means they have little security in their right to reside in the country, as was demonstrated by expulsion orders against more than 300 Asians in 1967.

In mid-1971 the Tanzanian government decision was taken to acquire all rented property valued at over £5,800. If the property was built or acquired over ten years prior to the time the decision was taken, no compensation was to be paid. This affected the property of a number of Asians.

In Kenya, Uganda and Zambia the legislation regarding residence, employment and trade is even more comprehensive, their prototype being the pioneering Kenya models. The Kenya Immigration Act of 1967 stipulated that all non-citizen employees were liable to be asked to obtain work permits in order to continue in employment. As of January 1970, only employees falling within certain categories were called upon to obtain work permits. These categories, however, comprise the great bulk of Asian employees such as shop assistants, cashiers, accounts clerks, salesmen, typists, secretaries, stenographers and most kinds of skilled manual workers. Work permits are granted only after the Kenyanization Bureau has satisfied itself that no citizen with the requisite qualifications is available. At the same time, work permits are normally granted for periods of one to two years, during which time the employers are expected to train Kenyans to take over those jobs on the expiry of work permits; in Uganda they are issued for even shorter periods. It is likely that gradually other categories of employees will be called upon, as in Uganda where workers in all categories have been required to apply for permits. Kenya and Uganda have made the most use of this legislation; in Zambia it has been little applied so far, while at present Malawi has no plans for the repatriation of non-citizens.

The Trade Licensing Acts of Kenya, Uganda and Zambia include two major provisions which affect non-citizen business-men. The Acts reserve certain areas – the non-scheduled or non-prescribed areas, which in effect include all areas outside the main shopping centres of a few large cities – for citizens only. Non-citizens are allowed to operate there only if they are granted a licence, which is given for one year at a time. It is only in the scheduled areas, which have been steadily shrinking, that non-citizens can carry on their trade. The second provision of the Acts restricts trade in certain commodities to citizens only. The list, which is periodically extended, now includes such commodities as maize meal, sugar, rice, fresh vegetables, lentils, cement, meat, cigarettes, blankets, milk, shoes and sandals.

How have these measures affected the Asian community? To attempt to answer, it is necessary to form some idea of the number of gainfully employed Asians. No figures are available, but in Kenya rough estimates indicate that the number might be in the range of 42,000. Of these, 11,000 to 12,000 are thought to be citizens of Kenya. Therefore, potentially about 30,000 Asians are likely to be affected by Africanization measures. In the first year of the Immigration Act's operation it has been estimated that out of nearly 10,000 applications for work permits, about 1,000 were turned down. It may be safely concluded that virtually all those rejected were Asian applications.

Similarly it was reported in early 1969 that during the first year of effective operation of the Trade Licensing Act nearly 3,000 Asian traders had been refused trade licences. It is likely that quite a few of them were subsequently granted licences, though

45

the exact figures are not known. Again in early 1970 it was reported that nearly 1,000 Asian traders had been refused licences, 600 of them from Nairobi. It is clear that if these figures are true, they imply a sharp reduction in the number of Asian traders. It should also be remembered that many of these firms are owned by several heads of families. Thus if in the period between 1968 and 1970 a total of 4,000 Asian traders were refused licences, this would affect roughly 15,000 to 18,000 Asians in Kenya.

In Uganda it is estimated that up to 10,000 trading firms will be affected. The policy in Zambia is even more far-reaching. In 1968 President Kaunda announced that as from the beginning of 1970, non-citizens would not be given licences to operate in non-urban areas. In 1970 this was followed by another announcement that they would not be allowed to operate in urban areas either. The deadline is the beginning of 1972, so it can be expected that by January 1972 wholesale and retail trade by non-citizen Asians will cease, thus closing to them an area where the great majority have found employment. In addition certain other activities are to be forbidden to non-citizens, such as baking, etc. If these measures were to be fully implemented, the great majority of Asians would be out of business. As this would seriously disrupt trade in the country, it may be expected that these measures will be implemented gradually.

In Malawi, despite the absence of new specific legislation, a somewhat similar process is taking place. In 1968 the Asian traders in the rural areas (none of whom was a citizen) were given two years in which to move away from the villages and rural trading centres and into towns and larger urban areas. Most Asians from the rural areas have since moved out and have been given licences to operate in urban areas. Many of the shops vacated by the departing Asians are still unoccupied and the government is understood to be having second thoughts about the pace of application of its policies. The government has announced plans, following the examples of Kenya, Uganda, Tanzania and Zambia, to set up an Import-Export Company as a subsidiary of the Malawi Development Corporation. One of its purposes would be to supply goods to African businessmen. In time it could be developed into an instrument to exclude Asian businessmen from importing or dealing in specified goods as has happened in the other countries.

It does not necessarily follow that all the Asians affected by these laws will be compelled to cease trading entirely. In Malawi the Asian traders are still allowed to operate in urban centres, and indeed no trader has been forced out of business as a result of removal from the rural areas. Moreover, it is possible they will be free to move into more specialized trade – hardware, automobiles or electric goods. In Zambia displaced Asian traders are being urged to move into industry.

In East Africa opportunities in industry still exist; it is unlikely, however, that industry will be an answer for most of these people. In Malawi all industrial projects have to be licensed under the Industrial Development Act, which is often used to confer monopolies. Asians who have applied for industrial licenses have met with refusal. Whatever the reasons – and it is possible that in many instances the Asian applicants did not command sufficient financial and technical resources – the feeling persists that the government discriminates against them, largely due to the influence of white expatriate civil servants who channel such licences to European firms. In Zambia few Asians are sufficiently organized to go into industry; the leap from retail trading to an industrial enterprise is a big and difficult one. Moreover, and this factor is present to some extent in all the countries except possibly Kenya, Asians fear that if they start an industrial project which is successful, the government will subsequently move in to take it over.

Additionally there is the feeling that their days in Africa are numbered anyway, and as it may be necessary to leave in a few years' time, it is better to go now while there are still possibilities of starting a new career elsewhere.

In Malawi, in particular, this feeling has been aggravated by what is regarded as arbitrary action by the government. Deportations at short notice are common, and the Business Licensing Act has been amended to provide that if a partner in a business is deported, the trade license of the entire partnership is automatically revoked. Perhaps the most dreaded legislation is the Forfeiture Act passed in 1966 which decrees that if the minister is satisfied that a person's conduct has been or may be prejudicial to public security or the national economy, all of the latter's property, commercial, real and personal, will be confiscated to the state. The decision of the minister cannot be questioned in court, nor can any other action taken under the Act. The recent spate of deportations and confiscations has lowered the morale of the community, and many are contemplating leaving Malawi.

In other countries as well, though to nothing like the same extent, there is a crisis of confidence. The result, therefore, of the legislative and policy measures of these governments and the known fears and anxieties of the Asians is that over the next ten years we can expect a large-scale emigration of the non-citizens at least.

POSSIBILITIES OF EMIGRATION

An immediate problem for these people is to find another place to settle. A whole series of restrictions have been imposed on their movements which were not expected a few years ago. Many of the Asians who did not take up local citizenship had hoped eventually to settle in Britain. A study undertaken in Kenya in 1968 showed that of the Asians who were contemplating eventual emigration, 18 per cent preferred to settle in Britain, while 67 per cent preferred India and 6 per cent chose Canada. The accuracy of these figures is questionable, however. The purpose of the survey was to try to show that Britain had panicked in passing its 1968 restrictions on immigration, as the number of Asians who wished to go there was quite small. The interviewees were aware of this, and their answers could well have been determined by the desire to prove that a large number was not indeed involved.

Another reason why only a small percentage opted for Britain could have been fear of encountering racialism there which had been stirred up in order to increase the pressure for immigration restrictions.

According to the survey's figures only 12,000 Asians would have wanted to go to Britain, though the number of Asians holding British passports was estimated at 67,000. A more accurate assessment would almost certainly have made Britain the first preference of the majority. It is also likely that proportionately more Asians in East Africa than Central Africa would have preferred Britain to India or Pakistan. Britain does appear to offer better prospects for them than the other two countries, but many of the Central African Asians still feel strong cultural and emotional ties with their countries of origin. Some are first generation immigrants and they lack the educational and other skills that would facilitate adaptation in a foreign country like Britain. Some are already said to have made investments in India.

The East African Asians, on the other hand, are more sophisticated and skilled, and more adjusted to a cosmopolitan environment. Conscious as they are of the benefits of education, they are also attracted by the excellent opportunities for the education of their children in Britain.

Until 1962 immigration into Britain from the Commonwealth was unrestricted, but in that year legislation was passed the effect of which was that only a limited number of immigrants would be allowed in annually. The legislation did not, however, affect British citizens, wherever they might be, provided they held passports issued by Her Majesty's Government in Britain. Before independence in this region of Africa, British citizens living there were affected by these restrictions, as their passports were not issued in Britain. The position of protected persons was similar. After independence, British citizens once again acquired the right of free immigration to Britain, as they became entitled to U.K. passports, although the British protected persons remained excluded from this category.

For a few years after independence only a small number of Asians from East Africa and fewer still from Central Africa went to Britain, but towards 1967 the flow increased, especially from Kenya and Uganda, so that while in 1965 and 1966 about 6,000 had emigrated annually, in the first two months of 1967 alone about the same number emigrated.

The reason for the increase was only partly the increasingly difficult conditions for them in East Africa; more important was the suspicion that Britain was soon to introduce legislation to restrict their right of entry into Britain, a suspicion which was encouraged by the rather racialistic stand of some leading British politicians.

Legislation was in fact introduced in February 1968 as an amendment to the 1962 Act. It provided that certain categories of British citizens overseas had no right to enter Britain, notably those who had no 'close connection' with Britain, in the sense, *inter alia*, that neither they nor their fathers or grandfathers had been born in Britain. Though this legislation was not couched in racial terms, its effect was to introduce racial discrimination for the first time into British nationality and immigration laws, and the overwhelming majority of British Asians were thereby deprived of the right to enter and settle in Britain.

The 1968 legislation did not, however, impose a total prohibition on the immigration of British Asians. The government announced a scheme of 1,500 special vouchers a year for heads of families. They are called special vouchers because, unlike the vouchers issued under the 1962 Act, they are not related to prior employment or professional qualifications, but confer a right of entry regardless.

British Asians can also apply for ordinary vouchers under the 1962 Act, but as they have few means of arranging employment before reaching England and as the categories of 'professionals' is rather limited, not much use can be made of them. In 1969, for example, only ten out of the 300 vouchers assigned to Kenya were taken up.

It became obvious that a ceiling of 1,500 special vouchers would cause considerable hardship, for it would leave a large number of Asians who would be unable either to obtain or hold employment or carry on trade in East and Central Africa and yet who would have no right to enter Britain.

Since the enactment of the 1968 amendment and the fixing of the quota at 1,500, the pressures of Africanization increased, though it was admitted privately in British government circles that it was hoped the amendment would have the effect of slowing down Africanization programmes. In fact after 1970/71 Africanization did somewhat slow down, especially in Kenya where there was no further revocation of trade licences of non-Kenya citizens. There was also a slowing down in the replacement of non-citizens in administration. As a consequence the number of U.K. passport holders applying to the British High Commission in Nairobi for vouchers to come to Britain had declined from around 200 per month to fifty per month. Whereas in 1968 virtually no Kenya citizenship was being granted to Asians, in 1971 they were being granted at the rate of about a dozen per week.

It is unlikely that the Kenya and Uganda governments will allow these Asians to stay for so long, though it is sometimes alleged that they have succumbed to British pressure to allow them to remain, even though deprived of the opportunity to earn a living. For instance, in October 1971 Uganda took back four Asians who had been refused entry to the U.K. It was the first time in several years that Uganda had done this. In December 1971 the Uganda government announced the cancellation of citizenship applications of 12,000 Ugandan Asians. But in January 1972 the British government intervened, and after discussions were held at leadership level between the two countries, the cancellation was withdrawn by Uganda.

As a result of discussions with the governments of Kenya and Uganda, from the beginning of June 1971 the rate of entry of U.K. passport holders from Kenya was doubled from 1,500 to 3,000 special vouchers a year, in addition to which there was a special 'once-for-all' bonus of 1,500 vouchers during the next six months. In May 1972 the special vouchers were further increased from 3,000 to 3,500. As dependants – an average of three per family – are admissible on the passport holder's voucher, it was estimated that the total number of entrants for settlement would rise from about 6,000 to 18,000 in 1971 and to 12,000 in each future year.

In 1971 the total number of East African Asians who entered

Britain was 11,564, an increase of 4,725 on the 1970 figure of 6,839.

	1970	1971
Employment voucher holders	*115*	*134*
Special voucher holders	*1,644*	*2,956*
Others	*614*	*740*
Dependants	*4,466*	*7,734*
TOTAL	*6,839*	*11,564*

In January 1972 1,256 U.K. passport holders from East Africa entered Britain, as compared to 470 in January 1971.

As British policy is now administered, priority for the right to enter under the voucher system is given to those whose entry permit is cancelled or not renewed. In practice therefore a person can be without any employment or place to live, and yet not qualify for a voucher. Only if he becomes destitute does he move up in the queue. The result is that unemployed Asians live on their savings or on charity, uncertain of their future and becoming increasingly desperate. A few even attempt illegal entry.

If they are refused entry into Britain, other countries can, and do, refuse to take them, so that Britain is ultimately forced to admit them, though, more as a punitive measure than anything else, not until they have been locked up in jail for twenty-eight days, this being the maximum period of detention pending inquiries allowed under the 1968 Act, after which a habeas corpus application would probably secure their release.

The preceding discussion about the right of entry into Britain and the restrictive legislation in existence applies only to Asians who are British citizens; it has no relevance to the British protected persons. Under British law these are aliens, and at no time had unrestricted right of entry into Britain. Nor are they eligible to apply for entry under the Commonwealth Immigrants Act. Thus their position is even worse than that of the citizens of other Commonwealth countries.

The status of British protected persons is anomalous both under international law and British law. They have no territorial connection with Britain, are not nationals, and yet, vis-à-vis third parties, Britain claims to speak for them and they can demand the protection of the British government in foreign countries. The device thus prevents a considerable number of persons from actually becoming stateless, yet the rights of such persons are minimal and they share many of the disabilities of stateless persons.

It is not clear what Britain's obligation to them is in the event of their deportation from East Africa. It is arguable that as the only country with which they have any links, Britain is obliged to take them. The problem does not appear to have arisen yet, and in several cases India has helped by admitting such persons.

Britain's international responsibility to her overseas citizens, even though they may be treated as second rate under her own domestic legislation, is clear. If no other country wants them, Britain should take them in. This position has indeed been accepted by the government, for when the Home Secretary was introducing the legislation he told Parliament that if a citizen 'was thrown out of work and ejected' from a country, Britain would have to take him. While this statement created a great deal of hope, it has in practice been interpreted as applying only to those actually ordered to leave the country, and not to those only put out of employment.

It is interesting to note that in recent months the British government has shown greater signs of flexibility in its policies regarding the entry of African Asians holders of British passports.

At least 300 such persons who have flown to Britain from India in the first four months of 1972 without entry vouchers have been permitted to remain on visitors' visas (they hold 'D' passports which do not entitle them to residence in Britain). Statistics have shown that no such cases leave Britain at the end of their legal stay.

Officially there is no change in British government policy towards these immigrants (the Home Secretary said in March 1972 that there will be no large-scale immigration to Britain). But unofficially it appears that the government attitude is one of not making a fuss, and to put a stop to their previous policy of sending unqualified immigrants back, who, as they were not being allowed back into the country they had left, were forced to become airborne 'shuttlecocks' flying backwards and forwards to Britain. It is not yet known if, under the new unofficial policy, the government will impose an annual limit on admittance of those without entry vouchers.

A further indication of the easing of attitude on the part of British political leadership is the recent Green paper produced by the Labour party* proposing a major reform of the law of citizenship which would give groups like the East African Asians free access to Britain. One of the proposals was 'that U.K. citizens with no colonial, dual or other citizenship should have the right to free entry to Britain on the same basis as other U.K. citizens'.

What are the alternative avenues of emigration? Many of the

Citizenship, Immigration and Integration (1970).

Asians who are equipped for a life in the U.K. could also fit into Canadian society, and most of them would be willing to emigrate there despite their greater ignorance of conditions in Canada. A certain amount of emigration to Canada does take place (approximately 5,000 went in 1968 alone), but immigration regulations are stringent, being related basically to Canada's manpower requirements, and it is unlikely that many Asians will qualify for settlement. The Asians who do qualify tend to be those with professional or commercial skills or with considerable financial means, groups which are very mobile in any case. So Canada cannot really be looked to for alleviation of hardship cases unless there is a significant change of policy.

The Common Market countries too are beginning to tighten up on immigration. A safeguard system to prevent too many immigrants in Britain seeking jobs in other Common Market countries after British entry was agreed to by Britain and the six in Brussels on 14 January 1972. This was at the special request of the Dutch government who feared that their high standard of social services would attract a large influx of immigrants.

A special clause is to be included in the Treaty of Accession allowing Community institutions to authorize a country receiving too many immigrants to call a halt. The decision on when a country can forbid entry of immigrant workers will be made by the Market Council of Ministers on a proposal from the Commission.

Commonwealth immigrants to Britain who have not applied for British citizenship will not be able to travel freely to work in Europe when Britain joins the Common Market. Britain's definition of 'nationality' made it clear that all immigrants who had been resident in the country for five years or who were not subject to immigration control could, under the Market rules as they stood, seek jobs in other Market countries after British entry. By this same definition patrials (citizens of the U.K. and colonies who are citizens by their birth or that of a parent or grandparent or by adoption, registration or naturalization) were excluded from travelling freely to work in Europe.

In the case of East African Asians, those who have lived long enough in Britain and met other requirements to be given full status as 'nationals' will qualify to benefit from Market rules. But those still in East Africa would not.

Small openings have existed for skilled and semi-skilled Asians in some developing African countries; Zambia, for example, wanted to use Asian railway workers and teachers to reduce her dependence on Europeans, and Ethiopia recruited a number of

Asians. These countries, however, cannot be expected to absorb more than a small fraction, and even that possibility has been in jeopardy since the 1968 amendment to British immigration laws, for these other countries have been anxious not to be burdened with U.K. Asians with nowhere else to go after their term of employment comes to an end. Pakistan has introduced similar restrictive regulations. Thus an unexpected consequence of the British legislation has been to reduce severely the possibility of Asians moving even to countries where their services are needed.

The most serious repercussion in this respect has been in relation to the right to settle in India, although so far this applies only to the Asians in Kenya. Many of them who had planned to emigrate to India found after enactment of the 1968 law that doors to India were also barred. Whatever the reason for this – it was generally assumed to be India's method of putting pressure on Britain to accept her legal obligation vis-à-vis the U.K. Asians – it introduced a further element of uncertainty and hardship. A partial solution was found in an agreement made between India and Britain in July 1968. Its terms cover 'persons of Indian origin holding U.K. passports and resident in Kenya who are compelled to leave and wish to go to India'. If such persons are denied permits for residence or opportunities of employment or trade, they can seek an endorsement on their passports from the British High Commission, and on the presentation of this endorsement to the Indian High Commission they become eligible for admission into India. The endorsement states that the person concerned has a right to enter the U.K. and will be issued with an entry certificate on application to the nearest British representative. Even in this case the applicant must be out of a job to be eligible.

In order to ensure that this procedure is not used to by-pass the quota set under the 1968 Act, the endorsement is given only when the British High Commission is convinced after careful investigation that the applicant genuinely wants to settle in India. The result is that most of those who go to India under this scheme seem to settle there; only 6 per cent of them have applied to go to Britain. But another result is that there is a waiting list for those wishing to go to India, while others who are not yet unemployed but may wish to move there have difficulty as well. With regard to those who do go to India but later change their minds and wish to avail themselves of the option to go to Britain, it has been alleged that they have found the endorsement useless and are forced to take their place in the queue for the 1,500 vouchers. Exact figures of those who have gone to India under this system are not available, but it is estimated that in the seven years up to 1968, 40,000 Asians have permanently settled there.

Even as recently as in mid-1971 India was allowing large numbers of Kenyan Asians to enter the country on six-month visitors' visas. But at the same time India indicated to Britain that she was not prepared to keep these Asians indefinitely; she requested the British government to take about 15,000 Asian holders of U.K. passports who had been admitted to India over the previous three years.

Unlike Kenya and Uganda the Indian government has not responded to pressure upon it by the British government to stop Asians with U.K. passports from leaving India. The Indian government's attitude has been a consistent one: that Britain should accept its responsibilities to its own citizens.

Since passage of the 1968 British law, much of the discussion about the plight of the non-citizen Asians has concerned the limited possibilities for emigration. While for large numbers this is the immediate problem, a longer term problem is that of establishing a new home and a new form of livelihood. Many of the people involved are of advanced age, have worked all or most of their lives in East Africa, and may now find it difficult to make a new start. This is more true of the shopkeeper or small wholesaler than of the white-collar worker or artisan. Most have put aside some capital which they hoped would help them make a start. But in many cases, due to their unemployment, such capital is rapidly eroded, while they wait their turn to go to Britain, India or elsewhere.

Even if substantial capital is available, only a limited amount can be taken out initially on emigration. In East Africa the sum used to be £5,000 per head of family, inclusive of personal belongings; and thereafter £2,000 a year until the entire amount was taken out. In 1968 the initial amount was reduced to £2,500 because there were fears of a severe drain on foreign exchange reserves at the time of the 'exodus'.

In Central Africa the provisions are still quite liberal. In Zambia a person is allowed £8,000 initially if he is over fifty-five or £6,000 if he is under fifty-five; thereafter £5,000 annually. In Malawi a person of fifty-five years or more can take out £7,500 initially, otherwise £4,000; and thereafter £4,000 annually. It should be mentioned, however, that out of fifteen families who applied recently to leave Malawi under these terms, only one application was approved.

For a person who intends to buy a house or set himself up in business abroad, the initial amount he can take with him is quite inadequate. Even if the intention is to form a joint family enterprise, the total capital available is unlikely to be adequate for anything but very limited enterprises.

In any event there is no guarantee that the various members of a family will find themselves in the same country abroad. One of the less publicized but unfortunate consequences of the tangle of various citizenship and immigration laws is the splitting of numerous families. Various members of a family have sometimes been ascribed different nationalities by the automatic operation of the law; certain members opted for local citizenship while others did not. The more educated members find that they can obtain a visa for settlement in Canada, while those less skilled cannot. Thus the tradition of family cohesion and mutual assistance which has been an important factor in the East African Asians' success in commerce and industry often breaks down when the family emigrates.

The question may well be asked as to how the Asians can expect to fare in their second migrations. Whether they return to their ancestral homes in India or Pakistan, settle in the harsher climate and strangeness of Canada or encounter colour-conscious Britain, will they not carry with them the sense of belonging to a minority group and its attendant difficulties? Will they be exchanging one set of problems for another?

It is of course difficult to answer this question. Asians who are leaving East Africa are doing so either because they are being forced out or because they feel the future there holds little for them or their children. Not many of them have had strong emotional attachments to East Africa, and the vindictiveness, as they perceive it, of the governments there have made many of them frustrated and bitter. Thus, while many will undoubtedly experience physical inconvenience, suffering and financial loss in leaving East Africa, only a few of the Asians will feel emotional regrets, except when families are forcibly split up.

Even if their new governments are not positively welcoming, the absence of those negative features is in itself encouraging. The Asian migrants are willing to make a fresh start and anxious to have a sense of security. They find they are not conspicuously more affluent than their new hosts. They are better equipped than many other immigrants, and with their advantages of education, skills and finance, they should not experience too much difficulty in establishing themselves in their new homes.

It may be that, in time, the only relevance East Africa will have for them is the lesson they may have learnt from their first experience of migration. It is not clear whether they have decided that for a minority rigid communal isolation is good or unwise; what does seem more obvious is that in their new countries the tendency towards integration and assimilation are much stronger than they have been in East Africa.

THE PROBLEM OF ASIAN CITIZENS

The most significant consideration for our purpose is the future of those Asians who are citizens of one of the East African countries. Most, if not all of them, expect to continue living there. Will they be allowed to carry on their pursuits and be treated on a basis of equality with the Africans? What economic prospects do they have? What role will they play in society? Will they continue in their communalistic ways or will there be greater integration with the other races? Answers to these questions depend on a variety of factors.

What are the policies of these governments in relation to the Asians? What is the attitude of the Asians? How will the economies of these countries develop? Will there be political stability?

The policies of these countries differ, and even within individual countries there have been fluctuations in policy during the short period since independence. Further, there is sometimes a disparity between policy and rhetoric, and between law and practice. An attempt will be made to describe the policies and to assess their implications for the Asians, but the above proviso should be kept in mind.

The official policy in all three countries of East Africa is one of equal treatment for the Asian citizens. Sometimes this policy is unclear because when official threats or warnings are pronounced, it is not always obvious that they pertain only to non-citizen Asians. Also, many statements of policy are couched in terms of 'Africanization', a concept which has similar terminological ambiguities and racial connotations, although on occasions its use has been defended on the basis that it refers to all citizens. But it is doubtful whether this policy is absolutely fair in its applications to Asians, for despite their high educational and technical skills, few Asians occupy really senior positions.

Attitudes of citizen Asians have developed in response to their environment, to the policies of the governments and to the opportunities open to them. It would be true to say that the situation at present is unsettled. It is unlikely that many citizen Asians will leave in the near future, and indeed some of them have done extremely well recently due to the removal of competition from the non-citizens. Thus, for the foreseeable future at least, the great majority of citizen Asians will remain in East and Central Africa.

In assessing their future prospects, particularly in regard to their relationship with the Africans, it would be best to consider various sectors individually: economics, education, politics and social relations.

ECONOMICS

This is perhaps the crucial area and may well determine whether Asians will stay on in Africa or not in the long-term; it also affects important aspects of the Asian-African relationship.

The role of Asians in the economic life of the region has decreased. One instance is the decline of their role in the marketing of cash crops, which was an important function of and source of income for Asian traders, especially in Uganda and Tanganyika. The marketing and ginning of cotton was in fact a virtual Asian monopoly during the inter-war period in Uganda, but later there was a steady increase in the share taken by co-operatives and individual growers in cotton marketing and ginning. This was the result in part of the natural growth of the co-operative movement but the process was also aided significantly by government legislation, even in the colonial period, which in effect compelled Asian ginners to sell out to co-operatives by its assigning control over the allocation of the cotton crop to ginneries in different zones. As a result by the early sixties the co-operatives and individual growers virtually controlled the marketing and ginning of the entire cotton crop.

A similar policy was applied to other cash crops. Coffee-curing and marketing, which until the fifties were largely in the hands of non-Africans, had been placed firmly in the hands of co-operatives by 1966. Likewise greater control was secured over the marketing of minor cash crops through creation of the Agricultural Produce Marketing Board.

In Tanzania co-operatives had played a more important role from an earlier period, particularly in the Chagga area. But here again official policy ensures that co-operatives and state marketing boards will take over the marketing and processing of all agricultural products as soon as possible.

As a consequence the Asian role in the marketing and processing of the important cash crops has been virtually eliminated in the East African countries.

There has been a similar decline in their participation in commerce. Initially Tanzania made an attempt rapidly to increase the share of co-operatives and African businessmen in wholesale and retail trade. The first Five Year Plan issued in 1964, for instance, aimed to increase the share of co-operatives to 10 per cent of wholesale and retail trade by 1970, and to between 30 and 40 per cent in the longer run. In order to further this objective, the International Trading and Credit Company of Tanganyika Ltd (INTRATA) and the Co-operative Supply Association of Tanganyika (COSATA) were set up by the government. However subsequent experience with COSATA proved to be disastrous as the organization incurred huge liabilities and sustained heavy losses. Thus the co-operative movement failed to make significant inroads into wholesale or retail trade.

Meanwhile the government's attitude toward private African enterprise was undergoing a fundamental change. This was defined in the famous Arusha Declaration of 1967 which, as is well known, called for a wide-ranging programme of nationalization of private banking, insurance and leading commercial and industrial enterprises. At the same time the leadership ethic effectively put an end to the incipient business activities of the African political and bureaucratic élite. The government had turned away from the policy of encouraging the emergence of an African business class; for the paradoxical result of this move towards socialism was to shield established Asian and European businessmen from the incipient competition of African traders. Long-term policy continued, however, to be one of eliminating capitalist elements in the commercial and industrial sectors and effecting their replacement by co-operative and state-owned enterprises.

It should be noted here that the majority of the enterprises nationalized at the time of the Arusha Declaration were large scale, expatriate-owned firms. The nationalized commercial firms were amalgamated with INTRATA to form the State Trading Corporation (S.T.C.). Soon after its inauguration the S.T.C. was handling 20 per cent of all imports and 7 per cent of total exports. It had also acquired distribution rights for certain locally manufactured products. Since that time the S.T.C. has steadily extended its operations in all these directions.

The logical extension of this policy was realized in February 1970, when the Tanzanian government announced that the entire wholesale trade would be handled by the S.T.C. This was bound to affect large numbers of Asian traders, many of whom would be forced to close down. Even retail traders may find operating under the new conditions less attractive and less profitable. In the early stages of the take-over of wholesale trade the S.T.C.

is expected to make considerable use of Asian merchants with experience in this field.

For the present, retail trade remains largely in private hands. The S.T.C.'s policy thus far has been not to extend exclusive distribution rights to a few selected traders, nor to give preference to African or citizen businessmen. It does, however, give preference to co-operatives if they are efficient distributors. Long-term policy in the retail sector is to replace private enterprise by co-operative and state enterprise. It is likely that the S.T.C. will move into retail business in the years ahead, and in that event the last stronghold of Asian business will be liquidated.

The thrust of Tanzanian policies has been to transform the colonial economy into a socialist economy. In sharp contrast to this, Kenya has followed a vigorous policy of Africanization in commerce and industry and has pioneered many techniques in this area which are being adopted by other Eastern and Central African states facing similar problems. Even where state institutions have been created in the fields of commerce and industry, they have been used more to further Africanization than to extend state control and ownership. In the earlier period the emphasis was on increasing the competitiveness of African businessmen through training, subsidized loans, commercial extension services, etc. But this approach did not yield rapid results and the government introduced new legislation under which non-citizen employees and traders had to obtain work permits and trade licences in order to continue in gainful employment. This we have already examined.

In addition to these tools, the government has also created other institutions and policies to help accelerate Africanization. The Industrial and Commercial Development Corporation (I.C.D.C.) has, among its other functions, the responsibility for promoting African business enterprises through loans, advisory services and equity participation. The Kenya National Trading Corporation (K.N.T.C.) has monopoly rights over the import and distribution of certain commodities, and it assists African businessmen by granting them distributive rights in these commodities. It also provides training facilities for them. Local manufacturers of some important products have been persuaded or required to distribute their products through K.N.T.C. and hence through African traders. Under the Transport Licensing Act non-citizen businessmen must obtain licences to operate carriers. Various steps have been taken to accelerate African participation in the construction industry as well.

Uganda has followed policies and practices very similar

to Kenya's, namely the promotion of African, as opposed to more generally citizen, business activities. Their effect, as in Kenya, will be the Africanization of small-scale capitalism. However, unlike the position in Kenya but in accordance with the spirit of the Arusha Declaration, the Uganda government announced in May 1970 the complete or partial nationalization of major sectors of the economy, including import and export trade, all manufacturing and plantation industries, banks, oil companies, public transport and mining companies. The implementation of these measures will have the most far-reaching effects on the economic prospects of the Asian community.

Whereas policies aimed at greater localization affect only the non-citizen Asians and in fact may temporarily help citizen Asians by reducing competition in business and employment from non-citizens, measures of a socialist nature adversely affect all capitalist enterprises, whether owned by citizens or non-citizens. The ultimate goal of a socialist economy is of course the complete elimination of all capitalist elements in the society.

It remains to be seen whether the Uganda government will follow up its nationalization measures by curbing incipient African capitalism. As it is, there are some unresolved conflicts inherent in the government's present policies which aim at increasing the socialist sector of the economy while simultaneously promoting African capitalism.

The change of regime in Uganda has introduced further uncertainty. It is too early to speculate about the economic policy of the new government. While restrictions against non-citizen Asians are unlikely to be modified, there may be greater scope for Asian citizen private enterprise than under the old regime.

In Zambia the position is similar to that in Uganda; President Kaunda has nationalized the major sectors of the economy, while retaining strong incentives for the growth of local capitalism.

Some years ago business families usually planned for their sons to enter the family business. Now more and more the Asian parent plans for his children careers other than commerce. Higher education is regarded as more vital than ever before, while increasing importance is also attached to the acquisition of technical skills. It is realized that there will be increasing unemployment for school leavers. While many Asian youths will be able to avoid unemployment because they possess special skills, others will inevitably fail to find jobs. Some sections of the community will suffer a drastic reduction in their standard of living. There do not seem to be many alternative ways of earning a

E

living. In Kenya and Uganda land is scarce, and it seems impossible that Asians will have a chance to go into agriculture.

Such a possibility does however exist in Tanzania where land is more plentiful. A number of young Asians have been recently trained in agriculture, and initial experiments in settling Asians on land and introducing them to farming have been successful. The government has encouraged such activities and has offered Asians technical assistance. This is a promising development.

Another area where Asians could make an important contribution is in the more technical and skilled areas of public and semi-public employment. As the East African countries move towards greater state ownership and control and as parastatal institutions proliferate, there is an increasing demand for personnel skilled in the ways of commerce, insurance and accounting. At present most of such persons are to be found among the Asian communities. To an important extent the success of experiments in state enterprise could depend on these Asians. It is another question, however, whether they will be allowed to make such a contribution. In Tanzania the services of Asians have been used, and it is generally acknowledged that the success of nationalization owes a great deal to their work. Kenya and Uganda have so far shown little inclination to employ Asians in similar ways.

It would be idle to speculate further about the future. A key determinant will be the scope and nature of educational facilities, and the extent of access to them, a subject to which we now turn.

EDUCATION

As we have seen, the educational systems in colonial times operated along racial and segregated lines. In addition there were enormous disparities in the standards of education available to children of different races. Equally, there was great disparity in access to educational facilities. While practically every Asian and European child attended primary school and most of them (at least in East Africa) had access to secondary education, the primary school enrolment for Africans in the fifties was considerably below 50 per cent, while only a tiny fraction of the relevant age group could obtain secondary education. The educational system for all three races was based on the British school system, with similar curricula and examinations.

It was to be expected that after independence the national governments would introduce major changes in the systems inherited from the colonial era. Education is a key instrument for forging national unity and promoting development of the economy. In addition, because of the almost universal desire for more and better education, it has also become a highly sensitive issue in national politics. There have been many important changes in the educational systems of these countries during the last decade. Our purpose here is to focus on these changes in so far as they affect the Asian community.

The first major reform was integration of the school system. This has affected both government and communal state-aided schools. This integration has been brought about by opening the formerly Asian and European schools to African children, and in these schools preference is given to African children. Quotas have been set, so that already most of the former Asian schools have a predominance of African children. Even as between children of citizens, Africans receive preference. Under this policy the proportion of African children admitted to such schools in Kenya has been raised from 33 per cent in 1966 to 80 per cent in 1970. As a result it is now much more difficult for Asian children to enter school. The pressure is felt particularly in the secondary schools; most children are able to get into primary schools.

The situation is most critical in Tanzania, where the government has taken over all schools. In Uganda and Zambia, because of the big expansion in educational facilities just before and after independence, the situation is much better and most Asian children are admitted to secondary schools. In Malawi it is becoming increasingly difficult to find secondary school places.

The response of the Asian community to these reduced educational opportunities has been to establish their own unaided schools, as they had done at the turn of the century. It has been estimated that in Tanzania alone no less than twenty-four secondary schools have sprung up all over the country since 1964 to cope with the educational crisis. Similarly in Kenya several new secondary schools have been built or are being contemplated.

In addition to community-run schools, private schools run on commercial lines have mushroomed in the last fifteen years. In Malawi a company has been set up in which shares can be bought, which entitle one to a place in the secondary schools financed by the company's funds. While such schools answer a real need, they tend to be inferior to government schools; and as they receive little or no subsidy, even when they are not profit-making organizations, the fees tend to be relatively high, and so preclude most children of poor parents. Some parents manage to send their children overseas, but apart from the cost factor governments have been restricting the use of foreign exchange for this purpose.

For instance in August 1970 Tanzania refused to provide foreign exchange for the overseas education of residents of Tanzania.

The second comprehensive reform has been in the direction of 'nationalization' of the educational systems. The curricula are being redrafted to reflect local history, geography, zoology, etc. In Tanzania and Kenya Swahili is increasing in importance, and already the first eight years or so of schooling in Tanzania is conducted in Swahili. There is more stress on the relevance of education to the problems of these countries, and here again Tanzania takes the lead. There is now considerable emphasis on rural and agricultural education, and the school entry age has been raised from five or six to seven so that towards the end of primary school students are old enough to learn skills like carpentry and farming. The function of primary schools is no longer regarded as that of preparing an élite for secondary and university education. School leaving and higher school certificate examinations for East Africans are conducted locally.

While these changes undoubtedly represent a step forward from the national point of view, their effect on the Asian community has been a mixed one. On the one hand, Asian citizens should benefit from an educational system which is more tailored to local conditions and more attuned to the needs of the economy. On the other hand, such education reduces their mobility. It renders a little more difficult the acquisition of higher education and technical skills which the community feels are becoming increasingly indispensable to its survival. Also the new emphasis on agriculture is less relevant for the Asian community which has always been and will continue to be highly urbanized.

At the post-secondary level, the children of citizen Asians have done well. The universities have been able to absorb all the candidates qualified for entry, and because of the earlier favourable position of the Asians a disproportionately large number of university students are or have been Asians.

This situation does not apply in Malawi and Zambia, however. The former has about twelve and the latter ten Asian university students, not all of them local Asians. Lack of financial means has been no barrier. In Malawi university education is free and in Zambia it is heavily subsidized, while in East Africa all qualified citizens are able to secure government bursaries to supplement whatever funds the parents can afford.

In the last few years a considerable number of Asians have graduated from the University of East Africa (now divided into national universities). Most have taken degrees in medicine, engineering, architecture and other science-based professions –

areas where there is a dearth of qualified people in East Africa. It remains to be seen how long Asians will retain this lead in university education. In time the results of changes in the primary and secondary school system will no doubt be reflected in the university intake.

POLITICS

In East Africa Asians actively participated in politics before independence. As we have seen, this was largely because political representation was on a communal basis. At independence communal and fancy franchises were abolished, and at the same time political rights were reserved to citizens. These two factors combined to reduce Asian interest and effectiveness in politics. Politics are now a matter of political parties, where the role of the individual politician is less important than before. Politics are also based on tribal or regional support and alliances.

In this context Asians feel there is no scope for a distinctively Asian contribution. Asian political parties have been voluntarily dissolved. Many Asians, particularly in Zambia and Malawi, feel there is safety in low visibility and that avoiding an active role in politics will prevent their involvement in controversy and factionalism. In these two countries there are no prominent Asians in political life.

This is unlike the situation in East Africa where some of the Asians active in politics before independence still have a role. While their abilities are not in question, they have, with one or two rare exceptions, been kept on solely to reward their past services or in order to present a picture of non-racialism or to strengthen party prospects. These Asians have probably reached the limits of their careers and the majority can be expected to leave politics in the foreseeable future.

At present it seems unlikely that an element of fresh Asian blood will be injected into East African politics. Many young Asians who are committed to East Africa are also those with superior education and skills; while in former times these people might well have gone into politics, they now feel they can best serve their country by working in the universities or the public services. A few might have considered politics if the circumstances had been more propitious. As long as the rewards in politics are as attractive as they are, at least in Kenya and Uganda, an effective Asian entrance will be difficult, while the restrictions placed by Tanzania on the commercial activities of politicians may discourage propertied Asians there.

Another characteristic of politics in East and Central African countries is the trend towards a one-party system: both in law and in practice there is one effective political party which controls most institutions of the state and the instruments of propaganda. In such conditions, free from fears of rival political parties, the leaders can impose on the country decisions that might otherwise be politically risky. Theoretically such a system should be more favourable than the two-party system both to Asian politicians and to the Asian population in general. In a two-party system it is difficult for Asians to decide which party to support, for whichever party they do not support threatens them with reprisals.

As Asians in East Africa have generally been divided in their support between the two parties in a particular country, they have become the target of abuse and threats from both sides. A one-party system eliminates the need for this agonizing choice; Asian loyalties to the political system can be manifested more readily and more fearlessly. This theoretical proposition may not apply in reality, however, for the single party is seldom as monolithic as it seems. It could be disastrous for the Asians to become involved in the subterranean struggles for power within the single party.

It is interesting to look at the actual political participation of Asians since independence. Tanzania is perhaps the country in which Asian participation at grass-roots level is most pronounced. This is partly due to the fact that local politics have been more important in Tanzania than elsewhere as a result of TANU's structure, but in part it is a reflection of the determination of the Asians there to involve themselves in the affairs of the country. While a considerable number of Asians are members of TANU, especially in the smaller urban centres, only comparatively few have played an active part in its management. But their number is larger than is generally supposed.

A study conducted in Dar es Salaam in 1968 found that there was a significant degree of Asian participation in the affairs of TANU. Several political leaders as well as branch and cell leaders were interviewed and the general opinion was that since independence Asians had shown greater willingness to join in political activities. A large number of cell leaders were found to be Asians; it was estimated that they comprised 10 per cent of the total in the capital, though exact figures were not available. One Ismaili leader stated that 90 per cent of his community had joined TANU.

At the national level, too, Asian participation had been significant and the general elections of 1965 and 1970 showed that it was still possible for an Asian candidate to defeat an African rival in a predominantly African constituency. One of those elected in 1965 and again in 1970 is Amir Janal, the Minister for Finance.

In Kenya, Uganda, Zambia and Malawi there is less Asian participation. In the 1969 general elections in Kenya not a single non-African candidate was elected, and it is doubtful whether results would be different if similar elections took place in Uganda. Perhaps it is not merely a coincidence that the Asians in these countries are so highly involved in organizations like Lions and Rotary Clubs; feeling unable to participate in the national political system, they look to these organizations for excitement and prestige.

SOCIAL

Social relations cover a wide spectrum, ranging from behaviour toward a domestic servant to inter-racial marriages. African leaders say that Asians must integrate themselves with the host society. Asians agree – so long as integration does not mean inter-racial marriages, forms of forced association, or a threat to their own culture. Thus there is a great deal of uncertainty about what is meant by or involved in integration.

Integration presumably means a state of affairs where the various communities live in harmony, owing common loyalty to key political and administrative institutions. Beyond that, it can take the form either of pluralism, where each group retains its own cultural and social institutions, or assimilation, where the cultures mix and merge, which in most cases means that the culture of the majority group will dominate. On this important issue there has been little meaningful discussion. What the Asians prefer is perhaps clearer than what the Africans want, but even among the former attitudes are changing.

The Asians have a predilection for pluralism, and this is more marked in Central Africa than East Africa. This attitude is rooted deeply in their culture, and the difference with regard to pluralism between the Asians in East and Central Africa is due to the greater hold of tradition on the latter group. Colonial rule served merely to reinforce cultural isolation and social and economic divisions.

We have already discussed various changes taking place since independence that should have the effect of breaking down these divisions. Perhaps the most important of these changes is the integration of the educational system. The emphasis on education in the early years of Asian settlement owed as much to cultural

67

as to economic factors. The early educational system for Asians laid much emphasis on religious instruction, Indian languages and on the transmission of traditional Indian values and culture generally. But over the years the Asian educational system has been steadily Westernized, and education has played a key, if unintended, role in promoting social change within the Asian community.

Almost within a generation the Asian population has been wrenched from a traditional society into a Western-orientated one. Thus any enquiry into, for example, the extent of change from the joint family to the nuclear family, with its profound social consequences, must devote attention to the impact of education.

In this connection it is particularly relevant to assess the role played by education for girls. In the last twenty years there has been a virtual social revolution in the status of women in Asian society. Increasing educational opportunities, which in turn led to a large number of Asian women seeking paid employment, has been a vital element in this process. The recent moves towards nationalization of the educational systems, accompanied by greater emphasis on local problems, will further accelerate the detachment of the Asian community from their inherited traditions. The rapid disappearance of Indian languages from primary and secondary school curricula will also prove in the long run a powerful factor in the erosion of Indian cultural influences.

The integration of the educational system from kindergarten to university will have a profound effect on the attitudes and positions of the new generation of East African Asians. It is bound to lead to better race relations, to improved understanding of the diverse cultures of East African societies and to increased social contact across racial lines. The reduction or elimination of differential educational facilities for different races can also be expected in the long run to lead to a corresponding reduction of racial inequalities in income and wealth.

What of the preference of Africans? Some African leaders have asked for total assimilation, as signified by inter-racial marriage. Others have shown no marked preference for this degree of social integration, and it is significant that the rising African élite prefers to socialize *inter se*; and its members prefer to marry girls of their own tribe. It is therefore difficult to say whether or not the Africans want total assimilation.

The policies of the governments have been ill-defined. The Zanzibar government comes nearest to demanding complete assimilation. And characteristically it is in the sphere of marriage that the government there has applied most pressure. President

Karume has brought pressure on the Asian community in an attempt to promote the marriage of its daughters to Africans and a decree passed in 1970 dispenses with the necessity for the consent of both parties to the marriage.

The mainland Tanzanian government has also shown itself to be favourably inclined toward assimilation, though not one so drastic in nature, and has been careful to avoid giving the impression of employing coercion. It has frequently attacked communal cultural and social institutions, stopped radio broadcasts in Indian languages, and insisted on active Asian participation in local self-help schemes and in the rallies and other activities of the TANU party. The emphasis on Swahili as the national language also helps to bring the Asians more into the mainstream of national life, as does an integrated system of schooling.

Kenya and Uganda, despite their imposing economic pressures on the community, have done little to accelerate integration. Communal institutions flourish, including schools. Fewer efforts have been made to get the Asians involved in political parties or schemes of self-help, and women's and youth organizations have not really become multi-racial.

Even greater isolation is tolerated in Zambia and Malawi. In those countries Asian housing is still largely segregated, and few even of the educated Asians participate in the cosmopolitan life of the capitals.

One of the difficulties involved in discussing policies of assimilation in the East and Central African context is the absence of a homogeneous predominant culture. The various tribes have differences, and in any case the African way of life is itself undergoing profound changes. In the absence of a stable dominant culture, total assimilation is not very practicable. The irony of the situation is that the common meeting-ground of the two communities may well prove to be Western culture.

If one is to judge by trends since independence, one can say that the earlier pressures on the Asian community to 'integrate' are weakening. Perhaps Asian exclusiveness in the past has been resented not so much for itself as for its implications of racial arrogance and superiority. As more and more Africans move into positions of responsibility and wealth, they acquire greater confidence and seem less disturbed by this traditional practice. So far there has been no concerted attack on the exclusiveness of any communities. The Asian community regarded as having made the most progress in integration with the Africans is the Ismaili group which has responded to the able leadership of the Aga Khan and his administrators. For example almost all 8,000

Kenyan Ismailis took out citizenship at the time of independence. Yet the Ismailis are as culturally bound as other Asian groups, and their social organization is even more cohesive and exclusive than that of others. With greater political freedom and increasing African prosperity, there is less concern with social distance between the races, except in Zanzibar.

It is unlikely, however, that the pattern of inter-racial social relations will remain unchanged. There are many forces at work which should lead to the breakdown of isolation. The abolition or reduction of communal schools and other services is bringing the different Asian sub-communities together. The unfreezing of the structure governing the distribution of wealth and jobs is of profound significance. What was often a class problem tended to be viewed as racial, for such were the economic disparities between the races that social contact was barely conceivable. Now the former strict segregation of residential areas is breaking down as the African élite moves into the more fashionable sections. Even in the less desirable areas the Asians and the Africans have become neighbours. There is increasing contact in a great many spheres of life, not least in the trade unions, which until recently have been inclined to practise racialism but now tend to bring together the working members of the two races.

In Tanzania the government has introduced a system of national service, during which the service men and women live in camps for five months of the two-year period. The scheme is optional for certain groups, compulsory for others. It is unlikely that many Asians would have volunteered for national service but a number of them come under the compulsory scheme and have been in the service.

Quite apart from helping the image of the community by this conspicuous commitment to the nation, the experience of the youth of various races living together in such close proximity for five months while engaged in work often referred to as nation-building cannot but increase racial understanding and produce a spirit of comradeship which transcends racial differences. Other significant factors, already discussed, are at work in the newly integrated kindergartens, schools, and universities.

It is doubtful whether Asians will establish contacts with Africans at all levels of society, or only in the upper reaches. While the pattern of social relationships will change, it may well be a long time before this happens on a significant scale. There appears to be less and less direct pressure on the communities to get together. Most groups in East Africa show a preference for social exclusiveness or at least for establishing social contacts with their own kind. This will not in itself harm the future of Asians so long as the colonial coincidence of race and wealth changes.

What is important is that the hostility directed against the Asians should disappear or at least diminish. With the advent of prosperous African middle and upper classes a state of stability may be reached in which social diversities will be accepted within a wider framework of political and economic integration. As far as divisions within the Asian communities themselves are concerned, it is likely that these will become less .important as communal institutions decline.

CONCLUSION

Increasing pressures on the Asian community have brought their problems into the foreground; the issues involved are becoming clearer. Solutions, however, may not become obvious for some time. While government actions have brought the issues to a head, there is little evidence that the governments concerned have given sufficient consideration to the role and place of the Asian. Nor have the Asians themselves a clear idea of the solutions needed; they seem to feel that all depends on government policies. By abolishing racial barriers and racial institutions the governments have set in motion forces for integration. They must now ensure that integration takes place in a meaningful way, and accept their responsibility for ensuring equality and justice among all citizens.

Future prospects for the Asians remain in doubt, but certain developments seem likely. First, over the next few years there will be a significant reduction in the number of Asians in East Africa. Their shops in the rural areas will disappear, leading, at least temporarily, to further concentration in the more highly urban areas. Second, the Asian dominance of commerce will decrease further, giving way either to African enterprise or to state enterprise. In professions as well as other forms of employment there will be increasing participation by Africans.

These changes are likely to result in a lessening of the tension and controversy surrounding Asians as a group. As a consequence pressures on their community to change and to integrate, which were strong at independence, may ease or disappear.

In that case the Asian predilection for communal exclusiveness will assert itself, further postponing integration between the two communities.

APPENDIX:

Most statistics concerning the number of Asians in East Africa and the number who opted for citizenship are estimates and vary widely. For example, the figures given below for 1969/70 are extracted from the *'The "D" Valued Passport'* by Mariyam Harris (a Christian Action/Race Relations pamphlet published in 1971). Mrs Harris in March 1971 said that as people are constantly leaving East Africa these estimated figures are only approximate ones.

The statistics given below are estimates gathered from various sources and are as accurate as any statistics in these circumstances can be.

ASIANS IN EAST AFRICA

Kenya:	*Total Asian population*	*182,000*
	Indian citizens	*24,000*
	Kenya citizens	*70,000*
	British passport holders	*82,000*
	Status to be determined	*6,000*

Source: Kenya statistical Digest quarterly economic report published by the Ministry of Economic Planning and Development and Surendra Pal Singh, Deputy Minister, External Affairs, India.

Tanzania:	*Total Asian population*	*105,000*
	Indian citizens	*5,000*
	Tanzanian citizens	*35,000*
	British passport holders	*50,000*
	Stateless or status to be determined	*12,000*

Sources: Office of the Chief Immigration Officer, Tanzania. Indian High Commission and British High Commission. Surendra Pal Singh, Deputy Minister, External Affairs, India.

Uganda:	*Total Asian population*	*80,000*
	Indian citizens	*1,000*
	Uganda citizens	*30,000*
	British passport holders	*40,000*
	Stateless or status to be determined	*9,000*

Sources: Office of the Chief Immigration Officer, Uganda. Indian Association and Surendra Pal Singh, Deputy Minister, External Affairs, India.

2 THE SOUTHERN SUDAN AND ERITREA:

ASPECTS OF WIDER AFRICAN PROBLEMS

by Godfrey Morrison

Godfrey Morrison has been Editor of
African Confidential *since 1968, and from 1964–67*
was a Reuter correspondent in Africa. In 1971 he
revisited the Sudan, Eritrea and Uganda to write his
report for the M.R.G.

THE SOUTHERN SUDAN AND ERITREA

INTRODUCTION

Across Africa from the Red Sea coast of Ethiopia's Eritrea Province to the west coast of Mauritania there runs a human fissure. In a fluctuating line through Ethiopia, Sudan, Chad, Niger, Mali, and Mauritania the black and brown races of Africa meet. In several cases ethnic differences are aggravated by the clash of Islam with Christianity and various pagan beliefs.

In some of the countries the tensions are under control. But in others, notably the Sudan and Ethiopia, they have flared into armed conflict. These conflicts are relatively forgotten.

This study looks at them. The Sudanese problem is dealt with at greatest length: it is the most serious and cost the most lives. The problem of Eritrea is examined more briefly. Finally the international implications of both conflicts are considered.

PART ONE

THE SOUTHERN SUDAN

'*It is, of course, as difficult to judge what is going on in the Upper Nile as it is to judge what is going on on the other side of the moon.*' Lord Salisbury, British Prime Minister, in a telegram to his envoy in Cairo, in 1897.

The Sudan is an immense country. At almost one million square miles (about 2½m. sq. km.) it is the African continent's largest state. Its total area is not much less than that of Western Europe. Population is estimated in 1971 at about 16 millions. Slightly over one quarter of both population and area is accounted for by what is generally referred to as 'the South'. This consists of the three provinces of Upper Nile, Bahr el Ghazal and Equatoria. The differences between the South and the rest of the country are not just administrative; they are ethnic, geographic, political and religious, with their roots firmly embedded in a long history. So profound are these differences that they have led to an armed

74

THE SUDAN

200 mls

- ▬ Sudan borders
- ░ Southern provinces
- • Towns
- ◉ Capital
- ～ Rivers
- +++ Railways

EGYPT

SAUDI ARABIA

Red Sea

LIBYA

Nile

Wadi Halfa

Port Sudan

CHAD

Dongola

Merowe

Nile

Atbara

Shendi

Eritrea

Massawa

Keren

Omdurman

KHARTOUM

Agordat

Asmara

Kordofan

El Obeid

White Nile

Nyala

Renk

Roseires

NUBA MOUNTAINS

Melut

Blue Nile

Kodok
Fashoda

Malakal

ADDIS ABABA

Raga

Bahr El Gazal

Tonga

Bahr El Ghazal

Wau

Upper Nile

Gambela

ETHIOPIA

CENTRAL AFRICAN REPUBLIC

Rumbek

Maridi

Equatoria

Juba

Nagishot

Yei

Torit

CONGO (Kinshasa)

Aba

W. Nile

UGANDA

KENYA

Lake Rudolf

Lake Albert

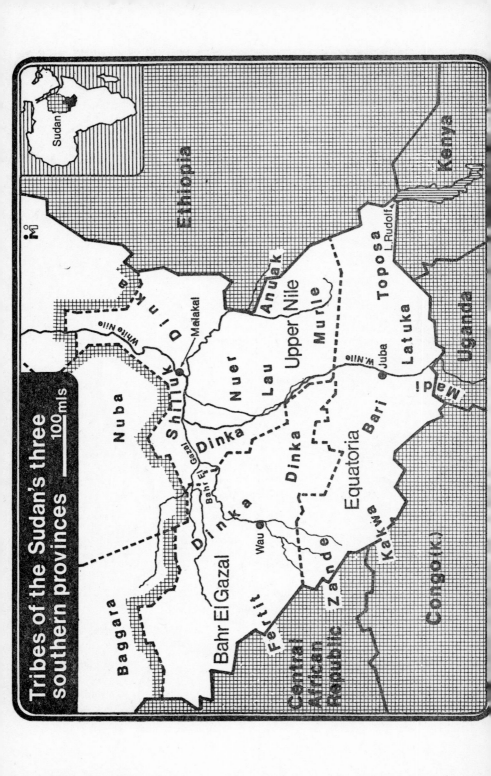

Tribes of the Sudan's three southern provinces

100 mls

conflict which claimed many thousands of lives between 1955 and 1972.

Almost the whole country, except the eastern coastal region, is part of the Nile basin, and this great river has traditionally provided the country with its main communications. So large is the Sudan that its parts enjoy (if that is the word) the most disparate climates, from desert in the far North to rain forest in the far South.

The climatic differences are matched by an even sharper ethnic divide. The people of the North are (mostly) brown-skinned Hamito-Semites who think of themselves as Arabs. In the South the native population is exclusively negroid.

History and geography have compounded the ethnic differences. While the Northern Sudan has for several thousand years been in regular contact with the peoples of the Mediterranean and the Middle East, the people of most of what is now the South were totally ignorant of the outside world until the middle of the nineteenth century.

For centuries the Northern Sudan had been crossed by camel caravan routes. Great markets such as that at Shendi were in contact with Lake Chad and Timbuktu in West Africa, with the Red Sea and Arabia, and by means of the Nile with Egypt and the Mediterranean. Contacts with Upper Egypt were frequent and normal for much of the Northern Sudan. Nineteenth-century European explorers were amazed to find plentiful evidence of ancient civilization such as the strange pyramids at Merowe. But in the South they found nothing like this. Indeed it was not until 1841 that an outsider really penetrated the Southern Sudan.

Another difference between North and South which has its roots deep in history is religion. Most of what we know today as the North was converted to Islam comparatively early on. By the second half of the fourteenth century Islam had reached Dongola; a century later it was established in what is now Berber Province, and in the sixteenth century Islamic schools had been established up the White Nile at least two hundred miles from its confluence with the Blue Nile.

But the South remained a pagan world, with the different tribes holding varying beliefs, until the arrival of missionaries in the nineteenth century. And despite the latter's work the South remains predominantly pagan even today. This religious contrast was to add yet another dimension to the North-South problem.

Though the White Nile and the Blue Nile, which come together

F

at the modern capital of Khartoum, have always provided the Sudan with its main lines of communication, until well into the nineteenth century the White Nile was effectively blocked to travellers from the North by the *sudd*, south of the present-day town of Malakal. The *sudd* is a huge swamp where the channels of the Nile are lost in a mass of floating papyrus and decomposing vegetation which forms islands and hampers navigation. Even today constant work is needed to keep the channels open and in the last few years navigation of the Upper Nile has been further complicated by the mysterious appearance and extraordinary growth of the floating water hyacinth. Though a railway now links Wau, capital of Bahr el Ghazal Province, with the North, the White Nile remains the main line of communication between the Northern and Southern Sudan. There are no tarmac roads whatsoever in the whole of the South and the gravel and dirt roads in most of Upper Nile Province are impassable in the rainy season because of the clay subsoil. Because of the density of the water hyacinth the river steamers do not usually now travel at night. This inevitably lengthens the journey time with the consequence that it is now more difficult to move supplies from the North to Juba than it was twenty years ago. It is almost as if nature were today conspiring to cut off the South once again from the North.

THE PEOPLE

The people of the South are exclusively negroid. They are divided however into three main linguistic groups and the differences between them have had, in the past, very far-reaching social and political consequences. The three groups are generally described as:

(a) The *Nilotics*, who include the Dinka, Nuer, Shilluk and Anuak. They live mostly in the Bahr el Ghazal and Upper Nile Provinces. These main groups are further divided into tribes (e.g. the Dinka include distinct sub-tribes such as Cic, Bor and Agar). The Dinka are the largest single tribal group in the South, numbering over one million. They are cattle raisers rather than tillers of the soil.

(b) The *Nilo-Hamitics*, who include the Murle, Didinga, Boya, Toposa, Bari, Lotuko, Mundari, Kakwe, etc., living mostly in Equatoria. The degree of social organization in these tribes is rather less than in the tribes of the previous group; affairs are generally run by councils of elders, while the Shilluk, for example, boast a *reth* or king.

(c) The *Sudanic*, who include the Azande, Kreish, Bongo,

Moru, and Madi tribes. They live in the extreme south-western part of the Sudan towards the border with the Congo whence they are believed originally to have come.

The division of the Sudan into brown Moslem Arabic-speakers on the one hand, and black pagan or Christian Africans on the other, is a neat and broadly useful generalization. But like all generalizations it is not entirely accurate. For example in the North there are the people of the Nuba mountains who are very black but are nonetheless mostly Moslems. And of course over the centuries there has been much mixing of blood. The Baggara of southern Darfur, though a very dark-skinned people, show their mixed ancestry by the way their features vary from the obviously negroid to the aquiline.

Until the middle of the nineteenth century the South was effectively cut off from the North even though population movements were going on all the time, with the Shilluk sometimes moving quite far down the Nile only to be pushed back later to their swampy heartland.

Throughout much of the nineteenth century most of the Northern Sudan was under Turco-Egyptian rule and it is to this period that some of the origins and causes of today's troubles in the Southern Sudan can be traced. The successful penetration of the *sudd* in 1941 and the subsequent journeys of discovery by such explorers as Baker, Burton and Speke to the source of the White Nile shattered forever the isolation of the South. Once discovered, it was quickly realized that the South could supply in quantity two valuable commodities: ivory and slaves.

Expeditions to the South to find ivory followed very rapidly. At first it was fairly easy to extract. The traders from outside were able to barter with local chiefs quite close to the Nile. But gradually expeditions had to go deeper and deeper into the interior, and slowly the trade in ivory gave way to trade in slaves.

Black slavery was not, of course, created by the penetration of the South. Black slaves had been prized possessions for centuries in Egypt, Arabia, and the Northern Sudan. Ethiopians were for some reason particularly valued. Nor, of course, was slavery an exclusively Arab vice. When Napoleon conquered Cairo in 1798 the Sultan of Darfur sent an emissary to congratulate him. In answer Napoleon sent a request for 2,000 able-bodied black slaves.

Once discovered, it was clear to all that the Southern Sudan was a rich new source of something which was still seen as a commodity to be traded like any other. Not only in their slaving activities, but even in their ordinary trading practices, the new intruders in the South, whatever their nationality or race, used very strong-arm methods. To the Southerners the new arrivals were unwelcome intruders; and inevitably in this hostile environment the intruders often had to resort to force merely to survive.

The early traders also invariably used Arabs as porters and bodyguards. The latter were often permitted to take back to the North a couple of slaves. The attitude of superiority displayed by Northern Sudanese towards Southerners at that time persists among Northern Sudanese even to this day. It certainly seems that the old slave practices laid the foundations for many of today's troubles. The Northerners' habit of describing Southerners as *abid* (slaves) is very much less prevalent than it was. But it remains an issue even today in the minds of many Southerners.

As the nineteenth century wore on, Europe exerted pressure on Cairo in an effort to halt the slave trade and some attempts to this end were carried out by such pro-consuls in the South as Emin Pasha, Colonel Gordon and Romolo Gessi.

In 1885 Cairo's hold over the Sudan was swept away by the establishment of rule by the Mahdi, the religious leader, and his successor, the Khalifa. The period of the Mahdiya saw the Northern Sudan and parts of the South under Mahdist rule. This did little to increase the chances of future North-South co-operation; slavery was again permitted, and the attempts at forced Islamic proselytization of Southerners aroused considerable hostility. Kitchener's defeat of the Mahdist forces at the Battle of Omdurman in 1898 brought the Mahdiya to an end and ushered in the era of Anglo-Egyptian condominium rule which was to last until the Sudan became independent in 1956. For the next half-century the British in effect ruled the Sudan. By the end of the nineteenth century the Southerners had already come to regard the Northern Sudanese as people who abducted their women and property, who thought of them as naturally inferior, and referred to them as *abid*.

From my own conversations with Southerners it is clear that their society has made up for a lack of formal education and written history by a wealth of oral tradition. Thus memories of the latter part of the nineteenth century are still very much alive. Because of this, friction between North and South was probably inevitable in an independent Sudan even if Britain had foreseen how soon independence would come and even if, from the very start, British policies had had as their principal aim the creation of a viable cohesive single Sudan. In the event British policymakers did not foresee how rapidly events would move. And (often from excellent motives) they did little to weld the country into one nation.

THE BRITISH IN THE SUDAN

The first task of the British in the South was pacification and the re-establishment of basic communications which had not flourished during the Mahdiya. The White Nile had become almost blocked by the *sudd* and tribal clashes were frequent. In the Southern Sudan as elsewhere in Africa the British favoured 'indirect rule'. This involves ruling as far as possible through existing political and social structures and using tribal chiefs as agents of the colonial power. Such a system, as opposed to the more 'direct' methods of rule adopted by other colonial powers (notably France), is advantageous for the colonial power in that it is cheap. Also, in that it preserves or even accentuates traditional tribal and social divisions, it is a system which is conducive to rapid pacification of an area and one which helps make security relatively easy to preserve. Indirect rule also has some advantages for the ruled. Because their political and social structures are left intact, the period of colonial rule is not so culturally cataclysmic. Many Africans believe that indirect colonial rule was less traumatic psychologically and, because existing structures were left untouched, that the 'African-ness' of the states so ruled has been less impaired than elsewhere.

However that may be, for countries ruled in this way the system also has serious, practical disadvantages after they reach independence. Geographically almost all African states are the creation of Europeans: that is to say, they are 'artificial' in that they are the product, not of their own people's history, but of the struggles and rivalries of distant European powers. Because of this almost all of them suffer from serious internal divisions. And because indirect rule depended on and retained ancient tribal differences, states thus ruled were left almost as divided at independence as at the moment colonial rule began. It is noteworthy that tribal rivalries have played a much more important role in post independence history in English-speaking Africa than in the states once ruled from Paris.

In the Sudan indirect rule meant that little was done to weld together North and South. And, whatever their merits and demerits, British colonial methods also meant that little was done to unite Southerners even *among themselves*. (Ironically greater success has been achieved in this direction by the Northern Sudanese, though not in the way they would have wished.)

During the period of British rule Christian missionaries, who had already penetrated the country, were encouraged to pursue their work in the South. The whole area was divided into 'spheres of influence' for the various denominations such as Roman Catholic, Anglican and Presbyterian. Of particular importance for the future were the missions' educational activities. Among the educated, English gradually replaced pidgin Arabic as the main *lingua franca* of the area.

As the twentieth century progressed the influences tending to divide the North from the South grew steadily. Local languages and English were encouraged; Arabic was discouraged. The missionaries, because they taught the Christian Gospel, inevitably intensified their converts' sense of difference from the Moslem Northerners.

By 1930 Sir Harold MacMichael, Civil Secretary in the Khartoum administration, could write a memorandum which defined the main principles of policy towards the South as:

(a) The building up in the Southern Sudan of 'a series of self-contained racial or tribal units' whose structure and organization would be based on traditional usage and beliefs.

(b) The gradual elimination from the South of the Northern Sudanese administrators, clerks and technicians, and their replacement by people from the South.

(c) The use of English where communication in the local vernaculars was impossible.

As early as 1911 the British had begun to recruit men from the South for a local Equatoria Corps. By 1918 this had entirely replaced the Northern army in the South. The Southern troops were regarded as a useful insurance policy against any possible unrest in the North and remained the sole military force in the South until they were replaced by Northern units following the 1955 mutiny of Southern troops and the subsequent troubles.

By the Closed Districts Order much of the South was forbidden territory to foreigners and Northern Sudanese. In addition the Permits to Trade Order of 1925 forbade any person to trade in the South without a permit. A general policy of discouraging the 'Gellaba' or Northern Sudanese traders was effected. These measures were aimed at protecting Southerners from exploitation by Northerners. But they probably also hampered the economic development of the South. Even at the top administrative level, divisions between North and South were already solidifying quite early in the century. By 1921 the Governors of the three Southern Provinces were no longer required to attend all the meetings of Sudanese Provincial Governors held annually in Khartoum. Instead they held their own meetings in the South and were directed to keep in touch with their opposite numbers in Kenya and Uganda. Even the British District Commissioners who worked in the South were regarded as something of a race apart by their Northern colleagues who referred to them as the 'Bog Barons'.

Less impressive were the practical results of education in the South. A D.C. wrote in 1941 that 'perhaps the most disappointing aspect of the working of Southern policy is the failure to produce in ten years any Southern staff trained for executive work.' Oliver Albino, in his book *The Sudan – A Southern Viewpoint*, writes that it was not even clear that Southerners were being encouraged to seek jobs in the administration. 'Not until 1942 was the first Southerner . . . allowed to sit for the Civil (now the Public) Service examination,' he writes. One man was selected in 1944, two in 1946, and a larger group of twelve sat in 1948. Albino comments, 'It is difficult to understand why progress towards localising the staff was so gradual.' The most probable explanation is quite simply that the administrators were not worried; they felt no sense of urgency because they did not foresee just how rapidly events were to move. Whatever the reason, the educational backwardness of the South as compared to the North has had dire consequences, contributing even at the present time to the other points of division, and sharpening the superiority/inferiority syndrome which seems still to lie at the heart of the Southern problem.

Thus by the end of the Second World War British policy was firmly based on operating two quite different administrations in the Sudan. An educationally and economically backward South, whose traditional tribal structures were relatively unchanged and most of whose people were pagan but whose educated élite was largely Christian, had to be carefully guided forward and protected at all times from the more advanced North.

And then in 1946 – only ten years (as it turned out) from independence – Britain's policy towards the South was reversed.

A CHANGE OF POLICY

A number of factors induced the change: a growing political awareness in the North; fear that the North would be swallowed by Egypt if left on her own; an increasing use of Northerners in development schemes in the South; and a distinct coolness on the part of colonial authorities in Kenya and Uganda towards any suggestion that the Southern Sudan, with its many administrative and economic problems, should be annexed by East Africa.

The new policy was defined by the Civil Secretary in a memorandum dated 16 December 1946. It ruled out integration of the whole or parts of the South with East Africa and stated: 'The policy of the Sudan Government regarding the Southern Sudan is to act upon the facts that the peoples of the Southern Sudan are distinctly African and Negroid but that geography and economics combine (so far as can be seen at the present time) to render them inextricably bound for future development to the Middle Eastern and Arabicized Northern Sudan: and therefore to ensure that they should, by educational and economic development, be equipped to stand up for themselves as socially and economically the equals of their partners in the Sudan of the future.'

This statement dating from 1946 describes the essential dilemma of the South today.

The new policy seems to have been generally well received though major doubts and reservations were immediately expressed by some of the British administrators in the South. They foresaw that a unitary Sudan would inevitably be dominated by the Northerners, not merely because of their superior number but also because of their greater sophistication. Mr B. V. Marwood, Governor of Equatoria Province, agreed with the new policy, saying that neither isolation nor attachment to East Africa were practical. However he proposed that there should be safeguards and a period of 'trusteeship' until the South 'knows its own mind'. These were admirable sentiments but unfortunately events were already moving fast and there was just not sufficient time for the British to prepare the South to enter as an equal partner with the North into an independent Sudan. Even at this stage, however, the likelihood that difficulties might arise in the future was foreseen and federation was proposed.

In 1947 a conference was held at Juba attended by a small number of Southern Chiefs and educated people, a few Northerners and British officials. From this conference it became clear that articulate Southerners were worried about possible domination by the North in the future. Southerners also expressed fear that Northern traders might exploit the South. During the conference a number of the Southerners present changed their minds about the nature of their future relations with the North and the conference came out generally in favour of 'one Sudan'. This was the first time that Southerners from different parts of the South had come together – even among themselves – to discuss their future and some Southerners allege today that the Southern delegates were threatened, bribed or blackmailed by Northerners during the conference. Whatever the truth of these allegations it is clear from reading the minutes of the conference that many of the Southerners expressed general forebodings about their future and, in particular, made it clear that 'one Sudan' was acceptable to them only on condition that the South was accorded special safeguards.

When the 95-member Sudan legislative assembly opened in 1948, thirteen Southerners were appointed to it. Belated efforts were made to give the South a special economic boost. The Zande scheme was started and some moves aimed at accelerating education were implemented, including the opening of the first secondary school. Arabic was introduced as a subject in all schools.

But by 1950 political events were moving so quickly in the North that the old British hope of preparing the South to enter an independent Sudan as 'an equal partner' with the North had become impossible to realize. In 1953 the British ratified an agreement between the Northern political parties and the Egyptians concerning the future independence of the Sudan. The South was not consulted about this nor was it allowed to take part in the negotiations (on the grounds that Southerners had no officially registered political party). The same year saw the formation of the Southern Party which was to change its name to the Liberal Party in 1954.

In October 1953, elections were held for the Sudan's first Parliament which was to have twenty-two Southern members, roughly a quarter of the total. Most seats were won by the Southern Party despite the energetic efforts of others, including the pro-Egyptian N.U.P. (At this time the outside world's attention was drawn to Sudanese affairs mainly by Major Salah Salim, an Egyptian Government Minister, who became widely known as the 'dancing major' because of his shirtless participation in a Dinka dance. His aim appears to have been to prove that whatever the colours of their skins the peoples of the Nile were one.)

By the time of this election campaign the main factors which would contribute to the deterioration of North-South relations were apparent. Major Salah Salim promised Southerners forty posts as Governor, D.C. and Assistant D.C. when the British departed. And other politicians, both Northern and Southern, were not above playing on Southerners' memories of slavery and on old grudges. Following all the promises, the report of the Sudanization Committee, which had been set up to deal with the replacement of British officials by Sudanese, came as a great disappointment to Southerners when it was published in October 1954. Only four Southerners were appointed Assistant District Commissioners out of a total of 800 senior posts, together with two to the minor position of *Mamur*. Mohamed Omer Beshir observes in his book *The Southern Sudan* that the Committee 'in the best traditions of the British Civil Service, allocated jobs and made promotions in accordance with seniority, experience and qualifications. As the posts held by the Southerners, at the time, were by far fewer and more junior than those held by the Northerners, and as the Southerners lacked seniority, they were not much affected by Sudanization.'

Experience from the last twenty years in the new African states has vividly shown that the distribution of government employment (and thus in a sense government patronage) has been one of the most sensitive political areas. In societies where the private sector is underdeveloped in terms of employment opportunities the potency of what may be described as the 'jobs-for-the-boys factor' in politics is very great.

Mohamed Omer Beshir, himself a Northerner, writes that the result of Sudanization 'was not only disappointing to the educated Southerners but it was also looked upon as the changing of one master for another and a new colonization by the North. It was also looked upon as a breach of promises made by the Northerners . . . What the Southerners finally got was much less than they were promised or made to believe that they would get. The Southern educated class was thus alienated and even the illiterate and ignorant were becoming hostile to the Government authority and to the presence of the Northern administrators.'

Against this background relations between North and South steadily deteriorated. In late July 1955, 300 Southern workers were dismissed from the cotton industry in Nzara. Demonstrations occurred during which at least twenty people died when the security forces opened fire.

Some Southerners now talk of this incident as marking the outbreak of hostilities between North and South. The following month the Southern Corps of the army mutinied following rumours that they were going to be disarmed and sent to the North. In the disturbances which followed many people died. According to Northern Sudanese the total casualties were 261 Northern Sudanese and seventy-five Southerners. Southerners put the figure of Southerners killed – particularly in the weeks following the mutiny – much higher. Eight thousand Northern troops were airlifted to the South and in the middle of December Sir Knox Helm, the British Governor-General, whom many Southern Sudanese regarded as the only remaining independent guarantor of their rights, left the Sudan.

On 19 December the Sudanese Parliament adopted a resolution stating that once independence arrived 'full consideration'
would be given to Southern demands for federation. In return
Southern members voted for independence, which came into
force on 1 January, 1956. But the prospects for North-South
co-operation in an independent Sudan were far from promising.

INDEPENDENCE

It proved very difficult to reach agreement on the exact form that
a permanent Sudan constitution should take. Indeed the matter
remains unresolved even to this day. In any event, the Southerners'
pressure for some form of federalism was not heeded by a Constitution Committee which studied the problem. By December
1957 a majority of the Committee, whose membership was heavily
weighted in favour of the North, decided that the disadvantages
of regionalism outweighed its benefits. The 1958 elections were
fought in the South by a new Federal Party which won forty of the
forty-six Southern seats. North-South relations within the resulting Constituent Assembly soon ruptured and in June 1958
Southern members walked out.

The following November civilian parliamentary rule collapsed
and the army, led by General Ibrahim Abboud, took over.
Military rule, which lasted for six years (November 1958 to
October 1964), brought no solution to the Southern problem.
Instead the situation steadily worsened. The Abboud regime
appears to have believed that all that was required for solution
of the problem was firm handling of the South. That this policy
failed so dismally proved once and for all that the problem of
the South was deeply political in nature and not simply one of
security. With the advent of military rule the belief that the
forced 'Arabicization' of the South would solve all difficulties
became fashionable in Khartoum. In 1960 the weekly holiday
which, since 1918, had been observed on Sunday in the South
was changed to Friday so that it would coincide with the Northern
observance of a Friday holiday.

Efforts were made to force the South to respond more readily
to Northern wishes. Privately-owned (i.e. mission) schools had
been nationalized in 1957, though they continued to be allowed
in the North. The South's two boys' secondary schools had been
moved after the 1955 mutiny (and even today Juba Commercial
and Rumbek Secondary schools continue to function in the
North). During the military regime military governors and
administrators in the South spent much of their energy on efforts
to spread Islam and promote the use of Arabic in the belief that

87

this would produce national unity. Six intermediate Islamic Institutes were started and a Secondary Islamic Institute was opened in Juba.

Measures designed to harass the Christian missionaries working in the South were gradually adopted. In February 1964 the Government announced the expulsion of all Christian missionaries from the Southern Sudan. Understandably there was much hostile international reaction to this move and the Sudan Government set out its case for the missionaries' expulsion in a Black Book, published by the Ministry of the Interior. This accused the missionaries of deliberately hampering national integration by fostering a civilization and culture which were different from those in the rest of the country 'and by implanting in the Southern Sudanese, Christianity, the use of English hatred of the North and separatism'. The Black Book went on to make some very wild accusations against the missionaries, some of which had been found unsubstantiated in the enquiry into the 1955 mutiny and disturbances. The weakness of many of the Black Book's accusations and the ease with which many of its assertions have since been refuted by missionaries and others has led inevitably to a widespread belief that the expulsion was ordered by the military authorities because (a) they believed that forced inculcation of Islam and Arabic was the only practical way to unite the country, (b) they were badly rattled by the deterioration of the security position in the South and foreign scapegoats would be useful, and (c) they felt it would be better if foreign independent witnesses were not present to report the methods used by the security forces in their attempts to restore order.

It would be foolish, however, to pretend that the missionaries had always acted wisely. For example, the Roman Catholics' hard line on the question of the Church's divine rights with regard to education of their members in the South inevitably touched a very sensitive spot. The governments of newly independent African states are as sensitive as Henry VIII was when it comes to questions of sovereignty.

The deterioration of the security situation in the South went hand in hand with a growing exodus of the educated élite and the establishment outside the Sudan of Southern exile political movements. (During the military regime the political parties of the South, as of the North, were banned.) The exodus of Southern politicians began when Father Saturnino Lohure, a senior Southern political leader who had been elected President of the Federal Party in 1958, as well as Joseph Oduho, William Deng, Aggrey Jaden and others left the country. In 1962 this group founded in the Congo capital the Sudan African Closed Districts National Union (S.A.C.D.N.U.) which the following year changed its name to the more euphonious Sudan African National Union (SANU).

The worsening security situation and the growth of guerrilla activity in the South had their origins in the 1955 mutiny. Although conditions became more normal in districts where Southern officials were appointed, some of the soldiers who took part in the mutiny fled into the bush after it collapsed and they formed the nucleus of the guerrilla forces which are fighting the Sudanese security forces today. In 1961 the Southern prisoners who had been taken north following the mutiny, about 800 in all, were released and many of them, being soldiers, joined the guerrillas. The latter were referred to by Northerners at the time (and still are) as 'outlaws'. There was then, and probably still is, an element of simple banditry in the Southern troubles. But as time went on it became increasingly obvious that the troubles were essentially political. The Khartoum authorities were slow to accept this fact.

The first serious incidents occurred in September 1963 with attacks by dissidents on the police posts of Pachola, near the Ethiopian border, and Kajo Kaji, near the Uganda border. In January 1964 a larger force tried unsuccessfully to capture Wau, capital of Bahr el Ghazal Province. By this time the guerrillas were becoming generally known as the Anya-Nya, a name derived from a word for the poison of the Gabon viper.

The Abboud regime fell in October and the unrest in the South was a contributing factor, as the regime's collapse occurred following riots which had been sparked off by police trying to break up a students' meeting in Khartoum which was discussing the situation in the South. This was not the first time that a change in regime had been vitally influenced by the persistence of the Southern problem. And the same could well occur again.

A caretaker civilian regime took over, led by Sirr el-Khatim el Khalifa. Freedom of the press and at the University was restored and party political activity was again permitted. Despite its care-taker nature the government initiated some striking changes in the Sudan's foreign policy, which up until then had been cautiously non-committal. Active support was promised to the rebels in the Congo and to Eritreans who were rebelling against Ethiopian rule. These assurances were accompanied by other generally anti-Western declarations and can be seen as the start of the Sudan's swing to the left in foreign policy which has gone so much further today. The promises and the aid given to Congolese and Eritrean guerrillas were, in the event, to complicate and aggravate still further the Southern problem.

The caretaker government included three Southerners who were members of the Southern Front, a political party formed by Southerners educated in Khartoum and closely linked with SANU, which by this time had its headquarters in Kampala, Uganda. On Sunday, 6 December 1964 there occurred another of those disastrous events which have bedevilled North-South relations. Serious clashes broke out between Northerners and Southerners in Khartoum and the accounts of these carried south immediately afterwards deepened Southerners' fears and suspicions.

Despite this, a Round Table Conference to discuss the South was convened in Khartoum in March 1965. Divisions among Southerners revealed themselves when SANU split between those, led by William Deng, who favoured accepting the invitation to the conference, and those who did not. In the end both groups decided to attend and when the conference opened it also included representatives of the Southern Front and six Northern political parties, as well as observers from seven African countries. The Southerners demanded a plebiscite for the South while the Northerners would not go beyond proposals for some form of regionalism. In the event no final solution could be arrived at though the conference did pass a number of resolutions calling for the Southernization of the public services in the South, the establishment of a university there and the stepping up of educational facilities in the area. Subsequent elections in the North brought to power an Umma-NUP coalition government led by Muhammed Ahmed Mahgoub. Conditions in the South continued to deteriorate and few of the practical proposals aired at the Round Table Conference were ever carried out.

On 9 July 1965 an argument in Juba between a Northern soldier and a Southerner led to a night of killing and burning by army personnel during which between 1,000 and 3,000 people lost their lives. Much of the African quarter of the town was burned. Three days later in Wau seventy-six people were gunned down at a wedding reception by Northern soldiers. Understandably these events, which marked something of a watershed, completely shattered Southerners' confidence in their rulers and the exodus of Southerners from the South into Ethiopia, Uganda, the Congo and the Central African Republic speeded up.

In June 1966 Mahgoub was replaced by Sadik el-Mahdi and in March 1967 elections in the South were contested successfully by SANU. In April 1968 elections were held throughout the

Sudan but the turnout and the results in the South showed that they were no longer very effective in projecting the popular will of Southerners. In three of the sixty Southern constituencies no voting took place because of the security situation and in most of the others the voting figures were tiny. The Southern Front won ten seats, the Independents four, various Northern political parties twenty-eight, and SANU fifteen. In fact William Deng polled more votes than any other candidate in the South. Relations between him and Sadik were hopeful and showed mutual trust. Tragically, however, the following month Deng was murdered by persons unknown. This was a serious loss to the Sudan as he was an effective political leader whose moderation, coupled with a determination to establish his people's rights, might well have made him a figure of key importance to any solution of the Southern problem.

Many of the Southern politicians returned to exile after the Round Table Conference. And, as seems to be endemic in exile movements, they were plagued by dissension. A group including Joseph Oduho broke away from SANU (in exile) and formed the Azania Liberation Front. An uneasy reconciliation occurred and in April 1966 the newly merged ALF moved its headquarters into Equatoria Province. In August of the following year a clandestine convention of Southerners, held at Angudri between Maridi and Yei near the Congo border, merged many Southern political parties in exile into the Southern Sudan Provisional Government with Aggrey Jaden as President. In March 1969 this body was replaced by the Nile Provisional Government which was subsequently rivalled by another body, the Anyidi Provisional Government.

Despite all the rivalries based on personalities and tribal animosities, a surprising degree of basic administration was maintained throughout the latter sixties by the various groups operating in the Southern Sudan. Despite shortages of cash and other resources, it is clear from eyewitnesses (including a number of Western journalists who travelled through the region on foot) that the Southerners maintained a large number of bush schools and dispensaries, and even administered a system of justice over considerable areas.

In May 1969 a military coup in Khartoum brought to power a left-wing military junta led by General Nimeiry. Coincidentally power in the South passed from the political movements to the Anya-Nya and the overall leadership of Colonel Joseph Lagu became generally recognized.

One of the first major announcements of General Nimeiry's

Revolution Command Council concerned Southern policy. On 9 June 1969 he promised regional autonomy for the South together with an intensive programme for the social, economic and cultural advancement of the area. Other aspects of the new policy would be: the appointment of a Minister of Southern Affairs, the continuation and widening of the amnesty declared by the previous regime, and the training of Southerners to take up positions of responsibility. This statement was welcomed by most Southerners.

The man named Minister of Southern Affairs, Joseph Garang, was himself a Southerner and a veteran Communist politician. The South was also represented in the largely civilian government set up under the ruling military junta by another Southerner, Abel Alier, Minister of Works. For the year ending July 1970 £3 million was specially allocated for the repair of war damage in the South; this sum included £250,000 for the repair of damaged schools and the building of new ones, and most of the rest was earmarked for various agricultural projects. Within the police a definite policy of Southernization was adopted and at the time of writing the provincial commanders of both Upper Nile and Equatoria are Southerners. General Nimeiry's regime also reintroduced army recruiting in the South and in January 1971 a dozen Southern army officers graduated, the first for some years.

The Southern problem was of political importance to General Nimeiry's regime just as it had been to its predecessors. Nimeiry, however, had staked a lot on finding a solution, as he had justified his own coup in part by previous regimes' failures to settle the Southern question. Nimeiry's regime with its strong Marxist contingent naturally placed considerable emphasis on the economic development of the South as a means of solving the political problem. One of the difficulties involved in this approach, however, is the fact that the South is caught in a political/economic vicious circle. The argument runs that the solution of the political problem demands more than anything else economic development which would provide employment; if economic activity were sharply increased then political discontent would wither away. In order to carry out a programme of economic improvement, however, a high degree of political stability is needed (not unreminiscent of the situation in Ireland). And the South's terrain, climate and lack of communications make it an area far from easy to develop even it there were no political complications.

So far it is not clear that General Nimeiry's regime has achieved decisive enough progress on either the political or the economic front to break the vicious circle. Reviewing the government's social and economic achievements in the South in an interview published in the government newspaper *Nile Mirror* on 29 April 1971, the Southern Affairs Minister Garang cited what are fairly modest achievements. In the medical field the sixty-bed hospital at Gogrial in Bahr el Ghazal was in operation. A health centre and dental clinics had been completed at Wau and the provincial capital's hospital had been provided with specialists. The extended Aweil rice scheme, a jute plantation at Tonj and a tomato farm at Wau were 'progressing well'. In Upper Nile Province a hospital at Kodok was under construction, the hospitals at Nasir and Doro had been re-opened and an eye clinic had been established at Malakal. Other achievements included the opening of a school for medical assistants at Juba, while coffee farms at Maridi, Oba, Matika and Kargullu 'had been reviewed'.

Meanwhile the precise form which Southern autonomy will take remains uncertain. The present regime is on record as recognizing the historic and ethnic differences between North and South and a ministerial committee, which includes Nimeiry himself as well as Garang and Alier, is charged with working out details. First tentative results of the autonomy programme include the establishment of a planning and co-ordination council for the South whose budget is separate from the national development budget. Nevertheless, the nub of the problem – to what extent Southerners will decide their own affairs *politically*– remains unresolved. Indeed it seems likely to remain an unsolved problem so long as the arrangements for the political future of the whole of the Sudan also remain undecided.

A 'People's Committee for a National Charter' which aims to draw up a political blueprint for the years ahead has been meeting for several months but it is not yet clear what will emerge. For the moment the country is exposed to left-wing slogans while the economy appears to run slowly down. In the South itself the amount of employment available is very small. As a result the government faces a serious problem with regard to those Southern refugees who return to the Sudan at the government's urging and then discover there are no jobs for them. This problem is openly acknowledged. Indeed one of the most positive features of the present regime is its readiness to acknowledge that problems exist. This readiness struggles uneasily with a tendency shown by some officials to blame all the Sudan's troubles, whether in the North or South, on the 'imperialists'.

Within the government service itself the present regime has made greater efforts than any of its predecessors to promote Southerners and find jobs for them. Critics say that this is merely an attempt to buy off educated Southern and foreign opinion –

G

and no doubt there is an element of truth in this. Nevertheless the regime's moves to bring Southerners into government service must be the correct policy if any policy which does not involve the secession of the South is to succeed. Apart from the two government ministers who have already been mentioned, other Southerners prominent at the present time include: Jervase Yak, who again holds the influential post of Governor of Khartoum Province, Othwon Dak, Head of the Publications Bureau of the Ministry of Southern Affairs and Franco Garang, Director of Education for the Southern Provinces. Others such as Samuel Aru (a former President of SANU), Hilary Paul Logali (a Minister of Labour in the second Mahgoub government), and Lubari Ramba (a former Southern Front MP) are directors of state corporations. The present regime has also appointed a number of Southerners to the foreign service including Philip Obang, who is counsellor at the embassy in London. The appointment of Southerners to senior jobs in the administration has been facilitated by the erosion of civil service personnel resulting from the various coups d'état since independence: each change of regime has been followed by a purge of civil servants.

Attempts have also been made to speed up education for Southerners but at university level, for example, the South is still under-represented in proportion to its population. And despite the efforts made in the civil service the same remains true there. In the religious field the present regime has not pursued the forced pro-Islam policies followed by some of its predecessors in the South. In the schools which are operating in the South, time is set aside for religious instruction in Islam, Roman Catholicism or Protestant Christianity, according to choice. The foreign missionaries are still forbidden to return to the South but otherwise the activities of the Christian churches are not hampered. Curiously enough the Verona Fathers (who are often represented as the Vatican's arch-agents in encouraging the Anya-Nya and other Southern separatists) still have over 200 expatriate staff and continue to pursue their activities in the Northern Sudan where they run a number of schools as well as medical services.

The present regime appears to be very concerned about its international image. A considerable number of journalists (including the author) have been allowed or even encouraged to visit the South, and in May 1971 a delegation representing the World Council of Churches was permitted to visit the region.

THE MILITARY SITUATION

The Southern Sudan covers a huge area. The total area of the three provinces of Equatoria, Upper Nile and Bahr el Ghazal is appreciably larger than that of South Vietnam, Cambodia and Laos combined. As already noted, communications are very difficult. Much of the country is thickly covered with vegetation for much or all of the year, making it excellent guerrilla terrain. The total number of armed men the Anya-Nya can put in the field at the present time is probably between 5,000 and 6,000. The total numbers of Sudanese army forces in the South are (probably) about 14,000 men in three brigades. In addition there are probably about 6,000 police. Given the immense size of the South, its poor communications and its suitability for guerrilla activities, it is inconceivable that security forces totalling around 20,000 men can remove by military means the threat to security posed by 5,000 guerrillas so long as the latter remain determined to fight.

In the last three months of 1970 and in early 1971 the security forces scored some notable successes in their cat-and-mouse tactics with the guerrillas. The rebel headquarters at Owiny-Ni-Bul, where the Israelis are reported to have dropped supplies by air, was attacked; and the German mercenary Rolf Steiner was captured. A number of rebel camps were captured, together with large quantities of arms and ammunition. The fact that two of the camps were equipped with crude airstrips demonstrates just how large an installation can be hidden in the vastness of the Southern Sudan. In addition to their ground forces the Sudanese possess a couple of dozen Mig 21's and eight large M18 Soviet helicopters. Though no recent figures are available, it is certain that the military campaign in the South represents a serious financial drain on Sudanese government finances (the problems of supply are very great) especially in view of the present depressed state of the economy.

Accounts by journalists who have recently been with the Anya-Nya in the Southern Sudan make it clear that (a) the guerrillas are not well equipped but (b) their morale appears to remain high in the sense that their hatred for the Northern Sudanese soldiers continues as strong as ever. Despite the enormity of the task, the Sudanese military authorities in the South say they believe they are winning the battle to restore normal security to the area. Major General Mubarak Osman Rahama, Commander of the forces in the South, told me in March that he was optimistic about the outcome. He added, however: 'We need time. It is a chronic problem. We don't expect quick success.' That the relations between the security forces and the civilian population are a key factor has been realized. The General said emphasis had been placed on the civilian aspect of the army's role ever

The Fourth World

since the 1969 coup d'état. In view of this the army, apart from its security duties, was engaged in various road-building projects and other activities designed to improve its relations with civilians. Observers say some improvement has been achieved in civilian-military relations within the towns during the last couple of years. Results appear to have been less impressive.

General Mubarak said it was 'difficult' to turn his soldiers into diplomats vis-à-vis the civil population. This is probably a considerable understatement. Even if only five per cent of the stories concerning military atrocities and intimidation of the rural population in the Southern Sudan were true, it would still be abundantly clear that discipline has left much to be desired. Probably the truth is that however praiseworthy the leadership's motives it is very hard to control the troops once they are out in the field. Counter-insurgency is one of the most difficult of the military arts. To be successful it demands a greater degree of discipline, self-restraint and patience than any other kind of military operation. Northern Sudanese in the South feel themselves to be in a foreign and basically hostile environment. For their part the Anya-Nya fight a ruthless war. They do not take prisoners and according to a recent account by a Western journalist who accompanied a guerrilla party into the Southern Sudan the standard Anya-Nya treatment for a captured Northern soldier is a bullet in the back of the head. This goes some way to explain the savage nature of the conflict though it does not excuse the many well-authenticated attacks on civilians.

The Sudanese authorities support their contention that life is returning to normal in the South by pointing to the growing population in most of the main towns. Juba, which had a population of 14,000 in 1962, now contains 60,000. Maridi, which had 5,000 in 1968, by 1971 has 30,000. They also point to the numbers of former refugees who have been persuaded to return from abroad.

This picture is complicated, however, by the fact that officials in neighbouring countries report a continuing net inflow of Sudanese refugees. Ethiopia, which had about 18,000 of them in early 1970, had some 20,000 in 1971; in 1971 there were an estimated 178,000 Sudanese refugees in Uganda, again a slight increase. In the Congo in 1971 there were about 66,000 and in the Central African Republic about 22,000 compared to about 18,000 in July 1969. If these figures are correct, and if the figures given by the Sudanese for returning refugees and growing urban populations are also correct, there can be only one conclusion, which is that the rural population of the Southern Sudan is moving (a) into the towns and (b) into neighbouring countries as well. If this is indeed the case then the prospects for a return to normal life in the South are bleak; for the implication is quite simply that the countryside of the South is steadily losing its inhabitants.

Clearly there are political and social dangers too in the growing numbers of unemployed in the towns. In a town such as Juba the unemployed blacks will form an increasing contrast to the Northern Sudanese merchant and bureaucratic class who, though of the same nationality, are seen by many Southerners as essentially colonists. Whether or not such a view is justified matters less for practical purposes than the fact that such a view is held.

Social divisions are visible even in the South's educational system. Since 1969 all instruction has been in Arabic and at the Juba girls' intermediate school which I visited there are two streams. The higher stream, containing 150 of the 400 pupils, consists of those students for whom Arabic is the first language; the second stream is comprised of those girls for whom Arabic is a language which has to be learned. Inevitably stream A contained the daughters of Northern merchants and Northern civil servants, while stream B consisted of the local Southern girls. No doubt this system makes sense educationally, but it is easy to guess at its divisive social effects.*

Inevitably too, the Northerners in the South make up their own community socially since they, for the most part, feel that they are living in an almost foreign land. When saying goodbye to a Northern Sudanese teacher who had helped me in Juba, I remarked that I hoped to see him again if I came back in a year or two. 'I'm afraid not,' he said and added: 'I've done my two years down here.' He said this with a 'roll on demob' satisfaction very reminiscent of those in compulsory military service.

I am also bound to record that the Southerners to whom I spoke remained sceptical about the North's intentions. Though not necessarily hostile, a number of the people were frankly cynical. They had heard too many promises from too many governments and now will believe the promised political and economic results only when they see them. Given the historical background this suspicion of outsiders – whether they come from London, Khartoum or Moscow – is very understandable. On

---

* Despite all the encouragement given to Arabic, English retains its uses in the South. Educated Southerners, if they are from different tribes, tend to speak it. Though most of the official signs in the South are now in Arabic, 'MEN' and 'WOMEN' decorate the public lavatories. And in a village I visited, the only sign on the local shop said: 'NO CREDIT'.

the other hand, a conference concerned with the South's social and economic advancement, held at Juba at the beginning of 1971, showed that the area does have considerable latent potential – in sugar, coffee, cotton, tobacco, maize, fishing and cattle – which could be developed if confidence can be restored.

THE ADDIS ABABA AGREEMENT

In February 1972, following earlier secret and informal soundings, representatives of the Sudanese government and the Anya-Nya and exiled Southern political groups met in Addis Ababa. Aided by the mediatory efforts of the All-Africa Conference of Churches, the World Council of Churches, and Emperor Haile Selassie of Ethiopia, the two sides finally ratified an agreement on 27 March to end the war. Khartoum secured its most essential demand – that the Sudan's territorial integrity be preserved – but President Nimeiry's Government displayed great political courage by granting very important concessions to the Southerners, many of which could have proved unpopular in the North. Under the agreement a very real measure of regional autonomy was granted to the South, which in effect was to have its own government. Elections were to be held in eighteen months and special provisions were made to prevent subsequent amendment to the South's special position without its consent. The central government would supervise legislation on national defence, foreign policy and trade, currency, certain communications matters and economic and social planning. However, very important powers were to be retained in Southern hands, notably internal security and police. The agreement contained provisions for a cease-fire and arrangements for its implementation. Khartoum's determination to bring the war to an end was seen in the very rapid 'Southernization' of government posts within the South. The provisional Southern government was established in Juba in April with Abel Alier, a Southerner and the Sudan's Vice-President at its head. He had been one of the principal architects of the Addis Ababa agreement and President Nimeiry's trust in him had been shown by the fact that he had been appointed to head the Khartoum delegation at the Addis talks. Despite this Alier was no 'Northern stooge' and by late April 1972 it was possible to be optimistic about the Addis agreement 'sticking'. Much would obviously depend on the actions of the army and the guerrillas in subsequent months. The Addis agreement provided that, following Southern recruiting and the absorbtion of Anya-Nya elements into the army, half of all those stationed in the South would be Southerners.

It was also clear that the eventual success of the agreement would also depend on success in dealing with the very great refugee problems and on the economic rehabilitation of the area. Much in turn would obviously depend on the response of the rest of the world to Sudanese appeals for help.

PART TWO

ERITREA

THE LAND

Ethiopia is an empire. It says so in the country's most recent constitution, that of 1955. Nor is this mere idle terminology, for in Ethiopia, despite the changes during Emperor Haile Selassie's forty-year reign, the methods of government remain essentially imperial. Under the political theory which is implicit in Ethiopian politics all power emanates from the Emperor (it comes to him from God), and Ethiopian history for the last couple of centuries has essentially been the story of various Emperors' differing success in consolidating and centralizing their power.

The same period has seen the ebb and flow of the Ethiopian Empire's frontiers. Ethiopia is a very ancient nation (the Lion of Judah claims royal descent from Solomon and the name Ethiopia has been known since Biblical times), but the location of the country's modern frontiers is the product of countless conquests, defeats and movements by the various rulers of the country. Much of the country's history has consisted of violent struggles between rival rulers of parts of what is now Ethiopia. In earlier times Ethiopian rulers sometimes claimed, and even exercised, a vague suzerainty over huge areas which are no longer a part of the country (including for example parts of what is now the Sudan).

In terms of the Africa of today Ethiopia is unique in that it was never entirely conquered by a European power. Ethiopians point out that even the five-year occupation of the country by the Italians (1936–1941) did not amount to total conquest because armed resistance continued during that period in the remoter areas of the country. The absence of a colonial past, though a matter of pride for modern Ethiopians, has meant that in some ways the struggle to modernize the country has been more difficult than in other African states. Elsewhere in Africa the colonial period was a cataclysmic event in that it was accompanied by the forcible entry of Western ideas and technology. In Ethiopia ancient political and social structures remain; and to some extent they have acted as a brake on modernization. This

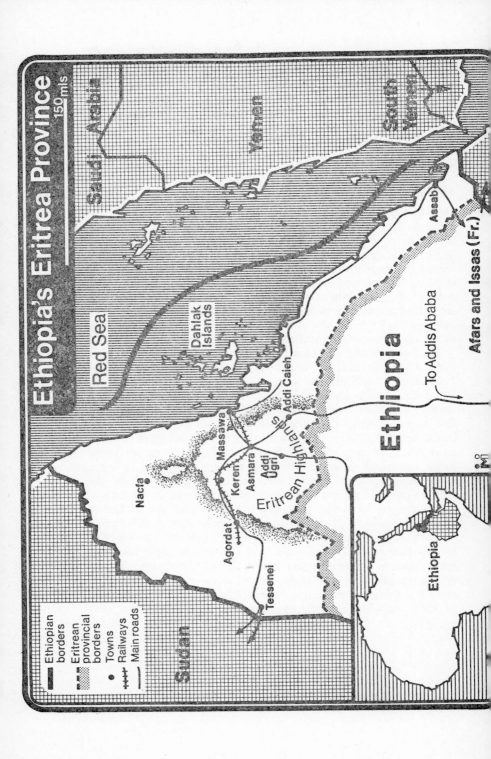

Ethiopia's Eritrea Province

150 mls

Saudi Arabia

Yemen

South Yemen

Red Sea

Dahlak Islands

Assab

To Addis Ababa

Afars and Issas (Fr.)

Massawa

Nacfa

Kerem

Asmara

Addi Ugri

Addi Caieh

Eritrean Highlands

Ethiopia

Agordat

Tessenei

Sudan

Ethiopia

Ethiopian borders
Eritrean provincial borders
Towns
Railways
Main roads

can be seen in such diverse aspects of Ethiopian life today as the difficulty in modernizing administrative and political methods and changing ancient systems of land tenure.

Geographically the country consists, for its larger part, of a huge plateau rising many thousand feet, which is cut in two by the Great Rift Valley running from the Red Sea to East Africa. The Western part of the plateau drains by means of the Blue Nile and other rivers into the Sudan. The eastern part drains into the Indian Ocean. One of the most striking features of Ethiopia's main plateau uplands is the way they are frequently and sharply cut by large fissures and deep valleys. This aspect of Ethiopian geography has had a most profound effect on the whole history of the country. Communications have always been made very difficult by the topography. This in turn made it extremely difficult for early rulers to unify even the central upland area of what is now modern Ethiopia. But it also made incursions from outside very difficult, whether these were by other African peoples in earlier times, or by European peoples in the colonial era.

Helped by its geographic isolation another remarkable feature of Ethiopia was also able to survive. This was the Ethiopian Orthodox Church which, despite its connections with the Christian Coptic Church of Alexandria, is *sui generis*. By modern times the country had become in effect a beleaguered Christian island surrounded by Islam. This fact, as well as memories of their external history which consisted for centuries of struggles with the Moslem peoples who were on their eastern, northern and western borders (to the South were pagan Bantu peoples), make Ethiopians even today instinctively suspicious of the Sudanese, Somalis, Egyptians and all other Arabs and Moslems. This suspicion remains a factor in the country's foreign policy.

THE PEOPLE

The Ethiopian people are believed to originate from a migration of Semitic people from Arabia into the highlands of the country several thousand years ago. The immigrants mixed with Hamitic people already there who had earlier displaced southwards negroid peoples.

Today Ethiopia contains a mixture of peoples, divided, as elsewhere in Africa, by tribe and religion. Ethnically it is not a particularly homogeneous country. However, the main peoples of the highlands of Ethiopia (including Eritrea province) do share general facial characteristics which make them easily recognizable at, for example, international African gatherings. Blacker than the peoples of the Northern Sudan or North Africa, their features

101

are more aquiline than those of most peoples of eastern, southern or western Africa.

There has never been a full or detailed census, but the total population in 1971 is thought to be about 25 million. The most important (that is to say the most influential, though not the most numerous) people are the Amhara of the central Ethiopian highlands. North of them are the Tigreans, related to the Amhara and also professing Ethiopian Orthodox Christianity. They also speak a related language, Tigrinya. Both of these languages are descended from Ge'ez, a dead language still used for church liturgy. The relationship of Amharic and Tigrinya to Ge'ez is comparable to that of French and Italian to Latin. Tigrinya is spoken not only in Tigre Province but also in the highland areas of Eritrea Province. Most of Southern Ethiopia is peopled by the Gallas, who extend from Walaga in the West to the ancient city of Harar in the East. They are by far the most numerous people in Ethiopia; estimates put their number at between 40 per cent and 50 per cent of the total population. Among the leading families, notably the Emperor's, there has been some intermingling of these three main peoples. Other important peoples of Ethiopia include the nomadic Danakil of Eritrea's Red Sea plain and the Somalis of Eastern Ethiopia who regularly move across the border between the Ogaden Province and the Somali Republic.

ERITREA

There are two opposing historical views of Eritrea. One, held by Eritrean separatists, maintains that what is now Eritrea Province of Ethiopia is 'naturally' and historically a separate entity which should rightly be independent of Ethiopia for ethnic, religious and historical reasons. The other extreme, the Ethiopian view, is that Eritrea's federation with Ethiopia by a United Nations decision of 1952 represented the natural return to Ethiopia of a 'lost' province which was naturally and rightfully hers for ethnic, religious and historical reasons. The facts do not appear to bear out either of these conflicting views (or, put another way: a good case for either can be made out by a careful selection of the facts). For the key to Eritrea is that it is a territory divided within itself.

The central mountainous region of Eritrea, which contains the capital Asmara, is geographically a part of the Ethiopian plateau. Its people speak Tigrinya, a language they share with people of the neighbouring Ethiopian province of Tigre. They are Christians and have participated in the mainstream of Ethiopian civilization for thousands of years. Today not only by language but in physical appearance, dress, customs and diet they appear to outsiders as 'Ethiopian'.

However, in the north and west of the province and along the margin of the Red Sea – in other words in lowland Eritrea – the people are largely Moslem. In the far west the tribes of the Northern Sudan spill over into what is now Eritrea. Even in lowland Eritrea the majority of people are not primarily Arabic-speaking but retain their own languages such as Tigre and Dankili. But in these areas Arabic is widely used in commerce and the language is current enough for the Ethiopian authorities to consider it worth publishing an Arabic newspaper.

The unification of Eritrea and the demarcation of its present boundaries were only achieved in 1890 by the Italians. Until then it was not really a separate political entity. The highlands had been part of the Christian Kingdom of Tigre (itself intermittently under the control of Ethiopian rulers) and the lowlands had been penetrated successively by Turks, Egyptians and the Mahdi's forces from the Sudan. In 1890 the Italians formally declared the creation of their colony Eritrea (it was named after the Roman name for the Red Sea). They remained until 1941 when they were defeated by British forces during the Second World War. The period of Italian rule was (in retrospect) beneficial to Eritrea in certain ways. Economic development came to the area, unlike the rest of Ethiopia. Eritrea benefited from the Italian genius for road building, and these roads remain today an asset (even though some of the most important ones were built for a sinister purpose – the invasion of Ethiopia in 1935). An Italian settler population arrived, some of whose basic technological skills have rubbed off on to the local population. A modern capital grew up and today Asmara is in many ways Ethiopia's finest city, even though it seems to have an atmosphere more of the Mediterranean than of Africa. Eritrea's two ports Assab and Massawa also grew and they represent much of Eritrea's importance to the rest of the Empire: without this province Ethiopia would have no territory of her own on the Red Sea. The fear of being land-locked has undoubtedly been one of the greatest factors in Ethiopia's determination to gain control of the area.

Despite several ambitious and successful agricultural schemes, including cotton and vegetable plantations, the countryside in Eritrea remains today a bleak and intimidating landscape. Rainfall is lower than in most of the rest of Ethiopia and even subsistence agriculture is hard, demanding great persistence from the inhabitants. In the lowlands many of the people remain nomadic while in the highlands the population is more sedentary. For both, mere survival is difficult in a bad year. Bandits or *shifta* have been a feature of Eritrea since ancient times and neither the Italians nor the British ever successfully controlled the problem. The extreme harshness of life, which provides a strong incentive to lawlessness, and the dramatically 'folded' nature of much of the terrain, which assists the escape of any lawbreaker, have conspired to make Eritrea a difficult area to which to bring complete security. This has undoubtedly aggravated the political problem which exists today.

By 1941, when the British military administration took over Eritrea, there were about 60,000 Italians in the territory. Their number has gradually declined over the years until today there are fewer than 5,000 and this figure is likely to decrease still further. After the British took over, Italy continued to take a great interest in Eritrea for she not only had a sizeable colony of her nationals there but also had considerable economic interests. It is not an over-simplification to describe the period of British rule as one of struggle between Italy and Ethiopia for future control of the country. At one stage the Italians hoped to restore their colonial presence in the guise of administering the U.N. trusteeship of the country (as they did in Somalia) but they failed because of local and international opposition. Later they came to support the idea of an independent Eritrea, which inevitably would have retained close links with Italy. Despite the fact that this did not happen Italian interests remain very strong in Eritrea. Indeed her links with rest of Ethiopia have grown steadily and relations beween Rome and Addis Ababa are currently very cordial.

Visiting Eritrea today it is hard to imagine that the territory was ever administered by the British. In fact the British did not change things very much; most of the laws were left unaltered as were many administrative practices. Some impetus was given to education and – of even greater significance for the future – a measure of political freedom was accorded to the population.

Three main parties grew up: the Independence Bloc, which benefited from some Italian support; the Unionist Party, which represented the mainly Christian pro-Ethiopian section of the population and received support from Addis Ababa; and the Moslem League, whose main power base was, naturally enough, Western Eritrea.

FEDERATION

By the end of the 1940s the political temperature in Eritrea had risen sharply, and externally it had become an international problem. The four-power Commission of Investigation, consisting of France, the Soviet Union, Britain and the U.S.A., could not agree about the territory's future. Discussion, both within and outside Eritrea, envisaged many different possibilities for the future: full independence, union with Ethiopia, partition, with the Christian highlands becoming part of Ethiopia and the Moslem lowlands going to the Sudan, or a trusteeship perhaps under Britain. The U.N. finally decided that the best answer to the problem was a compromise which took account of Ethiopia's special interest and the fact that the Unionists were the strongest party within the territory but which at the same time recognized the special nature of Eritrea. This compromise was that Eritrea should enter into federation with Ethiopia. The country was to have its own Parliament and a largely separate administration. Most internal affairs were to be handled by the Eritrean government but the Imperial government of Addis Ababa would have control of defence, foreign affairs, trade and (because of the special importance of the outlet to the sea) communications.

Throughout the 1950s Addis Ababa kept up a steady pressure in favour of its gaining greater control over Eritrea's day-to-day affairs, and it is clear that many of the local officials and politicians did little to resist this trend. In any case they were under strong pressure as the Imperial government had at its disposal great power of patronage. In a way the end of federation could have been foreseen because of the friction that was bound to occur when a small state with a Western-style democratic constitution federated with a much larger autocracy.

By 1955 the situation had changed to such an extent that the Emperor's representative could tell the Eritrean Assembly that there were 'no internal or external affairs as far as the office of His Imperial Majesty's Representative is concerned and there will be none in the future. The affairs of Eritrea concern Ethiopia as a whole . . . and the Emperor.' During this period economic development continued in Eritrea and there appears to have been no question of its being treated as a poor relation. Indeed the territory's special status gave it an edge over other parts of the Empire. It retained sufficient political influence as a separate entity to make concessions by the federal government necessary. The authorities in Addis Ababa were well aware that Eritrea, if allowed to continue to exercise its democratic freedom, could pose a serious threat to the Imperial concept. Democratic ideas have always shown themselves to be highly contagious; there was clearly a danger that other parts of the Empire might demand similar rights. After all it was not as if Eritrea were a particularly large part of Ethiopia either in area or population. Today there are estimated to be at most about 25 million people in Ethiopia; Eritreans number around two million or at most about 10 per cent of the total. The territory's area is 45,000 square miles compared with Ethiopia's total of 395,000 square miles. The Empire contained then, as it does today, several more important minorities such as the Galla or the Somalis.

In May 1960 the Eritrean Assembly voted unanimously to change the name 'Eritrean Government' to 'Eritrean Administration'. The chief executive became the chief of administration and other symbolic changes involving the territory's insignia were made, all with the effect of reducing the territory's real autonomy. In 1962 the Assembly accepted the end of its autonomy and Eritrea became Ethiopia's fourteenth province. In the closing years of federation political unrest had grown steadily in Eritrea, partly due to Addis Ababa's efforts to crush local autonomy and partly because of discontent among urban workers. The latter was mainly due to the deteriorating economic situation, aggravated by the departure of large numbers of the Italian community. Many Eritreans maintain that the Eritrean Assembly destroyed federation under duress, responding to bribery and other pressures from Addis Ababa. These allegations are denied by Ethiopian officials. Whatever their truth, the end of federation destroyed the Eritreans' special position within the Empire as well as the political rights which they had enjoyed and other Ethiopians had not.

The political developments which had taken place during the period of British rule and the period of federation could not be wholly undone, however, even by cancellation of Eritrea's special status and the imposition of direct rule from Addis Ababa. A people who have experienced political rights and freedoms appear to remember them even if subsequent rulers do their best to make them forget. Trade unionism developed in Eritrea long before it did in Ethiopia, where it was formally legalized only in 1963; and even today Eritreans are prominent in the labour movement.

With federation dead and political and press freedoms curtailed it was inevitable that opposition to the Imperial government should go underground. The Eritrean Liberation Front (E.L.F.) arose in the last years of federation when it became clear that Eritrea would lose its autonomy. Opposition to the government was particularly strong among the Moslem population of western Eritrea and it is here that the E.L.F. gained its first recruits and scored its initial success. The Moslems were markedly hostile because they believed (correctly) that they were about to be dominated by a Christian-orientated government.

Almost since its inception the E.L.F. has been plagued by internal dissension. This has arisen from differences based on personalities, ideologies and religion. Much of the action in the mid-sixties took place in western Eritrea, as the guerrillas could operate from bases inside the Sudan to which they could withdraw if the need arose. Mostly the guerrillas' tactics have been to ambush small security units or attack government installations such as posts, highway depots, bridges, and roads. Their most spectacular attacks have been made on the railway which links Asmara with the two important inland towns of Keren and Agordat. In late 1970 they stopped a train on this line and having disembarked the passengers, ran it off the rails into a ravine. Pictures of this exploit, which appeared in the press throughout the world at the end of December, represented one of the few recent occasions – together with the hijacking of Ethiopian airliners – when this obscure conflict has gained any widespread publicity.

THE SITUATION IN 1971

The E.L.F.'s fortunes have fluctuated ever since its beginnings according to the degree of internal unity it managed to achieve and the amount of external support it received. 1970 saw a sharp rise in E.L.F. activity. In April an E.L.F. gunman walked into a restaurant-bar in the centre of Asmara and shot dead three retired civil servants and three other people. In October and November there were a number of attacks on Christian villages many of whose inhabitants were killed by the guerrillas. On 21 November, E.L.F. elements ambushed a convoy on the Asmara–Keren road and the dead included the commanding general of Ethiopia's 2nd Division (which is based in Eritrea).

The Ethiopian government's response was to declare martial law and a state of emergency throughout much of the province. This step placed more discretionary power in the hands of the military and imposed curfews and travel checks, though many thousands of refugees crossed the border into the Sudan. In January 1971 a new Governor-General, appointed by the Emperor, took up his post. Lt Gen. Debebe Haile Mariam has so far impressed local observers as a man likely to take sterner steps than his more conciliatory predecessor (a relative of the Emperor's) to restore security in Eritrea. He has already taken measures to impose better discipline among security forces, particularly with regard to their treatment of, and attitude towards, the local population. In 1969 public hangings, including that of a fifteen-year-old boy, were reported at Agordat; and in the last few months of 1970 there were reports of My-Lai-type atrocities in Eritrea. Despite Ethiopian government silence and official denials, it seems extremely probable (on the basis of information from independent sources) that some very grave incidents have taken place including the following:

27 November 1970: At a village called Bascadara security forces herded 120 people into a mosque (ostensibly in order to safeguard them from a planned air strike). The security forces then shot dead 112. The story could only be told because there were eight survivors, who had feigned death.

1 December 1970: At a village near Keren 625 people were killed in two days. Boy Scouts from Keren buried the dead.

27 January 1971: About sixty people were killed in a mosque at a village not far from Elaberte.

(In at least one of these cases the actions of the security forces were in retaliation for villagers having betrayed them to the E.L.F. It is said that before the incident near Keren a party of soldiers had been welcomed by villagers, who had given them food and drink. While the soldiers were relaxing, E.L.F. guerrillas, alerted to the troops' presence by the villagers, arrived and shot several of the soldiers dead.)

In the early months of this year, following the declaration of a state of emergency, the 2nd Division was 'beefed up' (to quote one Ethiopian official) so that, together with the police commandos, the security forces probably now total around 20,000 men. In addition there are local militia units which are said to play quite an important role because their members receive money, titles*, or other rewards for killing or capturing guerrillas. As noted earlier in this report, the terrain over which both guerrillas and security forces have to operate is extremely wild and affords excellent cover. On balance the difficulty of the terrain is probably to the advantage of the guerrillas when it comes to actual fighting or setting up ambushes and then making a quick escape. However, the land's extreme aridity and harshness probably favour the security forces in the long term because it makes it difficult for the guerrillas to 'live off the country'.

In addition to their ground forces, by African standards the Ethiopians possess a highly developed air force. A considerable part of this is stationed in Asmara, including about eight F86

---

* As far as the author knows, Britain is the only country which can currently rival Ethiopia for the hierarchical elaborateness of its system of titles.

single-engine jet strike aircraft, about a dozen T29 piston-engine bombers and a number of transports. Together with the army they also have a number of light aircraft and helicopters.

The main consequence of the declaration of a state of emergency seems to have been that army units have penetrated the countryside more than previously. It also appears that since November 1970 they have pursued a more 'active' strategy, going out regularly with patrols and operating travel checks rather than, as before, waiting for the guerrillas to attack.

There is little doubt that the Ethiopian forces have been more successful in the first months of 1971. This is evidenced by decreased checks and restrictions on travel (single vehicles were again using the main Asmara/Keren/Agordat road without military escort), and by the absence of serious incidents in the early months of the year. E.L.F. activity continued, however. This was admitted in one of the rare official communiques on the fighting which appeared in the Eritrean press. (To read the government-controlled press in Addis Ababa one would hardly be aware that there was any trouble in the province.) The official statement, which seemed to cover a five-week period, reported:

5 February 1971: At 10.30 a.m. a group of guerrillas attacked an army patrol post at Haberenqua village in Hamasen district and killed fourteen people including twelve civilians. Five other people were wounded. The guerrillas lost ten dead.
5 March 1971: The residents of Halib Menal in Keren district captured 'two out of four brigands after a brief exchange of fire'.
7 March 1971: The guerrillas returned in large numbers and plundered the village, taking away cattle. In a subsequent encounter between a contingent composed of the police and army, the guerrillas withdrew taking their dead and wounded with them. The security forces lost one dead and five were wounded.
8 March 1971: An army squad surprised a guerrilla base camp in a cave called Silu near Emba Soyira Mountain, 20 km. east of Senafe Wereda. The army lost one man during the raid and the 'bandits' withdrew to Geradif valley carrying their casualties.
11 March 1971: A mine laid by guerrillas destroyed a large part of an Imperial Highways Authority camp 8 km. east of Teseney. Four people were wounded by the explosion. Of the two who were rushed to hospital in Asmara, one died.

The above is probably a fair picture of the nature of the Eritrean conflict at the present time. Although the account was issued by an Ethiopian government official (who might normally be

H

expected to be biased), it has the ring of truth if only because it reflects some credit on the fighting abilities of the guerrillas and acknowledges their practice of carrying away their dead and wounded. It certainly is a more accurate picture of the nature of the fighting than that which emerges from the E.L.F. By the time their own accounts of incidents have reached one of their exile bases and then have been passed on for broadcast by Baghdad or Damascus Radio, they have become so embellished that they often take on an almost surrealist tone. At various times they have claimed to control up to 40 per cent of Eritrea and to have 'liberated' Keren. The E.L.F. have always exaggerated the number of armed men they have in the field; a reasonable estimate is that in the middle of 1970 there were about 3,000 armed guerrillas and since then at least one third have been driven out of the country (either across the Sudanese frontier or across the Red Sea to Yemen and South Yemen).

In the early months of 1971 the Ethiopian army's main aim was to try to cut off the guerrillas' external sources of supply, arms and other help. This military objective has been accompanied by diplomatic initiatives aimed at discouraging the E.L.F.'s foreign supporters (see below under 'The Wider Implications'). But attempts to halt the supply of arms to the E.L.F. do not seem to have been successful; indeed there is evidence that recently the quality of their weapons has greatly improved, with the acquisition of FN rifles, Czech sub-machine guns, light rockets and Russian and Chinese mines.

That in recent months there has been an exodus of Eritreans into the Sudan is borne out by reports from the Eastern Sudan where the influx has been causing problems for Sudanese and U.N. refugee officials. In the Tokar area near the Red Sea a stream of refugees, 90 per cent of them women and children, has been reported. Many of the new arrivals are emaciated and in very poor condition. One visiting official from a U.N. agency reported recently that he had counted over 1,000 graves immediately on the Sudanese side of the frontier. The World Food Programme, a specialized agency of the U.N., is distributing emergency food supplies to about 17,000 of these refugees. The recent influx brings to about 43,000 the total number of Eritrean refugees in the Sudan, according to Sudanese government estimates. The Sudanese government's policy is to keep the refugees well clear of the frontier so as to avoid incidents.

Despite the Ethiopians' relative success in the military field, underlying political problems remain. Some of these are due simply to the repetition in Eritrea of problems common to the rest of Ethiopia: an example of this is the economic stagnation caused by the closure of the Suez Canal, which has reduced the competitiveness of some of Eritrea's exports to Europe. Nor has Eritrea been fortunate with its weather for the last two years; poor rainfall and the resulting hardship have inevitably affected popular feeling. There are also more permanent problems. One is the feeling of many Eritreans that, because the Empire's official language is Amharic, they are discriminated against in education (e.g. entry to university is by Amharic exams), as well as in government service. They also point to the preponderance of Amharic speakers rather than native Eritreans in top positions in the civil service – even within the civil service in Eritrea itself: at present most departments in Asmara appear to be headed by someone from Ethiopia proper who has as his deputy a local Eritrean. These grievances, though they have a certain justification, need to be set in the context of the situation of other and larger minority peoples within the Empire. Compared to these the Eritreans, thanks (a) to the political pressures they have been able to exert in the past and (b) the relatively large number of them who are educated people, have fared favourably. In terms of education and representation in the government it is not so much a question of Eritrean under-representation as of Amharic over-representation. The latter enjoy a huge preponderance in the government and the higher reaches of the civil service. But as Christopher Clapham has shown in his book *Haile Selassie's Government*, Eritreans have been by far the best represented group in the highest ranks of government after the Amhara of Shoa Province. It should also be pointed out that many Eritreans were in the habit of migrating to Ethiopia proper even before federation and many of these had very good jobs. Today Eritreans are found throughout the Empire. They are particularly prominent in technical and junior managerial positions.

It would be fair to say, however, that *Moslem* Eritreans have been discriminated against. For historical reasons mentioned earlier the feelings of the Ethiopian political establishment fall short of goodwill towards Moslems. Though there has been no recent census in Eritrea (there has never been any census in Ethiopia), officials maintain that about 35 per cent of the population of Eritrea Province is Moslem and 65 per cent is Christian. This could well be incorrect: in 1952 the British Administration estimated that there were 514,000 Moslems and 510,000 Christians. It is quite probable that a similar balance, some 40 per cent of the population belonging to each group, exists today. Within Eritrea the Moslems have not progressed as fast as the Christians, partly for reasons of education. It should be added, however, that the Eritrean who is a member of Ethiopia's Council of Ministers is a Moslem.

The E.L.F. itself has been affected by Eritrea's Moslem/Christian division. At one time it looked as if the E.L.F. would manage to unite all Eritrean dissident feelings, regardless of religion. The Eritrean Independence Party was originally led by a Tigre Christian, Michael Woldemariam; later, the Christian Tedla Bairu (a former president of the Eritrean Federal Assembly) became vice-president of the Front. But dissension, has arisen recently because only one of the E.L.F.'s divisions has been led by a Christian. A number of E.L.F. attacks on churches have been very badly received by Christian Eritreans. In addition the increasingly Pan-Arab tone of E.L.F. propaganda has done much to alienate Christian support. The E.L.F. has adopted this tone because it has been the militant Arab states, notably Syria, Iraq and Libya, who have provided the Front with most of its financial and other help. Some observers – and not just Ethiopians – believe that if Eritrea were granted independence it might fall apart because of the age-old antipathy between Christian and Moslem.

Despite this division a measure of genuinely 'Eritrean' feeling persists. For the present the division of Eritrea should enable Addis Ababa at least to keep the E.L.F. at bay. But in a country where the dominance of an Amharic minority is so preponderant it is likely that the 'edges' of Ethiopia (there is also a Moslem Irredentist movement among the Galla in the south) will increasingly demand a greater say in running their affairs.

PART THREE

THE WIDER IMPLICATIONS

At one time the problems of minorities within nation states could be classified as 'internal' matters which the outside world was obliged to leave alone. But in recent years the absolute right of sovereign states to order their own affairs as they see fit has come under increasing fire. It is not my intention to discuss whether or not this is a desirable tendency; it is merely to observe that this change has occurred. The international concern with South Africa's domestic policy is a fair example. And in both the Nigerian and Pakistani civil wars voices were raised in many parts of the world suggesting intervention of one kind or another.

Part of the reason for this increased 'interference' in other peoples' affairs is probably a realization that in the second half of the twentieth century 'internal' problems tend to become international in scope by reason of the effects they exert on nations outside the sovereign state in question. The internal problems concerning the Sudan and Ethiopia described in this report are good examples of this. Humanitarian concern about the victims of the situation in Southern Sudan is not the only reason for international interest even though estimates of the number of people who have lost their lives directly or indirectly as a result of the troubles range up to one and a half million. The main reason for the first signs of the internationalization of both conflicts is that they have become involved with the Arab-Israeli struggle and, more distantly and as yet more tenuously, with East-West rivalry. The two local conflicts have also interacted so as to involve each other.

In the purely African context, that is to say in terms of the Organization of African Unity (O.A.U.), both disputes are accepted almost unanimously as internal affairs with which no state or person has any right to interfere. The reason for this is the African states' agreement that Africa's present national frontiers are sacred and inviolable. This position, which is enshrined in the O.A.U. charter, is motivated by a very justifiable fear that if ever there were any serious questioning of the present frontiers a diplomatic and possibly military Pandora's box would be flung open. The basis of this fear is the knowledge that Africa's frontiers are artificial (the creation of foreigners) and therefore weak and open to challenge.

The troubles in the Southern Sudan and Eritrea are aspects of a wider problem which concerns most of Africa. But their difficulties are not only more active, and in human terms more serious, than any of the others; they are also of greater international importance because of the number of nations involved.

THE SOVIET UNION

One result of the Soviet Union's important role in Egypt has been a natural desire to spread this influence up the Nile. North-East Africa is currently Moscow's favoured area on that continent. For some years the Sudan has had Africa's best organized and most powerful Communist Party. This party, which is broadly pro-Soviet, is the only one in Africa to have a member within the government. These considerations, together with Moscow's pro-Arab stand in the Middle East, have made the Russians a strong ally of the government in Khartoum, despite Nimeiry's recent anti-communist moves.

The Russians supply the Sudan with military equipment and

training in accordance with an agreement dating from 1968. Although talk of the Southern Sudan conflict as 'Russia's Vietnam' is undoubtedly exaggerated, the Russians are involved in an indirect way with an estimated 700 of their military experts on training duties within the country. A count of entries in the Juba Hotel register early in 1971 revealed there had been 123 Russians out of a total of 800 visitors to the hotel during the preceding six-month period.

As far as Eritrea is concerned, Russia is indirectly engaged on the side of the Eritrean rebels in that the guerrillas receive most of their support from militant Arab states which in turn are supported by the Soviets. The Russians are somewhat concerned about being pre-empted by the Chinese, who also aid the E.L.F.

THE UNITED STATES

Ethiopia is one of the African states where Washington concentrates her aid, which reportedly amounts to more than $150 million (economic) and a further $100 million (military) a year. The U.S. offers this aid for a number of reasons, including that of defence commitments between the two countries. In particular the U.S. maintains a communications base at Kagnew, near Asmara in Ethiopia's Eritrea Province, where some 3,800 Americans live. This base is a valuable facility for the U.S. which uses it for satellite communications, its space programme, and presumably to eavesdrop on the Arab world. The Ethiopian armed forces are largely supplied with American equipment. In 1965 the Eritrean guerrillas reported shooting down a U.S. helicopter which was carrying out a reconnaissance mission against them, and in April 1971 they claimed to have shot down an American reconnaissance plane.

ISRAEL

Israel too has chosen to make Ethiopia one of the countries it aids most in Africa. Its aid includes that for many well-publicized projects. Less publicized are the arms and training provided for police commandos in action in Eritrea, and a political official in the Governor-General's office in Asmara. Eritrea is of interest to Israel because its Red Sea coastline is the only area of the coast 'friendly' to Israel, and also because, without Eritrea, Israel could not overfly Africa. Naturally the Israelis wish to discourage the E.L.F., which has links with Palestinian guerrilla movements.

The Israelis are also alleged to have provided clandestine support to the Southern Sudanese Anya-Nya since at least 1969.

Though I myself have no evidence of this, it is likely to be true because (a) Southern Sudanese have told me this; (b) a number of journalists who have visited the Southern Sudan from the guerrilla side have said there is Israeli support; and (c) it is obviously in Israel's strategic interest to embarrass the Arab states by opening a 'second front' away to the South. (Roughly half the Sudanese army of 50,000 is at present tied up in the South.) The reported route for Israeli support is through Ethiopia.

UGANDA

When President Idi Amin overthrew Milton Obote in January 1971 Kampala-Khartoum relations sank to a new low following a number of anti-Khartoum and pro-Anya-Nya declarations by the new President. The Anya-Nya continued to use Uganda as their main refuge outside the South and by December 1971 relations had become critical, with Amin accusing Sudanese troops of crossing into Uganda. The main reason for Amin's hostility to Khartoum was his justified fear that the Sudanese were aiding elements still sympathetic to Obote. Reports that pro-Obote guerrillas were receiving training in the Southern Sudan probably contributed to Amin's volte-face in his relations with Israel and the Arab states in March/April 1972 and his decision to mend his fences with Khartoum. It seems not impossible that some sort of deal between Khartoum and Kampala was arrived at; and it was interesting to note that Amin urged the Anya-Nya to ratify the Addis Ababa agreement.

ETHIOPIA

Traditionally hostile to Moslem powers in general, Ethiopia has also at times been hostile to the Sudanese government because of suspicions that it helps the Eritrean guerrillas. In the last couple of years Ethiopia has felt increasingly beleaguered as left-wing coups occurred in the Sudan and Somalia – both areas from which she traditionally expects trouble. Ethiopia also fears that U.S. enthusiasm for supporting her may be waning. Washington, after its experience in Vietnam, is more wary of foreign involvements of any kind, particularly if they affect the Middle East question. Kagnew Base in Eritrea, the Americans hint, is not essential; the development of Diego Garcia in the Indian Ocean, with the co-operation of Britain, could make it expendable. The U.S. has also resisted some of Ethiopia's requests for arms aid. When a U.S. serviceman was shot dead early in 1971 on the Asmara-Massawa road some Machiavellian observers speculated that perhaps he was not a victim of the E.L.F. but had been shot by the Ethiopians in the hope that the Americans, attributing the act to E.L.F., would react sharply and increase their support for Ethiopia.

Ethiopian friendship with Israel is motivated mainly by the need to have a counterweight against the Arab states, but Addis Ababa holds a good card in the shape of its strong position within the O.A.U. At an African summit conference a couple of years ago something of an Ethiopian/Arab crisis occurred because the Arab states opposed an Ethiopian-sponsored resolution condemning hijacking. Another card up Ethiopia's sleeve is her ability to assist Southern Sudanese rebels in retaliation for any Sudanese help to Eritrean rebels. The Ethiopian Foreign Minister visited Khartoum in March 1971 at which time the two countries agreed on a mutual 'I won't help your rebels if you don't help mine' pact. Border incidents occur, and the two wars were interconnected by the fact that some of the peoples of the Southern Sudan (such as the Anuak) straddle the frontier with western Ethiopia. Ethiopian officials are believed to have threatened the sizeable community of South Yemenis in Ethiopia with expulsion if they continue to help the E.L.F.

In Eritrea, the Emperor personally commands greater respect than his troops, many of whom have alienated the local population who dislike living under military rule.

3 THE AFRICANS' PREDICAMENT IN RHODESIA

by G. C. Grant

*G. C. (Jack) Grant is a Rhodesian citizen and lives
in Salisbury. Born in Trinidad and educated at
Dalhousie, Cambridge and Yale Universities, he first
went to Rhodesia as a school teacher in 1931. He was
Principal of Adams College, Natal, between 1949 and
1956. In 1960–62 he was the Secretary-Treasurer of
the Rhodesian Christian Conference; in 1964–69 the
Treasurer of the Christian Council of Rhodesia;
and from 1968 until 1972 he was the Field
Secretary of the United Church Board of Rhodesia.
He also captained the West Indies cricket team from
1930 to 1935.*

THE AFRICANS'
PREDICAMENT IN RHODESIA

INTRODUCTION

To understand the position of Africans in Rhodesia today it is necessary to go back in history at least to the closing years of the last century, when European settlers – symbolized by Cecil Rhodes and his followers – began to enter the country from the south and to take it over. This is not the place to pass judgement on that invasion. But its outcome was that a portion of Africa, at that time still unnamed yet inhabited solely by Africans of the Mashona and Matabele peoples, was occupied by Europeans and named Rhodesia. The arrival of these foreigners totally changed the history of the country and began a new era.

Conquered peoples cannot help but learn from their conquerors, especially if the latter bring with them capital, skills, a more advanced technology, and a challenging and comforting faith. That the victors of the Matabele War of 1893 and the Mashona and Matabele Rebellions of 1896–7 did much to bring the vanquished into a more modern world cannot be denied. For instance, they established a new pattern of law and order – if not always justice; they introduced western educational and medical services, as well as sophisticated commercial and mining methods; and they brought the Christian religion. In addition they developed the natural resources as never before; they provided road, rail, telephone and postal links both within the country and with the outside world. Their actions transferred, if not catapulted, Rhodesia's original inhabitants from their traditional ways into the problems of the twentieth century.

The reaction of the conquered to their conquest was mixed (rebellions were put down with resultant heavy bloodshed). The Africans experienced both bewilderment and excitement, resentment and admiration, resistance and attraction. Occasionally they expressed gratitude and acceptance of the new ways. But always there was a measure of hesitancy. Nonetheless, a case could be made out that the Africans regarded the invaders as 'an attractively creative minority' (Toynbee).

Many Africans believe that they were deceived, rather than

118

conquered by Rhodes and his followers*. But conquerors who do not totally eliminate the conquered sooner or later have to decide how they are going to treat them. They can, for instance, regard them as serfs – that is as permanently underprivileged, intellectually inferior, and culturally barbaric. They can, on the other hand, see them as potential equals who one day will be full fellow citizens in the land of their birth. But to treat them as potential equals requires an outlook which is not primarily self-regarding and which is prepared to share privileges and opportunities. This kind of outlook recognizes that in the course of time conquerors and conquered will become one people.

This recognition presents difficulties, even in a racially homogeneous society; but when the invaders differ in colour and culture from the subjected the difficulties are compounded. The problems are further bedevilled when the invaders bring with them emotional and unscientific convictions that their superiority derives primarily from the pigmentation of their skin (exemplified for instance by the persistent, if vain, white attempt to deny that the remarkable Zimbabwe ruins could have been built by blacks). Such attitudes are hard to combat. Worse still, they cannot but provoke racial animosity as well as widen the gap between the two races; the fruits of such myths are conceit on the part of the invader and hatred on the part of the subjected.

A glance at the history of Rhodesia since the 1897 conquest will show that white Rhodesians – hereafter referred to as Europeans – have usually been divided in their attitude to, and in their treatment of, black Rhodesians – hereafter referred to as Africans. Some Europeans, such as many missionaries, have regarded Africans as fellow men and fellow citizens: in religious language, they have regarded Africans as fellow children of God. A much larger number of Europeans, however, have regarded Africans as lesser breeds with whom there can be no equality and with whom there must be as little intermingling as is economically convenient. The following extract from the leading article of *Property and Finance*, a Rhodesian monthly (December 1971) is typical of this attitude:

The word 'Rhodesian', for decades referring to the people who have created the country, now means something very

* Rhodes ambiguously offered 'equal rights for all civilized people'. See, *inter alia*, the books by Professor T. Ranger and Philip Mason's *Birth of a Dilemma* (O.U.P., 1958). The roots of many of Rhodesia's current problems stem from its never having been administered by the Colonial Office, but instead first by a commercial company and then, from 1923, by settlers.

different: the most rabid Black nationalist as well as the most primitive tribesman is now as much a Rhodesian as anyone else.

A third group of Europeans have wavered between benevolence and contempt, at one time accepting the notion of 'African advancement', while at other times equally vehemently pursuing a policy of 'keeping Africans in their place' – a wavering reflected in the policies and practices of successive Rhodesian governments. In the late 1950s and early 1960s these Europeans tended to emphasize partnership and genuine development. Since the Rhodesian Front took power in 1962, however, they have exhibited a quite different attitude, emphasizing racial separation and differences, and development only in racially divided areas. This party, the Rhodesian Front, which now has overwhelming European support, was created in 1962 explicitly in order to oppose any kind of advance to majority rule. It believes strongly in racial discrimination, and is thought not to have a single African member. In other words, it represents a European society which is aware that its privileged economic and social position depends on retaining power in white hands. This is borne out by the 1969 Constitution – the third in less than a decade – which is blatantly racial. (No less a person than the Prime Minister, Mr Ian Smith, has boasted that this is so.)

This Constitution did away with the common roll and substituted two rolls – one for Europeans and the other for Africans. From the 1969 Constitution also emanated a Land Tenure Act which divided the country into two racial areas of approximately the same size – one portion of some 45,000,000 acres for a quarter of a million Europeans, and the other portion also of 45,000,000 acres for over five million Africans. The Act makes it a punishable offence for a member of one race to 'occupy' land in the other area or even to visit the other area without proper permission. This division of the land gratified the government's European supporters, who have proudly described such a division as creating 'parity'.

A similar instance of 'parity' is to be found in the Education Vote, where again approximately the same amount of money is set aside for African education ($18,194,000* in 1970/71) as is allocated for non-African education ($16,270,000). This takes no account of the fact that the number of children in African schools (660,000) far outnumbers the children in European schools (just over 56,000). There would, of course, be a vastly greater

* One Rhodesian dollar = approximately £0.60 Sterling.

number of African children at school if they were provided with education to the same level as the Europeans. For one of the main aims of the government in Rhodesia is to 'maintain the Rhodesian way of life', which in essence means preserving white privilege and white supremacy. In Rhodesia such aims are expressed by euphemistic phrases like 'preserving Christian standards' or 'keeping government in civilized hands'.

A further illustration of this kind of racialist thinking is to be found in the proposed 'Residential Property Owners (Protection) Bill'. Its ostensible purpose is to promote racial harmony by preventing people of different races from living in the same area. Another of its alleged aims is to give each racial community the freedom to develop in its own way. In actuality, the real purpose is to keep the races apart and to remove those few Indians and Coloureds who have managed, within the law, to infiltrate into what the Europeans consider to be European areas.

What stands out in Rhodesian life after eighty years of European rule is that life is racially orientated, with the Europeans ruling and the Africans being ruled.* Coupled with this feature is the determination of the Europeans to keep economic and political power for as long as possible. This means that Africans must remain in a subservient position. Consequently, most Africans of calibre (of whom there are many in Rhodesia) no longer look on Europeans as, in Toynbee's words, 'an attractively creative minority' but as 'an odiously dominant minority'.

Many of Rhodesia's discriminatory practices are unwritten:

* Racial discrimination has been prevalent in Rhodesia since the arrival of the first white settlers in 1889. Laws such as the Immorality Suppression Act of 1903 made sexual relations between a black man and a white woman a criminal offence. In 1953, when Rhodesia joined the Central African Federation, the Federal Constitution provided for an African Affairs Board to report on 'differentiating' legislation. The 1961 Rhodesian Constitution introduced an elaborate Declaration of Rights. It was made justiciable and specially entrenched so as to make amendment impossible without the approval of all racial groups through four referenda. There was also an independent Constitutional Council to scrutinize legislation. These provisions were repeated *verbatim* in the 1965 Constitution adopted by the Rhodesians after their unilateral declaration of independence. But in the 1969 republican Constitution the Declaration of Rights was made non-justiciable. Furthermore, a special section was inserted to make discrimination legal if 'such treatment is fair and will promote harmonious relations between such persons or communities . . .'

It was Winston Churchill who said of Rhodesia, fifty years ago: 'It will be an ill day for the native races when their fortunes are removed from the impartial and august administration of the Crown and abandoned to the sea of self-interest of a small white population. Such an event is no doubt very remote. Yet the speculator, the planter and the settler are knocking at the door.'

for example, no black Rhodesian at present holds a commission in the armed forces or the police, or is allowed any position of seniority in the civil service – despite many vacancies for these continually being advertised.* Asians in Rhodesia have for a long time found that building societies refuse them loans to buy houses in white areas while offering generous credits for the purchase of homes in Asian areas. Similarly, although the Immigration Act does not say so in specific terms, only white immigrants have been allowed into the country for the last twenty years. The final ignominy for a black Rhodesian is the 'rights of admission reserved' signs which appear in most places of public entertainment, signalling to him that he is not wanted.

---

* David Holden, of the *Sunday Times*, recently reported: 'The Government persistently refuses to employ African graduates in senior grades of the Civil Service in spite of a shortage of other suitable candidates. Salisbury has been for months without an Assistant Medical Officer of Health because the best qualified applicant – who was actually offered the post by the City Council – was a coloured doctor from South Africa who was refused permission by the Government to enter Rhodesia.

'In answer to protests from the Rhodesian National Association for Coloured People over this and at least three other similar recent incidents an official spokesman declared last month: "Asiatics, coloured people and Indians are not admitted as immigrants to this country. Parties to a mixed marriage are similarly not welcome as immigrants. Government in principle does not favour mixed marriages . . .

'At the same time, the Minister of Justice, Mr Lardner-Burke, warned the House of Assembly (Parliament) that European immigrants found consorting with non-white women could be deported and that miscegenation was frowned upon.

'Actions under the Land Tenure Act against African 'occupation' of 'white' land include several cases of African institutions such as commercial colleges and medical clinics being refused permission to operate in 'European' areas; threats of prosecution for Europeans who permit resident African servants to live on their property with their families; and an attempt (so far thwarted) to force the churches to register as 'voluntary associations' which would then have to request permission to hold multi-racial services in 'white' areas.'

Sir Roy Welensky, the former Prime Minister of Rhodesia, has commented: 'Men who were once scarcely even visible on the lunatic fringe of racialism now have to be taken seriously.'

The sort of device that has served Salisbury's multi-racial cinemas for years is providing two public lavatories for each sex, one labelled 'Europeans Only' and the other 'All Races'. (No prize for guessing who uses the latter.)

It is true that as yet Africans can still attend cinemas in European Salisbury, still use a multi-racial swimming pool, still share park benches and buses with whites, still spend their money in white shops and even – if they can afford it and can stand the stares and glares of other customers – eat, drink and sleep in Salisbury's three most expensive hotels. With the exception of the capital's three main hotels it is virtually impossible for an African to get a meal or a bed in a hotel or motel.

THE PRESENT POSITION

Against this background, let us look at some facts which give an insight into the position of Africans in Rhodesia today.

Population: The latest figures, as given in the Digest of Statistics for November 1971, are: 5,220,000 Africans; 249,000 Europeans; 9,300 Indians; and 16,900 Coloureds. It is obvious that the Africans outnumber all other people by about twenty to one. In addition, the annual increase of 3·6 per cent in the African population is so great – 279,000 in 1970 – that every year it exceeds the total number of all other races in the country. By comparison the whites are increasing, from a smaller base, by a mere 1·1 per cent a year. Consequently, even the most vigorous of government-sponsored schemes for attracting European immigrants is not going appreciably to alter the present overwhelming preponderance of Africans. Nearly half the African population is under sixteen years of age. A recent government campaign to encourage birth control among Africans got off to a poor start. Africans resisted it and are still resisting it because they regard the campaign as politically and racially motivated, designed to reduce the number of blacks. Numerically, therefore, Africans will always be well in the lead. No doubt this is one reason why the wishes of the people as a whole are not to be tested by a referendum. It is also significant that in 1960–1970 Rhodesia lost 88,210 of its white population to gain only 82,170 replacements. Only 6 out of 50 white M.P.s in Parliament had been born in the country.

Land: The latest division of the land as laid down in the Land Tenure Act of 1969 sets aside some 6,000,000 acres as National Land, 45,000,000 acres as European Areas, and 45,000,000 acres as African Areas. Included in this Act is a provision stating that these allocations of land cannot be altered beyond a maximum of 2 per cent. The division is as unfair in quality as it is in quantity: a much larger portion of the land with the best soil and the best rainfall has been included within the European Areas. At the same time the main road and rail links definitely favour European farmers, and all towns (where 80 per cent of the whites live) fall within the European Areas.

The harshness with which this law is implemented is reflected in the recent forced closure of Cold Comfort Farm and in the measures taken against Chief Rekayi Tangwena and his people – who for four years have been harried from their ancestral homelands of Inyanga in the Eastern Highlands because their land had been designated a European Area (although no white man had lived there, and the Tangwena had been in continuous occupation). In 1968 Chief Tangwena won his case of appeal against eviction in the Rhodesian High Court; whereupon Mr Dupont purported to issue an Order in Council setting aside the Court's decision. Although their homes were razed and they were repeatedly evicted by the police and the army, most of the Tangwena returned and, remaining in the mountains, continue to assert their claim to their homeland.

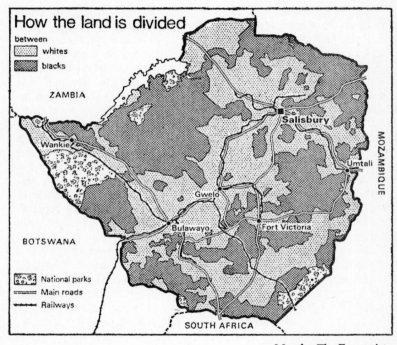

Map by *The Economist*

About two-thirds of the African population live in the African rural areas and by far the greater number of them live in what are known as Tribal Trust Lands, where land cannot be individually owned. Though many own a few head of cattle and though an increasing number are growing cotton as a cash crop, the total picture is one of bare subsistence. There are also a small number of Africans who own land in what is known as African Purchase

Areas, but the following figures* speak for themselves:

	TRIBAL TRUST LAND	PURCHASE AREA	TOTAL
Area in acres	39,900,000	3,700,000	43,600,000
Number of farmers	600,000	8,000	608,000

Certain officials of the Government Agricultural Department have become increasingly alive to the fact that African rural areas have been sadly neglected and are deteriorating rapidly as the population increases and pressures on the land become greater. But their schemes intended to improve the situation have too often been imposed from above without consultation with the African farmers concerned, and have thus been resented and resisted even when they have been demonstrably sound. In some instances the law has had to be invoked, even to carry out such necessary measures as contour-ridging and the culling of cattle.

Another agency at work is the Tribal Trust Lands Development Corporation (TILCOR), which is a profit-making organization. The TILCOR schemes in specially selected areas are still in their infancy, so it is too early to assess their worth. But one criticism that can be levelled at them is that they tend to be schemes conceived by Europeans for Africans: so far African participation in them has only been at the lower levels. Unless this tendency is modified and corrected quickly, the results will leave much to be desired. Good schemes often come to grief through poor imagination, and the latter is reflected in this case by too much European domination and too little African apprenticeship or management.

The Churches own considerable stretches of land – about 400,000 acres. Their titles were obtained by outright gift from the authorities in the early days of European rule or by later purchases. These lands were acquired by the Church in order to support the early missionaries and to enable them to carry on their mission work among the African people. On these lands today are to be found churches, schools, hospitals, homes and other buildings. On these lands, too, are to be found thousands of African tenants, usually eking out a living by subsistence farming. But because the Churches have given priority to preaching, teaching, and healing, they have not given the same attention to their land. Through this understandable neglect, the Churches are now faced with some major problems concerning land use and land ownership. The choices before them are two: either they produce imaginative development programmes, which would involve major injections

* Taken from a paper on *Land Apportionment and African Voting Qualifications in Rhodesia* by H. Dunlop, Senior Lecturer in Economics at the University of Rhodesia.

of capital, or they hand the land over to the government or to the Chiefs or to their tenants. The present writer favours a development programme leading to tenant ownership of their plots. The Tribal Trust Lands will remain Rhodesia's biggest problem whether or not the Proposals are accepted. Declining productivity has resulted in increasing numbers of Africans moving to the urban areas in search of employment, and for the main part they have been unsuccessful.

As far as land in Rhodesia is concerned, however, the whole question is bedevilled by the inability of those in authority to think in other than racial categories – as exemplified by the Land Tenure and Land Apportionments Acts (which, of course, predate U.D.I.), the TILCOR projects by Europeans for Africans, and the drought relief compensation which is mainly for European farmers and not African peasants. Until such thinking disappears the land question will continue to be a potentially explosive problem in Rhodesia.

Employment and Income: The following is a comparison of some of the more important data, taken from the Monthly Digest of Statistics for June 1971:

	NO. OF EMPLOYED		AVERAGE ANNUAL WAGE		AV.AN. INCREASE (1963–1970) FOR AFRICANS
	AFRICAN	EUROPEAN*	AFRICAN $	EUROPEAN* $	$
Agriculture	306,300	4,360	153	2,457	2·2
Mining	52,200	3,650	334	4,456	8·7
Manufacturing	103,600	20,100	478	3,606	14·4
Electricity/Water	4,200	1,520	448	3,840	15·5
Building	48,400	8,560	428	3,273	15·3
Finance/Insurance	2,800	7,140	714	3,280	35·5
Restaurants/ Hotels	46,600	20,460	454	2,654	20·3
Transport	17,500	4,910	626	3,600	13·6
Public Administration	27,600	11,960	409	3,129	10·6
Education	20,600	6,400	590	2,709	19·0
Health	7,600	3,310	579	2,388	28·4
Domestic	113,100	NIL	256	——	5·5
Other	25,300	9,320	430	2,442	10·6
TOTAL	775,800	106,700	312	3,104	9·75

* Includes Asians and Coloureds.

These figures show that there is a dramatic difference between the average annual earnings of Africans and Europeans – nearly ten times as much.

The proportion of Africans in employment has fallen from 17 per cent to 14 per cent in the last decade. The latest figures show that there are now at least a million Africans unemployed: their numbers have increased by 45,000 a year for many years. The figures show, too, that over half of all African workers are in the two lowest paid categories of agricultural and domestic employment. Consequently, to base voting qualification on a combination of income earned, property owned (values being much higher in areas reserved for whites), and education attained greatly favours the European voters. Further, the figures show that the average annual increase in wages for most African workers is minimal.

Education: Surprisingly, some ten years ago there occurred a promising, little-noticed innovation in the African Education Department. Almost overnight all African teachers with 'standard qualifications' – that is a recognized university degree, etc. – were placed on the same salary scales as European teachers. Africans rejoiced and hoped that this change for the better would soon apply to all teachers, however few their qualifications. Unfortunately, no further change in the general direction of equal pay for equal qualifications occurred. Instead, a few months ago, the clock was turned back. At that time a commission of inquiry into salary scales of all government employees recommended certain rises for teachers which were more favourable to European teachers than to Africans. The Government denied that this was an act of racial discrimination because the different rises did not apply to African and Europeans as such, but to teachers in government schools and teachers in aided schools. But as most European teachers are in government schools and most African teachers are in aided schools the general effect was to the advantage of European teachers. One example will make the point clear: a certified four-year-trained teacher, European, in an African or European government schools will be on the scale which begins at $3,540 and rises to $6,660. An African teacher or a European teacher with the same qualifications working in an aided school will be on the scale which begins at $2,820 and rises to $4,824. This shows a salary differentiation of $720 on starting and a disadvantage of $1,836 on reaching the top of the scale.

It was the introduction of these new pay rises that sparked off a series of demonstrations by students from the University, the Gwelo Teacher Training College, and several secondary schools. Though the demonstrations were peaceful and orderly, the government took immediate and harsh retaliatory measures. Some students were expelled from their colleges;

127

others had their government scholarships taken away; and many received six cuts of the cane from the police or their principals.

In assessing the provision of education for Africans it is important to establish a basis of comparison. For instance, if one compares the educational facilities for Africans in Rhodesia with the facilities in poorer countries such as Chad, then the facilities for Africans in Rhodesia are of course better. But if one compares the facilities for Africans in Rhodesia with the facilities for Europeans in Rhodesia, then the facilities for Africans are worse.* The following figures are taken from the Reports of the Secretaries for African and European Education of 1970 and from the November 1971 issue of the Monthly Digest of Statistics:

	AFRICANS	EUROPEANS
1971 *Primary Schools*	*637,000*	*33,046*
Junior Secondary	*3,807*	*NIL*
Senior Secondary	*22,376*	*23,365*
Teachers in Training	*2,024*	*520*

Local University: 937 — of whom nearly half are Africans.†
In addition there are some 1,865 European students attending South African universities.

Immediately we note that whereas 637,000 African children are in primary schools, there are only 33,046 European children in primary schools. Yet the number of African children in secondary schools is not much different from the number of European children in secondary schools – 26,183 compared to 23,365. But whereas it is almost impossible for African students to go to South Africa for higher education, it is comparatively easy for

---

* It is interesting, however, that there were more holders of university degrees amongst the African nationalist leaders in detention than amongst the Rhodesian Front cabinet. And of course there were many more qualified Africans in Rhodesia than there were in Zambia, Malawi, Tanzania or Kenya when Britain gave them independence. Although education in Rhodesia is better than in several poorer African states, it is gradually declining both in quantity and in quality. Enrolment in schools has declined: 713,170 in 1968 to 703,729 in 1970. The reduction of teachers from 22,900 in 1966 to 20,300 in 1969 has affected the quality of education. There are 3.7 million Africans under sixteen years of age; if their education had been administered with the same enthusiasm as in East or West Africa the present enrolment of African children should have been higher.

† University College, Salisbury, is a unique institution in Rhodesia, being one of the few places where a large number of Africans and Europeans can live and work on an equal basis. For most Africans it represents their only chance to acquire a university education. But in 1966 following U.D.I. several of its lecturers were deported from Rhodesia, and many of its African students have since been restricted, detained or harassed.

European students to do so: the figure of 1,865 students at South African universities proves this.

Another important factor in the African educational system is that some seven years ago the Rhodesian government introduced what it chose to call 'A Dynamic Plan for African Education'. Yet, in the same breath, it pegged the African Education Vote to 2 per cent of the Gross National Product – thus making the plan more static than dynamic. Furthermore, one of the main provisions of the new plan was reduction of the primary school course in African schools from eight years to seven, in order to bring it in line with the seven-year course for Europeans. But this change was spoilt at the outset by reducing the number of teachers for the primary course not from eight to seven, but from eight to six. This meant that one of the seven classes was without a class teacher. The new plan also envisaged the provision within ten years of 300 junior secondary schools, which would offer a two-year course with a technical rather than an academic bias. But after some seven years the total number of junior secondary schools was only twenty-one. Furthermore, in length and content the course has been so unsatisfactory that the educational authorities are about to increase the course to four years and to make the curriculum much more technical.

Of the one hundred schools which provide any form of second-ary education to Africans, eighty-three continue to be run by the Churches. Of the five schools which offer sixth-form education, three are run by missions and two by the government.

In 1970 the government made it known that as from 1971 it would pay only 95 per cent of the salaries earned by teachers in African aided primary schools, though this provision would not apply in the case of teachers in African government schools. This new policy also included the condition that if aided schools were to continue under their present management, the school authorities would have to make good the 5 per cent deduction. Faced with this ultimatum a large majority of aided-school authorities, almost all of which were Churches, decided reluctantly to re-linquish control of their schools; they refused to be held respons-ible themselves for the financing withdrawn by unilateral decision of the government. One result was that a major change in the control of primary schools for Africans occurred at the end of 1970 and the beginning of 1971 – namely, that the Churches' role ceased to be dominant. It is estimated that of the 3,116 primary schools now operating, only 640 are still under Church auspices; and even some of these 640 will soon be handed over to the government or to local councils.

One other point to note about African and European education is the level of government expenditure. In 1970 the amount spent on African education was $17,104,380, while that on European education, including Indians and Coloureds, was $16,329,652. In other words the amount spent on each African child is about one-tenth that spent on a European child. Yet because the total amounts for African and European children are reasonably close, this is also called 'parity'.

Sport: This is the one field where inter-racial activities have been allowed, accepted, and sometimes encouraged. Soccer, for instance, is inter-racial as far as control, players and spectators are concerned. It is common practice for European teams to play African teams or for some teams, especially professional ones, to include both European and African players. Athletics, too, is an inter-racial activity, so much so that for the last ten years or so Rhodesian athletic teams have always included Europeans and Africans. But following U.D.I. in 1965 the Rhodesian athletic team was barred from the 1968 Olympics and it may also be barred from the 1972 Olympics. Even in athletics, however, racialism is reappearing. For instance, the European Education Department has issued instructions to all headmasters that no inter-racial athletic competition can be permitted at their schools unless the principal is assured that it is the wish of the parents. On the other hand, with the recent gradual relaxation (under pressure) of the apartheid sport rules in South Africa, it may not be long before Rhodesian athletic teams will be visiting South Africa and vice versa.

Tennis is another game that Africans are playing more and more, but almost entirely among themselves. Boxing is also a uni-racial activity. As far as cricket, rugby, hockey, and swimming are concerned few Africans participate, while yachting, motor-racing, and the like are of course beyond the financial means of Africans.

The Church: It is almost impossible to estimate how many Africans are full members of the Church, partly because the figures are denominationally collected and partly because the method of determining what constitutes full membership varies from denomination to denomination. Nonetheless, it can be said that in one way or another most Africans come under some Church influence and that they now far outnumber Europeans in church membership.

One of the most significant changes in the last ten years has been the slow but steady movement towards Africanization of the Church. Today there are no fewer than five churches belonging to the Christian Council of Rhodesia whose Heads are African – i.e. the British Methodists, the American Methodists, the

Disciples, the African Reformed Church, and the United Church of Christ. African clergymen and laymen are playing an increasingly vital role in the work of their respective Churches. When a delegation from the Christian Council seeks an interview with the Prime Minister or a visiting Foreign Secretary, the membership of the delegation is always inter-racial. At meetings of the Council or at meetings of the Heads of Churches the African voice is both heard and heeded. For example, an Anglican bishop with more enthusiasm than discretion claimed at a meeting that the Christian Council had passed so many resolutions that nobody listened to the Council any more. Whereupon an African bishop rose to his feet and said quietly: 'Mr Chairman, with all due respect to the last speaker, I would have him know that Africans not only listen to the Christian Council but expect the Council to give them a lead.' Such a rejoinder could well have been considered impertinent a couple of decades ago. Today it is accepted as part of the give and take of ecumenical debate.

Another remarkable change in recent years is the growing understanding and willing co-operation of Church leaders on matters of moment. One example is their united stand – that is Protestant and Roman Catholic – on the Land Tenure Act. Their firmness made the government think again, for they said with one voice, 'we cannot in conscience and we will not in practice' obey some of the provisions of the Act, especially those which relate to registration under the Act and to movement of clergy between, and within, areas designed for one racial group only. By acting in unison the Church leaders were strong enough to embarrass the government, although not strong enough to effect a change in its position. In all these endeavours African leaders played a major part.

Local theological training for Africans has, on the whole, not been of a sufficiently high standard. But due to the Theological Faculty at the University and a reorganization of the standards at Epworth Theological College much has been done to improve matters. Epworth, for instance, is no longer a Methodist College but an ecumenical one, with students and staff coming from Methodist, Lutheran, Congregational, and Presbyterian backgrounds. Moreover, the door is open to members of other denominations. But so far no African theologian of eminence has appeared. What is encouraging, however, is that several promising Africans now undergoing further theological training overseas are shortly to return to Rhodesia to engage in theological teaching. One other matter of significance is that the newly trained Epworth Theological College graduates are no longer simply of the pietist school, which emphasizes individual salvation. These graduates, with their modern training, are more aware of the harsh realities which confront their parishioners in the political, economic, and social spheres. They are therefore better able to offer help that is relevant to this day and generation; and in the forthcoming 'test of acceptability' concerning the Proposals for a Settlement they are likely to play an important, if not a decisive, role.

The Chiefs: Before Europeans entered the country, the Chiefs' role was considerable, both spiritually and politically. With the advent of Europeans and the break-up of traditional patterns of behaviour, their power diminished; the European invaders replaced the militant Chiefs with collaborators. In recent years, however – largely influenced by ideas from the South – government policy has been to revive the authority of the Chiefs. This has been done by increasing their pay, by extending their legal and administrative powers, and by giving them more protection. The independently-minded ones have been deposed. At the same time the government has been at pains to claim that the Chiefs are the true leaders of the African people and that they can speak for their people. Not satisfied with this enhancement of the position of the Chiefs, the government has gone one step further. The 1969 Constitution gave them power to select from among themselves all ten African members of the Senate, and to help choose eight of the sixteen African members of the Lower House (who are elected by Colleges consisting of Chiefs, headmen and councillors). But all that government has done to try to boost the morale of the Chiefs has done little to improve their competence. For the most part they remain uneducated and illiterate – certainly as far as parliamentary English is concerned. Politically they are backward-looking, and intellectually they do not belong to the eighth decade of the twentieth century. Their salaries are paid by the central government. Yet these are the men the government alleges are the real African leaders. The writer of this article remembers Mr Wilson saying after his session with the Chiefs during his visit to Rhodesia in October 1965: 'They are not much good.' Lord Malvern, the former Rhodesian Prime Minister, put it even more bluntly: 'As for the Indaba, that was a swindle . . . many of the Shona Chiefs are rather dodderers. Their real powers and influence were destroyed at the time of the Rebellion in 1896.' In 1964 Sir Alec Douglas-Home refused to accept that government-paid Chiefs represented black Rhodesians. In fact they are little more than glorified anachronisms.

Politics: At the central government level Africans have no political power in spite of their numbers. This is due to a number of reasons, some of their own making, but not all. For example, in their quest for political power Africans have often wasted their time and energy fighting each other rather than opposing the government. They have also lacked proper organization and adequate funds. Too often they, like Britain, have underrated the determination, the ability, and the strength of those in office. But having said all this, let us look at their difficulties and handicaps. They are considerable.

The Industrial Conciliation Act, for instance, is so heavily weighted on the side of the government and big business that it has prevented the African politicians and trade unionists from gaining better wages and conditions of employment for Africans in lower-paid jobs. As is stated in *Rhodesian Perspective**: 'The employer is in every way – socially, politically and economically – the boss.' Now even the limited power of the trade unions is likely to be further reduced by a recent bill designed to prevent strikes without prior government permission.

Government legislation, such as the Law and Order Maintenance Act† and the Unlawful Organizations Act, has time and time again been used to crush any nationalist opposition. Emergency powers have been used continuously since U.D.I. African trades union officials have been intimidated; African leaders have been arrested without stated reason, detained without trial, and restricted to camps or prisons for years on end. Their supporters have been given long terms of imprisonment for alleged intimidation; their parties have been banned and on each occasion their assets in the form of bank balances, office and other equipment, transport vehicles, and so on have been confiscated. Worse still, informers in their ranks have repeatedly devastated the plans of African opposition leaders. Add to this the censorship of the press, and the well trained and equipped security forces and it is easier to appreciate the difficulties. Consequently all attempts so far to disturb the government either from within the country or from without have made little or no progress. The holding of political rallies, the printing and dissemination of political literature, and the propagating of any essentially alternative political ideas have for years been forbidden by the authorities. Not surprisingly most African political parties are in disarray and quiescent. But one fact remains. It is that the leaders of the two banned parties –

---

* T. Bull, ed. (London, Michael Joseph, 1967), page 14.

† This Act led to the resignation of the respected Rhodesian Chief Justice Sir Robert Tredgold. He said of it: 'This Bill outrages every basic human right and is in addition an unwarranted invasion by the Executive of the sphere of the Judiciary.'

Mr Joshua Nkomo and the Rev. Ndabaningi Sithole – in spite of their long incarceration and isolation remain the real leaders of the African Rhodesians. No one has usurped their place.*

Yet in Parliament, acting as leaders, are sixteen Africans in the Lower House and ten in the Senate. By no stretch of the imagination can it be said that these twenty-six speak for the mass of the African people.† Most, though not all, of these twenty-six Africans in Parliament are likely to accept the Proposals for a Settlement 'under protest', oblivious of the fact that there is no place for protest: they can only totally accept or totally reject the Proposals.

It will be seen therefore that the position of the African Nationalist in politics is an invidious one. The main question he has to answer is whether he will seek political power peacefully or violently. If he chooses the former method then he will have at the very least many hard years ahead, and must accept that he will only gain political power if he can persuade the Europeans voluntarily to renounce it in his favour. If he chooses the latter he will need substantial outside help and at the same time will have to be prepared for much loss of life among his followers. Further, if he chooses violence, Rhodesia could easily become the flashpoint of the continent, with an all-out struggle between

* For an account of the history and estimated support of the African nationalist parties before they were banned, see Appendix 2. Mr Nkomo once summarized his policy as follows:

'As I have stated from time to time, we do not regard the white people in this country as a separate entity, but as part and parcel of the entire community who are fully entitled to all human and property rights as is any indigenous member of the community. We know that there are many Europeans who were born and bred here and have their homes in this country. These and many others are as good citizens of this country as any indigenous people – but we do not accept the principle of special privileges at the expense of the majority of the people.

'We do not seek to revenge, dispossess, oppress, dominate or subjugate anybody or any group of people. But rather we seek to establish a just society with opportunities for all, irrespective of colour or creed – based on the freedom of the individual. But there can be no just society where over 95 per cent of the country's population are denied the basic human rights.'

His most recent reported statement (the *Observer*, 28 November 1971) is that he remains firmly committed to 'No independence before majority rule'.

† The eight who were directly elected received a total of 2,279 votes in the election held on 10 April 1970. This is the total number of Africans, out of more than 5 million, who at present enjoy parliamentary representation. The current African M.P.s carry little weight in Parliament. They have never succeeded in significantly amending any controversial legislation. In both theory and practice there is no scope for an effective Opposition within the present parliamentary system where the government is responsible to a totally different electorate.

Africa north of the Zambezi and Africa south of the Zambezi. Either of these choices demands of the Africans considerable organization, and suffering, before they can hope to see any satisfactory improvement in their status.

THE PROPOSALS FOR A SETTLEMENT

Let us turn to 'The Proposals for a Settlement' to be found in the White Paper, Cmnd. 4835, 25 November 1971 (see Appendix 1).

As far as Africans are concerned, it can be taken for granted that most (but not all) of the Chiefs, Headmen, and other such government employees will accept the Proposals. It must be remembered that these men are government appointed, government paid, and open to government dismissal. Therefore, even if they wished to oppose the government, they feel they could not do so with impunity. Other Africans who will not hesitate to accept the Proposals include many of the M.P.s, Senators, businessmen, large property owners, and others who are prepared to mortgage political rights for economic prospects.

There is another side to the picture as well. For opposing the Proposals will be many African trade-unionists, teachers, ministers of religion, professional men, workers and small farmers, and a great number of urban people. But for the voice of these men to be heard effectively one condition must be fulfilled, namely the undertaking given in the White Paper that 'before and during the test of acceptability normal political activities will be permitted.' Indeed, the manner in which this promise is interpreted and carried out will be a decisive factor in the outcome of the 'test of acceptability'.

Let us look at the Proposals from the African point of view.

First of all, the Proposals have been arrived at with very little African participation, much less consent.* This is an insult to politically minded Africans as men and an affront to them as citizens of Rhodesia. That English diplomats with years of colonial experience could fall in with the thinking of European Rhodesians and ignore Africans to this extent must be construed as a cynical act. Surely they should have insisted that Africans must have their say in matters so vitally affecting their welfare. The failure of the two governments to pay due regard to Africans as people is a

---

* Only a very small number of Africans were heard. They presented Sir Alec Douglas-Home with a memorandum laying down the following conditions for a settlement: (i) immediate black-white parity in Parliament, followed by an election on a basis of permitting majority rule; (ii) the abolition of the Land Tenure Act; (iii) the outlawing of all forms of discrimination; (iv) a judicial Bill of Rights; (v) Rhodesia's reversion to the status of a British colony.

major cause of the Africans' likely rejection of the Proposals.

The Coloured and Asian Rhodesians, who – proportionately – should be entitled to five of the fifty white seats in Parliament, are not mentioned in the settlement Proposals.

Secondly, in terms of real power to influence government policy the Proposals offer Africans not even a political half-loaf. The reality is that no nation which is granted independence while its constitution withholds immediate majority rule and is based on a qualified franchise can guarantee unimpeded progress to majority rule. The reason is simple: the qualified franchise itself gives the Europeans, through their control of wages, job opportunities and of the educational system, absolute power over access to the vote. In other words, if the government provided many more secondary schools and the white employers decided to employ Africans at wages equivalent to those paid whites, more Africans would qualify for the vote; but nothing in the Proposals compels Europeans to do this. The pace of African advance, if any, is left entirely to the discretion of the Europeans, and it can also be set back at any time by increasing white immigration. Discussion of how long it will take to attain majority rule is therefore meaningless, though Professor Claire Palley has estimated (London *Sunday Times*, 28 November 1971) that the earliest conceivable date under the present Proposals is the year 2035.

Thirdly, the Proposals are not accompanied by any valid guarantees – merely by promises, assurances, and intentions of which there are eight. The fulfilment of the Proposals rests almost entirely on the goodwill and good faith of a government which is unashamedly racial and which openly sponsors racial discrimination.* One of Mr Smith's latest statements runs thus: 'It is possible for discrimination to continue as long as it is justifiable

* No objective person can consider the precedents for trusting Mr Smith as encouraging. He pledged he would not declare independence without consulting the country — and in the event failed to consult even the Rhodesian Parliament.

He stated 'As long as I am Prime Minister there will be no interference with the Press' not long before introducing rigid censorship. And he obtained the signature of the then Governor, Sir Humphrey Gibbs, authorizing emergency powers by specifically pledging there would be no U.D.I. – and then declared U.D.I. twenty-four hours later.

The principle of racial discrimination is included explicitly among the founding principles of the Rhodesian Front party, and much of the party's electoral success in 1962 was due to their rivals' proposal to abolish racial segregation. Smith's Declaration of Independence followed George Washington's with the significant exception of these words: 'We hold these truths to be self-evident, that all men are created equal, that they are endowed by their creator with inalienable rights, that among these are life, liberty, and the pursuit of happiness.'

and reasonable.' To believe that a government of such a party, with such a leader, will actively pursue a policy of African advancement is unrealistic. To the racist the supreme good is the preservation of his race and of his privileged economic position, and a promise is likely to be binding only as long as it is politically profitable. The following words of the Rev. Michael Appleyard are relevant: 'Justice must be protected by the law, not by expressions of good-will as expressions of good-will can be lawfully superseded. Therefore expressions of good-will are no basis for a Constitution.' To the African it will seem folly to rely on the promises of a racist regime.

Fourthly, if Africans accept the Proposals, even with reluctance, Mr Smith will of course maintain that he has full African support for his policies. Britain, South Africa and Portugal can be expected to recognize Rhodesia's independence immediately the acceptability finding has been made and the legislation required by the terms of the settlement proposals has been enacted. Doubtless other countries will follow suit and will consider themselves precluded from interfering in Rhodesia's internal affairs from then on. Rhodesia, it is clear, will no longer be a member of the Commonwealth, and in future none of her people will enjoy the benefits of Commonwealth membership, such as the educational and development funds granted exclusively to Commonwealth members, and from which Rhodesians, particularly Africans, have benefited both before and after U.D.I.

Fifthly, the Proposals themselves are a travesty, if not a negation, of the Five Principles which the British Foreign Secretary Sir Alec Douglas-Home himself drew up in 1964 as a prerequisite for the granting of independence to Rhodesia. To claim, as Sir Alec Douglas-Home and Mr Smith have done, that the Proposals are fair and just and in keeping with the Five Principles is simply not true – certainly in their spirit, if not in their letter. Had Sir Alec said, 'I have capitulated; I had to,' then we might have some sympathy for him. But the claim that the Proposals are honourable is harder to accept.

We now must look at each of the Five Principles to see what the Proposals have in common with them. The exact wording of these Principles is:

1. The principle and intention of unimpeded progress to majority rule, already enshrined in the 1961 Constitution, would have to be maintained and guaranteed.
2. There would also have to be guarantees against retrogressive amendment of the Constitution.

3. There would have to be immediate improvement in the political status of the African population.
4. There would have to be progress towards ending racial discrimination.
5. The British Government would need to be satisfied that any basis proposed for independence was acceptable to the people of Rhodesia as a whole.

1. UNIMPEDED PROGRESS TO MAJORITY RULE

The only major change is to provide for further African seats in the Lower House on a new Upper Roll, qualifications for which are the same as those applicable to European voters. That is to say, anyone with an income of not less than $1,800 p.a. or owning immovable property of not less than $3,600 can qualify for this vote. Also anyone with four years of secondary education of prescribed standard, having an income of $1,200 p.a. or immovable property of not less than $2,400 can qualify. This means that only the comparatively well-off Africans can qualify for the Upper Roll. Further, these additional seats will only be available if the number of Africans on the Upper Roll reaches 6 per cent of the number of European voters. Thereafter a further two seats will be added when the percentage rises to 12, 18, 24, and so on. Even so, only half of these seats will be elected by African voters. The other half will be selected by Electoral Colleges influenced by the Chiefs. Estimates as to how long it will take before 'parity' is reached in the House vary considerably, simply because there are so many unknown factors.* But all

---

* As Professor Roland Oliver has pointed out (in a letter to *The Times*, 26 November 1971):

'In order to achieve parity of representation, the African community has to find roughly the same number of qualified electors as the European community, and essentially the test is to be four years of secondary education. But whereas four years of secondary education is provided compulsorily for every white child in Rhodesia, it is provided for perhaps 2 per cent of black children, and the number of black children reaching this level in the future remains squarely in the control of the Rhodesian government with its overwhelming majority of white electors, who will not be inclined to hurry things along towards their own political extinction.

'Furthermore, it is to be noted that the stages in the increase of African representation are to take place not when the African community succeeds in producing certain absolute numbers of qualified electors, but when it achieves certain *percentages* of the number of *European* electors. This means that every additional European immigrant attracted to Rhodesia will raise the number of qualified Africans necessary to secure an increase in African representation. When one recalls how far the policies of past Rhodesian governments have been designed to promote white immigration, this must be a cause for great concern.

'Mr Smith is reported to have asssured his supporters that there will be little change in the lifetime of the present generation. This looks like an understatement.'

estimates agree that it will be a long time – definitely not during this century and almost certainly not within present Africans' lifetime. To call this extra representation 'unimpeded progress to majority rule' is far-fetched: it is much more akin to impeded progress.

2. GUARANTEES AGAINST RETROGRESSIVE AMENDMENT OF THE CONSTITUTION

The Proposals promise that there will be no amendment of the Constitution for three years, or until two additional Africans sit in Parliament, whichever is the sooner. But after that date all but the entrenched clauses of the Constitution can easily be changed by European M.P.s who have the necessary two-thirds majority in the House and a majority in the Senate. The Proposals also promise that certain parts of the Constitution will be specially entrenched. These include the Declaration of Rights, the qualifications for voting, the composition of the Senate, the House of Assembly, and the Tribal Electoral Colleges. These provisions can be changed only if two-thirds of the Senate and two-thirds of the Assembly, including over half of each racial group, vote for a change. But this is a weak safeguard, as only eight of the sixty-six members of the Assembly and none of the twenty-three Senators are directly elected by Africans. On the other hand, these provisions could just as readily be used to block progressive amendments in favour of Africans. Nor is there any external guarantee that a future government will not alter the Constitution once independence is granted.

3. IMMEDIATE IMPROVEMENT IN THE POLITICAL STATUS OF AFRICANS

The writer has looked in vain for any substantive immediate improvement. It is true that there is to be a Declaration of Rights which will be justifiable, in contrast to the Declaration in the 1969 Constitution which was not.* But nearly three-quarters of the Proposals is taken up with exceptions. Moreover, rights

* Harish Magan, a Rhodesian barrister, comments in *Race Today* (January 1972, Institute of Race Relations, London): 'The new section 84 A(1) will provide that if any person complains that the Declaration is being contravened in relation to him, then, 'without prejudice to any other action with respect to the same matter which is lawfully available that person may ... apply to the Appellate Division (of the High Court of Rhodesia) for redress.

'But the 1961 Constitution had a justiciable Declaration *and* a Constitutional Council to supervise its enforcement. The Constitutional Council was an independent, non-parliamentary multi-racial body which could delay for six months the enactment of bills contravening the Declaration (unless overruled

(Continued overleaf)

can be suspended by declaring a state of emergency – as they often have in the past.†

Further, there is no provision for repeal of the Preventive Detention Act, of the Law and Order Maintenance Act, or for the release of all detainees. The Rhodesian government says that it has already released twenty-three detainees this year and that it is about to release a further thirty-four. But it seems likely that the other sixty-four will remain in detention. Their cases will be referred again to the Review Tribunal which has on more than one occasion considered their appeal for release and turned it down. Even those who are released will still be barred from voting and from standing for Parliament for a period of five years. This means that many of the recognized African leaders will not be able to be with their people before and during the period when British Commissioners are conducting their test of acceptability.

That there will be little immediate change for the better in the political status of Africans is borne out by a remark made by Mr Smith in an interview published in the *Rhodesia Herald* on

by a two-thirds majority in Parliament). An even more valuable provision enabled the Constitutional Council to issue a certificate to any suitable test case where the litigant was alleging a contravention of the Declaration. In such cases the litigant would be reimbursed for his expenses out of the Consolidated Revenue Fund. No explanation has been offered for omitting these safeguards from the proposed new Declaration. These limitations will deter potential litigants from going to court because legal costs are very high and the scant provision made for legal aid in Rhodesia is highly unsatisfactory.' For his detailed analysis of the proposed Declaration, see Appendix 3.

† J. R. C. Fieldsend, formerly a respected judge of the Rhodesian High Court, has written in a recent letter to the London *Times:* 'It may be that the proposals for a Rhodesian settlement are the best that can now be obtained, but if we are honest we must recognize that their full implementation will depend solely upon the willingness of the European minority in Rhodesia.

'A justiciable declaration of rights is some small safeguard, but it is so hedged about with provisos and qualifications that any administration could drive a herd of cattle through its loopholes without resort to illegality. Furthermore, the record shows that the administration would, if necessary, undoubtedly act in defiance of a court order which frustrated their policy in any vital sphere; and if precedent is binding the court would be unlikely to force a confrontation if it appreciated that its order would be disregarded.

'If these proposals are not interpreted and administered in the spirit in which they were formulated by the Foreign Secretary and Lord Goodman they will certainly not satisfy even moderate African opinion. The sad conclusion is that those most vitally affected are now faced with the necessity of putting their trust in those whom Lord Goodman found to have principles and social morality so divorced from his own that there was nothing for it but to shelve discussion on that level and to confine negotiation to the technical issues.

'Is this any basis upon which to ask a simple people whether the technical proposals are acceptable?'

7 December 1971: He 'did not think that the new Declaration of Rights would mean any dramatic change in the way of life in Rhodesia'. As a leading African clergyman said: 'There is something very fishy about the Proposals because no-one has resigned from the Rhodesian Front. Mr Smith must have assured them that they need not take the Proposals too seriously.'

4. PROGRESS TOWARDS ENDING RACIAL DISCRIMINATION

Provision is made for a Commission of three (all Rhodesians, one of whom must be an African) to examine this question. In addition there will be an observer from the United Kingdom. Included in the functions of this Commission is a 'special duty to scrutinise the provisions of the Land Tenure Act'. The Rhodesian government has insisted, however, that any move towards the removal of discrimination may be vetoed by 'overriding considerations'. The work of this Commission will be hamstrung from the outset, for the Proposals state categorically that 'the Constitution of Rhodesia will be the Constitution adopted in Rhodesia in 1969'. In other words, Rhodesians will have to continue to live under a Constitution which is essentially racial. How then can this Commission make progress towards ending racial discrimination? Again, this Commission has to present its findings to a Parliament composed of fifty Europeans and at the most eighteen Africans whose members are left free to reject any recommendations which might bring to an end the kind of discrimination they regard as part of the natural order. Furthermore, there is no specific mention of altering the recently introduced differential salary scales for teachers. This is a burning issue, yet it is totally by-passed. The work of this Commission, therefore, can be of only limited significance.

5. ACCEPTABILITY TO THE PEOPLE OF RHODESIA AS A WHOLE

According to the White Paper all the Proposals will be subjected to a 'test of acceptability' before they can be implemented. The White Paper states: 'To carry out this test a special commission from the United Kingdom is to come to Rhodesia. It will travel extensively throughout the country visiting in particular all centres of population, local councils, and traditional meeting places in the Tribal Trust Lands. The Commission will carry out its inquiries in public or in private as it deems appropriate.' Beyond these statements, nothing is laid down about the methods which the members of the Commission will adopt to test the acceptability of the Proposals. But what we do know is that they will not hold a referendum.

141

K

Another point to be noted is that the key phrase 'the people as a whole' remains undefined. Does it mean citizens only or residents as well? (This is particularly important because a very high proportion of the Europeans are recent immigrants.)* There is an even more important question – namely, if merely the Chiefs are not to be allowed to speak for the people as a whole, how are the people to be given opportunities to speak for themselves? And if Rhodesian Africans are thought sufficiently responsible to pass judgement on the fundamental complexities of the new constitution, why are they not considered responsible to elect their own government now or in the near future?

There is a further question, concerning how much time the testing of acceptability will take. Will it be rushed through before the Africans are able to speak to their people and muster their forces? The officials and allies of the government are already at work in the Tribal Trust Lands where the majority or Africans live.† They have at their disposal machinery for getting across

---

* The Unlawful Organizations Amendment Act (1971), which provides for the prosecution of political exiles who return to Rhodesia, seems likely to remain in force. Rhodesians living abroad (e.g. in Britain) have been invited by the Pearce Commission to give their views on whether the settlement proposals are acceptable as a basis for independence. For the problems facing the Commission, and its proposed methods, see Appendix 4.

† The District Commissioners, the civil servants who run the Tribal Trust Lands, have been explaining to Chiefs and Headmen in the past few weeks the advantages of the Proposals, such as more jobs and more education. But, according to both the nationalists and the African Centre Party M.P.s (who support the Proposals), the District Commissioners have been misrepresenting the benefits by adding that the settlement will mean an end to racial discrimination, the reinstatement of the Queen, and the advent of African political power. On 11 January 1972 Bishop Abel Muzorewa, Chairman of the African National Council, sent a letter to Lord Pearce complaining that obstacles have been placed in the way of its meetings and that Africans have been threatened by Rhodesian officials. The letter said: 'If your task is not to be a mockery, the commission should press the Rhodesian Government to relax the restrictions on the holding of meetings, and to inform its district commissioners to stop frustrating the A.N.C. campaign.' While the A.N.C. had been able to hold a few meetings in the urban areas, 'attempts to hold meetings in the Tribal Trust Lands are being vigorously obstructed by the district commissioners,' Bishop Muzorewa wrote. 'The Government is doing all it can to prevent all persons opposed to the Proposals from holding meetings.' Bishop Muzorewa alleged that the district commissioners had refused permits for meetings. 'Their tactics range from bold statements that the A.N.C. could not be permitted to hold a meeting in the area, to threats that if they found anyone gathering people to ask them to reject the Proposals he would be arrested and imprisoned for a long time.' Bishop Muzorewa said the A.N.C.'s campaign was being 'deliberately frustrated by the authorities' and that the commission had a duty to see that all shades of opinion were canvassed freely.

Continued opposite

to the people the official point of view. They can move from place to place without let or hindrance. They can use the mass media. But what of the African Nationalists? For seven years and more their parties have been banned and their leaders imprisoned or exiled. They have been unable to hold public meetings, much less political rallies. At the present time it will obviously be difficult for them to lead a counter-offensive against the government's propaganda. But given time, funds, and freedom of movement and freedom of expression, they could build up an effective opposition to the Proposals. Sometime – sufficient time – is a most important factor in the test of acceptability's credibility.

Let us note, too, that 'radio and television time will be made available to political parties represented in the House of Assembly.' As there are no African Nationalists in the House, they will not be able to use these media. This deprivation is hardly in keeping with the promise contained in the White Paper 'that in the period before and during the test of acceptability normal political activities will be permitted to the satisfaction of the Commission.' From this it will be seen that the com-

Besides Sir Dingle Foot, Q.C., who wished to represent Africans before the Pearce Commission but was refused entry by the Rhodesian government, four black United States Congressmen have been told that they are not welcome in Rhodesia (although two white Congressmen were told that they were welcome). Mr Edson Sithole, an African A.N.C. lawyer, alleged on 13 January: 'We have applied for a meeting in every Tribal Trust Land, sometimes orally, sometimes in writing, and we have never been allowed to hold a single meeting. There are more than 200 Tribal Trust Lands.' He said the reasons for refusing permission varied. Some District Commissioners said they did not understand the Proposals themselves and did not see how ordinary Africans would be able to understand them. Others maintained that it was not permitted to explain the Proposals, and that anyone doing so would be arrested and imprisoned 'for a long time'. Still others claimed that only counsellors, Headmen and Chiefs were allowed to hold meetings. A report from an A.N.C. official alleged that following police action at a meeting called to discuss the settlement proposals, armed soldiers had been brought into the Belingwe area, about 300 miles from Salisbury. The report added: 'There have been indiscriminate arrests. People have been taken out of buses. It is estimated that 300 people have been taken by police and there is a very hostile campaign against the A.N.C.' Another report, from the Beitbridge area, near the South African border, alleged that a sixty-year-old African had been assaulted by police for distributing A.N.C literature and 'stating categorically that he would reject the proposals.' Mr Sithole said a headmaster in the Wedza district, about 100 miles south of Salisbury, had been dismissed from his post after being found explaining the settlement proposals to people at an African kraal; and a Headman in the district was said to have been arrested and fined eight dollars for holding a meeting on the White Paper at his kraal. A.N.C. members allege that on several occasions District Commissioners have told them that 'higher authority' had given instructions that no A.N.C. meetings were to be permitted.

munications cards are heavily stacked in favour of the government. All in all, the best that can be said of the Proposals is that in the long run – and it is a very long run – they offer some hope for peaceful political change and a definite hope of economic improvement. (Already British businessmen are hastening to Salisbury in the hope of regaining markets lost to foreign competitors.) Unlike the 1969 Constitution, the Proposals will not actually prevent the Europeans from giving power to the Africans if the Europeans should ever wish to do so. The possibility that such a change of heart will ever take place, however, remains extremely remote. At the same time if the Proposals were approved, the granting of legal independence and the ending of sanctions which would follow would bring an inflow of foreign capital; and this, together with the legitimizing of the present regime, would result in an influx of white immigrants. The combined effect would be to strengthen considerably the white power structure, economically, politically and numerically, thus making majority rule even less likely in the foreseeable future. Those Africans who are aware that they can only achieve full social and economic justice by obtaining political control – and I believe them to be the great majority – will answer with an emphatic 'no'.

The Proposals provide limited protection under the new Declaration of Rights in that a person can no longer be arrested and detained without his being told within a reasonable time what the charge against him is and when and where it will be made. This will put some restraint on the Minister of Law and Order, who for nearly a decade has been wont to detain people for lengthy periods without stated reason or without trial – though even this gain could be negated if the government continued its present practice of imposing a virtually perpetual state of emergency.

One feature of the Proposals is that they include an unspecified offer of £5,000,000 a year over the next ten years for a development programme primarily intended to 'stimulate economic growth in the Tribal Trust Lands'. This amount is to be 'matched appropriately' ('appropriately' is not defined) by sums provided by the Rhodesian government. Even so, among over five million people this amounts to very little per capita. Nor is there anything in the wording of this proposal to prevent the money being used for 'separate development'. In economic terms some Africans would undoubtedly benefit from the aid and from the ending of sanctions, though white immigrants are likely to fill many of the newly generated jobs But the political benefit to Africans is only hypothetical if the British government will have no control over how its funds are spent.

The two governments seem to have forgotten that charity is no substitute for political justice; and that what people require is not merely bread but also the rights of citizenship in their own country. These proposals are entirely lacking in anything that would make Africans say with pride: 'We are Rhodesian citizens.' On this score alone the Proposals deserve to be rejected.

Are bad terms better than none? There is one crucial point to be noted about the Proposals: they cannot be amended. They must either be accepted in their entirety or rejected. Only one of two answers is allowed – 'yes' or 'no'. In presenting these Proposals to Parliament and recommending their acceptance Mr Smith said: 'The Commissioners' sole role will be to assess the acceptability of these Proposals, and they will have no mandate to consider any other proposals. The alternative to accepting this agreement is to maintain the status quo, which means retaining the present Constitution without amendment.' The choice before Africans is thus an unenviable one.

To most politically minded Africans – and this cannot include the Chiefs – the Proposals bring no joy. In fact many Africans openly speak of the Proposals as a sell-out, a fraud, a disgrace. If they have to accept the Proposals it will not be willingly. The Christian Council of Rhodesia resolved in September 1971: 'While we hope for a settlement, our prayer is that there will be no sacrifice of justice and of human dignity and rights. Indeed, we would prefer no settlement to an unjust one.'*

* Martin Meredith (the *Observer*, 8 January 1972) reported: 'The Churches in Rhodesia are divided. Almost all are critical of the proposals, but disagree over what action should be taken. Some Church leaders like the Anglican Bishop of Mashonaland, the Rt. Rev. Paul Burroughs, and the Methodist Church's Fred Rea, consider that although the proposals are based on the 1969 constitution, which the Churches have already condemned as racial and unjust, they nevertheless could mean a decisive check in the Rhodesian Government's course towards apartheid. Church advocates of acceptance believe that rejection would lead to a right-wing backlash and a fast move towards a South African system of government. In addition, they say, Rhodesia would lose British aid, sanctions would continue and the groundwork would be laid for a violent racial conflict. The multi-racial Centre Party faces the same dilemma. It is critical of many of the proposals, but nevertheless regards acceptance of them as the lesser evil.' On the other hand, the A.N.C. believes that if the five million black majority rejects the settlement terms, Mr Ian Smith will be forced to renegotiate a more favourable agreement. Fears that the anti-settlement faction will be able to overturn the agreement – which took almost a year to formulate – have led to a campaign among white businessmen to try to persuade their African employees to approach the Pearce

(Continued overleaf)

APPENDIX 1: THE PROPOSALS FOR A SETTLEMENT

The United Kingdom's White Paper describes the proposed terms (verbatim) as follows:

'The proposals for a settlement contain provisions which are summarized below under each of the Five Principles.

The First Principle

The 1969 Constitution expressly precludes the Africans from ever attaining more than parity of representation with the Europeans in the House of Assembly. It also relates any increase in African representation to the amount of income tax paid by the Africans. Under the proposed terms for a settlement, these provisions will be repealed and replaced by new provisions securing unimpeded progress to majority rule. The Africans will proceed to parity of representation in the House of Assembly through the creation of a new African higher roll, with the same income, property and educational qualifications as the European roll. As the numbers registered on this roll increase, additional seats will be created on a basis that will ensure that when parity of

Commission with 'Yes' votes. A group of leading anonymous businessmen has collected funds to support its drive, and the multi-racial Centre Party is also stepping up its activities.'

But Peter Nieswand (the *Guardian*, 4 January 1972) reported that Bishop Muzorewa, the chairman of the African National Council, informed a press conference that the A.N.C. had studied the terms in depth from political, economic and legal angles, and had found them to be a sell-out of the African people. 'This is the first and last opportunity for the African people to say whether they wish to participate in their own auction at the hands of British political merchantmen. The A.N.C. calls upon every African to say 'No' to these harmful and treacherous proposals. They spell doom, destruction, and forfeiture of our heritage as a nation.' Bishop Muzorewa said the terms offered independence to a minority, whereas the African people had always demanded that there be no independence before majority rule. The Bishop said the A.N.C.'s aim was to force the rejection of the settlement terms, and pave the way for more negotiations. 'I think there will be further negotiations,' he said. He said the A.N.C. had absolutely no interest in the cynical mathematics of how long it would take to reach majority rule under the present proposals. 'We are convinced that minority rule will remain in this country in perpetuity.' The Bishop said the Pearce Commission, which will test the acceptability of the settlement terms, could not be a substitute for a referendum on a one-man, one-vote basis. He also criticized the composition of the commission: 'It is to comprise only white men.' The proposed settlement has resulted in a united movement representing almost all of Rhodesia's Africans for virtually the first time in the country's history.

Under the Rhodesian government's regulations, the A.N.C.'s meetings cannot be held out of doors; and indoor meetings must, the government insists, be held only in halls which are insured. But the A.N.C. complains that no insurance company is willing to give the A.N.C. the necessary cover.

146

representation is reached the number of voters on the African higher and the European rolls will be approximately equal. The first two additional African members will be elected by the voters registered on the new African higher roll and the next two by indirect election under the existing system of Electoral Colleges, of Chiefs, Headmen and elected Councillors, and this sequence will be repeated in relation to further additional African members. By this means parity of representation will be reached with fifty European members and fifty African members in the House of Assembly. The latter will then comprise twenty-four indirectly elected, eighteen directly elected by the new African higher roll and eight directly elected, as at present, by the African lower roll. At this point a referendum will be held among all Africans registered on the two African rolls to decide whether or not the indirectly elected Africans should be replaced by directly elected Africans.

The Constitution will provide that, after the referendum and any elections necessary to give effect to the result, ten Common Roll seats will be created in the House of Assembly. After the result of this referendum has been implemented an independent Commission will be appointed to ascertain whether the creation of the Common Roll seats provided for in the Constitution is acceptable to the Rhodesian people at that time. But the adoption of any recommendation of this Commission to vary these arrangements will be a matter for the Rhodesian Parliament and will be subject to the normal procedure for amending specially entrenched provisions of the Constitution. Failing any such agreed amendment, the Common Roll seats will be filled by an election in a single nationwide constituency by the voters on a roll consisting of all registered voters on the African higher and the European rolls. As the number of African voters increases, they will be able to determine the result of elections to a majority of these seats, thus achieving majority rule.

The Second Principle

At all stages in the progress to majority rule it will be necessary to obtain the approval of a substantial proportion of the African representatives in the House of Assembly for any amendment to the specially entrenched provisions of the Constitution which will include all the arrangements which affect African political advance. Until the Commission appointed after parity reports, such Constitutional amendments will require, in addition to a two-thirds majority of all the members of the House of Assembly and the Senate voting separately, the affirmative votes of a majority of

147

the total European membership and of a majority of the total African membership in the House of Assembly. This will ensure that, in the unlikely event of all the indirectly elected Africans voting in favour of a retrogressive amendment to the specially entrenched provisions of the Constitution, the blocking mechanism will still rest in the hands of the directly elected African members of the Lower House. As African representation increases the two-thirds majority will require an increasing number of African votes. Thus after parity has been reached and the referendum on the future of the indirectly elected Africans has taken place, the need for an additional safeguard over and above the requirement of a two-thirds majority will disappear and it will be dropped. At this stage the support of at least seventeen African members in the House of Assembly will be required to pass any amendment of a specially entrenched provision.

The Third Principle

The creation of the new African higher roll will bring with it the prospect in the near future of increased African representation in the House of Assembly. The reduction in the franchise qualifications for the existing African lower roll will enfranchise a large number of additional Africans. These two measures amount to a substantial improvement in the political status of the Africans. In addition there is provision for the British Government to allocate substantial sums of money for an aid programme for Rhodesia over the next ten years in order to improve educational facilities for Africans and to help with the economic development of the Tribal Trust Lands, thus increasing job opportunities available for Africans. As a result of this aid the rate at which additional Africans will attain the income and educational qualifications required for the franchise will be accelerated. There will also be a new special Review of the cases of the remaining detainees by the existing Tribunal with a British observer present.

The Fourth Principle

There will be a new and strengthened Declaration of Rights, which will be enforceable in the courts. There will also be an independent Review Commission to examine forthwith the problem of racial discrimination in all fields, including the special problem of the allocation and use of land. The Rhodesians have undertaken to commend to Parliament legislation to give effect to the recommendations of this Commission subject to considerations that any Government would regard as overriding.

Meanwhile they have made it clear that they are prepared to allocate additional land for African use as the need arises and have given an assurance that with the exception of a limited number of unauthorized occupants in certain areas, there will be no further evictions of Africans until the recommendations of the Review Commission have been considered.

The Fifth Principle

These proposals for a settlement will only be confirmed and implemented after the British Government have satisfied themselves that they are acceptable to the people of Rhodesia as a whole. Accordingly, the British Government have appointed a Commission with Lord Pearce as Chairman to canvass as thoroughly and as impartially as possible the views of all sections of Rhodesian opinion, including Rhodesians resident abroad or in detention. The Commission will start its work in the near future. Before and during this test of acceptability normal political activities will be permitted to the satisfaction of the Commission provided they are conducted in a peaceful and democratic manner. The Rhodesians will be releasing a substantial number of detainees. If the British Government are satisfied that the proposed terms are acceptable to the Rhodesian people as a whole, the Rhodesians will take the necessary steps to enact the legislative changes required to implement them. After these have been completed the British Government will recommend to Parliament that independence should be granted to Southern Rhodesia on this basis and that in these circumstances sanctions will no longer be required.'

(Reprinted by permission of H.M. Stationery Office)
For the detailed text of the terms, and of the Proposed Declaration of Rights, see Cmnd. 4835 (H.M.S.O., London).

For a critical analysis of the White Paper, see *The Black Paper on Rhodesia* by M. Christie (Southern African Research Office, 1 Wickersley Road, London S.W.11).

APPENDIX 2: THE AFRICAN NATIONALIST PARTIES

The following account has been written by Dr Edwin Lichtenstein, a Rhodesian lawyer:

The African National Congress was launched in September 1957. It was proscribed less than twenty months later, in February 1959, its assets seized and more than five hundred of its officials detained and restricted. During the brief period that its existence was condoned by the Rhodesian government, then led by Sir Edgar Whitehead, the A.N.C. attracted a membership of about 17,000. This figure is, however, not a clear guide to the support enjoyed by the A.N.C. An African-led party, rejecting European tutelage and voicing African aspirations, was at that time a novel concept for most Africans and only the most politically committed felt impelled to seek membership. But for every member there were many more supporters. The strength of the A.N.C. was felt most markedly in rural areas where there was increasing discontent arising out of the implementation of the Native Land Husbandry Act of 1951, in terms of which native commissioners were empowered to enforce destocking of African-held land. Indeed George Nyandoro described this Act as the A.N.C.'s best recruiting officer, and the threat to the authority of the native commissioners posed by the growth of the A.N.C. was perhaps the strongest motive for its banning.

The A.N.C. was succeeded in January 1960 by the National Democratic Party. Its growth was even more rapid than that of its predecessor. The N.D.P. had a legal existence of less than two years. The extent of the support it attracted during that period is reflected in the events of 1960 and 1961. Its membership, about a year after its formation, was approximately 87,000. (I was given this figure at the time by the party's secretary general. I was then treasurer of the Bulawayo branch and this overall figure was consistent with the membership figures for my own branch.) The membership was growing steadily at the time of the ban and again for every member there were many more supporters, indicated inter alia by the size of audiences at meetings called by the N.D.P.

During 1960 it became clear that the Whitehead government seriously underestimated the popular support of the N.D.P. and completely misjudged the mood of the African people. The arrest in mid-1960 of several N.D.P. leaders led to serious riots in Salisbury – where some 20,000 Africans attempted to march to the centre of the city – and subsequently in Bulawayo. These riots, the worst in Rhodesia's history, occurred incidentally some six weeks after Sir Edgar Whitehead had described Rhodesia in a broadcast as the still centre of the cyclone in Africa.

A further indication of the mass basis being established by the N.D.P. was given when, prior to the official referendum conducted by the Whitehead government amongst an almost entirely white electorate to decide on the adoption of what is now the constitution, an unofficial referendum was conducted by the N.D.P. About 400,000 Africans voted at this referendum, virtually all of whom disapproved the constitution.

The N.D.P. was banned in December 1961 and within weeks was succeeded by the Zimbabwe African People's Union. The development of ZAPU was again marked by massive attendances at its public meetings (the holding of which was being made increasingly difficult under the severe provisions of the Law and Order (Maintenance) Act), and by the rapid gaining of members.

I estimate that the membership at the time of the banning was between 150,000 and 200,000 and probably closer to the latter. I was at the time treasurer of the Salisbury district council of ZAPU and I base my assessment on the fact that 200,000 membership cards were printed at ZAPU's inception and all were used. The rapid growth of ZAPU, despite the constant harassing of its officials by prosecution under the Law and Order (Maintenance) Act, was not something that the Whitehead government could long tolerate and, in September 1962, ZAPU in its turn was declared an unlawful organization.

It was inevitable that, as a result of repeated arrests of their leaders, prosecution of their officials and proscription of their organizations, African political militants should come to regard themselves as being in a state of war with the existing order. It was a concomitant of this that a break by any group or individual was regarded as a serious threat to African solidarity, a desertion to the enemy. During the existence of the N.D.P. a splinter group broke away from the party and formed a new organization styled the Zimbabwe National Party.

This party was founded by former N.D.P. members who expressed dissatisfaction with the leadership of Joshua Nkomo. Michael Mawema, who had been the N.D.P.'s first president, became a leading official of the Z.N.P. Despite the unimpeachable dedication of some, but by no means all, of its leaders, a splinter party such as the Z.N.P. and its successor, the short-lived Pan African Union, incurred the uncompromising hostility of N.D.P. militants who regarded breakaway activities as little short of treason. Its meetings were broken up and its leaders subjected to vilification and attack. It is of course a persistent feature of political struggle throughout the world that where people regard themselves as being locked in a life and death struggle with a powerful oppressor, they show scant tolerance for any who are believed to threaten the strength of their movement.

The present rift in the African nationalist movement is fraught with these attitudes. The formation of the Zimbabwe African National Union (ZANU – not to be confused with the aforementioned Z.N.P.) in 1963 resulted largely from dissatisfaction with Joshua Nkomo's leadership, when many of the most able

leaders of ZAPU felt obliged to break with their former organization and found a new party. It would appear that at the outset
many, perhaps the majority, of officials at branch level supported
the newly formed ZANU, but the mass of supporters refused to
desert Nkomo who for years had been held up to them as the
leader who would guide them to political emancipation. It was
perhaps naive of the ZANU leaders to imagine that mass support
would desert Nkomo. At present therefore the split persists,
almost entirely on the grounds of personality, with Nkomo
retaining the mass following, but ZANU having within its ranks
many of the most able and tested leaders (such as the Rev. N.
Sithole).

(From *Venture*, 11 Dartmouth Street, London S.W.1)

The African National Congress summed up its policy as follows:
'The African National Congress of Southern Rhodesia is
a people's movement . . . Its aim is NATIONAL UNITY of all
inhabitants of the country in true partnership regardless of race,
colour and creed. It stands for a completely integrated society,
equality of opportunity in every sphere and the social, economic
and political advancement of all . . .

'Congress is not a racial movement. It is equally opposed to
tribalism and racism.

'It welcomes as members all of any race . . .

'It recognizes the rights of all who are citizens of the country
whether African, European, Coloured or Asian, to retain permanently the fullest citizenship.

'It believes that this country can only advance through non-
racial thinking and acting, and that an integrated society provides
the only alternative to tribalism and racialism . . .

'Congress believes that in the whole of Southern and Eastern
Africa there are outstanding needs which it is supremely important
to meet:

(a) The standard of living of millions of people must be raised
in a short space of time through their rapid social, economic
and political advancement.

(b) This is only possible with the aid of skills, techniques and
capital from overseas. These must be attracted to this country
not only by the offer of material advantages but also by appeal
to the altruism and sense of service prevalent in the world. This
is a challenge to the more advanced and privileged people in the
world whose help is required in the interests of world peace and
the total development of mankind.

'Congress realizes that to meet these needs is a task of gigantic proportions, but believes that nothing short of this can ensure the peaceful development of this country for the benefit of all its inhabitants. Congress is therefore dedicated to the fulfilment of these needs and regards it as a matter of the most urgent necessity . . .'

Recently there have been two further developments. FROLIZI (the Front for the Liberation of Zimbabwe) has been formed under Shelton Siwela in an attempt to unite the ZAPU and ZANU exiles in Zambia. It has the support of James Chikerema and George Nyandoro of ZAPU, and of Nathan Shamuyarira and Godfrey Savanhu of ZANU. In Rhodesia the African National Council, under the chairmanship of Bishop Abel Muzorewa, has been formed and has taken a lead in criticizing the Proposed Settlement.

APPENDIX 3: THE PROPOSED DECLARATION OF RIGHTS

by Harish Magan, a Rhodesian barrister:

The new Declaration lists the same freedoms as those protected by the 1961 Constitution, namely: the right to life and personal liberty; protection from slavery, forced labour and inhuman treatment; protection from deprivation of property, and from arbitrary search and entry; protection of the due process of law; protection of freedom of conscience; protection from discrimination. But all these freedoms are subject to the overriding proviso that, as in the 1961 Constitution, all existing laws are exempted. Section 13 (1) of the new Declaration exempts a law if it:

> (b) is a law . . . that has had effect as part of the law of Rhodesia before the fixed date and has continued to have effect as part of the law of Rhodesia at all times since that date; or
>
> (c) repeats and re-enacts an existing law without alteration; or
>
> (d) alters an existing law and does not thereby render that law inconsistent with any provision of paragraphs 1 to 11 of this schedule in a manner in which or to an extent to which it was not previously so inconsistent.

This provision ensures that the status quo will continue unaltered; a bewildering net of laws renders virtually every protection in the Declaration meaningless. The infamous Land Tenure Act * divides the country into black and white areas of almost

* The Land Tenure Act No. 55, of 1969.

153

equal size, whereas the five million black Rhodesians outnumber the whites fifteen to one. Health and social services have always been segregated. In education the discrepancy between the services provided for the whites and the blacks is blatant and only education for white children is made compulsory.*

One glance at the Law and Order (Maintenance) Act† reveals how it negates the freedoms of assembly and association promised by the Declaration. Section 6 (1) of the Act allows a regulating authority to 'issue directions for the purpose of controlling the conduct of public processions within his area and the route by which and the times at which public procession may pass'. Section 12 (1) empowers the Minister, if he deems it desirable for the maintenance of law and order, to:

(a) prohibit the assembly of a particular public gathering;
(b) prohibit all public gatherings for such period, not exceeding three months, as may be specified in the order . . .

The list continues in similar vein until it reaches sub-section (g). Section 15 (1) of the Act states that:

If three or more persons are assembled in a public place or at a public meeting and conduct themselves in such a manner that a police officer has reasonable grounds for believing a breach of the peace is likely to occur or that public disorder is likely to be occasioned, he may call upon the persons assembled to disperse . . . if any person fails so to depart immediately after an order is so given and repeated, the persons so remaining shall be deemed to be an unlawful gathering, and to have taken part in an unlawful gathering.

The Unlawful Organizations Act, passed only a few months ago, goes even further. It declares unlawful all the former African nationalist political parties of Rhodesia, as well as any organization which associates in any way with bodies such as the World Federation of Trade Unions and the International Union of Students. The President may ban any successor organization or one directed by former officials of an unlawful organization. Anyone who has been an official of an unlawful organization can be ordered to resign from any other organization. This means that all the nationalist political leaders of Rhodesia can now be permanently barred from active politics simply at the whim of

* Compare Federal Education Act No. 15, of 1956, Sections 2, 40 and 7 (1) (now adminstered as a Rhodesian statute) with the Rhodesian African Education Act, Cap. 97.
† Act No. 55, of 1971.

'he President. In fact, the Act contravenes not only freedom of expression and association but virtually every other provision of the Declaration as well. The protection of the due process of law is meaningless when mere attendance at a meeting of members of an unlawful organization creates a presumption of membership in that organization; * nor is the President's order, declaring an organization unlawful, open to question in any court of law.†

It should be remembered too that with regard to future legislation the Declaration leaves sufficient exceptions to permit a very wide range of legislation limiting individual freedoms. And in times of emergency all measures may contravene the Declaration as long as it 'could reasonably have been thought to be required for the purpose of dealing with the situation in question'.

Each section of the Declaration contains its own exceptions. The right to personal liberty is subject to the Minister's right to order the preventive detention of any individual, whereas the latter right is unfettered since no conditions for preventive detention are stipulated in the Constitution save a review within nine months. The protection from arbitrary search or entry is subject to anything done 'in the interests of defence, public safety, public order, public morality, public health or town and country planning.'

In four sections of the Declaration,‡ a litigant has to go much further than simply showing a contravention of his rights. He has to show that 'the court should not accept that the provision of the law concerned is *reasonably justified* in a democratic society . . . without proof to its satisfaction.' The court will then call upon the Minister to show cause why the provision should not be declared inconsistent with the Constitution. Reasonable justification requires the Minister simply to show that the provision is not obviously unreasonable. This is a much lower level of proof than the equivalent sections in the 1961 Declaration, which required the Minister to show 'in a society which has a proper respect for the rights and freedoms of the individual, the *necessity* of that law . . .'

Finally one must consider the implications of the curiosity drafted section 84 (A) (9) of the proposed constitutional amendments. It states that a court 'shall not declare any provision of an Act enacted or statutory instrument made after the fixed date . . . to be inconsistent with any provision of the Declaration of Rights if the provision concerned has been in force for a period of at least

* Act No. 55, of 1971, section 12.
† *Op.cit.*, section 3 (3).
‡ Sections 6, 8, 9 and 10.

155

ten years, whether as part of the Act or statutory instrument concerned or of any previous Act or statutory instrument repealed or amended and substituted by the Act or statutory instrument concerned.'

This means that Acts passed after the Declaration comes into force will not be declared invalid as contravening the Declaration if they have been in force for ten years by the time a case is taken to court. An individual, of course, cannot go to court unless the Declaration has been 'contravened in relation to him'. Therefore the government could, if it wishes, pass an enabling act contravening the Declaration, not take action affecting any particular individual for ten years, and then do exactly as it pleases with immunity.

(Extracted, by permission, from *Race Today*, January 1972)

APPENDIX 4: THE PEARCE COMMISSION

Hugo Young has described the difficulties facing the Commission:

The Pearce Commission faces a task of monumental gravity. It has been convened as nothing less than a substitute for and improvement upon the democratic process, to discover whether the Smith-Home agreement is acceptable to the Rhodesian people. Its job is not to study and evaluate the suitability of particular constitutional proposals but to replace the secret and universal ballot as the very fount of democracy. Pearce rests on the belief that four wise men are better able than the normal processes of political action and democratic vote to divine the popular will. It is meant to achieve a democratic expression without using a democratic method.

Pearce is given the invidious task of ratifying or cancelling a political decision which has already been taken, and doing so in the name of the Rhodesian people.

This has only happened, it is said, because Rhodesia is a country where the secret and universal ballot cannot work. If that is true, however, so is another proposition: that Rhodesia is a country where a Commission may very well not work either.

The impediments challenging the commissioners' powers of divination are formidable indeed. Rhodesia is a police state, which has lived for many years under emergency powers. Political life has been stultified, political leaders are in prison. Political education has therefore largely ceased, and it is unlikely that in the time available political activity can do much to crystallize views and thus assist the Commission. Any political reawakening among African nationalists has in fact been specifically impeded by the settlement terms. By denying access to the radio to all nationalist parties the terms exclude at a stroke the most committed critics of settlement from the most potent medium of communication.

The emergency powers have already stimulated police interference with discussion of the settlement. They have given the Government a grip on action and opinion which the Commission is unlikely to be able to break. In particular, few detached observers with Rhodesian experience expect the Commission to be able to fulfil the British undertaking that everyone would have access to it. In the tribal areas the chiefs and district commissioners, all Rhodesian Government employees, are likely to remain the prime guardians of access to tribal opinion.

Ever since it was set up it has been apparent that the Commission, although nominally independent, would be heavily dependent on the two Governments who now have in common a powerful vested interest in the settlement. The Commission cannot be blamed for having no time to assemble a bureaucracy of its own. But its role as trustee for five million Africans who had no part in making the settlement is surely not best carried out by permitting all the interpreters, for example, to be recruited in Rhodesia by Rhodesians before the Commission has started work there.

A further hindrance to a credible verdict will spring from the Foreign Office's choice of the sixteen assessors, all but one of them former members of the colonial service, and seven of them still in Government jobs. Can they gain the confidence of the African?

Even with a chairman of greater political experience, the Commission would have little chance of altering the basic conditions of Rhodesian life as they have developed over six years and more. It must use its limited room for manoeuvre to the utmost if it is to reach a credible conclusion. Plainly the most fruitful area where this flexibility exists is not in the matter of assessment at all but rather in the first and less-noticed aspect of the Commission's work, its duty to explain the settlement.

Explanation is what the settlement document demands above all. It is, to begin with, exceedingly complicated. The White Paper leaves many questions unanswered – intentionally – and the omissions of the shortened version, which is to be distributed to the Rhodesian people, make it if anything even more tendentious. Its many *lacunae* of detail are matched by a characteristic which is understandable in an outline agreement but fatal to an explanation of it: it contains nothing about the disadvantages of a settlement or the consequences of turning this settlement down.

L

The central unanswered question is how long the settlement is likely to delay majority rule. Both Governments have made their estimates of this, but both shelter behind their imprecision as an excuse for not publishing them. There is no reason nor any justification for the Commission to do likewise. Varying estimates have been made, on various assumptions. They cannot be exact, but they offer some guide. By publishing them Pearce need not endorse them. If it fails to publish them, it will be pretending to give an account of the opinion of people who have been deprived of the minimum data on which to reach one. It is not good enough to say, as the shortened version of the White Paper says, that majority rule 'will come about by steady steps' – as if that is an incontestable certainty.

Related to this is another fundamental point. If the settlement goes through there may be more jobs, but there may also be far more European Rhodesians; if it is rejected, there may be fewer jobs but also very much less European immigration. That too must be part of the context of any intelligible explanation. If it is relevant for Sir Alec Douglas-Home to urge that the settlement is Rhodesia's last best hope, it is also relevant for the Commission to point out that it will be the final exclusion of any outside responsibility for the future of the Rhodesian African.

These and other basic issues would lead the Commission away from the safe but profoundly deceptive aridities of the Governments' version of the settlement. It is ground where some commissioners may therefore be unwilling to tread. But if they do run away from it, they will surely find that the Commission has become the creature of the status quo, which is marked by ignorance, repression, political fear, and the determination of both Governments that no information shall be made available and no discussion encouraged which might imperil the appearance of consensus.

The test of acceptability, the fifth of the principles governing the settlement, was always incapable of perfect fulfilment. Certainly this method matches the Tory demand in October, 1964, just before leaving office, for a referendum or nothing. The Commission is put in the bizarre position of discovering whether the generality of Africans support the proposition that they are unfit to vote and will remain unfit to hold power for many years. Only by adopting a positive, urgent and patient approach to its explanatory task can the Commission hope to prevent gravity being shattered into abject farce.

(Extracted, by permission, from the *Sunday Times* of 9 January 1972)

On 12 January 1972 Lord Pearce announced the Commission's proposed method of working in Salisbury. He said he hoped there would be full, free and fair discussion, and peaceful and constructive debate on the terms of the settlement: 'We deplore intimidation or obstruction from whatever quarter it is expressed and in whatever form it is applied.'

Lord Pearce stated that if the Commission decided that the population of Rhodesia was divided fifty-fifty on the Proposals, or that it could not be sure of Rhodesian opinion, the finding would be negative. He said that the Commission could not estimate how long it would be before majority rule might be achieved under the Proposals, because of the imponderables, but that he hoped there would be intelligent debate on this question while the Commission was at work.

The Commission, Lord Pearce said, would respect all requests for privacy and strict confidence while taking evidence, and that even interpreters would be excluded if people wished. On the other hand, the press and public would be allowed to attend where witnesses wanted them. He stated that in going into rural areas the Commissioners aimed to bring their presence to the attention of everyone and to find a centre where they could be reached by everybody who wanted to see them. He said the Commissioners would 'use their commonsense' in determining how many people were represented by the views of leaders or people in authority.

He concluded: 'Finally, may I implore you to believe that we are completely impartial and that our one aim and ambition is to interpret accurately the true voice of Rhodesia.'

4 THE POSITION OF BLACKS IN BRAZILIAN SOCIETY

by Anani Dzidzienyo

Anani Dzidzienyo was born in Ghana in 1941, and after studying in Ghana, the United States, and the United Kingdom, did research in Brazil between 1970 and 1971. He is currently a research fellow at the Institute of Race Relations in London.

THE POSITION OF BLACKS
IN BRAZILIAN SOCIETY

INTRODUCTION

In 1500 Pedro Alves Cabral of Portugal landed in what is now Porto Seguro, near Salvador, the capital of the state of Bahia. But it was not until 1530 that the first Portuguese colonists arrived. Two years later the Portuguese founded São Vicente (near Santos, the port of São Paulo), later destined to become an important sugar-cane centre. In 1548 a government for the new possession was created in Salvador, Bahia, which became the first capital of Brazil in 1549 and was to remain so until 1763.

African slaves were imported into Brazil by the colonists to work in the sugar-cane plantations, just as they were brought to other parts of the New World. Slavery continued in Brazil until 1888, sixty-six years after Brazil had attained independence from Portugal and one year before it became a republic. During the course of the transatlantic slave trade it is estimated that about 3,647,000 men, women and children were imported into Brazil, of whom about 1,200,200 went to Bahia alone. Salvador, Bahia was thus to become the most African of Brazilian cities, and even today aspects of African culture and customs (Afro-Brazilian religious cult-houses, folklore, dietary habits, etc.) are visible in everyday life.

Close connections were maintained between Brazil and the west coast of Africa, and some ex-Bahians (Baianos, Baianas) returned to West Africa and became master craftsmen, traders, and so on. Brazilian influence is especially noticeable in Lagos, which has a Brazilian quarter where Bahian customs are observed and where buildings have a distinctive Bahian flavour. A similar situation exists in Dahomey, while in Nigeria, Ghana and Togo there are families which descend from the Brazilians who returned to West Africa in the last century.

Other parts of Brazil which had received sizeable numbers of African slaves are Rio de Janeiro, Minas Gerais, São Paulo, Pernambuco, Rio Grande do Sul and Paraná. In the early 1870s Brazil's population was estimated to be about ten million, of which the following were slaves:

BRAZIL'S SLAVE POPULATION IN THE EARLY 1870s

STATE OR PROVINCE	NUMBER OF SLAVES
Rio de Janeiro	*304,744*
Minas Gerais	*235,155*
Bahia	*173,639*
São Paulo	*169,964*
Pernambuco	*92,855*
Rio Grande do Sul	*69,366*
Paraná	*10,560*

According to the 1872 census, which was the first general census taken in Brazil, the population consisted of 3,787,289 (38·14 per cent) whites, 1,954,543 (19·68 per cent) blacks, and 4,188,737 (42·18 per cent) of mixed blood.

In 1890 the figures were: 6,308,198 (43·97 per cent) whites, 2,097,426 (14·63 per cent) blacks, and 5,934,291 (41·40 per cent) of mixed blood.

By 1940 the figures were: 26,171,778 (63·47 per cent) whites, 6,035,869 (14·64 per cent) blacks and 8,744,365 (21·20 per cent) of mixed blood. In 1950, when it was estimated that the Brazilian population had risen to 51,944,397, there were 32,027,661 (61·66 per cent) whites, 5,692,657 (10·96 per cent) blacks and 13,786,742 (26·52 per cent) of mixed blood.*

At this time, in terms of geographical regions, the east had 15·6 per cent blacks in a population of over 18 million, the north-east had 11 per cent out of more than 12 million, the south 6·5 per cent out of nearly 17 million, and the central west 10 per cent out of almost 2 million.

In 1960 the Brazilian population was estimated at 70,967,185 and the projected figure for the 1970 census is 96.000,000.†

With this number of people and an area of 8,515,965 square kilometres, Brazil ranks as one of the largest countries in the world, and as a potentially major power.

It is said that the black or 'blacker' proportion of the Brazilian population has been decreasing as a result of *branqueamento* (whitening), or the tendency for marriages and unions to involve greater racial and colour mixing, which results in more people of mixed blood, or of generally whiter complexion. There has also been a significant European migration. In the case of São Paulo, for example, it is estimated that in 1854 immigrants constituted only 3 per cent of its population (922 people); by 1886, however, the figure had increased to 25 per cent (12,985 people). The period

* do Nascimento, Abdias, *O Negro Revoltado* (Ediçoes GRD, Rio de Janeiro, 1968), p. 31.

† Brazilian Institute of Geography and Statistics 1970 Census, Perspectives (Rio de Janeiro, 1970).

between 1872 and 1886 continued to show a rapid rise in the city's white population. The proportion of foreigners in the national population as a whole reached its peak in the 1900 census when it had grown to 6·16 per cent. Thereafter, however, the figures showed this downward progression:

1920	—	*4·94%*
1940	—	*3·11%*
1950	—	*2·09%*

One factor in this decrease is the large number of those, originally classed as foreigners, who have chosen to take on Brazilian nationality. Portuguese, Italians, Spaniards and Germans form the largest immigrant groups who have done so. There is also a large Japanese community, centred mainly in São Paulo (both the city and state). It may be said that there has been no significant black migration to Brazil since the days of slavery and that blacks in the population today are descendants of the slaves.

The terms 'black' and 'dark' are used throughout to refer to those who are recognizably black, and is more accurate than the expression 'people of colour' which is the umbrella expression commonly used in Brazil to describe all non-white people, with perhaps the exception of Chinese or Japanese.

THE POSITION OF BLACKS IN BRAZILIAN SOCIETY

'In Brazil, there is no racism: the Negro knows his place.'

(*A popular Brazilian saying*)

The usual description of Brazil as the one country in the world where people of different races live together in harmony and where opportunities are open to all, irrespective of racial background, is definitely misleading, if not completely inaccurate. The most effective way of ascertaining the reality of the Brazilian racial situation is to look at the socio-economic and political positions of black or dark Brazilians in their society. But before doing this it is necessary to question the validity of another widely held opinion which is that the successful intermingling of the races has gone on for so long that it is now impossible to say with any degree of certainty who is black and who is white in Brazil. In fact, a sizeable proportion of the Brazilian population – approximately 10 per cent out of 96 million people – are recognizably black or distinctly dark. Their presence does not belie the extent to which racial intermingling has taken place, but it does bring out the bias which has been a hallmark of the much-vaunted Brazilian 'racial democracy' – the bias that white is best and black is worst and therefore the nearer one is to white, the better.

The hold which this view has on Brazilian society is all-pervasive, affecting stereotypes, role-playing, job opportunities, and life-styles; and, what is even more important, it serves as the corner-stone of the closely observed 'etiquette' of race relations in Brazil.

This etiquette dictates strongly against any discussion, especially in a controversial manner, of the racial situation, and thus it effectively helps to perpetuate the pattern of relationships which has been in existence since the days of slavery. Traditionally the blacks are expected to be grateful to the whites for the kindnesses shown to them and to continue to depend on the whites acting as their patrons and benefactors; it is also expected that the blacks will continue to accept the whites as the nation's official mouth-piece, explaining to outsiders the 'unique' nature of Brazilian race relations. The etiquette also decrees that official platitudes used to describe the Brazilian situation, like 'racial democracy', are to be accepted without question, while critical analysis or open discussion of this delicate subject is strongly discouraged.

Until the Brazilian society frees itself from this self-imposed prohibition against open discussion the present idyllic picture of Brazilian race relations will continue to predominate. Until then, the black Brazilian's position will indeed continue to be unique among New World blacks in that he alone will appear not to have profited from the new consciousness which Africans and other blacks throughout the world are experiencing, nor will he seem to have attained a greater consciousness of his position in relation to the overall society in which he lives. The growth of black consciousness is discouraged by the society's refusal to grant the black citizen the opportunity to realize his whole identity – including his black self – by denying the significance which black development (political, social and cultural) holds for him in particular and for Brazil in general.

At present the black man's position in Brazil can only be described as being virtually outside the mainstream of society. He is almost completely unrepresented in any area involving decision-making; with relatively few exceptions he is not to be seen in government, administration, business, or commerce, except at the lowest levels where manual labour is required. The only areas where he plays a significant rather than menial role are in football and entertainment. The reasons for his prominence here will be discussed later. It is enough to note at this point that the availability of these two particular avenues to blacks who wish to have a successful career and thereby benefit socially and economically is not peculiar to Brazil; nor is this a new phenomenon. The implication is that there are more parallels between the racial situation in Brazil and those in other multi-racial countries than is generally acknowledged. Until Brazilian blacks have an opportunity to assert themselves in all sectors of their society any claim that *as a group* they possess equal rights must remain highly questionable; the voice of a solitary Pelé in a white wilderness or that of the exceptional musician or entertainer who has 'made it' through his exceptional ability or good fortune is not enough to validate such a claim.*

Until Brazilians stop reacting, both officially and unofficially, with hurt pride and dismay when questions are asked about the position of black citizens, Brazil will continue undisturbed in its present ostrich-like posture, making any real improvement in its racial situation unlikely, if not impossible.† A real opportunity to create a more egalitarian society does exist, but the way to achieve this is not by reiterating often meaningless and misleading statements about the absence of overt racist practices in Brazil, the existence of a twenty-year-old anti-discrimination law,‡ and the greater inter-racial friendliness and mingling to be seen on the streets, particularly at carnival-time.§ Even if all this were true, such things are not in themselves conclusive proof that racial discrimination does not exist in Brazil, particularly in its more subtle manifestations. In a society where social control mechanisms have traditionally been used with great effect to ensure that one group remains dominant and the other dominated it has not been found necessary to enact rigid rules in order to ensure the continuance of the dominant-dominated relationship. Were legal precepts alone proof that racial justice and harmony exist, it would be a completely different story. The distinction between theory and practice is very important in an assessment of the black Brazilian's position, because there are no legal provisions which force him to remain in a disadvantaged position; there is, in fact, no need for them because the economic, social and political structures of Brazil are such that, by their very nature, they operate against the interests of the blacks. This kind of

---

* *Diário de Notícias* (daily newspaper), Salvador, Bahia, 11 October 1970.

† *O Cruzeiro* (weekly magazine), Rio de Janeiro, 8 September 1970. Article by Theophilo de Andrade.

‡The Afonso Arinos Law, passed in 1951 (Lei no. 1,390, 3 July 1951). This law makes discrimination based on race or colour in public establishments, education and employment a criminal offence punishable by jail term or fine.

§ Edwards, Franklin, ed., *Franklin Frazier on Race Relations* (The University of Chicago Press, 1968), pp. 98–99.

politico-socio-economic structure can effectively handle the rare black person who manages to succeed despite all the odds against him, because his example does not threaten to upset the fixed nature of existing unequal relationships. If anything, because he has managed to 'make it', he will be used by the society as a 'pin-up' to support the contention that Brazil is indeed a racial democracy. In fact a certain few names are often cited to show that some 'people of colour' have been successful – the implication being of course that the rest could follow suit if they would only try harder. Ignored here is the fact that had these few black Brazilians not been exceptionally gifted or fortunate, they would not have attained success.*

The term 'people of colour' is itself probably the greatest single factor contributing to the myth of the 'racial democracy',† for it is used to describe all non-white people or 'mixed-bloods' – a group which ranges from those completely black to those almost white. What must be noted here is that, in practice, Brazilians make extremely fine distinctions between subtle variations in skin tone, and that lighter-skinned Brazilians do not consider it a compliment to be classified with dark or black people. So to group all of them together under a blanket term is to distort the real situation.‡ In theory a third category is recognized – that of the *mulato*, which applies to those neither black nor white. This middle category is further broken down into light and dark *mulatos*, with the lightest-skinned passing over to the 'white' category and the darkest being included among the 'blacks'. It should be noted that even this tripartite classification does not mean that the dark-skinned *mulato* would consider himself to be black; quite the contrary in fact. Moreover, because of this Brazilian obsession with whiteness and blackness and the shades in between, with a concomitant emphasis on hair texture, nose shape and size of lips, there exist further race and colour break-downs to the point where Brazilians have more than twenty different expressions to distinguish colour variations between the two extremes of black and white.§ When the claim is made that Brazil has always

* *A Tarde* (daily newspaper), Salvador, Bahia, 6 December 1932.

† Pereira, João Baptista Borges, *Côr Profissão e Mobilidade: O Negro e o Radio em São Paulo* (São Paulo, 1967). Between pages 17 and 35 the terms 'negro' (black), prêto' and 'de côr' (coloured) are used 45 times: negro – 27 times, de côr –12 times, prêto – 6 times. (These terms are used interchangeably.)

‡ Harris, Marvin, *Pattern of Race in the Americas* (Walker & Co., New York, 1964).

§ Ianni, Octávio & Fernando Henrique Cardoso, *Côr e Mobilidade em Florianópolis* (São Paulo, 1960). Florianópolis is the capital of the state of Santa Catarina, in the south, and has a large European element in its population.

offered the 'person of colour'* or mixed blood equal opportunities, there is a deceptive lumping together of all these people who in fact are not generally considered to be in the same racial/colour category and who therefore are not accorded the same treatment. Hence, the claim that 'people of colour' are to be found at all levels of society is inaccurate if black or dark people are included in the term.

Another factor which has contributed to creating a false impression about the Brazilian situation is the practice of denying the existence of significant racial similarities between Brazil and the United States. This is done on the one hand by choosing to emphasize certain points about the Brazilian racial scene which invariably bring out its better aspects, while on the other hand stressing the worst aspects of the racial situation in the United States. It is argued that what distinguishes Brazil from the United States is the fact that in Brazil there is 'prejudice against appearance', while in the United States one finds 'prejudice against origins'. The validity of this claim can best be tested if we apply it to the Brazilians who *look* black. In their case appearance and origin cannot meaningfully be separated and the distinction is therefore false.

There is a further element involved in this distinction: the existence of 'prejudice' may be admitted but not the action to which it leads, that is, 'discrimination'. 'Prejudice' is a state of mind while 'discrimination' involves prejudical action, so that prejudice need not necessarily be followed by discrimination nor be concomitant with it. Thus people can be prejudiced without translating their prejudices into discriminatory action, i.e. making distinctions in one's treatment of others that are not based on fair and objective criteria equally applicable to everyone.† In a situation where it is considered inadvisable to indulge in overt discrimination refuge may be taken in the explanation that it is prejudice, not discrimination, which exists. In the Brazilian case in particular, although it is often admitted that a certain amount of prejudice is felt against dark persons, it is claimed that such prejudice does not involve actual discrimination.

It is further argued that this prejudice is not really directed against darker people as such (that is, not on the basis of their

* In Brazil the term 'black' is rarely used to mean 'Negro'. Hence the resort to words and terms denoting non-whiteness or darkness. 'Pessoas' or 'gente de côr' (people of colour, coloured people) is thus very convenient as a descriptive term.

†Pierson, Donald, *Negroes in Brazil* (Southern Illinois University Press, 1967, and Feffer & Simons Inc., London and Amsterdam, 1967).

colour), but rather against their low position in society (that is, their socio-economic standing). The blacks, having originally been brought to Brazil as slaves, were of course at the very bottom of the socio-economic and, by implication, political pyramid; and with the abolition of slavery in 1888 they were immediately thrown into a competitive socio-economic situation for which they were quite unprepared. They were handicapped even before they could begin.* Thanks to the system of valorizing individuals as they begin to move up economically, it would be assumed that those blacks and dark people who began to acquire technical and professional skills could gradually move away from the base and edge upwards in the socio-economic pyramid. If the majority of blacks and dark-skinned people remained at the very base, as has happened, this would not necessarily be regarded as having a connection with their appearance and racial origins; instead the assumption would be that they were suffering because they were poor. The expression generally used in Brazil to characterize this phenomenon is 'money whitens', meaning that once an individual of dark colour acquires money he can literally buy himself out of the black category and into the white category; because, the argument goes, along with money come all the social benefits which are commonly associated with whiteness and success in Brazil.

Once again the reality is more complex. For example, the experience of one black professional in Salvador, Bahia (the city with the largest recognizably black population in Brazil) attests to the fact that for blacks professional qualifications and economic status are not always synonymous with social success as is normally the case with near-white and light-skinned people. The truth is, of course, that an individual's blackness does not suddenly become invisible simply because he has acquired some wealth.†

Of course it is unlikely that many blacks will be able to accumulate wealth, and therefore some of the exceptional few who do may be accepted within the white fold. Because of their small numbers and because they have achieved a certain measure of success within the existing system, such people are not likely to upset the overall pattern of relationships between whites and

* Fernandes, Florestan, *A Integração do Negro na Sociedade de Classes* (São Paulo, 1965). Ianni, Octávio, *As Metamorfoses do Escravo* (São Paulo, 1962).

† Pierson, *op. cit.*
He observes that the indelible character of colour makes it somewhat different from other criteria of rank.

blacks. Indeed, if anything, these people are more likely to conform to than to challenge the patterns of the group to which they have been admitted: firstly, because their success and inclusion in white society is proof of their personal abilities; and secondly, because it is unlikely that they will criticize the system which has just accorded them so signal an honour. Thus they become captives of the situation and are often called upon to testify to the efficacy of the 'racial democracy' which has enabled them to reach their relatively high positions.

This is one example of how most observers of the Brazilian racial scene can be, and have been seduced by outward appearances. Also contributing to the image of racial equality is the mingling of the races in the shanty-towns (*favelas*) and in the streets and public places where people of the most beautiful colour combinations are to be seen. There also seems to be a general acceptance of the myth that the Portuguese somehow managed to initiate good race relations in Brazil, despite their own history as slave-traders and the inegalitarian nature of their own society.

The Portuguese are said to have been much less bigoted than their Anglo-Saxon counterparts in North America about mingling their blood with that of Indian and African slave-women. Furthermore, the Catholic religion is thought to have had a humanizing influence on the slave-masters in that it recognized the humanity of the slave and the possibility that he had a soul which could be saved. In addition to this ecclesiastical recognition that the slave was not wholly without human rights, in the secular sphere his rights were acknowledged in law. Theoretically the slave was legally permitted to buy himself out of bondage, to get another slave to take his place (presumably by coercion or persuasion), and even to lodge complaints against his master. Because these legal rights were known to exist, the position of black Brazilians has often been described in a way which makes no distinction between theory and practice; in reality the two have not been identical.*
For example, legal rights notwithstanding, in practice a slave could not lodge a complaint against his master, could not testify in court, and, even if he were freed, his freedom was subject to revocation at his ex-master's discretion. Furthermore, since Brazilian society was governed and led by slave-owners for the greater part of the period during which slavery was legal, it would be naive to expect

---

* (a) Freyre, Gilberto, *The Masters and the Slaves: A Study in the Development of Brazilian Civilisation* (Alfred Knopf, New York, 1946) and *New World in the Tropics: the Culture of Modern Brazil* (New York, 1959).
(b) Tannenbaum, Frank, *Slave and Citizen: the Negro in the Americas* (New York, 1946).

that these slave-owners would be concerned about the legal rights of slaves when this would not only damage their own economic interests but would also undermine the system upon which their power had been built.

The sexual relationship between the slave-master and his slaves was also intrinsically unequal. With few, if any, Portuguese women in the colonies, it is not surprising that the male colonists should have had sexual relations with their slave-women who, of course, were in no position to repulse their master's advances. Such behaviour would be common even in the case of slave-masters who did have European wives. A slave-woman, being in a weak, unprotected and 'inferior' position, was considered by white males to be easy prey; this view of her has lasted through succeeding generations to include her descendants even today. The *mulata*, who is the subject of many popular Brazilian songs, is the living example of this. Despite the contention that she is the symbol of Brazil, she is in fact commonly spoken of and treated as being sexually approachable and promiscuous; these attributed qualities are thought to make her desirable as a sexual partner but unsuitable as a wife. The term *mulata* is now used so loosely that it means any non-white woman who is relatively dark; it is even used to describe a near-black woman and is a polite way of avoiding the term 'black' (*prêta* or *negra*), which is considered uncomplimentary. For this reason, in a magazine claiming to present the 'hottest mulatas in Brazil' some of the women photographed were obviously black but had been called 'mulata'. In 1960 when a 'people of colour' club in Rio de Janeiro decided to enter a girl for the 'Miss Rio de Janeiro' contest – a preliminary round for the 'Miss Brazil' contest – some other clubs threatened to withdraw from the competition. They seemed to fear that if a *mulata* was allowed to enter the contest that year, then before long really black girls might compete as well. * It is clear from this that while *mulatas* may be considered suitable as dancers during carnival-time, they are not thought to be proper representatives of Brazilian beauty whose epitome is generally considered to be *morena* (sunburnt in appearance but not actually black or very dark).

The praises sung to the *mulata* in many Brazilian songs do not reflect either the position of the majority of dark and black women in Brazil. Most *mulatas* have to work as housemaids and cooks in a clearly defined role which remains essentially

* *Cadernos Brasileiros* (special edition entitled '80 Anos de Abolição' (Instituto Latino Americano de Relações Internacionais, 1968). Contribution by Paula Assis.

unchanged despite the acts of friendliness on the part of their employers. Here too a tradition is cited in an attempt to show how warm and friendly master–slave relations have been in Brazil: the *mãe prêta* (black mother), who nursed her master's children, is still spoken of sentimentally by many who were brought up by her and who claim, for that reason, to be free from racial prejudice. What appears to have been forgotten is the fact that the *mãe prêta* was looked upon with affection because of her fidelity and service to her master and his family regardless of her own wants or comfort; her counterpart was to be found in the southern United States as the 'black mammy'. Although mutual affection might have existed, her role was firmly fixed and there was no question of her ever improving the unequal basis of her relationship with her master and his peers. The existence of the *mãe prêta* cannot therefore be said to confirm the absence of racial discrimination in Brazil – particularly when one remembers that, in this role, her feelings as mother to her own children and her desire for her own family life were deliberately stifled.

All this, however, is not to dispute the existence of a few Brazilians who have publicly expounded views contrary to the accepted traditional, official and popular concept of Brazilian race relations. The works of people like Florestan Fernandes, who carried out a pioneer study of the *Relationship between Blacks and Whites in São Paulo** (the industrial capital of Brazil) in conjunction with the French scholar Roger Bastide, have examined Brazilian 'racial democracy' in a new and critical way. In his subsequent works, including *A Integração do Negro na Sociedade de Classes*† ‡ and *The Weight of the Past*,§ Florestan Fernandes has raised serious questions about racialism in Brazilian society. Following in his footsteps Octávio Ianni and Fernando Henrique Cardoso have studied *Colour and Social Mobility in Florianópolis‖* and Costa Pinto has examined the conditions of *The Negro in Rio de Janeiro*.¶

* Bastide, Roger & Florestan Fernandes, *Relações Raciais entre Negros e Brancos em São Paulo* (São Paulo, 1955).

† Fernandes, *op. cit.*

‡ *Ibid.* The English edition is: *The Negro in Brazilian Society* (Columbia University Press, New York, 1969).

§ *Daedalus* (special issue entitled 'Colour and Race') (American Academy of the Arts and Sciences, Harvard University, Spring 1967). Article entitled 'The Weight of the Past' by Fernandes.

‖ Ianni & Cardoso, *op. cit.*

¶ Costa Pinto, L., *O Negro no Rio de Janeiro* (Compania Editôra Nacional, São Paulo, 1952).

All these works share a recognition of the marginal position of the black in Brazilian society as a result of several major factors. The most important of these is the fact that abolition of slavery was not accompanied by any measures which would enable the ex-slave to take his place on equal terms in a highly competitive and rapidly expanding economy; thus he was left handicapped and unable to compete with even the newly arrived immigrants from Europe. This has been especially true in São Paulo.

Through the work of Florestan Fernandes and others, as well as recent historical research on Brazilian slavery (Vioti Costa, Stein, Degler, Graham), enough evidence has been presented to show the true nature of Brazilian race relations, both in the past and today; yet the old myths are still believed by Brazilians as well as foreigners. For instance, it is often said in Bahian intellectual circles that the analyses and conclusions of Fernandes and the 'São Paulo group' are applicable only to the southern part of Brazil where it is said relations are much worse than in the north-east (i.e. Bahia itself). The difference is attributed to the presence in the south of a greater number of recently arrived European immigrants, who are thought to have brought their prejudices with them.

RACIAL OR SOCIO-ECONOMIC PREJUDICE?

The work of Donald Pierson, the American sociologist who wrote *Negroes in Brazil: the history of race contact in Brazil*, and that of the well-known Bahian social scientist Thales de Azevedo,* may be said to represent the Bahian school of thought which holds that, slavery having ended, relations between whites and blacks, and (in Bahia) all those in the *mulato* (mixed) group, have been determined primarily by social and economic factors and that therefore it is not so much a question of racism as of social prejudice. It would follow that as soon as the blacks and dark Brazilians improve their low socio-economic status they will have no further problem in integrating fully into society. This school of thought agrees that there are rich and poor people and that the overwhelming majority of rich people are white while most of the blacks are poor, and it maintains that a rich black man becomes an 'honorary white' and a poor white man is considered to be 'black'.

* de Azevedo, Thales, *As Elites de Côr: Um Estudo de Ascensão Social* (São Paulo, 1953).
The socio-economic factor is the decisive one according to de Azevedo. There is an elite of coloured people in Bahia at the highest socio-economic and political lévels. He also contends that in Bahia there is a two-fold division, rich and poor. White was identified with the rich and black with the poor.

173

Two important points are to be noted here. The first is this group's acceptance of the view prevalent in Brazil that to be white is desirable and that 'whiteness' should be the eventual goal of all those unfortunate enough to be born black or dark. The second point about this school of thought is its view that the root of the problem is personal or social *prejudice* against low socio-economic status, which happens to be identified with being black but which, nevertheless, involves no racism or racial discrimination. Adopting this point of view means that any prejudice against, and negative stereotypes about, blacks – and their lack of participation at levels other than the lowest in Brazilian society – can be explained away with a minimum of discomfort to everyone.

As recently as August 1971 a leading Bahian newspaper carried an article entitled 'Where is Prejudice – in colour or in social position?', thus putting the emphasis on prejudice rather than discrimination. In this article the existence of racial prejudice was admitted, although it was added as usual that such prejudice has much more to do with class than with race. The article further admitted that some actual racism existed as well, as reflected in common racist expressions like 'He is black but intelligent'; 'A black man with a white soul'; and, of course, the ubiquitous question 'Would you let your daughter marry a black man?' A black maid was quoted as saying: 'My white bosses treat me well but I know my place.' The article also quoted Professor Thales de Azevedo who referred to the greater number of inter-racial marriages taking place and said that he himself believes racial prejudice is on the decrease; that is, there are now fewer obstacles in the way of 'people of colour' who wish to move towards integration into the white, class-based society, and that there is even a greater tendency towards such integration. 'Racial prejudice is something children learn from their elders; so, if it can be learned, it can also be unlearned,' the writer of this newspaper article affirmed, concluding: 'The *contribution* of people of colour in various fields of art, popular music, theatre, the arts, *and especially in football*, where they have become idols, will permit greater racial integration with less sensation [my emphasis].'* The limitations imposed on black people will be evident from the fact that their 'contribution' is confined to the worlds of entertainment and football which are quite remote from the decision-making areas of Brazilian society.

The process of 'whitening' is, of course, occurring in a more

* *Jornal da Bahia* (daily newspaper), 1 and 2 August 1971.
(Since the paper does not appear on Mondays, the Sunday issue is marked for Sunday and Monday: hence 1 and 2 August).

literal sense through more frequent intermarriage and miscegenation which in time will make it increasingly difficult to distinguish with certainty those who have black origins. The Brazilian policy of *branqueamento* encourages this tendency in the hope that it will eventually produce a new Brazilian all-white prototype. Certainly the encouragement given to European immigration will also contribute to this end.

In a society which officially denies the existence of discrimination, accusations that racially discriminatory acts have been carried out can be countered by the offender in two ways. If black or dark people complain that they are experiencing racial discrimination with regard to educational employment opportunities or housing, reasons other than the most obvious are advanced in explanation. For example, one finds that the expression *boa aparência* (good appearance) recurs in advertisements for salesmen, shop assistants, secretaries and other positions which involve contact with the public. This expression is commonly understood to mean that the applicant is more likely to be successful if he is white or near-white. There is nothing actually illegal about including the requirement *boa aparência* and the employer can always say that discrimination on the basis of race or colour was not intended. In one instance the owner of a boarding house in Salvador, Bahia, who was advertising for lodgers stipulated that people who were unemployed or dark-skinned need not apply. This restriction, he explained, arose simply from his concern for the well-being of his other lodgers who had had occasion in the past to complain about the behaviour of blacks living in his boarding house. He agreed, however, to accept as a lodger any black applicant who could prove his ability to pay the rent. 'Rich blacks' were therefore eligible, but whites or near-white applicants would not be required to undergo any such test.*

A second type of reaction often elicited by accusations of discrimination is one of great shock at the discovery of unfair practices. It is pointed out that such behaviour is completely contrary to the Brazilian tradition of race relations: 'How could any Brazilian do such an inhuman thing which goes against the very grain of our racial democracy?' or 'The guilty person should bear the full force of the anti-discrimination law.'†

The case of Jorge Fuad, the caretaker of a block of flats in Salvador, is worth noting here. In May 1971 when a black school-

* *Jornal da Bahia*, 20 May 1970.
† *Jornal da Bahia*, 28 May 1971.
Fotos e Fotos (weekly magazine), 17 June 1971.

teacher occupying one of the flats complained that Fuad had refused to let her use the residents' lift and had made racist comments about her, press reports stressed that he was a foreigner (of Arab descent) and therefore liable to deportation for his offence. Fuad filed a suit against the schoolteacher for alleged defamation of his character, and produced evidence to show that he had been born in Brazil. An interesting aspect of this case was the fact that some fifty-four residents of the building, none of whom had witnessed the incident, signed a document testifying to Fuad's reliability and efficiency; the document was meant to indicate that Fuad, being a responsible caretaker, could not possibly be a racist. Both the local and national press made much of the case, all of them condemning racism and expressing the hope that the law would take its full course and that the offender would be punished.* Up to the end of August 1971 the only development was the initiation of a police inquiry.

Shortly afterwards another incident occurred in Bahia, in which a resident complained that another resident in the same building had usurped her car-parking rights and had racially insulted her. She also stated that since it was the authorities' usual practice to put complaints about racism in limbo on the pretext of overwork and the need to deal with more important issues, she intended to take the matter further herself if she did not receive an immediate reply from the authorities.† The newspapers gave no indication of the nature of the action the complainant proposed to take.

In 1970 the B.B.C. televised a documentary 'Panorama' programme on race relations in Brazil which submitted that racial discrimination did exist. Following this an official protest was made to the B.B.C. by the Brazilian government, and the Brazilian press was aroused.‡ Great exception was taken to the fact that no black Brazilian had been interviewed on the programme, and that it was an American black girl (i.e. a foreigner) who had talked about discrimination. A columnist for the magazine *O Cruzeiro* wrote: 'It is unfair of the B.B.C. to accuse us of racial discrimination when we have the pride of being the only truly multi-racial society created in the tropics by the white man.'

Two important points emerged from the protest. The first was that no black Brazilian had been interviewed. In this regard it should be noted that in Brazil today, when even white political dissenters are forced to go underground, it would be difficult to

* *Jornal da Bahia*, 28 May 1971.
† *Jornal da Bahia*, 3 June 1971.
‡ *Jornal da Brasil* (daily newspaper), 18 August 1970.
Ref: An official protest delivered to the B.B.C. by the Brazilian Ambassador in London.

find black Brazilians willing to risk making public statements on television about their actual position in society for fear of possible reprisals against them. Two notable exceptions are Abdias do Nascimento and Gurreiro Ramos who, in addition to attacking the Brazilian racial situation, also hold political views which have made it necessary for them (like certain other Brazilian intellectuals) to live outside Brazil since the military takeover of 1964. Abdias do Nascimento, who is now lecturing at the State University of New York at Buffalo in the United States, is a playwright, author and founder of the Experimental Black Theatre in Rio de Janeiro (which he established in 1944). He has been uncompromising in his denunciation of what he calls the 'Kafka-esque nature' of the racial situation in Brazil. Gurreiro Ramos is a social scientist who has denounced with similar vigour and courage the insidiousness of Brazilian racism.

A second interesting point was raised during the protest directed against the B.B.C.: it was claimed that in Brazil the white man had created a 'world in the tropics'. This, in fact, is the dominant and most popular concept of Brazilian race relations, as orchestrated by the establishment sociologist Gilberto Freyre (*The Masters and the Slaves; New World in the Tropics*). Freyre's vivid descriptions of life as it was in the slave-master's house, and the affectionate relations between master and slave, have been highly effective in establishing Brazil's reputation as a multi-racial society free from racism. The Portuguese are alleged not to have considered dark people their inferiors as a result of having themselves been ruled at one time by the Moors. Proof of Portuguese open-mindedness is said to be found in their favour-able attitude towards miscegenation: they mated freely with their slaves, producing the *mulata*, symbol of Brazil. No one can discuss the nature of race relations in Brazil without paying due attention to Freyre's views, but his approach, limited as it is, is adopted without question by the majority of Brazilians.* It must be added, however, that even in Brazil itself Freyre's ideas are questioned by some historians and sociologists. But so per-vasive are his views generally – and so convenient to supporters of the status quo – that both Brazilians and foreigners tend to accept them as accurate description of Brazilian race relations. Recently, in June 1971, Freyre was quoted as saying that 'negritude' (i.e.

---

* Freyre, *op. cit.*
(N.B. Carl Degler rightly points out, in an article entitled 'Slavery in Brazil and the United States: an Essay in Comparative History', published in the *American Historical Review*, no. 4, April 1970, that Freyre's views constitute a highly conservative explanation of the Brazilian situation.)

black consciousness among Africans and people of African descent) is, no matter how it is defined, 'a mysticism which has no place in Brazil'. According to Freyre negritude may be relevant for the people of Africa who as a result of tribal divisions over the years could use it to strengthen national consciousness and encourage political integration; it might even be beneficial to black Americans who are seeking a new identity. As far as the black Brazilian is concerned, however, he thinks that this movement has no relevance at all. Freyre sees Brazil as a land made up principally of mixed racial and ethnic groups who live together on equal terms in a hybrid culture.*

The black Brazilian's position in white-dominated Brazil differs from that of blacks in similar societies elsewhere only to the extent that the official Brazilian ideology of non-discrimination, by not reflecting the reality and indeed by camouflaging it, achieves without tension the same results as do overtly racist societies. As for the reaction of the black Brazilian himself to a critical assessment of his position, it must be remembered that black and dark Brazilians have been brought up to accept the 'new world in the tropics' myth, so that they show signs of discomfort at any open and controversial discussion of the subject. More importantly, they have been encouraged to believe that they are the most fortunate blacks in the New World – especially in comparison with the 'poor black North American' – and perhaps for that reason they faithfully observe the etiquette of race relations and will readily point out the brotherly feelings which exist between them and white Brazilians. Of course an essential element in this attitude is the black's long-term subjection to racial stereotypes promulgated by the whites. Having been imposed upon the black man for so long, these negative images of himself have come to be accepted by him as true.

Those blacks and dark people who have been successful are regularly cited as evidencing the equality of opportunity which is said to exist in Brazil. Thus, because of his acceptance of the orthodox line, Pelé, the 'King of Football', is an invaluable ally of the Brazilian authorities and he is constantly used to demonstrate the validity of their 'racial democracy' propaganda. He himself claims that there is no racism in Brazil and that he personally has never experienced any acts against himself which could be construed as racist. Pelé happens to be the best known of these 'honourable exceptions' but he is by no means the only one. There are others in the world of football and entertainment who,

* *O Estado de São Paulo* (daily newspaper), 30 May 1971. Article by Freyre.

having themselves succeeded, avoid making any controversial pronouncements about the racial situation. It is not that these people lack racial consciousness; it is rather that they prefer not to place themselves in the firing line. Pelé can talk about racism in the United States and declare his agreement with the politics of Muhammad Ali, yet at the same time he cannot see that similar tactics might be equally applicable in Brazil.*

It has been said of Pelé that 'No black person in the whole world has done more to break racial barriers. He who claps hands for Pelé claps hands for black people.'† It is difficult to see how this statement could be justified: applause for a black football player disproves in no way the existence of racist or discriminatory practices in society. A black sportsman or musician may be required to play for audiences from which blacks have been deliberately excluded; the players themselves are present to provide entertainment for the white audience who, in return, may deign to admit the black players to their club-house and might even fete them as 'symbols'. None of this will affect the basic relationship between the white and black races.‡

What about the rare black person who, although relatively successful, begins openly to question the assumptions of 'racial democracy' in Brazil? How does the society respond? The following appeared in *A Tarde*, a Bahian afternoon newspaper:§

Frentes Negras (Black Fronts) – A new problem – Why? Men of colour and Brazil – Bahia and artificial problems – Anachronistic Impertinence . . . The problem does not exist. It is new, it is imagined, it is not real.

The article further maintained that it had always been a cause of surprise and admiration to foreigners visiting Brazil that any differentiation (discrimination) based on race (colour) was absent and that the black person, by virtue of his intelligence and ability, could freely reach any position including the highest offices in the political hierarchy, in administration and commerce; and that this

---

* *O Estado de São Paulo*, 16 April 1971.
Manchete (weekly magazine), 9 September 1971.
† Freyre, *op. cit.* (footnote on p. 178).
‡ This is relevant not only to the Brazilian situation but also to those in the U.S.A., Britain and France.
§ *A Tarde*, 6 December 1932.
The *Frente Negra Brasileira* was launched by Arlindo and Isaltino Veiga Santos, Jose Correira Leite, Gevasio Morais and Alberto Orland.
Fernandes, *op. cit.* (first footnote, p. 169) has written at length on black movements of that era in São Paulo.

had been the case even before the abolition of slavery. Therefore there was no need for 'black fronts' in Brazil. The idea was an artificial one, foreign-inspired, and it would only serve to upset the harmony of Brazilian (and Bahian) race relations.

This article was written in response to the launching in the 1930s of *A Frente Negra Brasileira* (The Black Brazilian Front) in São Paulo. This group proposed to unite 'people of colour' – blacks and *mulatos* – in order to secure better political, social and economic treatment for them all. It characterized itself as an 'organization with the principal objective of educating and socializing the race' and pledged that 'in the field of political action, we will vote for black candidates.' The Front gained considerable support and was registered with the supreme Electoral Tribunal as a political party. But following a coup d'etat its political activities were suspended, and when the ban was eventually lifted the movement re-emerged without its political programme; the emphasis was placed instead on organizing cultural and recreational activities.

Jorge Amado, himself a Bahian and a leading Brazilian author, now world-famous for his vivid accounts of Bahian life, wrote in *Pastôres da Noite* (Shepherds of the Night):

> Any child could have blue eyes, even when its father is black, because it is impossible to separate and classify the various bloods in a child born in Bahia. A blond appears amongst mulatos and a little black among whites. This is how we are. *

Despite the extensive racial mixing which characterizes Bahia, it is nevertheless true that there is so great an obsession with whiteness or near-whiteness among Bahians that a term exists – *branco da Bahia* (Bahian white) – to describe a near-white person who would be offended if he were referred to as a *mulato*, although strictly speaking the latter might be a truer description.† Similarly, in the streets of Bahia the unusual sight of a couple drawn from opposite poles of the race/colour spectrum will cause passers-by to stare and make disapproving comments. Yet even such reactions can be explained away, if rather illogically: 'Bahia is too traditional; patterns of relationships, ideas and behaviour have not responded to changes of the times.'

Even in the streets of São Paulo, however – a sophisticated metropolis and the economic capital of Brazil – identical reactions

* Amado, Jorge, *Os Pastôres da Noite* (Livraria Martins Editôra, São Paulo, 1970).
† Pierson, *op. cit.*

to the sight of such racially mixed couples are noticeable. A Bahian would comment, 'In São Paulo and in the south there is more racism generally'. It would be more accurate to say that here, unlike in Bahia, relationships have been challenged by changing economic patterns (e.g. blacks competing with whites on a large scale for skilled jobs). Because of this increased competition some of the whites' subtler discriminatory practices have given way to more overt manifestations of racism.

These more pronounced racist practices in the south are commonly attributed to the presence there of large numbers of non-Iberian European immigrants (Germans, Italians and East Europeans) and their descendants, who are thought to have imported their racist ideas. Florestan Fernandes has demonstrated, however, that far from this being so, the immigrant who comes to São Paulo is much more likely to be influenced by the existing patterns of inter-racial relationships which he encounters there. Fernandes found that in São Paulo there have been different stages in the white immigrant's relationship with blacks. Initially there was some feeling of solidarity between them since both, in different senses, were outsiders in Brazilian society. In time, however, as the immigrant raised himself from his initially low socio-economic position, he realized that continued association with blacks retarded his own upward mobility. At this point he tended to seek out new white and near-white friends as being more compatible with his improved circumstances.*

From the blacks' point of view the upward mobility of the white immigrant is, on the one hand, a source of encouragement and inspiration, for he is known to have arrived only recently and in most cases with little money and yet in a comparatively short period has managed to better his situation. On the other hand, the white immigrant's success reinforces the blacks' existing suspicions and doubts: why can the white immigrant advance so quickly when they, as Brazilians, have not succeeded in doing so despite all their efforts; is not this proof of prejudice and discrimination against them as blacks?† To say that they are victims of a competitive class society which places the highest premium on saleable skills is true. But this overlooks the fact that the vast majority of blacks were handicapped before they could even begin to compete with their fellow Brazilians in the

---

* Morner, Magnus, ed., *Race and Class in Latin America* (Columbia University Press, New York, 1970). Article entitled 'Immigration and Race Relations in São Paulo' by Fernandes.

  † (a) *Ibid.*

  (b) Bastide & Fernandes, *op. cit.*

private enterprise economy and that they continue in this position because of their colour. Simply to group them with other poor members of society (though undoubtedly they do share most of their problems) is to avoid acknowledging the special difficulties experienced by blacks today in an environment of confirmed racism.

Of course, Brazil is a rigidly stratified society within which upward mobility is quite difficult for all members of the proletariat. Decision-making and effective power remains the prerogative of a tiny élite. Traditionally this was composed of the large landowners but now includes new members drawn from industry, the armed forces, the church and intellectuals on the faculties of universities, colleges and secondary schools. About 50 per cent of the adult population is illiterate, and with a literacy bar most adults excluded from the ruling class are not even permitted to vote during elections. Furthermore, since April 1964 the country has been ruled by a military elite and there has been no open, free and direct election at either federal or state level. State governors are nominated by the 'ruling' party (ARENA) and there is an 'official' opposition party (MDB); but both parties operate strictly within a framework dictated by the armed forces. Many of the people who were actively involved in politics and in administrative and economic planning between 1946–1969 have been deprived of their political rights, as have others who were thought to have 'leftist, demagogic' leanings. Those suspected of either actively opposing the regime or endangering the 'honour' of Brazil are greatly harassed and most of this group have been forced to go into exile in Europe or elsewhere on the American continent.

There has been a consistent if perhaps not entirely intentional alliance of politicians, administrators, the aristocracy, academics, workers, artists and others – politically and ideologically at variance though they might be – vis-à-vis the plight of the black Brazilian. For their own reasons they all refuse to recognize that the special problems a black person encounters as a result of his colour and his heritage require special solutions.

Those who remain the chief beneficiaries of the inegalitarian socio-political and economic systems and are concerned about Brazil's image abroad find it highly desirable that no challenge is made to the status quo. The attitude of such people is that 'Brazil is a racial democracy and the subject is not open to discussion.'

On their part, politically and socially conscious intellectuals, students, progressive sections of the Church, and workers, recognize the gross inequalities in the socio-economic and political structures and want a just and egalitarian society with benefits and opportunities available to all. They are concerned primarily with the poor, the unemployed and the illiterate, but believe that to single out black Brazilians for special (i.e. preferential) treatment would be to deviate from the main course of reform. They certainly are not among those who believe that Brazil is a racial democracy, and they would agree that great prejudice as well as discrimination is directed against the blacks; but they believe that society must be seen as a whole and must be analysed in class terms. For this reason they regard blacks as part of the large sub-proletariat and not as a separate group meriting special treatment.

There is a third group in Brazil – and these people are in the majority – who accept without question the premise that racial prejudice and discrimination are not present. They feel that any problems experienced by blacks are a function of social and economic status alone. Such people believe in the 'money whitens' phenomenon, but unlike the second group they do not see their society in terms of class and consequently do not think in terms of restructuring it as a whole in a more egalitarian way.

And the blacks themselves? Those who have improved their economic and social positions would divide among the above three categories, probably with the majority in the third simply because continued personal advancement is not possible unless one avoids controversy. Those blacks who remain less fortunate – and the vast majority come into this category – vary in their outlook. Some are hopeful, trusting that the future will bring an improvement in their position or more probably in that of their children and grandchildren; some are convinced that racism exists and is responsible for their continued low position in society; others regard these questions as irrelevant to their daily lives.

Recently the following statement appeared in a Brazilian weekly magazine:

'The black person in Brazil has to learn to live like a black person. We have to spend less than we earn; we have to stop being workers and become employers.' These are the words of Raul Santos, a well-to-do black accountant in São Paulo who is involved in a movement aimed at uniting blacks. This organization has managed to have elected to the Federal Chamber of Deputies on an MBD (opposition party) ticket both Adalberto Camargo and Theodosina Ribeiro (as a State Deputy). Questioned about the movement Raul Santos has said: 'We are black and we rear children to understand they are black. It is only in this way that we can live without illusions and move towards greater integration in a society of whites.'* His is a call for black economic unity, as the magazine pointed out when it described the movement as working towards 'a form of "black capitalism" which does not accept the violence of Black Power'. But when the vast majority of blacks are still deprived of a strong economic base from which to work, how soon will it be possible for them to achieve and assert organized economic power?

THE FUTURE

Inasmuch as black Brazilians form part of that huge mass of the poor and disadvantaged which makes up the bulk of the Brazilian population, any solution to the problems of blacks will have to be worked out within this context. This is not to deny, however, that at the same time blacks face difficulties unique to themselves in Brazilian society.

On the surface, there would appear to be a great difference between the situations in the United States and Brazil because of the more open nature of racism in the United States. But as the American historian Carl Degler has demonstrated in his recent book *Neither Black Nor White*, there are many more comparable factors in the two situations than is suggested by posing them as opposites.†

Any black reaction to the Brazilian situation would appear to face two potent drawbacks: an official view considering 'racial activity' as subversive, and the overall attitude of society considering it divisive.

The Brazilian racial situation has been characterized by the openings offered to individuals to pull themselves out of the black or near-black category through marrying whites, becoming better educated, or improving their socio-economic status. But the individual path to escaping the black predicament (as in Brazil) certainly does not appear to improve the overall standing of blacks in society. It offers no meaningful way out for the masse*s* who are in a deprived position. Racism, whether openly or veiled, is not just an individual problem. The attainment of education, wealth and prestige, though mitigating some of the effects of racism on the individual who attains them, do not completely free him from his position in society as a black.

* *Veja* (weekly magazine), 13 January 1971.
† Degler, Carl, *Neither Black Nor White* (Collier-MacMillan, New York & London, 1971).

With the existence of mass communication and instant coverage of world events, the actions of blacks in other parts of the world cannot escape the attention of black Brazilians. It will be to the credit of Brazil if it allows the possibilities of black Brazilians becoming more conscious of what is happening in the United States and Black Africa, and their desire to become identified with these movements without in any way compromising or negating their Brazilianness.

5 THE TWO IRELANDS:

THE PROBLEM OF THE DOUBLE MINORITY - A DUAL STUDY IN INTER-GROUP TENSIONS

by Harold Jackson

Harold Jackson was born in 1932 and has been on the staff of the Guardian *in London since 1950. In 1966 he became the newspaper's roving reporter and covered the Middle East war, the Vietnam war, the Soviet invasion of Czechoslovakia as well as numerous lesser conflicts. In 1969 he was named Reporter of the Year by the International Publishing Corporation.*

He first went to Northern Ireland when rioting broke out in Londonderry in October 1968. He has returned many times since then and believes he has written more on that subject than on any other he has dealt with. Having had a rib cracked by rioters, been batoned by the police, gassed by the British army, and being agnostic in outlook, he claims to be totally neutral in his approach to the Irish question.

THE TWO
IRELANDS

PART ONE

NORTHERN IRELAND

There are no easy answers to the problems of Northern Ireland, and none is offered in this study. Its purpose is rather to bring out clearly for those who have only become aware of the place in the past troubled years the iceberg of political, religious, and social conflict which lies beneath the rioting, deaths, and material damage that have figured in the world's press.

The six counties of the province have existed as a separate political entity since the early 1920s, creeping reluctantly into life in the aftermath of the First World War and the achievement of independence for the major part of Ireland. The Protestant majority of Ulster did not want a separate Parliament, preferring to be totally integrated into the United Kingdom. But the Stormont legislature was imposed on them as part of the complex deal with which England hoped finally to rid itself of the Irish problem, a plague for three centuries or more.

The roots of the problem go almost as far back as the history of the islands. Ireland is a natural satellite of the British mainland – a fact that has contributed much to the intransigence of all the subsequent problems. It was colonized by the British who went to great pains to suppress any local rebellion against their rule. In the seventeenth century they offered grants of land, seized from the Irish, to any who were prepared to maintain forces to keep down the surrounding rebels, and thousands of Scots and English took up the offer – the so-called Protestant Plantation. For the most part they settled in the north-eastern counties, which were nearest their point of embarkation, and the Protestants there gradually evolved as a majority.

The differences of stock and religion and the circumstances of the newcomers' arrival ensured the enmity of their Catholic victims which survives to this day. It also created a siege mentality in the settlers themselves which has been just as durable. They were surrounded by people whose main discernible purpose was to obliterate them and the long campaign for Home Rule, primarily among the Catholics, in the nineteenth century heightened this paranoia. So Edward Carson, a diehard Protestant lawyer and politician (who later served in the British Cabinet) found a ready response among the Protestants when he promised to meet any surrender to the Home Rulers by the British government with force of arms. Not an inch of the soil was to fall under Catholic rule and these early slogans are ritually repeated on every formal occasion even now.

The birth of Northern Ireland was thus attended with all the suspicion of the English that has characterized the history of Ireland. The irony was that the people of the six counties who remained under the Crown felt more isolated than those who formed the Irish Free State. They saw themselves as the last stronghold of all the Protestant virtues which they had previously associated with England, and the subsequent years have accentuated this belief. This was made comically plain to me one day in Londonderry when an old woman, shaking with rage, seized my collar and screamed, 'We want to stay British, whether you bloody English like it or not.' Only with the safeguarding presence of Ulster within the kingdom, apparently, could an Ulsterman be sure of preserving his heritage.

But all this politicking also left the legacy that is found in some of the world's most intractable trouble spots – the problem of the double minority. Within their own enclave the Protestants of Ulster, one million strong, outnumber their Catholic brethren by two to one. But in the wider context of Ireland they themselves are easily outnumbered three to one. The inevitable and disastrous result was the advent of a ruling establishment with the reins of power in its hands but acting under the stresses of a besieged minority.

For its entire fifty years Northern Ireland has been ruled by the Unionist Party and for most of that time there has only been one issue – the preservation of the border with the Catholic Republic. Any real attempt at social, political and economic advance has hit this barrier and bounced back from it. And what has emerged has been a society suffering from a deep psychosis in which rational thought and action are invariably overtaken by emotional spasms the moment it comes under stress.

It is fatally easy for the detached observer to ask loftily why the two sides don't just do this or that to resolve their differences. There is always the calm assumption that reasonable men sitting round a table can come to terms with any problem. But it is vital to grasp that this sort of 'reason' is still far off in Ulster because of the enormous build-up in pressure created by the quite genuine

189

fears on each side. The fact that these fears are often based on incorrect assumptions does not mean that they are any less strongly felt.

Fifty years of failing to get any real say in the government of the province – and with little prospect of a change in the situation – have left the Catholics with a burning sense of grievance, reinforced by both institutionalized and informal discrimination. A man's first name – Sean, Liam, Eugene or whatever – is usually enough to reveal his religion and nothing will convince him that

a subsequent failure to get a job or a home was not governed by that fact.

Similarly, the Protestants see themselves confronted by a sullen minority which they believe only wants to destroy their constitution and put them in the hands of what they regard as one of Europe's most reactionary theocratic states. Article 2 of the Republic's constitution, for instance, says flatly that 'the national territory consists of the whole island of Ireland.' Every Catholic is thought to support that association wholly.

The Protestants in turn fear economic decline if they were to be taken over. The average wage in the Republic is some 20 per cent lower than in the north. They fear the loss of their relatively high standard of social services. Ulster spends £150 a head annually on education, housing, health and income benefits, the Republic only half of that.

They look alarmedly at the soaring Catholic birthrate – at 28·3 per thousand it is 40 per cent higher than their own – but omit to notice that the proportion of Catholics grows only slowly because they emigrate at more than twice the rate of Protestants.*

They look at the censorship in the Republic, at the need to smuggle in large quantities of contraceptives, at the prohibition of divorce, at the all-powerful influence of the Archbishop of Dublin, and they run terror-stricken to vote the straight Unionist ticket.

More subtly, they are intuitively aware of the urban working-class tradition of the industrialized north compared with that of the essentially peasant-orientated south, and they fear being swamped by 'the men from the bogs of Kerry and Connemara'.

And, let us be quite clear, the problem *is* one of the working-class. There have been no riots in the prosperous areas of Belmont or the Malone Road in Belfast. Here the well-to-do middle classes settle down in ecumenical harmony which has not broken down even under the tensions of the past years. Why should it? At the worst they are protected by their own mobility. They know that they have the resources to get up and go if they have to – and more of them are now contemplating it – to a calmer part of the province, to the Republic, or across to England.

But for the poverty-stricken ghettoes of the Shankill and Falls areas of Belfast, or the Bogside and Fountain districts of Londonderry, no such option is open. With a generally low level of

*A recent survey estimates that in fact Roman Catholics will not comprise a majority in the Northern Irish population before the year 2011 at the earliest, and possibly never; whereas almost all Protestants speak of it being in ten to twenty years' time.

industrial wages, high unemployment and an acute shortage of low-cost housing, the people trapped by their economic circumstances in these slums are ready victims of gut emotion whenever they feel a threat to what little stability they can cling to. It is those who have least to lose in material terms who need most to hug what they do have.

There were specific reasons for the riots which erupted in October 1968 and have continued more or less ever since. But, even if there had not been that particular spark, disorders would have come. They were endemic in the society and in the strains its people were facing. Conflict was present at the birth of Northern Ireland and it has remained part of its heritage, periodically breaking out into violence. Only recently, in the face of the latest trouble, have positive moves been made by the authorities to aim at the roots of the problem and due acknowledgement must be made to them. They have brought in equal voting rights for all elections, disarmed and reorganized the police, taken housing construction and allocation away from the bigots on the councils, introduced methods of complaint against the administration broader than those in England (though the Special Powers Act remains) and set up a Community Relations Commission to try to ease inter-group friction.

But, as so often happens with long-overdue reforms, no matter at what rate they are brought in they will never come fast enough for the deprived minority and, at the same time, they will represent a growing and unacceptable threat to the privileged.

The reasons for this is simply the total inability of either side to recognize the good intentions of the other. There was a notable example of this, again in Londonderry, following the usual senseless stone-throwing by Catholic youths in the Bogside. After some hours of skirmishing an English lieutenant-colonel called his troops back and approached the crowd. They stopped their bombardment and he talked to them, trying to calm the situation.

After about ten minutes a middle-aged man forced his way through the crowds and started haranguing the officer about three soldiers who had attacked a Catholic civilian who had given them a lift in his car. The man detailed the injuries the civilian had suffered and, when the officer said he had only recently arrived in the city and knew nothing of the incident, scornfully said, 'Well, it was in all the papers. You can read, can't you?'

It had, indeed, been in the papers. The account was of a court hearing in which each soldier was given a six-month sentence for the attack. But this fact had been entirely obliterated from the man's memory: all that remained was the 'atrocity' committed against a fellow-Catholic. The swift reaction of the establishment to the event had left no imprint at all and there was the sad feeling that it never would. Thus are the grievances tended and kept alive.

People believe what they need to believe. It is as important for the Catholic working-class to feel persecuted as it is for the Protestants to feel at risk from the enemy within and the Catholic hordes waiting over the border. This is what provides each side with the sense of community which is felt to be the only real security available. The manifestations of it have been seen on a hundred newsreels – the waving flags, the Orange sashes, the pictures of their folk-heroes, the Easter lily, the bowler hat, the incantations recalling the Troubles or the victory of King William III over the Jacobites in 1690.

The Ulsterman's passion for parades baffles the outsider. But it is a highly significant element in the sub-tribalism which is the kernel of the society. Its purpose is not only to display the trophies of each side's successes but also to delimit the territory each claims. The parades seldom cause trouble until they venture into areas regarded as the property of the other side. So a Civil Rights march cannot pass safely through the Protestant town of Claudy nor an Orange parade pass even the fringes of the Catholic Bogside area. Similarly, an attempt by the army or the police to stop a march over acknowledged territory produces a sense of outrage.

It is no use dismissing all this as primitive nonsense. Robert Ardrey has sought to show the importance of territory to all animals, man included, as a source of security. It cannot lightly be threatened, no matter how ritually, in a society as insecure as Northern Ireland.

So this is the first point to make: that virtually everyone in Ulster feels himself under threat and reacts accordingly. There is no inclination for reason or compromise simply because the most urgent need is to combat a threat which may seem small or non-existent to outsiders but looms obliteratingly over those locked into the situation. This is why so much of the effort of both sides is aimed against the established authority, be it the government, the police or the British army. Any action these bodies may take can be, and mostly is, interpreted as favouring the other camp and it produces the inevitable response.

But there are other reasons for this too. The political and economic geography of the six counties is relevant here. They are divided in both respects by the River Bann, which runs northwards to the sea more or less bisecting the province. To the east lie the counties of Antrim and Down and the city of Belfast, where Ulster's principal industries and main sources of employment are. These house the greater part of its population and are therefore overwhelmingly Protestant. The county of Armagh is a sort of halfway house, reasonably prosperous where it touches Down but increasingly depressed as one moves inland.

To the west of the river lie Londonderry, Tyrone and Fermanagh, mainly agricultural, underdeveloped, and containing large areas of Catholics. Most of the real bitterness of the conflict lies in these counties 'west of the Bann' and the very phrase conjures up a wealth of significance for an Ulsterman. Here is the longest history of discrimination and political thuggery. Because they felt themselves outnumbered the Protestants used every device to ensure their continued supremacy – rigging electoral boundaries, casting dead men's votes and seeing that jobs and homes went to their co-religionists. In the areas they controlled the Catholics did the same, though their power was obviously more restricted. But the combination bred an enmity which smoulders and flares and will continue to do so for years to come.

By its very nature Ulster is the poor relation of the U.K. Its location has attracted little outside industry from the mainland and it founded what prosperity it had on its ability to turn out great ships and fine linen. Both these occupations have declined catastrophically since the Second World War and the province has fought a desperate struggle to persuade reluctant Englishmen to take notice of its plight. Neither the British government nor industry has really responded – a penalty both of geography and of devolutionary government – and Ulster's unemployment rate of between seven and eight per cent has stayed far above the general British average.

But this overall figure masks the real internal problem in which the employment rate varies not only according to area but even, in some cases, from street to street. In the province's second city, Londonderry, the unemployment rate runs at 12·5 per cent and there are other places west of the Bann where it climbs even higher – to a peak of 23 per cent in Strabane. So the east survives at the expense of the west or, in Ulster terms, the Protestants at the expense of the Catholics. And the nature of employment in Londonderry exacerbates the social problem further. Its main work is the production of light textiles – shirts and other clothing – and most of those employed are women. The female unemployment rate is just over four per cent, that for men around 17·5 per cent.

This has meant that for years the main breadwinner in many

families has been the wife. A common sight in the city is to see groups of men lounging their day away in the desolate housing estates that lie above the centre. And what has grown out of this has been an embryo matriarchy in which the traditional dominance of the male has been steadily eroded. In a society which still observes the sort of cultural mores which persisted in England in the nineteenth century, this has had deep social and psychological effects. There is a constant need for the men to assert their masculinity.

Often this takes the form of excessive drinking and gambling. Pilot studies of the effects of long-term unemployment have suggested that it eventually saps virility in the strictly physical sense and this, too, may well have set up considerable stress. The result of it all has been a growing incidence of vandalism and blind destruction of public property – walls defaced, telephone kiosks destroyed – and a growing inclination to combat authority in the most flagrant way possible. This was one way to show that masculinity was still potent. Allied to the political grievances already simmering away it is evident why the riots that eventually broke out took the form they did.

There was an astonishing recklessness about the behaviour of the men involved. They seemed to lose all sense of personal safety as they hurled their stones and firebombs at the members of the Royal Ulster Constabulary. They were fired with the militant enthusiasm which Konrad Lorenz, in his seminal study 'On Aggression', discussed thus:

> One soars elated above all the ties of everyday life; one is ready to abandon all for what, in the moment of this specific emotion, seems to be a sacred duty. All obstacles in its path become unimportant: the instinctive inhibitions against hurting or killing one's fellows lose much of their power. Rational considerations, criticism, all reasonable arguments against the behaviour dictated by militant enthusiasm are silenced by an amazing reversal of all values, making them appear not only untenable but base and dishonourable. Men may enjoy the feeling of absolute righteousness even while they commit atrocities. Conceptual thought and moral responsibility are at their lowest ebb.

This has been true on both sides, of course. The militancy of the Catholics caused immediate reverberations among the Protestants and they responded in like fashion.

There have been few more shattering experiences in twenty years of reporting than to arrive among the smouldering remnants of Conway Street and Norfolk Street in the Catholic Falls area of Belfast. In a few hours at the height of the rioting in August 1969 ninety houses were methodically burned out by the Protestants from the nearby Shankill district. The inhabitants were first chased out of their homes – allegedly with the help of the Special Constabulary – and groups of men and youths then broke in and tossed petrol bombs in each home. I walked among the ruins with a middle-aged man who could only repeat time and again, 'They were decent working-class folk. What had they ever done?'

But the Protestant men of Second Street and Third Street, who were said to have been responsible, were also decent working-class folk as became evident when one talked to them later. Between the two groups lay a miasma of suspicion and misunderstanding which had far transcended any normal moral instinct. Some months afterwards a Protestant housewife stood with me contemplating the still-ruined streets and gave a long circumstantial account of how the Catholic savages had come marauding towards her home. She sincerely believed it and no amount of factual information – that there had been high barricades protecting her area, that no house in her street had been damaged, that all the losses had been on the Catholic side – could penetrate the mental barriers which the months had built up. Any action in defence of her tiny terraced house had been justified and the Catholics had brought on themselves the penalties they had suffered.

This, of course, is the material on which such militant leaders as Bernadette Devlin and Ian Paisley can work with such effect. Both have now become the ultimate symbols for each faction and both rely basically on the emotional responses they can draw from their followers. There are, in fact, curious similarities in their avowed dedication to the oppressed working classes and their radical opposition to the established regime. But they are not strictly comparable in quality, only in style. Miss Devlin's brand of revolutionary socialism is anathema to a large part of the Catholic working class who vote for her, as she herself admits. But her charisma in the sectarian politics of the province is what really counts. She is held to have beaten the system, to have shown that the underdog still has a bite, and that is all that matters.

Mr Paisley is working on easier material, if only because he is speaking to the majority. He is a demagogue of extraordinary talent and can gauge his audience's susceptibilities to a fine degree. To see him at work is to realize how simplistic is the view that the quarrel is religious. His speeches are spattered with references to the Reformation and attacks on the Church of Rome but these are a tribal shorthand for the real meat of his appeal. I have in fact never heard one person on either side make any reference to points of doctrinal difference. Only relatively late in the civil disorder did churches become a target for attack and, again, this was more because of their symbolic significance than because of any religious dispute as such. Once more it was the territorial nature of the buildings that mattered.

The bulk of Mr Paisley's speeches refer to the economic threat posed by the Catholics, to the competition they offer for jobs, homes and social benefits. He harps constantly on the virtues of the Protestant working-class and his attacks on the Unionist establishment are geared to its lack of contact with the grass roots of the constituencies. The Big House of the landed gentry who control the province is his real target and their vulnerability is heightened by a disparity of wealth between the social strata far greater than is usually found in Britain. His message is that those in authority are sapping the vitality of the country by their concessions to a minority which only wants to take over the hard-won perquisites of the Protestants. One of his favourite throwaway lines is that the Catholics are loyal 'not to the Crown but to the half-crown'. There is not much of a religious element in that.

The point about the emphasis on religion in the quarrel is simply that it is the handiest mark of difference available to the two sides. It is far easier to say that you don't like a man because he is of a different religion than to specify in detail all the things that are really resented. Much nearer the truth is that many Catholics dislike the Puritan virtues on which the majority group sets such store – an earnest approach to hard work, a rigid morality and an unforgiving attitude towards the transgression of cultural norms.

And the Protestant charges against the Catholics are that they are feckless and lazy, and they have too many children, that they expect everything to be handed to them on a plate and that they are dirty and smelly. These are precisely the charges which the English level against coloured immigrants and the Israelis against the Arabs. They are ill-defined and almost totally emotional in origin. They have nothing to do with the confessional persuasion of the group.

This fact is borne out in personal contact. At the individual level one never finds that these faults are singled out. No matter how viciously a man may attack the other religion as a group, he will always make an exception of those members he knows personally. The tensions are only generated at an impersonal level, a phenomenon again observed by Lorenz:

> The object which militant enthusiasm tends to defend has changed with cultural development. Originally it was certainly the community of concretely-known individuals of a group held together by a bond of personal love and friendship. With the growth of the social unit the social norms and rites held in common by all its members became the main factor holding it together as an entity and they automatically became the symbol of the unit.

The twin pillars of the Ulster problem are thus group loyalty and territorial integrity. If either or both these elements come under attack the response is total, unreasoning and devastating. Much of the trouble stems from the work of the Irish Republican Army or from the equally extreme Ulster Volunteer Force. But neither faction would make much headway if it did not have readily explosive material to work on and the reason for this volatility is a fine-crocheted network of interdependent tensions. These will only be unstitched over a long period of gradual reassurance for which no pace can be determined. It can only happen by consent: and consent in turn depends on the pace at which it happens. It is as simple but as complex as that.

One of the most fundamental and baffling aspects has been the apparently ineradicable tendency of the minority to attract discrimination. Not since the foundation of Ulster have they been prepared to contemplate assimilation. They rejected the concept of the state from the beginning and refused to participate in its institutions. Their need to retain their corporate identity was complete and has barely broken down since. The inevitable consequence has been that they have drawn to themselves the very antagonism and suspicion of which they complain.

Perhaps the clearest example of this, and the matter which many people take to be the root cause of the difficulties, has been in education. The Catholic hierarchy, as in many other countries, has insisted that its flock be taught in Catholic schools. This has meant that from the age of five years the two communities have led separate lives in the most formative area. They do not see one another, they are taught different aspects of their joint history, they inherit different cultural outlooks. The Catholic schools receive state support but there is a persistent allegation that they do not get as much money as the Protestant establishments. The government answers that this is simply because more pupils attend Protestant schools.

In spite of pressure, not least from the Catholics, that this system should be ended in favour of integrated education, the Roman Catholic Church has remained intransigent. Like many another exiled community – and this is in essence how it sees itself – it has a horror that unless its tenets are rigidly inculcated into its adherents they will gradually succumb to the mores of the major group.

There are any number of consequences that flow from this attitude. The main one, of course, is the alien quality which accrues to those who have not shared the experience of the majority. The system also ensures the ghetto herding of the Catholic population. It is a matter of administrative convenience for the parish priest that his parishioners and their institutions should be geographically close. The church is plainly the focal point and then the school. Around these two buildings cluster the population they serve, and so a ghetto is born. The Stormont government was not unaware of the problem but its energy in tackling it, never all that strong in any case, was sapped by the knowledge that any such attempt would be resisted root and branch by the church itself. To scatter the Catholics is seen as an attempt to dilute their tradition and absorb them, not least by the horror of intermarriage.

And the system has many attractions for the Protestants too. It has meant that the Catholics were handily grouped together for political purposes and could be manipulated more easily. The more flagrant case occurred in Londonderry before its political control was taken away and placed in the hands of an appointed commission. For local government purposes the city was divided into three districts – Waterside, North Ward, and South Ward. The first two had a predominantly Protestant population, the last was overwhelmingly Catholic. But the electoral boundaries were drawn in such a way that 4,300 Protestants in North Ward elected eight councillors, 3,600 Protestants in Waterside elected four, and 10,000 Catholics in South Ward elected eight. So, in a city whose population was 67 per cent Catholic and 33 per cent Protestant, there were twelve Protestant councillors to eight Catholic.

The gerrymandering cannot be defended. But it could not have been achieved so easily had it not been for the insistence of the Catholics in grouping together. The tradition goes back so far that there is no hope of eradicating it for generations; it is being perpetuated even now. The slum clearance schemes being carried out all over the province are achieved district by district. As new housing estates are completed, so the slum families are moved out to them to allow their former homes to be demolished. This means that the ghettoes are merely being transferred wholesale to another place and the problem revitalized for another eighty years or so.

The pressure to preserve things as they are often comes from the families themselves. Their disinclination to live in a mixed area has been heightened by the latest riots. As each outbreak has occurred families of one religion, isolated in a neighbourhood predominantly of the opposite persuasion, have received threats that they will be attacked unless they move out. These threats are often condemned by their neighbours but that gives little re-assurance. The family packs its belongings and seeks the security of living among its own kind, where there is both group and terri-torial protection. It is notable that in the new town of Craigavon, now being built as an industrial growth point, the grouping around the church will again be achieved when construction is finished. Economics is no guard against entrenched habits.

The point of this closeknit community emerges all too plainly when the situation boils over into crisis. Not the least astonishing manifestation to the outsider was the unbelievable rapidity with which protective barricades sprang up at the end of each street in the adjacent Falls and Shankill districts of Belfast once the rioting in Londonderry had started in August 1969. It was obvious that it would soon spread to the capital, so contagious was the fear it generated, and the inhabitants of the mean streets in the heart of the city prepared themselves within hours.

Within these enclaves a falsely cosy sense of belonging fell over the people. Bonfires flickering in the night helped to stoke the tribal quality and both Protestants and Catholics gathered around their separate pyres to seek comfort from the mass of their fellows. The taboos created by this marking of territory go deep. In Londonderry the police seemed totally inhibited from enter-ing the Bogside area though to the neutral observer there was no evident tactical reason for this reluctance.

At the height of the rioting I put the point to a head constable who was constantly urging his men not to pursue their tormentors. The government forces were strong enough and well-enough equipped to force a bridgehead down through the middle of the riot area and break the opposition into more manageable groups. 'You wouldn't understand, sir,' he said resignedly, 'not living here like we do.'

This reaction was also evident in the long period of the so-called Free Belfast and Free Derry regimes which operated in the Catholic areas of those cities. For months these enclaves were run by self-appointed vigilante groups who maintained order and refused all access to government forces. Both the Stormont administration and the British army came under intense pressure to reassert their rule but the political significance of such action was apparently more than they could contemplate and they held back.

This situation persisted in Belfast for nearly a year and was only ended when serious rioting developed and the troops were attacked with explosives. The effect on the Protestants of seeing the lawful authority of their province acquiescing in this territorial victory of their opponents was profound and lasting. They now felt they had no one they could trust to support them and there was the inevitable increase in their own militancy and readiness to use weapons.

Large quantities of arms were seized in the Catholic area and there was an immediate outcry that no search was being made of Protestant homes. The government introduced mandatory sentences for rioting and allied offences, but again the Catholics alleged that only their people had the appropriate charges brought against them while Protestants were brought before the courts on lesser counts which did not carry automatic penalties. 'After the recent riots in Shankill Road when seventy-six members of the security forces were injured,' said one statement by the Catholic defence committee, 'the police prosecutor chose to alter most charges to one which permitted nominal fines to be applied.' There was also the suspicion that Protestant juries would look after their co-religionists.

The cycle of action and reaction was therefore:

The Catholics alleged political and economic discrimination, which led to rioting;
Counter-riots broke out among the Protestants;
The government moved in to reassert its control;
Protestant action ceased;
The Catholics said that this proved the partisan outlook of the authorities and set up free zones;
The government came under sharp attack from the Protestants for permitting this defiance;
The Catholics reasserted their allegations of discrimination and more rioting occurred;
The authorities moved against it;
The Catholics said that no parallel action was being taken against Protestants who were stockpiling weapons;
The Protestants replied that they could not trust the government

to defend them and must rely on their own resources;
The government brought in measures to control both sides;
The Catholics alleged that these were being applied one-sidedly;
Both sides lost faith in the legal authority and further rioting
broke out in each camp.

Such a sequence allows all parties to claim that they were acting
under duress from the others and it is near enough impossible to
break, given the atmosphere of mistrust which prevails.

This mistrust often comes from factors which are beyond the
ability of the government to control. A crucial development in
Londonderry came through the decision of one manufacturing
company to close down its two factories there. It happened that
these employed large numbers of men from the huge Creggan
housing estate – the home of some 16,000 Catholics – and the loss
of the 2,000 jobs affected a majority of the families on the estate.
The reasons for the closure were never fully explained by the
complex turns in the affair, but seemed largely to hinge around
the efforts of the management to ensure continued low costs by
keeping wages down and by the determination of the employees
to achieve more efficient trade union organization to combat this
threat.

At heart it was an industrial dispute of a type familiar to every
advanced country but complicated by the fact that the company
received substantial government benefits as an inducement to operate in Ulster. The employees regarded these as enough of a
cost-cutting element to resist any encroachment on their earnings.
The dispute carried on for months and the government agreed to
place certain contracts with the firm to further its development.
But, in spite of this, the management declared 500 workers
redundant. A strike broke out over the issue and the decision to
close the factories was announced shortly afterwards.

There were immediate, and quite unprovable, allegations that
the government had acquiesced in a fraud which permitted the
firm to milk it of the concessionary benefits and close down
when these were nearing their end. The government responded by
saying that it had done all in its power to keep the plant open.
But the fact that it was Catholic families which had sustained the
blow, that it was again the men of the family who had fallen out
of work (and many found no further employment for years) and
that the government could find no alternative work to offer,
produced a fierce reaction against the authorities.

It apparently served to show once more that the Protestant
majority did not suffer, only the minority, though the government

was in fact powerless to exert any real control over events. It is just as powerless to stop industrialists deciding to site their new plants in the east of the province. The hard fact is that the administration is a supplicant to industry; it has to persuade manufacturers to bring work to Ulster when there are often sound reasons for them to go elsewhere.

Because three-quarters of the population lives in Belfast and the eastern counties, there is a greater pool of labour there, the communications are better, and that is where the factories tend to go. Houses are built where there are jobs, as are roads and all the rest of the industrial infrastructure. But, because 71 per cent of the people in the east are Protestant, all this is seen as positive discrimination by the Catholics.

There are the sins of omission too, though these operate in less tangible areas and are correspondingly difficult to bring home. Yet it is idle to pretend that they do not make an impact. Soon after the worst riots the then Prime Minister, Mr James Chichester-Clark, undertook a tour to inspect the damage. Not once did he enter a Catholic area, though they had been worst hit, and this simple fact incalculably set back the credibility of his government's genuine plans for reform.

Because of the nature of politics in Ulster they do not attract many men of real calibre, and this in turn perpetuates the inequities of the system. There have been any number of attempts to galvanize the inert middle-classes to see if they cannot retrieve the dwindling moral resources of Northern Ireland. But they have foundered on the rocks of dissociation to which the affluent (and therefore less tense) elements in the community cling as their last refuge.

There is no doubt that any who dare to advance towards the other community face considerable social and economic penalties for their temerity. In an introverted society the nuances of status are all-important and ostracism is a potent weapon. The Orange Order has become a widely known bogey to the world at large with its institutional dedication to anti-Catholicism. Its tentacles stretch deep into the province's establishment and its often baleful influence acts as a considerable brake on those who might otherwise come forward to work towards a settlement. The Order has the ability not only to expel transgressors, which it has done a number of times, but also to affect their business lives extensively. A Protestant businessman who became involved in the Civil Rights movement told me that a number of his customers had refused to trade with him as a result.

The same applies on the Catholic side. The government tried

to bring the minority more effectively into decision-making by a series of appointive commissions and similar statutory bodies. It was a sort of directed democracy but served, at least temporarily, to ease the inescapable political fact that one-third of the population is never going to reach the seats of power while factionalism determines the pattern of voting. However, many of those who agreed to be nominated were dismissed as Uncle Toms by their brethren and lost much of their credibility in consequence. This in turn set up the cry that the government was not sincere in its efforts, making use only of 'tame' Catholics. The total polarization of the communities brought about by the one-sided operation of the Special Powers Act to imprison Catholic suspects without trial made minority participation in government institutions virtually unthinkable, and many resigned as a protest.

The result of this refusal by the talent of the nation to take part in its own government is that decisions are taken by men of little insight or imagination. Their reactions to given stimuli are too often late and wrong, and they tend to make long-term judgements for short-term reasons. Thus the quality of life in Ulster suffers in a thousand subtle ways.

One example stands out vividly in my memory when there was an apparently inexplicable outbreak of rioting in a district of Belfast which had not till then given trouble and which had no evident reason to do so. There had been considerable tension in Northern Ireland in the period leading up to the anniversary of the Easter uprising in Dublin. Wide precautions were taken to ensure that the numerous Republican parades commemorating the event did not spark off more trouble.

There were small sporadic incidents but the period generally went off quietly. Then, on the last day, British troops were attacked quite unexpectedly by mobs of youths from the Ballymurphy estate which lies on the western outskirts of Belfast. The trouble persisted for three nights and a number of Protestant homes in the adjacent New Barnsley estate were evacuated by their occupants and subsequently ransacked by the rioters.

In a number of interviews with Cabinet ministers I found that all were completely baffled and put the trouble down to the usual scapegoat – Republican agitators. I also found that not one of them had visited the area. Subsequent interviews with the inhabitants over about four days seemed to me to make it all too plain what lay at the root of the riot.

The estate was comparatively new and the result of a slum clearance scheme. Its people had been moved from the city centre for resettlement and now found themselves largely isolated from their previous contacts. The bus services are infrequent and there is no entertainment available locally. The estate itself comprises a series of adequate but drab houses built in concentric circles so that it is wholly inward-looking. It also lies in a dip below the New Barnsley estate.

The picture that gradually emerged from my interviews showed that the Catholics had been expecting trouble in other parts of the province and were looking forward to seeing it on their television screens, a powerful medium for the fast transmission of community tension. There was a sort of vicarious involvement apparent and this was frustrated when nothing occurred. Whether as a result of agitation, which I doubt, or by some more mystic communication among the young men, they gradually assembled in the streets (notable for the signs prohibiting games in the open paved areas) and this in turn led to the rioting.

It is hard to convey to the men in power, who have had no direct contact with it, the lacklustre quality of life offered in a warren like Ballymurphy. It is equally hard to bring out the psychological effect on a minority group of their living literally beneath members of the majority. This factor certainly played a part in the Londonderry rioting when the people of Bogside grew increasingly outraged by the Protestants who peered down at them from the city walls towering above their enclave. This factor gave the people of Ballymurphy the feeling that their enemies could sweep down on them whenever they took the fancy, and induced a series of defensive responses in them.

It is this sort of complex reaction that calls for the delicate touch in governing which largely escapes those who control Ulster. Sometimes this is because of malice but far more often it arises from the blinkered attitudes inherent in their nature and upbringing. There is no ready cure for that.

Nor, for that matter, is there one which can resolve the province's deep-set problems. A major change might come if Ulster suddenly found itself with full employment and the modest affluence which most of the rest of the United Kingdom enjoys. But that is a hope on the far horizon and we shall have to wait long to see an end of this major aspect of the insecurity which accounts for some of the most primitive instincts in Ulster.

One of the effects of the recurrent upheavals has been to frighten away the industrialists most needed to help lower the tensions caused by too many people chasing too few jobs. Factories burned, work disrupted, production lost: no ordinary business-man will face that possibility. So the creation of new jobs falls behind target and the downward trend of economic and social forces quickens.

As the crisis has developed and quickened in pace its essentially emotional and irrational nature has become clearer and has led to a series of paradoxes which have increased the frustration of the participants. The response of the Catholics to the reforms introduced at the insistence of the Westminster government served to demonstrate that their political demands had been intended to establish that they had a grievance rather than that they were looking for redress. The original campaign for equal voting rights had carried the implicit undertone that they wished to operate the existing system. But, as attempts were made to meet this demand, so the Catholics rejected them and required that the Stormont government be abolished.

The massive military intervention of the I.R.A. in the political fight has enormously complicated the picture. Its political aims, in so far as they were ever stated by the most active element, were simplistic in the extreme and essentially nihilist. The removal of British rule and the reunification of the country were propounded as the total solution to the deep and complex problems of Ireland, ignoring the basic contradiction between nationalist aspirations and economic reality. The principal political leaders of the Catholic struggle are Social Democrats, yet the pressure under which they have come from the Provisional I.R.A. activists has forced them to campaign to join with one of the most deeply conservative governments of Western Europe. In as far as they have centred their struggle on the economic plight of their constituency, the solution they are offering would inevitably depress its material standards yet further to match those of the Republic, whose overall standard of living is only about 60 per cent of that in Britain.

On the Protestant side the Stormont government became enmeshed in an equally impossible dilemma. As violence increased and the climate for a reasoned political solution evaporated, the authorities committed themselves totally to the restoration of law and order. Only when peace had been reestablished would its leaders contemplate political negotiations. But the only way they could see to return the province to acceptance of the legal authority was to step outside the law. They introduced internment without trial, in contravention of the European Convention on Human Rights, and immediately sparked off a massive and militant reaction from the Catholic population. The scale of violence increased and, far from producing order, the move nearly threw Northern Ireland into civil war.

The treatment of the internees became a major issue and was eventually subjected to scrutiny by two tribunals appointed by the British government. The first acknowledged that the detainees' allegations of maltreatment were accurate but then lost itself in a semantic argument of what constituted brutality. The second was notable for a minority report by Lord Gardiner, a former Lord Chancellor, stating flatly that the methods used were illegal – a judgement apparently accepted by the British government, which promptly banned them. Then a decision of the Belfast High Court held that the actions of the British army in detaining and searching suspects were also illegal, an anomaly which had to be hurriedly righted in an overnight bill rushed through the Westminster parliament. So Stormont's commitment to law and order has simply produced a degree of official illegality, which has gravely undermined its credibility, and even greater disorder.

But the deepest paradox is, perhaps, that into which the British government has found itself dragged. Taking the original Catholic demands at their face value, Westminster insisted on the Stormont authorities introducing reforms to bring the practice of the province into line with accepted democratic norms. The perfectly rational foundation for this policy was that once the minority was reassured about its political and economic position within the community then the steam would go out of its campaign. A sense of bewilderment overtook British people at the apparently capricious refusal of the Catholics either to acknowledge or accept these measures. What the British have evidently failed to grasp is the essential inconsistency of the policy. The reason that Ulster was created was that the Irish Protestants did not believe in the possibility of the two communities living harmoniously together. Indeed, the very basis for the state was that the Catholics posed a threat to the Protestants which could only be forestalled by a separate jurisdiction with a Protestant majority. Since the underlying philosophy of London's policy now is that the Catholics do not pose a threat and can take their full part in the running of the state, it inevitably calls into question the whole basis on which Ulster was created. If the two communities can live peacefully together, why should partition survive?

Yet the Westminster government continues to proclaim its adherence to the existing constitutional position, failing to observe that neither community really accepts British rule. The Catholic leaders have called for British standards but do not want them implemented by the British: the Protestants avow their dedication to the British connection but resent direct rule from Westminster. On all sides the policies being pursued seem designed to produce the very results which their proponents do not want.

The inevitable frustrations engendered by these irrationalities have heightened the crescendo of violence and the targets chosen have become less and less relevant to the main issue. All the participants find themselves in what psychologists call a double-bind situation – the violence frustrates any political initiative and the lack of such initiatives increases the violence. The search for cause and effect has become a meaningless exercise but this does not stop the opposing elements from continuing to pursue it to establish their own case. The high degree of fantasy which has now entered the situation means that cool practical solutions have little apparent chance of success, since they would involve the abandonment of cherished illusions which offer those concerned an essential justification for their attitudes and actions. The likeliest element to fill this vacuum appears to be Realpolitik, which no one would welcome. This would mean that the violence of the I.R.A. would set off counter-violence from the Protestant extremists, that the British would ask themselves why they should remain in a situation which offers no visible advantage to them (particularly when their eyes are turning in the direction of Europe in any case), and that the Republic faces the prospect either of the northern Catholics being crushed or of acquiring an embittered Protestant minority which would throw an enormous political burden on its already-shaken institutions.

The imponderable question throughout has been how high a price anyone sets on his illusions, and we do not yet know the answer in Ireland.

PART TWO

THE REPUBLIC OF IRELAND

The situation of the Protestant population of the Republic of Ireland embraces another of those paradoxes which many regard as the main product of the island. They are a small and diminishing minority, their legal position is more evidently threatened than that of the Catholics in Northern Ireland, and yet they seem to be as content as can reasonably be expected.

There are now 130,000 adherents of the various Protestant denominations within the twenty-six countries – a noticeable drop even from ten years ago when the last census containing a question about religion was held. In 1961 the official return showed 145,000 Protestants. At the time of the census taken shortly after the partition of the island in 1920 the Protestants in the south were 221,000 strong. Sixty years before that, at the height of British rule in the days of what became known as the Protestant Ascendancy, there had been more than 800,000.

The present non-Catholic people of the Republic are, as might be expected, concentrated primarily in the counties immediately bordering Northern Ireland – Donegal, Cavan, Monaghan, and Leitrim. (The first three were once part of the ancient province of Ulster, which originally comprised nine counties.) The Protestants also form about nine per cent of the population of the capital, Dublin. Odd pockets are scattered elsewhere in the Republic, notably in the southern county of Cork, but their numbers are insignificant.

In many walks of life, however, the influence of this five per cent minority is out of all proportion to its size. The imposition of Protestant supremacy in Ireland still carries its historic aftermath and affects both groups in the old confrontation. For generations, for example, the banking business in the Republic was traditionally regarded as a Protestant preserve and this has started to break down only relatively recently.

It is not true to say that the Protestants act as an identifiable political force in any real sense – there is no such thing as a Protestant vote of any consequence – but they still maintain social distinctions which undoubtedly create irritation among the bulk of their countrymen.

It is hard to know how much of this springs from the clannishness of a religious group and how much is really based on the cultural nuances which are preserved in Ireland long after their disappearance in England, from where they were imported. The background of an economy leaning heavily on agriculture – which provides more than a third of the employment in the country – lends itself to the perpetuation of the class system based on land ownership and of all the associated exclusive leisure activities which were a notable feature of nineteenth-century England.

A social survey has shown that Protestants hold proportionately many more high-status jobs than the Catholic bulk of the country. There are 6·5 per cent of them working as company directors, managers, or company secretaries compared with less than one per cent of the Catholics. The proportion holding professional or technical positions is more than double that of the Catholics. About a fifth of the farmers working more than 200 acres turn out to be Protestants, four times as many as might be expected from their numbers in the whole population.

But there are indications that, like the Catholics in Northern Ireland, they do not wish to ally themselves with the apparatus of the state which took over from their forebears. In the senior ranks of the civil service they are greatly under-represented, holding only a little over one per cent of the posts. Their numbers in the army are miniscule, amounting to ·016 per cent of its strength. Only four of the 144 members of the Dail – the lower house of Parliament – are Protestants, and they are not there as representatives of their religion.

Some of this may arise from a positive rejection of the republican state. But undoubtedly there is also a feeling that the heavy nationalist fervour that has characterized the Republic since its birth may well work against a Protestant in jobs with evident political overtones. So they have tended to stay in the private sector.

In many ways their situation is the reverse of that facing the minority in Northern Ireland. There, though there are no overtly discriminatory measures written into Northern Irish law, the practice of the community puts the Catholics at a clear disadvantage. The notorious Special Powers Act, for instance, nominally applies equally to all citizens and allows the Government to detain anyone without trial. In reality it has only been invoked against those regarded as Catholic extremists.

In the Republic the potential for legal discrimination is much more clearly enshrined, but the affluence and social status of the Protestants largely tempers the effects of the restrictions. The most evident discriminatory measure is in Article 44 of the constitution, which declares that 'the State recognizes the special position of the Catholic church as the guardian of the faith professed by the great majority of the citizens.' Nobody seems quite clear just what this means but, equally, no one is in much doubt that it gives the hierarchy a tremendous ability to ensure that things go its way.

This in turn leads to other measures in the field of morals and religion in which the law of the state adheres to Catholic doctrine. Divorce is prohibited within the Republic and even the recognition of foreign divorces is not permitted. The manufacture, import, and sale of contraceptive devices is a criminal offence, even if the importation is for personal use. Blasphemy (which could well be committed by questioning Catholic doctrine) is a crime, though no one has so far had the nerve to put the law into action directly. A member of one Protestant sect was bound over to keep the peace for saying things 'offensive to the listeners' religious views'.

The censorship of books and films has the force of law and the standards by which the judgements are made relate closely to the requirements of the church. The climate seems to have improved noticeably lately and some of the more eccentric excesses to have stopped. But it is not open to a non-Catholic to have a free choice of reading matter.

Agreements between couples about what religion their children will follow are legally binding in the Republic. Since in practice only the Catholic church insists on such understandings in cases of intermarriage here again the reality of the law is discriminatory. The same is basically true of the laws about the adoption of children.

The fact is, however, that many of these laws are more or less openly flouted without penalty. The birthrate of the Protestants in the Republic is 13·2 per thousand, compared with 22·0 per thousand among Catholics. Part of the difference arises simply from the fact that a higher proportion of the Protestant population is elderly. But the massive smuggling of contraceptives is certainly reflected in the figures too. In parts of the country doctors are quite willing to supply the pill to those who want it, leaving it to the conscience of the individual to settle the religious problem. (A number of Catholic women get round the law by having the pill prescribed for skin complaints.)

The real problems of discrimination, however, come from the practices of the community rather than from legally defined areas. Both in the Supreme Court and in the High Court it was an unwritten understanding that at least one judge in each would be a Protestant. This has been quietly dropped and all the judges are now Catholics.

On paper the Republic's educational system also is eminently fair. All the country's secondary schools are privately owned and managed and the Government has introduced a scheme under which it agrees to pay £25 a year for every pupil, regardless of the denomination of the school. The reality of this is that the organization of the Catholic schools – around which the scheme was built – is such that the overhead costs are kept very low because they are integrated into religious orders. The Protestant schools employ lay teachers and, because of the small number of pupils, their incidental costs tend to come out high. The result is that, while the £25 really does provide a free education for Catholic children, it meets only about one-third of the Protestants' costs and parents must try to make up the difference.

This has produced a crisis in Protestant schools that is slowly strangling them. More and more children are gradually changing over to the Catholic schools because of their parents' despair at the standard of education and equipment in their own. The situation is often even worse in the primary schools, many of which can only afford one teacher to handle children ranging in age from five to fourteen. Some of the staff are untrained and unqualified and some are Catholics. As in Northern Ireland, it is arguable that integrated education is the best guarantee for future relations. But the essential element of choice is really being removed in the Republic.

A much knottier problem, and one at the heart of the Protestant situation in the Republic, comes with the question of inter-marriage and its consequences. Because of the isolation of so many Protestant families and because of the generally small representation of their religion in the country at large, it is inevitable that many will seek their partners from the majority group. This produces recurring personal crises.

The marriage of Catholics to those of another religion is governed by the Papal decree 'Ne temere'. This lays down a number of obligations which devolve on both parties and tend to be rigidly applied by the Catholic hierarchy in Ireland. One prominent Protestant cleric, Dr Kenneth Milne of the Church of Ireland, made his attitude to the way the decree is operated plain to an audience of Catholics at a seminar:

'I object to "*Ne temere*" not because it affects us numerically but because it strikes at the very root of family life. I would go almost so far as to suggest that it is contrary to the spirit, if not the letter, of the basic human rights. It is the great obstacle that exists to the integration of Catholic and Protestant society in Ireland, whatever it may achieve in terms of un-conditional surrender.'

The essence of the decree is that it makes the non-Catholic partner of the marriage a second-class element. In particular it extracts an undertaking that the children of the union will be raised in the Catholic faith – an undertaking, as already observed, enforceable in law.

Furthermore the spirit in which many priests approach an intermarriage also creates great tensions and resentments. A special dispensation for the Catholic partner is necessary, and there are often long and unexplained delays in providing it. In many cases an individual priest will simply refuse it altogether, though one in a neighbouring parish may well be more amenable.

The ceremony itself is not conducted in the body of the church but in the sacristy and the whole atmosphere has a sort of hole-and-corner quality highly offensive to religious susceptibilities.

The Irish Economic and Social Research Institute has estimated that in 1961 something like a third of the Protestant men married that year and a fifth of the women had a Catholic partner, and it concludes that intermarriage is having a major impact on the Protestant population in the Republic. Certainly, the fact that the children of those marriages are almost certain to join the Catholic majority means that there is a steady decline in the number of Protestants. The view taken of this development depends on the judgement of the observer, but it must be regarded as an actively discriminatory factor in normal life.

There are sporadic attempts by the Protestant communities to try to counter this trend by social exclusivity. A common instrument in this is the organization of functions whose under-lying purpose is to ensure that those of marriageable age have an opportunity to meet their co-religionists away from the influence of the majority group. The churches organize dances and the like at which no invitations are issued to Catholics. Inevitably it sets up hostility, less because it poses any real threat to anyone than because of the long and sad history of the relationships between the two religions. So one resentment feeds on another.

Here and there are dotted the almost fossilized survivors of the days before independence, the men and women who have been dubbed the West Britons. They are less strident than they were about their continued allegiance to England but they try to send their children to English schools, assiduously maintain as many barriers as they can to normal social interchange, and retain outlooks and intolerances that would make them totally out of place even in the country whose values they claim to follow. They are not numerically significant but the impact of their behaviour is disproportionate. As with the communal tension in Northern Ireland, the perceived reality overtakes actuality.

But perception, after all, is what matters in social development and it is foolish to imagine there is no potential for conflict despite the present reasonably relaxed position. There are few insuperable problems for the Protestants in the Republic be-cause they form only a twentieth of the whole population and because their general standard of wealth and social position is unusually advanced.

This happy compromise would change very rapidly if the constitutional claim of the Republic to rule the whole island became a reality. The position would then be that the Protestant minority would rise to 25 per cent of the overall population and institutional and informal discrimination would become far more potent.

A change in the provisions relating to the Catholic church is already a matter of active discussion in the Republic, though it is naturally meeting with considerable opposition. A committee of the Dail recently came to the unanimous conclusion that it was time to amend the laws on divorce and contraception, though again nothing active has been done about it.

These are the first signs of a willingness to attempt some sort of compromise in fundamental positions which could lead to better relations between the two sides in Ireland. But there remain many areas of potential friction which will need decades to eliminate.

In demographic terms the outlook for the Protestants in the Republic is gloomy. They are a disproportionately elderly group, they are declining numerically, the natural maintenance of their strength is heavily and adversely affected by their age and the pressures from the majority group, and their very problems are accentuating the rate of their decline. Their cohesion is apparently also failing now and there seems to be a far greater willingness to assimilate than when the Republic was founded fifty years ago.

Politically this may in the long run turn out to be beneficial. There has been little or no economic discrimination against Protestants as individuals, whatever may have been the case with their institutions, and they have continued to do rather well. Obviously, extremist attitudes towards them may be found here and there but they are far from typical of the broad pattern.

So, as Protestants become a less consequential element in the community, the pressure against them tends to slacken on the political front. And here may lie the route through the complexities that face the two communities in Ireland. If public opinion in the South can be persuaded that there is no further need to shield itself in law from Protestant encroachment, then there may be a corresponding softening of majority opinion in the North.

The rate at which private attitudes will also change is obviously unpredictable, but there is no reason why the Irish should turn out to be all that different from other communities facing tensions. Experience has shown that formal changes usually set the pattern for an easing of private intransigence.

This will do little to resolve one of the major underlying difficulties – the generally ailing economic state of the whole of Ireland and the gulf in prosperity between the North and the

South. But a little economic give here and a little social take there might at least produce a more amenable climate in which to start grappling with the fundamentals.

BASIC INFORMATION

Ireland (North and South)
  Area: 32, 595 square miles
  Population: 4,500,000
  Religions: Catholics 74·7 per cent. Protestants 25·3 per cent

Northern Ireland
  Area: 5,242 square miles
  Population: 1,500,000
  Religions: Protestants 65·1 per cent. Catholics 34·9 per cent

Administrative divisions:

	PROTESTANTS	CATHOLICS
Antrim	*75·6%*	*24·4%*
Belfast	*72·4%*	*27·6%*
Down	*71·5%*	*28·5%*
Armagh	*52·7%*	*47·3%*
Londonderry	*49·5%*	*50·5%*
Fermanagh	*47·0%*	*53·0%*
Tyrone	*45·4%*	*54·6%*

Government: There is a bicameral legislature consisting of a House of Commons with 52 members elected by universal adult suffrage and a Senate of 26 members elected by the lower house. The United Kingdom government retains responsibility for taxation, foreign relations, defence, and overseas trade and has a constitutional right to intervene in domestic government. The Stormont government was suspended for a year by Westminster in March 1972.

Republic of Ireland
  Area: 27,136 square miles
  Population: 3,000,000
  Religions: Catholics 94·9 per cent. Protestants 5·1 per cent
  Administrative divisions: There are 26 counties and the City of Dublin. The small Protestant population tends to be concentrated in the capital and in the counties of Donegal, Cavan, Monaghan, and Leitrim, which border on Northern Ireland.
  Government: There is a bicameral legislature consisting of the Dail Eireann, which has 144 members elected by universal adult suffrage by proportional representation. The Seanad Eireann has 11 members nominated by the government, 6 elected by the universities, and 43 elected by vocational and cultural interests.

CHRONOLOGY

1801. Ireland included as part of the United Kingdom and Irish Members of Parliament sit at Westminster.
Mid 19th century. Growing agitation for Home Rule for Ireland which is resisted by successive British governments.

The Fourth World

1916. Republicans stage an armed uprising in Dublin and declare a republic. Leaders subsequently executed.

1919. Republicans gain most of the Irish seats in the General Election and proclaim a National Parliament.

1919–20. A war of independence breaks out against the English.

1920. The Westminster parliament passes the Government of Ireland Act partitioning the country.

June 1921. First Northern Ireland parliament officially opened.

1922. The Irish Free State is formed.

1922–23. A civil war in the south between those who support and those who oppose the terms of the treaty between England and the Free State. The supporters win.

1932. The Free State becomes a republic.

1949. The Republic leaves the Commonwealth.

1968. Growing civil rights agitation in Northern Ireland culminates in serious rioting in Londonderry in October.

Feb. 1969. The Northern Ireland prime minister, Capt. Terence O'Neill, calls a general election to get a mandate for reforms, but the result is indecisive.

May 1969. O'Neill resigns and is replaced by a compromise candidate, Maj. James Chichester-Clark.

Aug. 1969. A Protestant parade in Londonderry leads to large-scale rioting which quickly spreads to the capital, Belfast. The British army is called in to restore order.

Sept. 1969. The Northern Ireland government embarks on reforms of the franchise, the police, and local government.

May 1970. The Republic's prime minister, Mr Jack Lynch, dismisses two members of his cabinet and they are put on trial for alleged complicity in smuggling arms into Northern Ireland. Both are acquitted.

July 1970. Armed rioting breaks out in the Catholic district of Belfast and the area is put under military curfew. Mandatory sentences for those causing civil disorders are introduced by the Northern Ireland government.

Sept. 1970. The reform of the housing administration, the last of the measures designed to meet Catholic demands, starts its passage through the Northern Ireland parliament, amid considerable Protestant opposition.

June 1971. A move by the Stormont government to create special parliamentary committees to increase Catholic participation is first welcomed by Opposition M.P.s but they later boycott Stormont altogether after the deaths of two men in a shooting incident in Londonderry.

Aug. 1971. Internment without trial introduced and a number of Catholic suspects arrested. It produces a violent reaction with many deaths and allegations that detainees have been maltreated.

Nov. 1971. The detainees' allegations are sustained by a Tribunal of Inquiry, and the British government appoints a committee to review interrogation methods. The Dublin government complains to European Commission on Human Rights.

Jan. 1972. Thirteen people shot dead by British troops after a march in Londonderry. The Dublin government recalls its ambassador from London and demonstrators burn down British Embassy in Dublin. The Lord Chief Justice of England appointed to inquire into shootings.

March 1972. Stormont is suspended, for one year, by the Westminster government; Mr Whitelaw is appointed Secretary of State for Northern Ireland.

6 RELIGIONS IN THE SOVIET UNION (1960–71)

by Michael Bourdeaux, Kathleen Matchett
and Cornelia Gerstenmaier

*Rev. Michael Bourdeaux is Director of the Centre for
the Study of Religion and Communism, and is also a
Research Fellow of the London School of Economics
and Political Science.
Kathleen Matchett and Cornelia Gerstenmaier both
work at the Centre for the Study of Religion and
Communism.*

RELIGIONS IN THE SOVIET UNION (1960–71)

INTRODUCTION

By Michael Bourdeaux

The Soviet regime clashed head-on with the Russian Orthodox Church after the Revolution of October 1917. It seemed obvious to the Revolutionaries that if the new era was going to engender a different society, the temporal power of the Church must be broken. They were wrong, however, in seeing the Church as nothing other than a negative force. The 'corruption' of the Church in 1917 has consistently been used as an excuse for what ensued, but the degree to which this was prevalent should not be exaggerated. On 19 January 1918, as one of the first acts of his reign, Patriarch Tikhon excommunicated those who were attacking church property and personnel. In view of the desecration which was occurring, moderation of language could hardly be expected:

> Recall yourselves, ye senseless, and cease your bloody deeds. For what you are doing is not only a cruel deed; it is in truth a satanic act, for which you shall suffer the fire of Gehenna in the life to come, beyond the grave, and the terrible curses of prosperity in this present, earthly life. By the authority given us by God, we forbid you to present yourselves for the sacraments of Christ and anathematize you . . . (Quoted in W. C. Fletcher's *A Study in Survival*, S.C.M. London, 1965, p.13).

Words such as these led to a hardening of attitude among religious people, but were not themselves the cause of the physical measures against the Church which the Bolsheviks had introduced at the very onset of the Revolution. It is doubtful whether these would have been avoided even if the attitude of Church leaders had been more conciliatory, given the militantly anti-religious character of Lenin's philosophy and of Bolshevik ideology.

Conversely, members of sectarian groups (Baptists, Seventh-Day Adventists and others) who had been badly treated under the Tsars, were treated leniently for a decade, but after 1927, when

Stalin began to bring every aspect of Soviet society under rigorous control, they suffered severely.

The 'dual allegiance' of some religious groups has also been cited by the Soviets as a reason to treat them with suspicion. Roman Catholics, Jews, Adventists, Jehovah's Witnesses do indeed have a focus outside the country, but many other governments, faced with the same fact, have still accepted people of these faiths as loyal citizens.

It was not until the Second World War, when Stalin made concessions to the Church in order to gain its maximum support during this time of national danger, that religious people gained any real respite, but even this was not to be permanent.

In 1960–64 Mr Khrushchev's government began (but could not finish) a new campaign of attempted liquidation against all religious groups. The Communist Party of the Soviet Union had, it seems, never relinquished its ultimate aim of rooting religion out of society altogether. Mr Khrushchev seems to have been disturbed by an increase in church weddings among *Komsomol* members and even some full Party members were known to be taking their children for baptism. This more active anti-religious policy was affirmed by an important meeting in January 1960 of the Society for the Dissemination of Political and Scientific Knowledge, which controlled atheist propaganda in the U.S.S.R. It was attended by several of the most senior politicians in the land, and it seems to have been the spearhead for the renewed attack against religion.

The call was for all Party and administrative organs to use the full force of the law against any religious practices which could be regarded as illegal. This meant, in the first instance, the disbanding of the numerous unregistered congregations which had grown up throughout the country, many of which had never received any satisfactory answer to their petitions to register. But in practice the local authorities received a *carte blanche* from Moscow to reduce religious practices in whatever way they thought most effective and without any particularly scrupulous regard for the law or the rights of believers. There seems to have been some local rivalry in chalking up anti-religious successes and the provincial newspapers gave prominence to articles claiming the closure of churches of all denominations and describing the court cases of priests and ministers who had allegedly broken the law or who were accused of moral dereliction.

At the highest administrative level, G. G. Karpov, head of the government's Council for Russian Orthodox Church Affairs, who had come almost to a 'live and let live' agreement with the

Moscow Patriarchate, was replaced by the much tougher V. A. Kuroyedov. Metropolitan Nikolai, who for many years had been responsible for the foreign policy of the Russian Orthodox Church and who was regarded by many as the most likely successor to the aged Patriarch, was dismissed without explanation and died in obscurity in 1961.

Mr Khrushchev himself re-affirmed the general direction of the campaign at the XXII Party Congress (*Pravda*, 18 November 1961), but its culmination did not come until early in 1964. Apparently what had been achieved so far was insufficient in the eyes of the Party. *Pravda* (2 March 1964) summed up the situation as follows:

Now that the building of communism has been broadly undertaken . . . the Party has put into its programme the task of fully and completely overcoming religious prejudices . . .

The resolution of this problem, as set out by N. S. Khrushchev at the XXII Congress of the C.P.S.U., envisages the elaboration of concrete measures to establish a system of atheist education and in every way to strengthen the programme of scientific atheism.

The Ideological Commission of the Central Committee of the C.P.S.U. has devoted an augmented session to the questions of forming a scientific world outlook for Soviet people, giving them an atheist education and creating a scientific system of atheist activity. L. F. Ilichov, Secretary of the Central Committee of the C.P.S.U., in his speech, and the participants at this meeting, discussed the question of atheist education from all angles. The practical recommendations worked out by the Ideological Commission have been approved by a decree of the Central Committee of the C.P.S.U., 'Measures to strengthen the atheist education of the people'.

Party organizations, ideological institutes, *soviets*, trade unions, the *Komsomol* and creative organizations now have a concrete plan of action which, when operated, will allow religious survivals to be very successfully overcome.

One may assess the nature of Mr Ilichov's advice from an article he wrote in *Kommunist* ('The Communist') in January 1964. He sanctioned the most direct resolution of the 'problem' by, for example, advocating the break-up of religious families:

We cannot and must not remain indifferent to the fate of children, upon whom fanatical religious parents are carrying out what is virtually spiritual rape.

The 'education programme' of which *Pravda* spoke in 1964 was implemented and is still in operation, but there has been a more careful approach to the whole question of religion in the Soviet Union since the beginning of 1965. Some imprisoned Baptists were granted an amnesty during that year, the nationwide closure of churches was halted, and there were a few exposures in the press of illegal or morally dubious acts against believers – such as the case of Alla Trubnikova, who was attacked by the chief atheist periodical, *Nauka i Religia* ('Science and Religion'), for having disguised herself as a pilgrim in order to insinuate herself into a convent (October 1965, p.14). V. N. Lentin, in his book *The Seventh-Day Adventists*, published in 1966, said that the overwhelming majority of the members of this sect were honest people, loyal in their attitude to the state (p. 37). Similar statements were made about the Baptists – almost always, however, excepting the group of reformers (see Chapter 4). More recently, nevertheless, one Soviet article almost justified this reform movement by saying that it grew up principally where churches had been 'closed without due reason' (*Questions of Scientific Atheism*, Vol. 9, 1970, p. 98).

After the fall of Mr Khrushchev there was a call for an end to the anti-religious excesses, not because there had been any basic change of heart by the regime, but because the physical measures which had been so widely employed were considered to be counter-productive. G. Kelt, an atheist lecturer writing in the central Soviet youth newspaper, *Komsomolskaya Pravda* ('Komsomol Truth'), on 15 August 1965, puts this succinctly:

Insults, violence and the forcible closing down of churches not only fail to reduce the number of believers, but they actually tend to increase their number, to make clandestine religious groups more widespread and to antagonize believers against the state.

The essential dilemma of Soviet atheism has never been more aptly summarized. Official policy did not allow this debate to continue long. There has again been a hardening of attitude over the last three or four years, accompanied by the arrest of numerous believers who are considered to have broken the law, but there has been no return to the massive repressions of the early 1960s.

The full evidence is lacking on why the Soviet State is still so actively hostile to religion – still, indeed, committed to eliminating it completely – while the historical circumstances of 1917 have so entirely changed.

The 1960–64 campaign might be partially explained as an

P

attempt by Mr Khrushchev to show that, although he was committed to de-Stalinize in the political field, he remained a 'good communist' at heart. As a practical demonstration, he picked upon religious believers, perhaps thinking they were the most defenceless sector of the population, among the most cowed and unlikely to hit back. If this was indeed his reasoning, he miscalculated. As Kelt indicated in the words quoted above, it was precisely the renewed pressure which caused believers to find a voice – indeed many voices – in their own defence. Even worse (from the Soviet point of view), this latter phenomenon seems to be directly connected with the widespread increase of interest in religion on the part of young people, to which the Soviet press now testifies almost weekly in some form or other.

There is probably also a more deep-seated reason for continued Soviet hostility to religion, a reason which perhaps the activists do not always fully realize themselves. This is that religion provides the only legal alternative ideology to communism in the Soviet Union. The church is persecuted, in fact, because it threatens the monolithic ideology, but the threat is, of course, more potential than actual. In a recent case, however, the state did feel itself more directly menaced. Extraordinarily severe sentences were imposed at a closed trial in Leningrad (November 1967) on leaders of the All-Russian Social-Christian Union for Liberation of the People (see Michael Bourdeaux, *Patriarch and Prophets: Persecution of the Russian Orthodox Church Today*, Macmillan, London, pp. 341–4). This is the one group known to have a definite political programme inspired by Christianity. Vladimir Ogurtsov, the leader, then aged thirty, was given a prison sentence of fifteen years, Mikhail Sado (30) thirteen, Yevgeni Vagin (30) ten and N. Averochkin (28) eight. In March–April 1968 a further seventeen young people were sentenced for up to seven years for belonging to the same group.

Because of the terms of reference, the pages which follow deal mainly with the 'negative' side of the situation. Every fact stated is fully documentable – but it remains important to remember that side by side with the continuing repression of religion in the Soviet Union, services go on in registered buildings of worship in virtually every major city of the country; a few religious publications appear; unofficially, religious literature is written and circulated to believers in whatever way is practicable – mostly in typescript – and this is increasing, despite the attempts of the authorities to stop it. A certain proportion of young people are turning to religion; the churches are, despite all obstacles, being regenerated in many ways.

A report similar to that which follows could have been written to document any of the above statements, but here a brief excursus is given on one of them only – the involvement of young people, as seen through the eyes of Soviet atheist writers.

A. I. Klibanov and L. N. Mitrokhin, the first being the most eminent and objective writer on religion and atheism in the Soviet Union, published an article in *Questions of Scientific Atheism* (Vol. 3, 1967), in which they stated:

> Among those Baptists under the influence of the 'Action Group'* there are more young people than in the other Baptist congregations. Sometimes members of the 'Action Group' have simply been called 'young Baptists'. Young people numbered more than half in some of these groups (p. 105).

More recently Volume 9 of the same publication (1970) has devoted a whole article to religious influence among the younger generation. It bears witness to an increase here by every major Christian denomination in the Soviet Union and by several minor ones as well. Here is a quotation from this book referring to religious instruction of the young:

> In the Russian Orthodox Church, similar functions are carried out by activists from the church or from church circles. Where there are no Orthodox churches, this is done by so-called 'nuns'.† They exercise surveillance over the internal, spiritual life of families, especially over the young, and they 'supply' children for baptism, creating public opinion and a 'micro-environment' of support for religious education (pp. 70–71).

To broaden the perspective, a very great deal of the unpublished writing being produced by younger authors in the Soviet Union today hints at a more than passing interest in religious themes. The poet-publicist, Yuri Galanskov, for instance, included a defence of the Pochaev Monastery in his unofficial periodical, *Phoenix* 1966. The Ukrainian nationalist writer Valentyn Moroz has written extensively about the persecution of the Eastern-Rite Catholic Church‡ in his homeland.

It has been necessary, in a work of this length, to take some arbitrary decisions. Not all religious 'minorities' could be included

---

* The same reform Baptists referred to above.

† The term *chernichki* is applied to women who keep religious life going in areas where there are no churches. Among them may be some 'nuns' (in the technical sense) who have done such work since the closure of their convents.

‡ Catholics who use the Slavonic liturgy (often called 'Uniates' or 'Greek Catholics').

for reasons of space. This report therefore excludes the Lutheran Church (Latvia and Estonia), the Georgian Orthodox Church and the Armenian Church, which, except for a few scattered communities, are confined to certain geographical areas where local factors play an important role. These could not be discussed without embarking on a study of general Soviet policy towards the relevant nationalities, which would have taken this report well beyond its terms of reference. Therefore it directs attention to those minorities which are spread more widely, even though the total number of their adherents may, in some instances, be smaller than those concentrated in a single defined area. Within these limitations, this report tries to maintain some sort of balance between various religious groups. Attention in the Western press has, up to now, been devoted mainly to the Jews, Baptists and the Russian Orthodox. While this study could not ignore these categories, it was felt to be important to direct attention at some length to other minorities, even though this meant leaving aside most of the massive available documentation on the Baptists and the Orthodox. In the case of the Jews, the Western press has principally drawn attention to them as an ethnic minority. This report treats them from the religious point of view and it therefore does not deal with the vast amount of evidence relating to other areas of Jewish life.

PART ONE

LAW AS AN INSTRUMENT OF SOVIET COMMUNIST PARTY POLICY

By Michael Bourdeaux

DISCRIMINATION AND THE LAW

It has sometimes been said that if only the authorities would abide by their own laws, the major areas of discrimination in the Soviet Union would disappear. Such statements are, at best, only partly true, for although there are certain guarantees of the individual's rights contained in the Constitution (technically the 'supreme law'), the fact is that, in practice, the Penal Code can negate what are supposed to be the superior freedoms of the Constitution. In no area is this contradiction more damaging to the rights of the individual than in that of religious life.

This study supports this last statement by a brief summary of the relevant laws, followed by a longer examination of the way these affect some of the major religious bodies.

The Soviet law, as at present formulated, declares church and state to be separated. Furthermore, it makes it quite clear that discrimination against the individual for reasons of his religious adherence is a punishable offence. These, originally, were Leninist principles. The first ever decree of the Soviet State on religion, in the formulation of which Lenin himself had a considerable say, proclaimed that it was illegal 'to restrain or limit freedom of conscience' and that 'every citizen may profess any religion or none at all'. This was logically reflected in the first Constitution (July 1918), which stated that 'the right to religious and anti-religious propaganda is recognized for all citizens'.

The right to 'religious propaganda' was obviously a highly significant principle – indeed, to Stalin it was an emotive one, which was not compatible with his policy of gathering every strand of Soviet public life under his personal scrutiny or the direct control of the secret police. The basic legislation, 'On Religious Associations', was promulgated on 8 April 1929 and it reflects, in almost every one of its sixty-eight paragraphs, the determination of an emergent dictatorship to impose itself totally upon religious life throughout the land. This law would obviously have made a mockery of the Constitution if the latter had been left unchanged. Therefore the Constitution was modified a month later (18 May 1929) to exclude the right to 'religious propaganda'; the right of 'religious profession' was substituted (contrasted to the right of anti-religious propaganda). The present Article 124 of the Constitution reads even more severely, with 'the freedom to hold religious services' as the believers' sole right. Significantly the Stalinist law, 'On Religious Associations', stands to the present day, not only unrepealed, but powerfully – if sporadically – enforced.

Even more significant for this report is the trend of penal (as opposed to civil) legislation in the 1960s. One of the old laws (Article 142 of the Penal Code) merely set a maximum sentence of one year's corrective labour or a fine of fifty (new) roubles for infringing the laws governing the separation of church and state. New and much harsher penalties were brought in on 27 June 1961 (Article 227) for certain specific offences. Leaders of groups proven to have encouraged religious activities 'harmful to the health of citizens or encroaching upon the person or the rights of individuals', or of inciting people 'to refuse to participate in social activity or fulfil their civic obligations', or of 'enticing minors' to participate in such activities, are now liable to a maximum sentence of five years' imprisonment or exile, with or without confiscation of all their property. Other participants in such activities (who are not leaders) are liable to serve up to three years in prison.

On 18 March 1966 the net was cast even wider, for the old Article 142 was emended to provide a maximum penalty of three years' imprisonment for second offenders – and such offences were designated as 'the performance of deceitful acts with the aim of arousing religious superstitions among the public', as well as the more expected ones of refusal to register congregations, the organization of religious education for the young and the printing and distribution of literature calling for an infringement of the law.

It is hardly possible to clarify what the published Soviet legislation envisages – not only because of certain glaring contradictions which we shall enumerate below, but also because of the imprecision of the wording. What offences, for example, are covered by the nebulous phrase, 'the performance of deceitful acts', which we quoted above? It is not impossible that at the height of some Soviet anti-religious campaign a prosecution counsel might stand up in court and claim that the celebration of Holy Communion in a Russian Orthodox church contained precisely the intention of 'arousing religious superstitions' – though this has never yet happened, as far as one knows. There would be no legal mechanism in the Soviet system for asserting at this point the technically superior guarantee of the 'right to hold religious services' contained in the Constitution.

Even supposing it were possible completely to clarify the published legislation, this would still not shed sufficient light upon current Soviet practice towards religion. This is because we know for a fact that some areas of religious life are regulated by secret laws. To quote the most obvious example, the very existence of the government's central controlling body, the Council on Religious Affairs, is nowhere allowed for in the published laws; even less, therefore, are its statutory powers publicly defined. This body is known to pass on to its local representatives series of secret instructions which sometimes go well beyond the public laws. Some of these instructions have become known to Soviet believers and have been sent out of the country. A translation of one set appears in *Religious Ferment in Russia* by Michael Bourdeaux (Macmillan, London, 1968, pp. 14–16) – and their authenticity was not denied by Metropolitan Nikodim of the Russian Orthodox Church when he was questioned on the subject in the West, nor subsequently by Soviet agencies when they reviewed this book. The late General Secretary of the Soviet Baptist Church, Alexander Karev, has referred to such unwritten laws. He spoke clearly of them during discussions with the reform Baptists in 1966.

Inevitably, therefore, if we approach Soviet practice towards religion from a purely legal standpoint, we find ourselves faced with many contradictions. It is all part of the pattern that the penalties for discriminating against believers on the grounds of their religion appear never – or at best very rarely – to have been invoked, though there has been occasional restitution of rights to believers who have been illegally deprived. Since 1966, for example, it has been an offence punishable by up to three years' imprisonment (Penal Code, Article 142) 'to refuse to accept citizens at work or into an educational institution, to dismiss them from work or exclude them from an educational institution, to deprive them of privileges or advantages guaranteed by law, or similarly to place material restrictions on the rights of citizens as a result of their religious adherence'. Hindering the celebration of religious rites which do not disturb public order has long been an offence (Article 143). Although the Soviet press has from time to time criticized the excesses of anti-religious zealots, there is no known documentable example of any penalties having been imposed for the offences cited. It is possible, however, that such penalties, when invoked, would not be publicized in the press. At the same time, every clause of the law which could restrict the basic human rights of Soviet believers has been exploited within the last decade, not to mention a number of practices which have no basis in public legality. The basic lot of the average Soviet believer seems to have been less severe under Brezhnev and Kosygin than it was under Khrushchev in his later years – yet the existing framework of past practice and present legislation offers no future security against a new physical anti-religious campaign such as took place in 1960–64.

Clearly, then, the empirical approach adopted in the rest of this study is of greater help to us in assessing the actual situation than a legalistic one.

Here are some signposts (not an exhaustive list) to the types of discrimination which have been practised towards religious believers in the Soviet Union within the last decade. Not all categories apply equally to all religious denominations, but every one is reflected at some point in the text. The list below gives some indication – though a far from exhaustive one – of the groups worst affected in each category.

1. OUTLAWING OF A WHOLE DENOMINATION. There is no published legal basis for this and it must be regulated by a secret

decree (Eastern-Rite Catholics in 1946, Pentecostals, Jehovah's Witnesses, many sectarian offshoots of the Orthodox Church and the Old Believers,* etc., throughout Soviet period).

2. ENFORCED MERGING WITH OTHER DENOMINATIONS, LOSING INDIVIDUAL TRADITIONS. There is no legal basis for this (Uniates from 1946 could continue to worship only by becoming Orthodox; the Pentecostals could become accepted from 1945 by merging with Baptists; similarly Evangelical Christians from 1944 and Mennonites† from 1963).

3. ENFORCED CLOSURE OF LEGALLY EXISTING PLACES OF WORSHIP. After the passing of the 1929 Law very few congregations could in fact register, but many did during and after the Second World War. In 1960–64 there was a massive illegal closure of places of worship throughout the Soviet Union, helped by state ownership of all religious buildings (1918 Decree, Article 13; 1929 Law, Articles 27–30). Only a very few of those churches closed have since been re-opened (all religious denominations, as far as is known).

4. STATE CONTROL OF ALL LEGALLY EXISTING PLACES OF WORSHIP. This is achieved by the registration regulations (1929 Law, Articles 2, 5 and 6), enforced by the supplying of lists of members to communist authorities (Article 8) and the right of veto by those authorities over the membership of the executive body (Article 14). These provisions, guaranteed in law, at the same time break the fundamental constitutional requirement of the separation of church and state (applies to every religious congregation in the U.S.S.R., except those which manage, illegally, to exist unregistered). There are many documented instances of refusal by the authorities to grant registration (Baptists and Orthodox). The authorities are not legally obliged to state reasons for refusing registration, but must say yes or no within a month of receiving the application (1929 Law, Article 7). Often they simply do not reply (Baptists, Orthodox). There seems to be no legal basis for the registering of clergy, but this is a further *de facto* control. There is known also to be illegal state interference in church appointments, but these last two are complex subjects which could not be discussed within the confines of this report.

5. BANNING OF ALL RELIGIOUS ACTIVITIES, EXCEPT WORSHIP WITHIN REGISTERED CHURCHES (Constitution, Article 124). (a) For worship

* The Old Believers went into schism with the Russian Orthodox Church in the seventeenth century, since when the Old Believers have splintered into at least fifty known groups.
† A Protestant Anabaptist group of Dutch-German origin.

anywhere else, permission must be sought two weeks in advance for each individual instance (1929 Law, Articles 59 and 61). Permission is often not granted (Baptists). (b) The clergy's activity is restricted to their own areas (1929 Law, Article 19). (c) There is an absolute ban on all relief work (1929 Law, Article 17). (d) No parish societies or discussion groups may be organized (1966 Decree). (e) Technically the law does not ban the production of religious literature, provided it does not call for 'infringement of the laws' (1966 Decree) – but *de facto* it is treated as illegal (Baptists, Orthodox, Roman Catholics) except for the single central periodical and occasional inadequate editions of calendars, the Bible, prayer and hymn books produced by some denominations. (f) All Sunday schools are banned – as is informal religious instruction for minors (1966 Decree); restrictions are placed even on that given by parents to their own children (1968 Marriage and Family Law). (g) Permission must be sought for any 'special theological courses' for the training of clergy (1929 Law, Article 18). The existence of permanent theological seminaries is not recognized in law and presumably their existence would end at once if the 'special permission' were to be withdrawn. Only Orthodox (three),* Roman Catholics (two), Armenians, Georgians and Moslems (one each), have formal institutions, though the Jewish *yeshivah* in Moscow is still reported from time to time to be nominally open. Lutherans and Baptists have correspondence courses, and the Russian Orthodox Church has also been able to increase its theological education by instituting one of these. (h) No other religious institutions whatever are recognized in law, though the Orthodox and Armenian Churches retain a few monasteries. Many existing monasteries were closed in the early 1960s (Orthodox). (These provisions relate to all religious groups.)

6. NO RELIGIOUS ASSOCIATION (PARISH) IS A PERSON AT LAW (1918 Decree, Article 12; 1929 Law, Article 4). Therefore no parish can contest its rights at law, nor can it formally apply for redress (all religions).

7. NO CENTRAL REPRESENTATIVE BODIES. No provision for these is recognized by the law. Discrimination is exercised here: Orthodox, Old Believers, Baptists; Moslems and Buddhists are allowed representative bodies; Jews and Roman Catholics are denied them. That of the Adventists was abolished in 1960. This is a violation of the constitutional principle of separation of church and state.

* If one counts the two academies for advanced education separately from the seminaries (although they occupy the same buildings as the institutions at Zagorsk and Leningrad) the figure would be five.

8. RESTRICTIONS ON LOCAL AND NATIONAL CONGRESSES. These may be held with especial permission (1929 Law, Article 20) – but *de facto* they take place only in the rarest instances. Baptists alone have, since 1963, established the principle of regular (in this case, triennial) congresses. Some denominations have never been permitted to hold a convention of any kind (Jews), while in 1946 the Uniates met under duress, only to abolish themselves! In May–June 1971 the Orthodox Church held its first congress since 1945.

(All the above restrictions are in some sense related to the law; those which follow have no basis whatever in law – indeed, the 1966 elaboration of Article 142 of the Penal Code theoretically protects religious believers from them.)

9. DEFAMATION IN THE PRESS WITH NO RIGHT OF REPLY. This has been frequently practised against all denominations; the worst instances since 1966 relate to Baptists, Adventists, Uniates, Jehovah's Witnesses and – less directly – to Jews.

10. ROOTING OUT OF OLD RELIGIOUS CUSTOMS. There has been an attempt to replace these by 'new socialist traditions' (*sic*). (Orthodox, Old Believers, Roman Catholics, Jews, Buddhists, Moslems are affected more than Protestant denominations.)

11. DISCRIMINATION AT PLACES OF WORK. This is strictly illegal, though still practised (Baptists and other sects, more than Orthodox and Moslems).

12. DISCRIMINATION IN HOUSING. There has sometimes been a refusal (strictly illegal) to grant adequate housing for religious believers; houses used – sometimes with permission – for religious gatherings have been attacked, windows smashed and doors broken down (Orthodox, Baptists, Adventists).

13. DISCRIMINATION IN EDUCATION. Quite apart from the restrictions on religious education noted in No. 5 (f) above, believers are often quite illegally denied equal opportunities in secular education (all denominations). Religious children at school often have to bear scorn from teachers and other pupils (Baptists, Orthodox). Students are often expelled from colleges and universities if their faith is discovered.

14. DISCRIMINATION IN PUBLIC LIFE. This is not dealt with in the text because known believers of all types are, with very few exceptions, effectively prevented from reaching positions of authority and therefore being discriminated against 'publicly', as it were. There are some known instances where believers have, for exam-

ple, been expelled from the Communist Party, from managerial positions or from teaching posts. It is a nationwide feature of Soviet life, however, that believers are almost always prevented from reaching such positions in the first place – even from entering higher education. This phenomenon is difficult to document, though it is made explicit in Party pronouncements on religion and is well known to all observers of the Soviet scene. It is mainly in the world of the arts that persons known to be believers are active in public life, though individual instances have been reported in the scientific sphere and even the higher military command. Such political and social discrimination at a very early stage in the person's life inevitably also leads to economic discrimination – the emergence of believers as a huge group of second-class citizens (in an economic as well as civil rights sense) throughout the Soviet Union.

PUNISHMENT FOR BREAKING THE LAW
Over the last decade, there have been thousands of documented instances in which the full force of the law has been used against believers, not to mention the existence of cases which we do not know about, in numbers which may only be guessed. Crippling fines have been widely imposed, often repeatedly on the same people, for organizing religious worship (the one 'constitutional right' of every Soviet believer) – often in cases where registration has been applied for but not granted. Most of our documented information here comes from Baptists.

Orthodox and Uniate believers (from bishops down), Jehovah's Witnesses, Roman Catholics, Baptists, Adventists and Pentecostals have been imprisoned for three or five years, sometimes even longer, for activities which are not considered criminal by the great majority of other countries in the world. Even some other communist countries permit religious practices which are considered illegal in the U.S.S.R. (for example, religious instruction for children). In many documentable instances false accusations of moral delinquency have been brought (see especially the case of the Orthodox Archbishop Iov of Kazan).

Special punishments have been meted out to those who have attempted to continue their religious observances in prison. There are a few known instances where the especially harsh conditions to which believers have often been subjected in prison or during interrogation have led to serious physical injury (the Baptist, Georgi Vins) or even to death under torture (the Baptist, Nikolai Khmara; the Orthodox monk, Grigori Unka). In January 1971 one of the most highly revered lay writers and reformers of the Russian Orthodox Church, Boris Talantov, of Kirov, died in prison as a result of his harsh treatment and inadequate medical attention.

PART TWO

THE RUSSIAN ORTHODOX CHURCH AND ITS OFFSHOOTS

By Michael Bourdeaux

One of the chief aims of Lenin's 1918 decree on the separation of church and state was to ensure that the special privileges which had been granted to the Russian Orthodox Church since the tenth century should be abolished and that henceforth all religious denominations should be treated as equal before the law. In practice, however, there are still certain privileges accorded to the Orthodox Church (reportedly still holding the allegiance of as many as 30 million people) not equally shared by other religious groups. There is no other denomination which is accorded all of these privileges: extensive representation abroad (at the World Council of Churches, the Vatican, numerous international religious conferences and through the staffing of certain parishes and bishoprics situated outside the frontiers of the Soviet Union); the publication of a journal; the maintenance of theological academies and seminaries. Admittedly, the extent of the last two was severely restricted within the decade of the 1960s, but at the same time the scope of the first was considerably increased. Despite the repeatedly avowed intention of the Soviet regime to eradicate religion in the long term, the central organization representing nationwide Orthodoxy (the Moscow Patriarchate) has become an integral part of foreign policy since the Second World War.

There is a danger, however, that the splendour of public display of ritual at home and the regular travel abroad of Orthodox dignitaries (usually young) may blind world public opinion to the realities behind this appearance.

Extensive documentation is now available, for example, about the nationwide enforced and illegal closure of churches during the latter part of Mr Khrushchev's regime (1960–64). Precise statistics are unobtainable, for we do not know for certain the number of open churches either before 1960 or now. However, the number of closures given by two young Orthodox priests resident in Moscow, Nikolai Eshliman and Gleb Yakunin, in a careful study of church-state relations during the early 1960s, is 10,000 – or roughly half of all those which existed at the beginning of the Khrushchev period. An official anti-religious publication in Moscow (*Propagandist's and Agitator's Handbook*, 1966, p. 149) said later that the number of churches remaining open was as low as 7,500, but there has been no subsequent confirmation of this. Since 1964 this mass closure of churches has ceased, but despite hints that individual buildings have been re-opened since then, the number is not substantial and there has been no return to the *status quo ante*. The most reliable source for information on the re-opening of churches since 1964 is Archbishop Basil (Krivoshein), of the Moscow jurisdiction, who has placed the number at 500 – or perhaps 5 per cent of those closed (*Episkepsis*, Geneva, 14 July 1970, p.7).

Exhaustive documentation on the enforced closure of churches in the Soviet Union will be found in the present author's *Patriarch and Prophets*, Chapter 4. Details in this are culled from a number of Soviet press reports, from the official *Zhurnal Moskovskoi Patriarkhii* ('Journal of the Moscow Patriarchate'), and from several accounts by Soviet citizens, unpublished in the Soviet Union. One of these is Alexander Solzhenitsyn, who has written a passionate lament on the closure of the churches, 'Along the Oka'. The late Boris Talantov, author of a detailed case-study of the strangulation of parish life in the Kirov diocese, states that forty churches there out of seventy-five were closed in the years 1960–64. He quotes the example of one village, Korshik, where 477 people complained fruitlessly at the closure of their church, thus proving that this action was quite illegal and demonstrating the damaging effect on believers of neither being able to own their own building nor being able to have legal representation as a religious body.

It is quite certain that many other parishes have unsuccessfully tried to gain registration since 1964, despite the legal provision that any group of twenty people of the same denomination has the right to be granted a building for worship. Especially well-documented is the case of 1,500 believers in the city of Gorky who applied in 1967 for the right to open a church. In a letter to Dr Eugene Carson Blake, General Secretary of the World Council of Churches (published in the *Church Times*, London, 1 August 1969), thirty-six of the petitioners state that in the whole of their city, with a population to 1,200,000, there are at least 120,000 Orthodox Christians. Yet they have between them only three small churches, all situated at a distance from the city centre and holding no more than 4,000 standing people altogether. They said that the provision of an extra church would help to relieve the dangerous overcrowding in the existing buildings. For months these petitioners received no answer whatsoever (despite the law which states that a reply must be received within a month) and finally they were told that the existing churches were sufficient. The application was repeated several times in 1967–8 and finally in desperation the case was made known to the outside world. It is not known whether Orthodox believers have since received back any of the thirty-seven churches in Gorky which had been expropriated under Lenin and Stalin.

Orthodox believers of Naro-Fominsk, near Moscow, have been trying for forty years to have a church registered. They recently appealed to Metropolitan (now Patriarch) Pimen and their cause was also taken up by the young civil rights leader, Valeri Chalidze (not known to be a Christian).

Chapter 3 of *Patriarch and Prophets* gives details of the closure at the beginning of the 1960s of most of the sixty-nine monasteries and convents and of five of the eight theological seminaries.

During the later 1960s there have been far fewer cases of slander against Orthodox believers in the Soviet newspapers than during the first part of the decade. It was formerly common practice to accuse Orthodox believers (from Archbishops down) of all kinds of debauchery and immorality. In the fifty-four years that such allegations have been made (with some intermissions), there has not been a single instance where the person slandered has been given any right of public reply. In many instances, the articles appear to have been written in order to pre-judge a forthcoming trial and to whip up public sentiment against the accused.

A most notable case of such public slander occurred in 1960 (*Izvestia*, 8 July). Archbishop Iov of Kazan, an Orthodox dignitary of nationwide reputation, was accused in the courts of financial dishonesty and of swindling the state of more than two million roubles' income tax. Not content with reporting such a charge, the author of the article, L. Zavelev, accused the Archbishop of being a fascist who supported Hitler when a large part of the Ukraine came under Nazi rule during the Second World War. Zavelev incidentally reveals the independent mind of the Archbishop in stating that he had refused to support the Kremlin-inspired 'peace campaign' in the late 1940s and 1950s, which was considered an essential part of the duty of every Orthodox bishop. Some such fact is likely to be the real (though undisclosed) basis of the charge against him. Zavelev also gives inadvertent testimony to the high regard in which his flock held the Archbishop, stating that many of his warmest supporters followed him from one diocese to another in succession to work for him. Iov allegedly received 840,000 roubles in 1958–9 in excess of his salary, which were used to support 'his luxurious villa, cars, drinking bouts and orgies'.

If all these accusations were true, his sentence of three years was extraordinarily mild, considering that many prople were shot for 'economic crimes' in the Khrushchev era.

Presumably Archbishop Iov was released in 1963, at the conclusion of his sentence, and retired quietly. But his story was not over. In November 1967 the Holy Synod appointed him Archbishop of Ufa. Such an act would have been inconceivable, either on juridical or on ecclesiastical grounds, if there had been any truth in the accusations. It virtually proves that the original accusations were a fabrication, backed up by the slander of the government newspaper, *Izvestia*.

This was very far from being an isolated episode at the time, but there have been no such scandals since the fall of Khrushchev (though Archbishop Yermogen was deposed and retired to a monastery in November 1965 for his opposition to illegal state interference in church affairs).

In November 1967 and April 1968, twenty-one young men were given sentences of up to fifteen years' imprisonment for belonging to a Christian political group sympathetic to Orthodoxy, the 'All-Russian Social-Christian Union for the Liberation of the People'. This was undoubtedly a special case.

In 1969 the prominent Orthodox layman Boris Talantov was imprisoned for three years, and did not survive his sentence. The lay church writer, Anatoli Levitin, was arrested soon after Talantov and was held without trial for nearly a year before being released. In 1971 he was arrested again and in May was sentenced to three years' imprisonment. He is now in a labour camp and because of ill health friends fear for his survival. In 1970 an article appeared attacking Father Pavel Adelgeim (*Pravda Vostoka* – 'Truth of the East' – 12 and 26 July) at the time of his trial and sentence for allegedly beating his wife and the daughter of another family. The parish priest of Kagan (Uzbekistan) appears, nevertheless, to have been a man of irreproachable character. No. 13 of the underground human rights journal *Chronicle of Current Events*, produced regularly in Moscow with painstaking accuracy, states:

Father Pavel Adelgeim was arrested in December 1969. He is widely known in church circles. Thanks to his initiative and energy, the believers in Kagan have been able to erect a new stone church in place of the old barn which had been serving as a local place of worship. Pavel Adelgeim, a young, well-educated priest, and a good preacher, enjoyed great love and authority among his parishioners. His ecclesiastical activity was beyond reproach from the viewpoint of the civil law.

Even the writer of the first *Truth of the East* article, before launching into his accusations, confirms the good character of his priest:

He did not indulge in even the smallest weaknesses, to which many old priests had succumbed. He did not drink and performed the religious rites earnestly. The faithful came from all parts of Kagan to hear Father Pavel's sermons: he spoke with eloquence.

In view of this testimony from an atheist writer, quite apart from what was written in the *Chronicle*, it is highly unlikely that there was any substance in the subsequent accusation of physical violence for which Father Adelgeim is now in prison. The second article in *Truth of the East* gives what is almost certainly the real reason for the sentence – the fact that this priest was a supporter of Fathers Eshliman and Yakunin and of Anatoli Levitin, all of whom have been campaigning for greater religious freedom in the Soviet Union. Their manuscripts were found among Father Adelgeim's private papers during a search of his flat.

A very recent report from reliable sources states that Father Boris Zalivako has been moved from a camp at Mordovia to the much harsher prison at Vladimir for spreading religious influence among other prisoners (*The Times*, 31 December 1971).

One of the best-documented instances of discrimination against Orthodox believers in the matter of housing is quoted in *Patriarch and Prophets* (p. 165). As an example of discrimination in education, the case of the Old Believer, Yevgeni Bobkov, is well known. Anatoli Levitin has described in some detail (*Dialogue with Religious Russia*, Paris, 1967, pp. 21–9) how this brilliant law student at Moscow University was expelled in 1959 because he was a standard-bearer in processions in the Old Believer church in the city.

In contrast to the Baptists, very little is known about the treatment of Orthodox believers in prison. It is quite certain, however, that there has been brutality, at least during the early part of the decade. For example, the Spiritual Council of the Pochaev Monastery described the death of their young novice, Grigori Unka, in prison in 1963:

His mother received a telegram from the prison administration in Chertkov . . . that her son had 'died suddenly' and she should come and take the body away . . . The mother collected the remains of her beloved martyr-son. Although the body was dead and silent, it still bore many visible marks – it was black and blue from bruises, the clothes were torn and pierced right through the side. He had never had any physical ailments, but had been tortured to death in his prime at twenty-five years of age.

This event does seem to be attributable to the sadism of an individual prison officer, rather than part of a planned campaign, for over the past decade we have hard evidence of the death of less than ten believers of all denominations in prison. In none of these instances, however, is there any record of the guilty officers having been brought to trial.

It seems most likely that the sects which have gone into schism this century (such as the 'True Orthodox Church') and which the Soviet State has rendered illegal, have been treated worse than the Orthodox Church itself in recent years, though at the moment we lack concerted information. No. 15 of the *Chronicle of Current Events* (August 1970), for example, contained information that three female members of the 'True Orthodox Church' were in Women's Camp 385/3 in Mordovia and were nearing the end of of their ten-year sentences. Despairing of justice within the system, members of this group have sought to organize their religious lives entirely underground – thus under prevailing conditions they may expect severe penalties when exposed, even though Soviet accusations against them of being 'monarchists' have not been backed up by evidence. An excellent new book, *The Russian Orthodox Church Underground* (1917–1970) by W. C. Fletcher appeared recently and its information considerably supplements what could be written here.

The Old Believers seem to have kept relatively in the background, as they have learned to do from long habit, and may not have suffered so much as some other denominations in the anti-religious campaign of Khrushchev. After 250 years of persecution under the Tsars, they are better adapted than most to ride out modern storms and await calmer times.

Q

PART THREE

THE ROMAN CATHOLIC CHURCH AND
THE UNIATES

By Cornelia Gerstenmaier

ROMAN CATHOLICS

Roman Catholics are persecuted in the Soviet Union today not only for their religious steadfastness but also for their international connections and because, to some extent, they are identified by the authorities with 'separatist' elements among Ukrainians, Belorussians, Latvians and above all Lithuanians, who make up the main body of professing Catholics in the U.S.S.R. The journal *Bezbozhnik* ('The Atheist') has said:

> A more bitter struggle is being waged against the Catholic clergy than against the Russian Church, because Catholic organization is more powerful than that of the Orthodox, and Catholic ideology is better adapted to the general conditions of life (18 March 1923).

In these words are written the whole tragedy of Roman Catholics as it was to unfold under Stalin.

Right up to the present time this Church has never been able to restore any central leadership. Ironically, the Russian Orthodox Church is today represented in Rome, but not the Soviet Catholics, though since the Second Vatican Council some bishops have been able to visit Rome.

The only dioceses functioning today are in Latvia and Lithuania, while the difficulties in remoter areas are more acute. It is also reported that outside the Baltic and the West Ukraine there are only four Catholic churches open. As a result of state control, contact between dioceses and congregations inside the U.S.S.R. has practically ceased. Thus, for example, young people from Belorussia may not study at the seminaries of Kaunas and Riga, although they come under Baltic jurisdiction.

There are probably over three million Roman Catholics in the Soviet Union today. Here we devote special attention to Lithuania, where the greatest concentration of them resides.

When Stalin annexed Lithuania shortly before Hitler invaded it, he took over a strong and impressively organized Church. But since then monasticism, once flourishing in over a hundred centres, has been abolished. Religious journals are no more. Only a prayerbook has been printed in an inadequate edition since the Soviet annexation. Almost half of the churches have been closed. The number of priests has fallen from 1,480 in 1940 to 864 in 1967. Of four seminaries, only the one at Kaunas remains. It is restricted to a maximum of thirty seminarists, so there are no more than five or six ordinations a year. Although the old dioceses remain in name, there are only four active bishops instead of fourteen, while two others are under permanent house arrest.

The Roman Catholics received fewer concessions than some other religious groups during 1954–7, while 1960–64 was a period of renewed physical persecution. Quite apart from slanderous attacks against individual priests and bishops in the press, such as we know from the examples quoted under the Orthodox Church, travel restrictions were placed on the clergy even within their own dioceses, which prevented them from holding confirmations and dispensing the sacraments. People known to attend church or who had had their children baptized found that discriminatory measures were taken against them. Writing to Mr Kosygin in 1969, forty Lithuanian priests described a young couple who were married in church and as a result had their permission to buy a piece of building land rescinded.

The Communist Party set up a special committee in Vilnius in 1963 with the special task of devising new secular 'rites' to replace traditional ones, but this campaign seems to have had even less success in Lithuania than in other parts of the Soviet Union.

Soon after the worst of the Khrushchev anti-religious crisis had passed, a very few concessions were made to the Lithuanian Catholics. The most important of these was the episcopal ordination in Rome of Mgr Labukas-Matulaitis, administrator of the archdiocese of Kaunas. He, in turn, was able to consecrate a new bishop of Telsiai in 1968 and two assistant bishops at the beginning of 1970.

These concessions should not, however, be taken as an indicator of a nationwide improvement in the situation. For example, the *Chronicle of Current Events* (No. 15, August 1970) reports the forcible closure by the police of two Catholics churches in Belorussia in 1969–70.

The most significant feature of the last decade is that the Lithuanian Catholics, like the Orthodox, the Baptists and the Jews, have found a voice. In January 1968, sixty-three Lithuanian priests (the number is given in Vatican sources) complained in a letter to the Soviet Council of Ministers and the Council for Religious Affairs about intrusions by the state into religious life. The specific case in point was the attempt by the authorities, through the enforced *numerus clausus* concerning the seminaries, to hinder the training of priests.

A few months later, in December 1968, priests of the diocese of Vilkaviskis addressed a similar petition to the Lithuanian bishops and diocesan administrators. They wrote:

The present seminary is obviously unable to fulfil the needs of the Lithuanian Catholic Church. Therefore a well-justified question arises: Who in the near future will proclaim God's word? Who will give the sacraments? Who will officiate at the mass? It is not the leadership of the seminary but government officials who have the decisive voice about the acceptance of candidates to the seminary. Those wishing to enter the seminary are dissuaded, many are forbidden outright to enter it, without any explanation (*East–West Digest*, 6, 1970, p. 181).

The authorities responded to this appeal with severe reprisals against many of the signatories. Some were dismissed from their posts, or forcibly transferred, others were imprisoned and sentenced in secret trials. The Dean of Vilkaviskis, Konstantinas Ambrasas, was dismissed from his post, charged with having neglected to inform the Council for Religious Affairs of the imminent protest by the priests of his diocese. Although more than a thousand members of the congregation signed an appeal on his behalf and sent a delegation to the diocesan administrative office at Kaunas and to the local official for religious affairs, Ambrasas was forcibly transferred to Leipalingis.

In September 1970 Fr A. Seskevicius was sentenced in Lithuania to one year's imprisonment for hearing children's catechism before first communion. A year later two more priests, Frs Zdebskis and Bubnis, also of Lithuania, were similarly sentenced. There have been mass protests about this by the Roman Catholic faithful.

Despite all the state oppression and notwithstanding the increased atheist 'education' campaigns, reports agree that church attendance remains very high. Even today only a few children in Lithuania are said to be unbaptized.

References to Catholic *samizdat* (clandestine) publications appear even in the official Soviet press:

A few priests – the best educated – sometimes write and try to distribute so-called memoirs, papers, discussions on theological questions and religious poems, regarding these 'works' as spiritual food for young, inexperienced priests and some of the believers (*Partiinaya Zhizn* – 'Party Life' – 5, 1970, p. 59).

THE EASTERN-RITE CATHOLICS (UNIATES)

The history of the Eastern-Rite Catholics is highly complex and so cannot be discussed here. Using the Orthodox rite and Slavonic language, but owing allegiance to Rome, they have been a constant subject of strife and have never fitted easily into either an Orthodox or Catholic framework.

About three and a half million of them came under Soviet rule with the annexation of the Western Ukraine in 1939. Their allegiance to Rome made them highly suspect to the Soviets, who saw a clear chance to 'resolve' the problem after the war. Metropolitan Andrei Szeptycki was falsely accused of being a Nazi collaborator. After his death in 1944 they imprisoned his successor, Metropolitan Joseph Slipyj, and with him all four Uniate bishops from the West Ukraine. In a secret trial Slipyj and his bishops were sentenced to between five and ten years' imprisonment and they were subsequently re-sentenced. Only Slipyj survived, spending seventeen years in concentration camps.

At the same time the Soviet authorities, with the active support of the Moscow Patriarchate, initiated a massive campaign for the 're-unification' of the Eastern-Rite Catholic Church with the Russian Orthodox Church. This takeover occurred most notably at the Synod of Lvov in 1946, attended by some of the Eastern-Rite clergy, but without a single bishop being present. Thus the Eastern-Rite Catholic Church was officially liquidated and in practice banished underground. About 300 Uniate priests managed to escape the ensuing mass terror by fleeing abroad. Between 1945 and 1953 half of the 2,950 diocesan priests who refused to submit to the Orthodox Church were imprisoned. Others continued to operate underground. Some died mysteriously. About 1,600 monks and nuns were expelled from their monasteries and convents and some were imprisoned. The same fate awaited the 540 seminarists, while the remaining believers were all forced into submission. All 4,440 churches and chapels either passed into Orthodox hands or were closed. More than a thousand schools and other social institutions were disbanded and all of their twenty-eight periodicals were banned.

In the course of attempts at a *detente* with the Vatican, the Soviet authorities released Metropolitan Slipyj in 1963 and allowed him to go to Rome. However, the officially hostile position towards the Eastern-Rite Catholics was in no way modified. While in the Orthodox *Journal of the Moscow Patriarchate* in 1966 the twentieth anniversary of 'reunion' was celebrated in triumphant articles, from about the same time atheist attacks against the increasing activity of the Eastern-Rite catacomb church began to appear.

Thus *Molod Ukrainy* ('Ukrainian Youth') on 12 November 1965 described a congress of members of the Eastern-Rite underground church, dubbed *Pokutniki* ('Penitents'). They had come not only from the Ukraine, but also from Belorussia and Moldavia and marched around Lvov with a brass band. An article in *Robitnycha Hazeta* ('The Workers' Newspaper') on 19 April 1970 states:

> Because of the reactionary essence of the Uniate Church, its loyalty to the ideals of the money bag, of imperialist circles, and of the Vatican, whom the Ukrainian bourgeois nationalists serve, the reactionary clergy of the Ukrainian Catholic Church are striving to reinstate the union . . . The clergy, allied with bourgeois nationalists, have completely exposed themselves and revealed their true face in their rotting philosophy and hostile acts. In spite of this, clerical-nationalistic organizations still exist abroad; so do various leaders who continue as in the past to please the imperialists; they distort the policies and ideology of the CPSU and slander our country. Naturally this 'song' is aimed at the politically backward, ideologically unstable people; among whom we find those who are not very familiar with the history of Uniatism.

'Uniatism,' says Professor V. Tancher of Kiev University in answer to a reader's letter in *Pravda Ukrainy* ('Ukrainian Truth'), 'will never have a place on Ukrainian soil. Remember this well, you who would revive the ideological corpse of the Uniates' (*Digest of the Soviet Ukrainian Press*, January 1969, p. 24).

The *Chronicle of Current Events* in its seventh and eighth issues (1969) reports on the most recent reprisals against the Eastern-Rite Catholic Church. Here we learn that at a meeting of Orthodox priests at Pochaev in 1968, the question of the 'illegal' operation of banned Eastern-Rite believers was discussed. All priests operating illegally, it was decided, should be located and reported to the authorities. The Orthodox Metropolitan Filaret promised to appeal to the top leadership of the Ukrainian Communist Party for an end to be put to the activity of this underground movement.

Doubtless as a result of this, house searches were carried out in October 1968 and at the beginning of 1969, involving numerous priests and former nuns in the Lvov area and the whole West Ukraine. Two Eastern-Rite priests were imprisoned and one of them, Pyotr Gorodetsky, was charged under Articles 138 and 187 of the Ukrainian Penal Code (slander of the Soviet State and the socialist system, and infringement of the laws on the separation of church and state).

The *Chronicle* No. 7, 1969, says:

The Eastern-Rite Church continues to function underground. It has become more active in recent years, and the number of its priests detained and beaten up by the police has grown. On 18 October 1968 ten of them had their homes searched: forbidden religious objects were confiscated, including even the Holy Sacrament – all this represents a flagrant encroachment into the sphere of religious observance.

At the end of 1968 Bishop Vasili Velichkovsky (already over seventy) was imprisoned at Kolomyya. 'In the course of his activity', says an official press commentary, 'he not only spread the word of God, but behind this screen he has been educating the faithful in the spirit of hate against everything Soviet' (*Slava Rodiny* – 'Glory of the Fatherland' – 15 November 1969). The report goes on to say that Velichkovsky was 'only' sentenced to three years because of his age and in accordance with the 'humane character of Soviet laws'. There have been various rumours that Bishop Velichkovsky has since died in prison, but these have not been substantiated.

'A priest of the Eastern-Rite was subjected to a house-search in connection with the recent arrest of Valentyn Moroz.'

Even excluding the question of those who try to maintain the Eastern-Rite under the severest repression, the Roman Catholic Church continues to face many difficulties – despite the diplomatic *rapprochement* between the Moscow Patriarchate and the Vatican in the last two years. Most recently, however, the situation has been potentially put in question once more by the outspokenness of Cardinal Slipyj. After the recent Synod of Bishops in Rome, he held his own Synod of Ukrainian Bishops and denounced the policy of the Vatican as a betrayal of Ukrainian Catholics. There is much pressure for Slipyj to be elevated to the office of Patriarch, which would certainly have repercussions in both West and East.

PART FOUR

BAPTISTS AND OTHER PROTESTANTS

By Michael Bourdeaux

The Mennonites are Anabaptists of Dutch and German origin who found sanctuary in Russia from the eighteenth century, and by and large were well treated under the Tsars. The Soviets found about 100,000 in their territory after the Revolution – and within a decade had set about rooting them out completely, a process accelerated during the purges. They were suspect partly because of their Western origins, but even more because of their traditional pacifism – a key feature in their religious outlook. It should be emphasized, however, that there is no hint of extremism in their religious make-up. A recent Soviet writer on the subject, F. Fedorenko (*Sects, their Faith and Practice*, p. 153) admits that 'a new wave of activity began in the sect in 1956–7, when active preachers began to return from prison' – in other words, Stalin's effort at total suppression had failed signally. The Soviet Union remains the only country in the world where there is a major Mennonite colony which has no right to set up an administrative body. Since 1963 they have been encouraged to throw in their lot with the Baptists, which means being forced to give up their pacifism and other special characteristics. In 1967 came the first news of the registration of a Mennonite congregation in its own right (*Bratsky Vestnik* – 'Fraternal Herald' – the official organ of the Russian Baptists, No. 4, 1967, p. 42). It is not yet clear whether this presages any major change in Soviet policy towards this denomination.

It seems to have been part of Soviet policy towards the Protestants since 1944 to force as many streams as possible to merge with what is now called the All-Union Council of Evangelical Christians and Baptists. Lutherans have never been pushed into such a union, however, which was instituted not primarily by the Protestants themselves for reasons of ecumenism, but by the state to facilitate its attempts at control.

Baptists – the term is normally used to signify Evangelical Christians as well – suffered as much under Khrushchev as the Orthodox did in the matter of enforced closure of churches. Possibly there was a drop of over half in the 5,400 congregations registered before 1960 (see Bourdeaux, *Religious Ferment in Russia*, p. 2).

The Minsk newspaper, *Sovetskaya Belorussia* ('Soviet Belorussia' – 12 May 1963), gave precise information about what had happened at Brest:

> In 1960 the Brest Baptist congregation united with a similar one at the village of Vulka-Podgorodskaya (Brest District). But only about 100 of the 380 believers would go to Vulka. The rest, incited by their spiritual pastors, Matveyuk, Shepetunko, Kotovich and Fedorchuk, began to organize illegal gatherings in private houses in the town.

Here is a clear revelation of an illegal act in an official Soviet source. The church at Brest had been abolished with no legal justification whatsoever. It needed, according to the 1929 Law, only twenty members to ensure its continuity, whereas it had 380. The so-called 'uniting' with a relatively inaccessible village church is irrelevant to this legal issue. Such events occurred all over the Soviet Union at the time. Since 1966 there has been scattered evidence about the re-registration of individual churches, but it is unlikely that the proportion of those recently 'legalized' again (in Soviet terminology) exceeds the 5 per cent figure suggested for the Orthodox.

A recent, but rather special, case of the total outlawing of a Protestant group is that of the Council of Churches of ,the Evangelical Christians and Baptists. Extensive documentation on this reform movement, which began in 1961, has been presented in *Religious Ferment in Russia*. This group went into schism from the All-Union Council not for any strictly theological or doctrinal reason, but because its members believed passionately that it was illegal for the state to interfere in church affairs. Its leaders constantly quoted the Leninist principle of the separation of church and state in support of their own position and two of them, Georgi Vins and Gennadi Kryuchkov, went on from this in a notable document (*Religious Ferment in Russia*, pp. 105–13) to claim that the 1929 Law was irreconcilable with this principle. This criticism of Soviet law, although justified and carefully presented, inevitably brought down the full wrath of the Soviet State upon the leaders of this movement. For almost a decade now they have been one of the most severely persecuted of all Soviet minorities and it is only recently that the number of those known to be in prison has fallen below 200. They have, however, themselves estimated that there could be the same number again imprisoned, about whom they have not been able to ascertain any details.

One of the accusations which has been constantly reiterated against these *Initsiativniki* ('Action-Group') Baptists, as they are commonly called in the Soviet Union, is that they 'refuse to keep the Soviet law'. Such allegations have not only been repeated incessantly in the Soviet press, but they have also been spread to foreign contacts by official representatives of the All-Union Council. In fact, these reform Baptists often know more about their legal rights than their detractors, but have rarely been able to avail themselves of them. They have, for example, consistently been unable to register their own congregations, although they have persistently sought this and are legally entitled to do so. Then the police move in to break up their meetings, claiming that they are illegal. The organizers have been heavily and repeatedly fined.

The reform Baptists have sought to establish their right to teach religion privately to their children and it was probably with their activities specifically in mind that one clause of the March 1966 revision of the Penal Code made the organization of any kind of Sunday school more explicitly illegal than ever before.

This law is now enforced with extreme severity and carried well beyond the limits of common sense. To quote a recent example (*Baptist Times*, London, 1 October 1970), Mikhail Khorev was sentenced to three years' imprisonment on 7 July 1970. The prosecution's case against him included an accusation that he had taken his children to a birthday party in a friend's house, where he probably said grace and may have offered a few other prayers. Khorev, whose sight is severely deficient, had suffered greatly during his previous spell in prison, after which he had had less than a year's freedom. It seems virtually certain that the real reason for Khorev's arrest was that he continued to occupy a position of leadership among the reform Baptists and took a prominent part in their consultations during his brief period of freedom.

The Baptists, at the time of writing, are the only religious group in the whole Soviet Union to have won the right to hold regular national congresses. These were held in 1963, 1966 and 1969. Although the reform Baptists considered that they were not truly representative (as only registered congregations could send delegates), it was undoubtedly as a direct result of continuous pressure from the reformers that they took place at all. Some Orthodox leaders have now condemned this Baptist initiative in establishing such a principle and would like to see their own Church follow suit. Even the reformers were given permission to hold a consultation at Tula in December 1969, but this does not seem to have been followed by an legalization of their position.

Nevertheless, the state-recognized Baptists have profited from the pressure exerted by the reformers. A series of decrees controlling the internal life of the Church which had been forced on the leadership in 1960 was annulled; Bibles and hymn books were printed (though in completely inadequate quantities); theological education for the ministry was re-introduced after a gap of forty years. This latter was no more than a correspondence course, but the Russian Baptists were thereby put on the same footing in this as the Lutherans in the Baltic States. A series of talks have also taken place with the aim of re-unifying the two

Baptist factions. The last-known took place in 1969, but after that relations seem to have broken down completely.

Paradoxically, Baptists are now at once among the most favoured and the most persecuted religious groups in the Soviet Union. It should not be imagined, however, that there is a clear division between the state-recognized Baptists and the others, nor that persecution is the lot exclusively of the latter. Not only are the state-recognized Baptists subjected to some types of discrimination (in university education, for example) – but this can extend even to non-Baptist relatives.

Komsomol Truth published an account of such a case (without criticism) on 25 March 1965. The non-believing wife of a man who became a Baptist preacher was victimized and demoted from her job as a waitress in a miners' canteen. 'They fired Olga from the snack-bar and transferred her to the scullery,' we are informed. When she applied for a vacant post of cashier, she was told, 'We would hire you with pleasure, Olga – but the administration of the mine wants you out.' In desperation, the article states, she was driven into the arms of the believers who showed sympathy for her predicament.

Meditsinskaya Gazeta ('The Medical Newspaper') stated on 4 August 1970 that a nurse at Rubtsovsk, Altai region, had been forced to resign from her hospital because of her Baptist beliefs, but the case was criticized by the doctor who wrote the article.

Discrimination has often been exercised against the children of religious believers at school – where the classes include compulsory lessons in atheism throughout the Soviet Union. There are hundreds of documented cases relating to many denominations, but an especially notorious recent case about which more is known than most was that of the chlidren of Ivan and Nadezhda Sloboda, from the village of Dubravy in Belorussia (see *The Times*, 6 November 1969). The two elder children were removed from their parents on 11 February 1966 and sent to a boarding school. Here they were badly treated and inadequately cared for physically, so they ran away and returned home. Before long the police arrived at the Sloboda home to carry off the children again screaming. Soon after this their mother was sentenced to four years' imprisonment and on 13 February 1970 the other children were removed, leaving only the father at home out of a family of seven.

Conditions for Baptists in prison have often been especially severe and there have been about 500 of them held at various times since 1960, with never less than 150 at any one time. This severity is probably due partly to the continuing attempts of the Soviet authorities to inflame nationwide feelings against the reformers and represent them as 'anti-Soviet'; partly to the determination of many of them to continue their religious observances in prison.

Pavel Overchuk was sentenced to two and a half years' imprisonment in 1966 when he was thirty-four (*Observer*, 19 November 1967). He was put in the *shizo* (punishment cell) because he 'prayed to God and talked about Him to other prisoners'. Overchuk described his treatment there and managed to have what he wrote taken out of the prison and eventually abroad. He wrote:

> What is the *shizo* like? It is a cell without windows, light or air, about fourteen to sixteen square yards in area. Electric light filters in from a corridor through a Judas-window with a narrow grille. In such a cell, deprived of air and light, about twelve to fifteen or more people are crowded, after they have had their warm clothes, handkerchiefs and bedding taken away from them . . . One may ask whether such treatment stopped me praying to God. On the contrary, I value all the more the divine gifts of air and light.

Some Baptist prisoners were treated even worse than this during their imprisonment. There was, for example, the case of the recent convert, Nikolai Khmara, known from an account in the Soviet press as well as from a number of documents from the Baptists themselves (see *Religious Ferment in Russia*, pp. 77–83). He was tortured to death in prison in January 1964, immediately after having been sentenced to three years for his religious activities. More recent deaths have been Ivan Afonin (died 1969), Alexei Iskovskikh (died 1970) and latterly, in July 1971, Pavel Zakharov died as a result of his sufferings in prison. The reform Baptists have recently mentioned a figure of eight deaths in prison 1961–71.

Georgi Vins, one of the two most prominent leaders of the reform Baptists, was so badly treated during his prison sentence which lasted from 1966–9 that at one stage his friends and supporters feared for his life. It is highly likely that when they made the facts known to the outside world, this persuaded the Soviet authorities to begin treating him better and he in fact survived to resume his leadership after a period of convalescence (though according to latest reports he is once again under investigation).

This excessively harsh treatment has not ceased even now. Ivan Afonin is the most recent of seven Baptists known to have died in prison in the last decade. He was sentenced to three years in 1967, when he was forty-one years old and his health was not good. He died in the Komsomolsky camp, Tula region, on 22 November as a result of being forced to do hard physical work when he was suffering from heart and rheumatic complaints. He left a widow and nine children.

Twenty-seven Baptists have been arrested in 1970 and the short-term prospects for those who are fighting to establish their human rights are still not good.

PART FIVE

THE JEWS AS A RELIGIOUS MINORITY

By Cornelia Gerstenmaier

In scarcely any case is the religious problem so closely bound up with the national as with the Jewish minority in the U.S.S.R. As Walter Kolarz writes: 'Much of the national oppression to which the Soviet Jews have been exposed is rooted in the communist assessment of Judaism as a reactionary religious force' (*Religion in the Soviet Union*, p. 372). 'Judaism', says M. S. Belenky, a Soviet commentator, 'has been and still is an enemy of progress and of the class struggle of the workers. The synagogue has always been the greatest obstacle on the path to the development of a truly democratic culture among the Jewish masses' (*Judaism*, p. 199).

After 1917 the first attempt to secularize the Jews consisted of a large-scale campaign against the Jewish festivals such as Passover, Rosh Hashanah (New Year), Yom Kippur (Day of Atonement). Keeping the Sabbath – that is, refusing to work – was strictly punished from that time. Study of Hebrew – the language of the Old Testament and the theologians – was banned. The Jews, like the Catholics, were deprived of any central organization, so that in practice contact with congregations abroad was made impossible. Except for some small calendars and the Peace Prayerbook of 1956, there have been no Jewish religious publications since 1917. In 1922 the *Hedarim* and *Yeshivot* (the Jewish elementary and higher schools) were closed, However, they continued to operate more or less secretly until 1938.

Towards the end of the 1920s there began a massive persecution of the rabbis and the *magids* (travelling preachers). At the same time synagogues were closed down *en masse*, after they had been represented in anti-religious propaganda as meeting-places for 'profiteers', 'parasitical' and 'anti-Soviet elements'. At a time when the persecution of Jews in Nazi Germany was reaching its peak, the Soviet authorities were persecuting the rabbis as alleged spies for fascist secret services.

Religious Jewry was badly hit (especially its important centre in Vilnius) when in 1939, with the annexation of the Baltic and the West Ukraine, over two million Jews came under Soviet rule. When between 1941 and 1945 the German occupation forces physically annihilated the majority of East European Jewry, a part of the rabbinate threw in their lot with the Soviet authorities in the active struggle against the fascists. Like other religious communities, religious Jewry was subject to much less persecution by the state during the war. This soon changed. Zhdanov's cultural policy (1946–53) was chauvinistic and essentially anti-semitic. Religious Jewry inevitably came under pressure at a time when an official campaign raged against specifically Jewish traditions and customs.

After Stalin's death the repression again lessened visibly, even towards religious Jews. For the first time in decades, a *Yeshivah* (seminary) was able to be legally opened in Moscow in 1956, even though the registration of students was limited and made extremely difficult. Indeed, doubts have been expressed as to whether it ever functioned in any meaningful sense. In the same year there appeared for the first time since 1917 a Jewish prayer-book (*Molitvennik Mir*) in 3,000 copies. Hardly any copies seem to have reached the provinces; it is likely that most copies went abroad to demonstrate the 'tolerance' of the Soviet authorities.

During the last fifteen years the situation for religious Jews has progressively deteriorated, though less rapidly since 1966. Had the rate of decline remained constant, then, as the synagogue statistics set out below illustrate, there would have long since been no synagogues whatsoever in the Soviet Union. These figures are based on a table quoted in the periodical *Russia Cristiana* (Milan, January 1970, pp. 53–4). They would seem to be a reasonably accurate estimate of the number of open synagogues, except possibly for the discrepancy between the 1956 and 1960 totals. The latter comes from a Moscow Radio broadcast of 22 July 1960, which, if accurate, may mean that the former is too high. It seems more likely that Moscow Radio's figure was too low, in which case there would have been more closures in the early 1960s.

1917	..	..	..	*3,000 (approximately)*
1941	..	..	..	*1,011*
July 1956	..	..	*450*
July 1960	..	..	*150*
February 1964	..	..	*97*
July 1964	..	..	*92*
1966	..	..	..	*62*
1969	..	..	..	*40/50*

Eighteen of these synagogues are in Georgia alone, although only 2·5 per cent of the Jewish population lives there. Seventeen more are in the Asiatic part of the U.S.S.R. and in parts of the Caucasus outside Georgia. This means that almost half of all the synagogues are in the non-Russian parts of the Soviet Union, in areas containing less than 10 per cent of the Soviet Jewish population. The region of Birobidjan, designated by Stalin as an area to which Jews would be moved, is almost completely secularized and as far as is known has no synagogue at all.

Even if these statistics should prove to be not entirely accurate, we have documented information about this progressive decline from Soviet sources, as well as certain events which were reported by eye-witnesses. It was reported, for example, that when the campaign against Jews was intensifying, the synagogues of Malakhovka (near Moscow) and Tskhakaya (Georgia) were burned down in 1959 and 1962 respectively. Money collected by Soviet Jews to build new synagogues was confiscated by the authorities. Extreme pressure was exerted against those who attempted to exploit their legal right of forming councils of twenty (*dvadtsatki*) and petitioning for the opening of synagogues, which meant that Jewish congregations were deprived of the one freedom which Lenin had unambiguously bequeathed to religious people.

Leningradskaya Pravda ('Leningrad Truth') on 11 November 1961 reported the sentencing of three members of the Leningrad synagogue to four, seven and twelve years' imprisonment. They were accused of having contacts with Westerners and of having furnished the latter with 'anti-Soviet' material. In 1962 the Lvov synagogue was closed after a series of attacks in the Soviet press. The press campaign against religious Jews went so far as to assert that some had been guilty of ritual murder.

In 1964 T. K. Kichko's book *Judaism Without Embellishment* (Kiev) was published. Its anti-semitic tone aroused protest from some Western Communist Parties and eventually it was officially condemned in the U.S.S.R. also. Yet a brochure by Yu. Ivanov, *Beware! Zionism* (Moscow, 1968: second edition 1970) has, not unjustly, been compared by Russian and foreign Jews to the notorious 'Protocols of the Elders of Zion'.

The baking of matzos and kosher butchery were made increasingly difficult for believing Jews. In 1962 the baking of matzos – 'counter-revolutionary bread' – was forbidden throughout the Soviet Union. In Moscow in 1963 three Jews were sentenced to prison for illegal baking of matzos. The packets of it which Western Jews sent their fellow-believers in the Soviet Union were seen as an 'ideological diversion'; they were frequently confiscated. Only after protest from abroad was the ban on baking of matzos lifted in some towns of the U.S.S.R. in 1964–5.

Since the Six-Day War of 1967 the general situation of Soviet Jews has become even more acute. There has been a general hardening of domestic policy as an inevitable corollary of the extreme anti-Israeli position of the Soviet government. Any sectors of the population with anti-semitic instincts believe that they can give vent to them with impunity under such circumstances.

There are about 40,000 Jews in Lvov and they seem to have maintained two *minyanim* (prayer groups) even after the onslaught against their synagogue in 1962. Nevertheless, these were forcibly closed at the beginning of 1970 (*Jewish Chronicle*, 27 February 1970).

Today religious Judaism has been reduced to its lowest point in Soviet history. There are probably no more than thirty-five to forty active rabbis. Moscow has half a million Jewish inhabitants – the largest number in any city of the world after New York – yet only one of its former eleven synagogues and two smaller prayer houses remain open. According to recent reports even the synagogue itself, seating 2,500 people, is endangered, since work has begun directly underneath it on the building of a new underground railway (*Jewish Chronicle*, 25 September 1970).

But there is one major new factor in the situation: Soviet Judaism, like Christianity, has recently found its voice. A large number of petitions have been reaching the West in recent months, addressed mostly to the U.N. and the Israeli government. In these Soviet citizens ask for active support for their attempts to emigrate to Israel. Most of the very recent pleas have come from Jews of Moscow, Leningrad, Georgia, Lithuania and Latvia. In many of these letters there is direct reference to religious discrimination; almost all the documents describe the struggle of the Soviet authorities against Jewish traditions that are thousands of years old. A number of these appeals have been published in the journal *Iskhod* ('Exodus') – modelled on the clandestine organ, *Chronicle of Current Events* – the first number of which began to circulate in April 1970.

One of the most important documents that has so far reached the West is a comprehensive analysis of the present situation of Jews in the U.S.S.R. (circulated in translation by the Institute of Jewish Affairs in May 1970). It states:

The basic aspects of the Jewish question in the Diaspora are

(a) discrimination; (b) assimilation . . . In the post-war years . . . discrimination, together with the liquidation of all forms of Jewish national existence in the U.S.S.R., resulted in national sentiments concentrating upon the only legally preserved institution, the synagogue. Against its own desire and even despite plain fear, the synagogue has become the centre of Jewish spiritual life. But it is unable to answer the people's questions and to satisfy their needs for the following fundamental reasons:

(a) The active hostility of the state towards all religions in the country is strongest perhaps against Judaism, the 'religion of the enemy from within' and has reduced the synagogue to a slavish degradation and to constant fear of repressions and, therefore, to a meek agreement to all the authorities' demands, however unjust.

(b) Advanced assimilation has raised a wall of linguistic and cultural alienation between the synagogue and the Jews. A Jew who does not know his own language, or his history, who has grown up in the traditions of Russian culture and who, moreover, has no opportunity for assistance or guidance by the Jewish religious community, moves, like a blind man, by his sense of touch. Under these circumstances, it is not surprising that an intellectual of Jewish origin who is seeking religion, not infrequently turns to Russian Orthodoxy which, in a final analysis, means one more step on the road to assimilation.

When the greetings of seven Moscow Jews for *Rosh Hashanah* reached the American Jewish Congress in September 1970, this was probably the first letter from Soviet citizens to an American Jewish organization. They wrote:

We are approaching the New Year with the confidence that in spite of the attempts to deprive us of our Jewishness and forcing us to live in, for us, an alien country, we will attain our rights to live in what is to us the holy land, the Land of Israel. And we repeat our centuries-old words with a renewed feeling of reality: 'Next year in Jerusalem' (*Jewish Chronicle*, 9 October 1970).

After the so-called 'hijack' trial in Leningrad (December 1970), which resulted in numerous convictions, the emigration figures to Israel began to show a sharp increase. A full documentation of this radical change in Soviet policy would require a great deal of space. However, information may be obtained from the Institute of Jewish Affairs, London.

Of all religious (and of course ethnic) minorities in the Soviet Union, the Jews are those whose destiny is worst affected by their government's external policies. These, in their turn, may be partly affected by the worst side of Russian and Ukranian nationalism. It is hard to foresee any substantial improvement while the Soviet 'anti-Zionist' campaign continues. It should be noted, however, that an increasing number of Soviet intellectuals dissociate themselves from anti-semitism in any form.

PART SIX

THE MOSLEMS

By Kathleen Matchett

The Moslem population of the Soviet Union is largely concentrated in the Central Asian republics, with other groups in the Caucasus, Bashkiria and the Kazan area. According to A. Puzin (*Religion in the U.S.S.R.*, Moscow, 1967) there is a 'Congress of Community Representatives' as the supreme Moslem body. It is not said how often this meets, but it held a conference in Tashkent in 1962. Under this central body there are four administrative districts, with muftis resident in Tashkent, Ufa, Buinaksk and Baku. At the recent death of Patriarch Alexi, these four muftis sent messages of condolence to the Patriarchate. Except for such unusual events and official publicity statements, almost nothing is heard of the activity of these administrations.

Another *Novosti* publication for foreign consumption, *Moslems in the Soviet Union*, says that Moslem monuments are being restored by the state as a part of its cultural heritage ('Historic Monuments', p. 2). The same claim is made by Constantine de Grunwald in his *God and the Soviets* (London, 1961) – quoting the words of the secretary-general of the Tashkent administration. However, in Puzin's book a Pakistani Moslem visitor is quoted as saying: 'Mosques are built and kept in repair by voluntary contributions of Moslems. The Moslem administration appoints imams and hatibs. The state does not in any way interfere in the internal affairs of religious communities.'

Whether or not there is a conflict here, there is certainly a sharp difference between the picture drawn by official publications for foreign readers, and the treatment of the Moslem faith as it emerges in Soviet publications for internal consumption. The book *Empirical Researches into Modern Religious Beliefs* (Moscow, 1967) contains a study of three areas in Azerbaijan Republic. Of these areas it says: 'The mosques and theological schools are almost all closed today' (see *Osteuropa*, 7, 1969, p. A48). Janis Sapiets, a B.B.C. commentator on Soviet affairs, said in December 1967 that the number of mosques had been decreased 'to twelve hundred by 1959 in the whole of Central Asia, compared with twelve thousand in the province of Turkestan alone before the Revolution' and that the clergy had been reduced 'to fewer than nine thousand for the whole of the Soviet Union, as against nine thousand in Bashkiria alone before the Revolution'. *Science and Religion* in September 1963 (p. 75) stated that there were eighteen mosques and sixty-nine imams (registered) for the whole of the Tadzhik republic (population one and a half million in 1959); in January the following year it said that there were then no more than thirty-nine imams working there officially (p. 22). In other words, nearly half of the imams had been barred from religious activity within a four-month period.

It is well known, however, that such direct action merely drives religious activity underground. For example, *Empirical Researches* states that in Zakatalsky *raion*, only seven mullahs were registered, but that many more preached (*Osteuropa* 7, 1969, p. A48). Newspaper articles make frequent reference to the existence of 'wandering mullahs', apparently unregistered religious preachers who keep moving and stay with local Moslem believers.

Press treatment of the Moslems is chiefly directed to accusations about harmful traditions that have survived amongst Moslem groups. There is for example the Moslem attitude to women; frequent attacks are made on the practice of *kalym* (enforced payment of dowry). One article tells how a report of the kidnapping of a girl was investigated, only to find that the young couple had eloped in order to avoid the ruinous wedding presents demanded by their families.

Another recurrent theme is the blood-feuds allegedly demanded by the Moslem religion – the shedding of blood to wipe out a first offence, and so on through generations. This custom is apparently still strong, according to the Soviet press, among the Checheno-Ingush people. An article in *Science and Religion* (December 1966, pp. 20–25) describes how many of these people were persuaded to accept reconciliation over outstanding feuds.

It is often said in the press that Moslem rituals endanger hygiene and health. One significant article in *Science and Religion* (March 1970, pp. 62–6) lists diseases that may be contracted through the observance of different rituals, including syphilis, malaria, artero-sclerosis and cancer. This is even worse than the accusations that have been made against Baptists that multiple baptisms are unhygienic!

The treatment of the Crimean Tatars (see later) raises the important point, however, of where religion ends and national entity begins. An article in *Science and Religion* of April 1967 has expressed this problem well: 'A word (Moslem) which indicates religious adherence is being used to define a group of nationalities, amongst whom this religion was once widely spread' (p. 50). And again: 'An incorrect understanding of the word Moslem not only complicates the process of the withering away of religious rituals and customs, but also opens up loopholes for ideas of nationalism and panislamism' (p. 51). This is an unusually frank treatment of a crucial point. The dilemma of the Soviet authorities with regard to Islam has been well defined by Janis Sapiets: 'Soviet policy towards Moslems is determined by two basic considerations: on the one hand, to convince foreign Moslems of Soviet friendship for Islam, and, on the other, to bring the day nearer when there will be no more Moslems left in the Soviet Union, because they will all have been "liberated from their religion", as the communists say. To reconcile these two aims requires a certain amount of ideological acrobatics . . .' This is apparent in the Soviet article mentioned above, as indeed the author seems to be aware towards the end when he remarks: 'In recent years our links with Arab countries have become significantly stronger. I have heard from those who have been there that they easily found a common language with the population of these countries: "As soon as they discovered that we were Moslems, our relations became most warm". Without wanting to say anything bad about our Arab friends, I would nevertheless like to point out that it did not become representatives of a socialist country to look to religious adherence as a basis for friendship between nations' (p. 52). Attempting to appear as champions of religious liberty to people in the Middle East and in Orthodox communities, while sounding the death-knell for religion at home, will continue to involve the Soviet authorities in the most complicated ideological manoeuvres.

PART SEVEN

THE SURVIVAL OF THE BUDDHISTS

By Michael Bourdeaux

As readers of Walter Kolarz's excellent chapter on the Buddhists in *Religion in the Soviet Union* will know, few religious denominations were as highly organized when the new regime took over in the Soviet Union. Only a brutal use of force could destroy the existing structure which bound half a million people into an integrated unit. The spiritual leader of the community, Avgan Dordzhiev, a man of outstanding calibre, believed, furthermore, that Buddhist teachings were compatible with the building of a 'socialist society' on the Leninist model.

Stalin, always as severe with his near-sympathizers as with his outright opponents, crushed the whole structure of Soviet Buddhism with a ruthlessness which was displayed towards few other religious groups in the U.S.S.R. The stock slander against the Buddhists in the 1930s, for which no evidence was ever produced, was that they were in the service of Japanese imperialism and were therefore enemies within. The Kalmyks suffered worst of all, being deported immediately after a decree abolishing their autonomous republic on 27 December 1943. They were not allowed to return until 1957 and not surprisingly found it impossible to rebuild their life along traditional lines.

This savage policy towards Buddhism has encouraged some commentators to go beyond the evidence, however. Nicholas Poppe wrote (*Religion in the U.S.S.R.*, Munich, 1960, p. 179) that the death of Dordzhiev in prison in 1938 'was the end of organized Buddhism in the U.S.S.R., of which not a single memorial remains . . . Nothing remains of the Buddhist temples in Buryatia and Kalmykia. The fate of Lamaism in the U.S.S.R. deserves attention as an example of the complete destruction of a religious group as a whole.'

Not even the combined might of the Soviet secret police, atheist agencies and political commissars could in fact achieve such a result. The evidence of a revival in Soviet Buddhism has been mounting in recent years. Very importantly, a Buddhist Central Council was re-established after the Second World War, based at Ivolginsk, twenty-five miles south of Ulan-Ude in Buryatia. This has not had the right of calling representative assemblies, except for the purpose of electing first Lama Sharapov and then later Lama Gomboev as head of the Soviet Buddhists (Bandido Hambo Lama). The former election, in 1956, may have been rigged, for Lama Darmaev, the former holder of the office, had retired and his deputy had gone at the same time. Lama Sharapov at once became a most successful mouthpiece for the Soviet cause when required, especially in dealings with the Buddhist peoples of Asia.

There has been much more to the revival of Buddhism than the establishment of a propagandist Central Council. There may now be as many as 300 active lamas on Soviet territory (excluding the Mongolian People's Republic, which falls outside the framework of the present study) though Soviet sources usually maintain there are no more than 'a few dozen'. What is certain, however, is that 'pilgrims constantly come to the *datsan* (monastery) at Ivolginsk, arriving on horseback, in cars and by aeroplane' (*Science and Religion*, Moscow, No. 7, 1961, p. 7). *The Propagandist's and Atheist's Handbook* (Moscow, 1966, p. 150) even admits that 'active religious propaganda in post-war years has succeeded in attracting a considerable number of young people into the religious communities'. Whether or not the recent claim of the Bandido Hambo Lama that 'practically every village' in Buryatia still has its own lama (*The Times*, 6 October 1970) is true, these small pieces of Soviet testimony demonstrate that the question of religious freedom for the Soviet Buddhists is still an important one.

A book published in Ulan-Ude in 1969, containing materials of a 1966 conference, made considerable reference to Buddhist survivals in Siberia, particularly Buryatia. Lamas are censured, for example, with exploiting the national festival, the *tsagalgan*, for religious ends and thus appearing to be upholders of national traditions.

The most recent Soviet book on the subject, *Buddhism*, by A. N. Kochetov (Moscow, 1968), which includes very few pages on the present internal situation, strongly suggests that normal religious practices undertaken by the lamas are treated as illegal. This implies that village communities are not able to exercise their legal right and become registered:

> Lamas and those acting as such are infringing the legislation on religous cults; they carry out religious rites even in believers' houses and some practise traditional medicine. The lamas are resurrecting barbarous old customs, such as giving minors in marriage, collecting bride-money, etc. (p. 156).

There has in recent years been a slanderous campaign against Buddhists in the Soviet press, though much of this has been in the local-language Buryat and Kalmyk newspapers which are not available in the West. But there have also been Russian-language articles, such as V. S. Ovchinnikov's 'The reactionary and anti-Soviet activities of the Buryat Lamaist priesthood' (published in the *Transbaikal Region Yearbook*, 1967).

The main burden of the literature on contemporary Soviet Buddhism which is available to us concerns the enforced rooting out of old customs and their replacement by new Soviet ones. Such campaigns are known to have had very limited success elsewhere and it seems most unlikely that the basic hostility of these Asian people to their European colonizers will have permitted them to embrace the ineptly named 'new traditions' with anything approaching enthusiasm. One atheist article will talk of 'coloured ribbons fluttering in the breeze above the roofs of houses, adorned with texts of prayers and incantations against evil spirits' as a common feature in the villages of Buryatia (*Science and Religion*, No. 7, 1961, p. 32). Another will describe the success of the secular replacements for just such old customs. There is contradiction and confusion among Soviet atheists – but Buddhism persists.

Running one's eye down a list of these Soviet rituals now being enforced among the Kalmyks (as published in *Questions of Overcoming Survivals of the Past and the Establishment of New Customs, Rituals and Traditions among the Peoples of Siberia*, ed. A. P. Okladnikov and D. D. Lubsanov, Ulan-Ude, 1968), one is amazed to see how little they relate to anything traditional in the lives of these people: Pension Ceremony, handing over of identity cards, farewell to those drafted into the Soviet Army, honouring the veterans of labour. Even the harvest festival seems to be by the Christian Church out of the Communist Party, with an insistent emphasis on the successful fulfilment of norms. At the most solemn moments, objects associated with Soviet power are venerated. This is what young men about to be enlisted into the Soviet Army must do:

> The most emotional moment of the ritual is the bringing-in of the Red Banner. The future soldiers come up to it one by one, kneel down, kiss the red flag and pronounce the words of solemn promise (p. 64).

The test quoted above makes no suggestion that religious feelings are in fact offended by such ceremonies, but where these are enforced this could well be the result.

PART EIGHT

SOME OTHER MINORITIES

By Kathleen Matchett

SEVENTH-DAY ADVENTISTS

The Seventh-Day Adventist movement reached Russia in the late nineteenth century; it is therefore one of the more established recent movements of Western origin to have taken root in that country. After the 1917 Revolution, there was a split in Adventist opinion regarding the new regime. One side declared its loyalty, another (according to recent Soviet sources) remained intransigently hostile to the Soviet system. This latter group has been called the 'Adventists of the True Remnant' and it is unknown how far it still exists. In so far as it does, it is totally underground.

The remainder of the movement, which accepted the new authority, has fared a little better, but still suffered badly during Khrushchev's anti-religious campaign. It has been estimated by Soviet sources to have around 20,000 members, but is probably larger. The Adventist central organization was banned in 1960 and the whole movement has occupied a penumbra between legality and illegality ever since. In some places, however, the Adventists are permitted to use the Baptist churches for worship on Saturdays, while in others they do have their own registered meeting places.

Numerous articles and books describe the Adventists as 'fanatics' and show that they are in conflict with the state over the question of religious education for children. Adventist parents are accused of keeping their children away from state schools – see for example an article in the newspaper *Komsomolets Tadzhikistana* ('Young Komsomol of Tadzhikistan' – 21 December 1969), where it is stated that Adventist parents have recently been brought to court for this alleged offence. No details are given of the outcome.

The Estonian newspaper *Noorte Hääl* ('Voice of Youth' – 22 February 1967) reported that a thirteen-year-old schoolgirl had committed suicide by swallowing a pestkiller, allegedly because of tension between Adventist religious teaching at home and school attitudes. The article says that the father was brought to court, but again no details are given.

Reports like this are typical of the accusations made against Adventists and others, who have no right of reply. Adventists have been accused of such diversified 'crimes' as adultery and causing deaths through adult baptisms in icy rivers.

The latter charge was made in a book on Soviet Adventists by A. V. Belov in 1964 (p. 131). The whole of this book is written in a crudely polemical fashion, in contrast to the book by V. N. Lentin in 1966. This latter even gives a picture of Adventists as the most progressive Christian group in the Soviet Union. The publication of such a work (short though it was) clearly reflected a thaw in government policy towards the Adventists. This, however, was short-lived. In 1968 another book by Belov appeared, not even mentioning Lentin's writing. It was admittedly less crude than the 1964 publication, but nevertheless marked a hardening of tone yet again.

On 31 July 1970 the Latvian newspaper *Cina* ('Struggle') reported the trial in Riga of a Latvian Adventist for using a private printing press to produce religious literature. Printed in Russian, this literature was apparently used in the Russian Republic, the Ukraine and even in Poland. The man was given a sentence of three years.

As with other religious groups, Adventists have to suffer discrimination in secular life simply because they are believers. *Science and Religion* in June 1966 (p. 8) condemned the authorities responsible for confiscating a house belonging to an Adventist family in the Ukraine (a traditional stronghold of this movement). In the same journal in February 1970, arbitrary discrimination is reported against Adventists in Moldavia, in the spheres of housing and work (pp. 29–33). It is stated that local authorities disregard law and morality simply in order to keep religious elements out of their jurisdiction.

The *Chronicle of Current Events* in its June 1970 number reported the case of Galina Trofimova of Vitebsk, Belorussia. It describes how she was detained arbitrarily by the police, searched, and a large sum of money confiscated without receipt. Subsequent attempts to reclaim the money have failed. This happened in December 1969; in April 1970 her house was searched and religious literature confiscated. The same report mentions the trial of the leader of the Vitebsk Adventists, Mikhail Sych, in December 1969.

Kazakhstan Truth on 16 June 1971 wrote about an Adventist community which is stated to have commissioned a large printing of religious literature from a state firm. The literature was printed in Alma-Ata and forwarded to Kuban but confiscated en route. The state printer was brought to court and undoubtedly members of the community were tried as well.

Despite official statements that this movement is declining, it is apparent that it is very much alive and that the authorities are still seriously concerned about its gains, particularly among young people.

PENTECOSTALS

The Pentecostal movement reached Russia at the beginning of the twentieth century. It first really began to spread in the 1920s. A wave of general religious persecution drove them largely underground in the 'thirties, but when the Union of Evangelical Christians and Baptists was created during the war, some Pentecostals joined. Later, however, some of these left the Union again.

V. D. Grazhdan (*Who Are the Pentecostals?*, Alma-Ata, 1965) claims that an underground network was set up in the 'fifties in Kazakhstan (p. 27). A. T. Moskalenko (*The Pentecostals*, Moscow, 1966) says that in 1956 an administrative body was set up in the Ukraine and even held a congress, at which Pentecostals were urged to leave the Union and form illegal congregations (pp. 83–4). As has been noted in the Introduction, Pentecostal congregations are *de facto* illegal. This is admitted by Soviet sources. *Basic Questions of Scientific Atheism* (Moscow, 1966, p. 136) says that 'The congregation does not have a regular prayer house and gathers for worship in believers' homes, in the forests, fields, etc.' It was, however, stated in 1970 by a Soviet Baptist leader and by returning travellers from the U.S.S.R. that fifteen Pentecostal churches have recently been registered.

It is generally admitted by Soviet sources that the Pentecostals are zealous in their worship and evangelization: 'Pentecostalism is one of the most active and fanatical religious sectarian movements' (*Questions of Scientific Atheism*, Vol. 1, Moscow, 1966, p. 231). 'The first thing that strikes you on acquaintance with the life of sectarian communities is the number and length of their prayer meetings. With the majority of Pentecostals, these are held daily or at least three times a week, in the evenings. In many congregations meetings are held twice daily: before work, usually from five to six a.m., and after work, from eight to ten p.m. Meetings last two, three or more hours. On Sundays and holidays Pentecostal meetings are held two or three times during the day, the total length reaching eight to twelve hours' (*Questions of Scientific Atheism*, Vol. 2, Moscow, 1966, pp. 285–6). 'The dynamism of the religious sects is noticeable from the age groups. Among the three sects, Evangelical Christians and Baptists, Jehovah's Witnesses and Pentecostals, the last two illegal sects are notably becoming younger in average age' (A. O. Yerishov: *Results of Sociological Investigations into Religious Observance*, Kiev, 1967; quoted in *Osteuropa*, Stuttgart, July 1969, p. A41). Such is the testimony of Soviet writing to the recent activity of Pentecostals.

They are continually being accused in Soviet writing of being 'anti-social' or even hostile to the Soviet political regime: 'In many Pentecostal congregations individuals come forward as "prophets" and leaders who are hostilely inclined to the Soviet system, therefore sometimes in these congregations there are harmful political sermons' (*Basic Questions of Scientific Atheism*, ed. I. D. Pantskhava, Moscow, 1966, p. 137). Occasionally accusations are even more violent, even going so far as to say that Pentecostals are guilty of ritual murder (Moskalenko, *op. cit.*, pp. 7–8, quoting from the newspaper *Izvestia*). As the Soviet public is so starved of genuine information about religion, this often has the effect of increasing general hostility.

We have very little independent information from Soviet Pentecostals, but what we do possess leads us to suggest that the more inflammatory accusations against them are totally without foundation. The best evidence on this is to be found in the documents which Pentecostals* from Chernogorsk (Siberia) left at the American embassy in Moscow in January 1963, when thirty-two of them (including fourteen children) pushed past the Soviet guards and unsuccessfully requested political asylum and assistance to emigrate. The documents they left (the texts of which were never published in full) lead us to believe that these people, although severely persecuted, with men imprisoned and children removed from their parents, were guilty of nothing except not being a registered congregation. Even this was not their fault. Least of all were the accusations of child-sacrifice justified, which had been published against them in the local press.

The Soviet press has even more recently witnessed to the trials of Pentecostal leaders. Grazhdan (*op. cit.*, p. 72) cites the case of the pastor D. Chaika, an old man of sixty in 1965. He says that Chaika had been sentenced three times, for alleged immorality.

On 8 May 1969 *Truth of the East* reported the trial of eight Pentecostals in the town of Angren. Among them were the leaders V. P. Frizen and P. G. Shmidt. The accused were charged with 'organizing illegal meetings of the sect, enticing minors into it, injuring the health of believers through fanatical rites and drawing believers away from participation in social life and from fulfilling their civic duty.' How did they achieve these things? 'In the experts' findings it was stated that the fanatical rites of the sect – the holy salutation, the washing of feet, the breaking of bread, speaking with God in tongues, and others not only facilitated the spread of infectious diseases, but also had a harmful effect on the human psyche.' How did the court prove that believers had been drawn away from society? By quoting Frizen's daughter, Vera, who testified that 'of all books she preferred to read the Bible'.

It was revealed that Frizen had already been in prison for five years. On this occasion he was again sentenced to five years, in strict-regime camps, with confiscation of property. Shmidt also received five years; the others, two or three.

On 20 September 1969 the newspaper *Kazakhstanskaya Pravda*

*They described themselves as 'Christians of the Evangelical Faith' – one of the two standard names for Pentecostals in Russian.

('Kazakhstan Truth') told the story of Alexandr Dering who went from the Baptists to the Pentecostals before leaving the Church. It is mentioned in passing that the leaders of the church in Ivanovka, including Alexandr's elder brother, were brought to court, and that the church then broke up.

The Belorussian newspaper *Banner of Youth* on 20 October 1970 wrote about the community in Pinsk. The man in whose home this unregistered group was meeting, Nikolai Abramchuk, has been sentenced. The article also states that many Pentecostals have ended up in a local mental hospital. This is perhaps an official admission of a new policy being used against 'dissidents' of all kinds, including Christians. It has also happened with the Baptist Ivan Lazuta of Belorussia and the Orthodox layman. G. M. Shimanov has graphically described his incarceration for religious reasons in a mental institution.

A Pentecostal girl, Anya Paramonova, who lived in Perm, was offered a flat to live in if she was prepared to give up her faith. She refused. When she took an exam for promotion in her job, she was failed because she was a Pentecostal (*Science and Religion*, November 1966, p. 30).

The government daily newspaper *Izvestia* (28 February 1968) reported how the children of a Pentecostal mother were taken away from her. Her husband divorced her and re-married. Therefore events such as those which led the Siberian Pentecostals to go to the American embassy in 1963 have by no means become a thing of the past.

JEHOVAH'S WITNESSES

This movement reached the Soviet Union as late as 1940. It spread, according to F. I. Fedorenko (*Sects, Their Faith and Practice*, p. 200) from the Western provinces of the Ukraine and Belorussia. W. Kolarz (*Religion in the Soviet Union*, p. 340) says that it also came in with Soviet prisoners returning from German camps where they had met Jehovah's Witnesses.

The sect is treated as strictly illegal, but there is no statement to this effect in the published Soviet law. The recent book by E. M. Bartoshevich and Ye. I. Borisoglebsky, published in Moscow in 1969, says that 'the real reason for this abnormal situation is their hostile position with respect to the socialist countries' (p. 166). It is argued that both Adventists and Baptists have their headquarters in America, so this is not *ipso facto* a reason for refusing registration. Fedorenko records the successive 'unmaskings' in 1947, 1952, 1957 and 1960, of the Witnesses' 'East European Bureau' in Lvov. Each time the organization re-emerged with new personnel. One of those mentioned as being among the staff before the 1947 arrests is P. G. Zyatek (pp. 202-3). Two later press articles claim that this man (the name is variously spelled Zyatek or Zyatik, although the writers are supposedly ex-leaders of the Witnesses themselves) was deputed to lead the Soviet movement, but that an opposition group formed accusing him of collaboration with the authorities. This finally led to a split in 1959.

The recurrent Soviet line is that the Witnesses' Brooklyn headquarters is a religious cover for political activity, and anti-communist activity at that. The Witnesses are regularly said to be linked with the C.I.A. Although Soviet writers ridicule the teachings of the Witnesses, the thrust of their attack is almost always political. One article, however, has suggested that the movement received instructions to relax its internal discipline because of 'socialist conditions'.

The continual hazard to Soviet believers, that of slander in the press without right of reply, applies very much to the Jehovah's Witnesses. They have been accused of political hostility, anti-social activity (persuading members not to join collectives, read newspapers or visit the cinema), maltreatment of children (by keeping them away from school, and even beating them when they join communist youth organizations), stealing state property (for example, printing and building materials), espionage, reprisals against those who leave the movement, and even murder.

This last charge was made in an article in the newspaper *Pravda Ukrainy* ('Truth of the Ukraine') on 13 June 1969. The subject of the article was a film which had been made about the Witnesses, entitled 'Made in America'. This film apparently showed scenes from trials of Witnesses. *Kazakhstan Truth* (16 June 1970) reported on a further film, this time 'unmasking' both Jehovah's Witnesses and reform Baptists.

Persecution has by no means been limited to press accusations. *Science and Religion* (February 1966, p. 2) recounted how a man was hounded out of his factory after an unsuccessful attempt to 're-educate' him. Official action has frequently gone to court level. There have been many trials of Jehovah's Witnesses in recent years. *Truth of the East* referred on 12 June 1969 to a trial of Witnesses in Angren; but in not untypical Soviet style, the reader is not told exactly how many of those mentioned were in fact in the dock, or what their sentence was. However, details are given of several individuals who had previously been sentenced. One is Vasili Russu, who was also mentioned in *Kazakhstan Truth* (16 March 1968). The latter article says that he had already been sentenced twice, the more recent one says that it was three times: once for desertion during the last war, once for anti-social activity and once for parasitism. In another case a father and four sons are mentioned, all of whom were sentenced for breaking Soviet laws (apparently because the father said his sons would not serve in the army). It is recorded that literature has been confiscated from Witnesses, as well as tapes and tape recorders. The *Chronicle of Current Events* No. 15 (August 1970) gives a list of women detained in camp 385/3, Mordovia, among them two Jehovah's Witnesses. Yevgenia Kislyachuk is about sixty-five and will complete a ten-year sentence in 1972. Vera Bozhar is forty-six and will complete seven years in camp in December 1970, to be followed by five years' exile. Both women were sentenced for belonging to the Witnesses.

The picture built up by Soviet atheist writers of the Jehovah's Witnesses is that of a fanatical underground political movement. But at the same time, a few sources do suggest that the majority of members are really honest workers who have merely been deceived by overseas manipulators. Gerald Brooke, the British lecturer who spent over four years in a Soviet camp, testifies to the scrupulous attention paid by the Witnesses to fulfilling their work norms while doing their sentences. It is difficult to be precise about the activities of Jehovah's Witnesses in the Soviet Union while the evidence remains so one-sided. This very one-sidedness, however, is itself evidence of discrimination.

Adventists, Pentecostals and Jehovah's Witnesses are all showing astonishing resilience in the face of a concerted effort by Soviet power to root them out completely.

CONCLUSION

The question of whether religious minorities in the Soviet Union are more threatened now than they were ten years ago may be endlessly debated. Soviet methods are less physical now, generally speaking, than they were under Khrushchev, but there is greater subtlety in the methods of persuasion. The evidence set out above demonstrates conclusively that the Soviet state has not even begun to reconsider its intention of ultimately rooting religion out of society altogether. Furthermore, the Soviet laws are designed to facilitate this, which means that a major infringement of human rights is written into the statute book. There is no clause in the basic 1929 Law designed to give the believer true rights or to ensure the implementation of the Leninist principle of separation of church and state. Nevertheless, it is unquestionable that Soviet people are becoming more aware of the rights they do possess, which may mean there will be less illegal discrimination against believers in housing and at work in the future.

Today's world has a long and sorry list of countries and situations where there is discrimination against minorities – ethnic, linguistic, religious, social. Some of the most glaring of these have received extensive publicity in recent years and the cases are written on the conscience of the world. Decades of injustice to the religious believer in the Soviet Union have resulted in remarkably little publicity, thanks partly, in recent years, to the clever exploitation by the Soviet regime of the international contacts which it has encouraged some of its Churches to promote, and partly to a fear that publicity might further harm those already in difficulties. Now the real situation has been extensively documented. The Soviet believer has begun to seek publicity in countries other than his own, and when this plea for attention has been granted it appears to have helped – or at least not to have hindered – the situation.

SELECT BIBLIOGRAPHY

A. *General*
Religion in the Soviet Union, by Walter Kolarz, London, 1961.
Religion in the U.S.S.R., ed. Robert Conquest, London, 1968.
Religion in the U.S.S.R., ed. Boris Iwanow, Munich, 1960.
Religion and the Soviet State, ed. M. Hayward & W. Fletcher, London, 1969.
Religion and the Search for New Ideals in the U.S.S.R., ed. W. Fletcher & A. Strover, New York & London, 1967.
Religion und Atheismus in der Ud.S.S.R., by Nadeshda Theodorowitsch, Munich, 1970. 'Freedom of Worship and the Law' by Peter Reddaway in *In Quest of Justice*, ed. Abraham Brumberg, New York, 1970.
'The Soviet Treatment of Dissenters and the Growth of a Civil Rights Movement' by Peter Reddaway in *Rights and Wrongs*, ed. Christopher Hill, London, 1969.
Uncensored Russia, ed. Peter Reddaway, published in London & New York, 1972 (based on the *Chronicle of Current Events*).
Voprosy Nauchnogo Ateizma ('Questions of Scientific Atheism'); series published in Moscow, Nos. 1–10 so far appeared, 1966–70.

B. *Russian Orthodox Church*
Christians in Contemporary Russia, by Nikita Struve, London, 1967.
Patriarch and Prophets: Persecution of the Russian Orthodox Church Today, by Michael Bourdeaux, London, 1970.
The Recent Activities of the Moscow Patriarchate Abroad and in the U.S.S.R., by John Dunlop, St. Nectarios Educational Series, Seattle, 1970.
Pravoslaviye ('Orthodoxy'), by V. Ye. Titov, Moscow, 1967.
Sovremennoye Pravoslaviye ('Modern Orthodoxy'), by N. S. Gordienko, Moscow, 1968.
The Russian Orthodox Church Underground 1917–70 by William C. Fletcher, London, 1971.

C. *Baptists*
The Christians from Siberia, by J. C. Pollock, London, 1964.
Religious Ferment in Russia, by Michael Bourdeaux, London, 1968.
Christian Appeals from Russia, ed. R. Harris & X. Howard-Johnston, London, 1969.
Faith on Trial in Russia, by Michael Bourdeaux, London, 1971.
Baptizm, by L. N. Mitrokhin, Moscow, 1966.

D. *Other Christian Denominations*
'Old Believers' by Michael Bourdeaux, in weekly encyclopaedia·*Man, Myth and Magic*, No. 73, London, 1971.
Staroobryadchestvo v Proshlom i Nastoyashchem ('Old Believers Yesterday and Today'), by V. F. Milovidov, Moscow, 1969.
Sekty, Ikh Vera i Dela ('The Sects, Their Faith and Practice'), by F. I. Fedorenko, Moscow, 1965.
Adventizm, by A. V. Belov, Moscow, 1968.
Adventisty Sedmogo Dnya ('Seventh-Day Adventists'), by V. N. Lentin, Moscow, 1966.
Pyatidesyatniki ('Pentecostals'), by A. T. Moskalenko, Moscow, 1966.
Kto Takiye Pyatidesyatniki? ('Who are the Pentecostals?'), by V. Grazhdan, Alma-Ata, 1965.
Svideteli Iegovy ('Jehovah's Witnesses'), by E. M. Bartoshevich & Ye. I. Borisoglebsky, Moscow, 1969.
Mennonity, by V. F. Krestyaninov, Moscow, 1967.

E. *Non-Christian Religions*
The Jews in Soviet Russia since 1917, ed. Lionel Kochan, London, 1970.
Iudaizm, by M. S. Belenky, Moscow, 1966.
Islam in the Soviet Union, by Alexandre Bennigsen and Chantal Lemercier-Quelquejay, London, 1967.
Islam, by R. R. Mavlyutov, Moscow, 1969.
Buddhas Wiederkehr und die Zukunft Asiens, by Ernst Benz, Munich, 1963.
Buddizm, by A. N. Kochetov, Moscow, 1968.

7 THE CRIMEAN TATARS AND VOLGA GERMANS:

SOVIET TREATMENT OF TWO NATIONAL MINORITIES

by Ann Sheehy

*Ann Sheehy has been a research associate at the
Central Asian Research Centre in London since 1960.
She served in the British Embassy in Moscow from
1957 to 1959.*

THE CRIMEAN TATARS
AND VOLGA GERMANS

INTRODUCTION

During the Second World War Stalin deported *en bloc* to the Urals, Siberia, Kazakhstan and the Soviet Central Asian republics a number of small nationalities, probably numbering some one and a half million persons in all. Of the seven nationalities who were simultaneously deprived of their national autonomy, the Volga Germans were deported in 1941 as a precautionary measure, and the remaining six – the Crimean Tatars, Kalmyks, and four Caucasian peoples (the Chechens, Ingush, Karachay and Balkars) – between October 1943 and May 1944 as a punishment for alleged wholesale collaboration with the Germans, although many of them had fought with distinction in the Soviet army or with the partisans. In his Secret Speech at the XX Party Congress in February 1956, Khrushchev included this deportation of whole nations in his catalogue of Stalin's crimes, but he mentioned only the Kalmyks and the four Caucasian nationalities. In January 1957 decrees were passed reconstituting the autonomous territories of these five nationalities, and assistance was provided for their repatriation. For the Crimean Tatars and the Volga Germans, however, there was and has been no such restitution. The Volga Germans were eventually politically rehabilitated in 1964, and the Crimean Tatars in September 1967, but in both instances the rehabilitation decrees made plain that there was no question of either repatriation or their national autonomy being restored.

When the decree rehabilitating the Crimean Tatars appeared it was conjectured, in view of their historic, cultural and ethnic ties with the Turks, that it might be a gesture to mark the improved relations between the Soviet Union and Turkey. But *samizdat* (unofficial) documents which began to come out of the Soviet Union in 1968 have shown that the Crimean Tatars, who probably now number some 250,000 to 350,000 and live mainly in Uzbekistan,*

*The Crimean Tatars claim to be over half a million strong, and this number is also quoted by their Russian supporters. But if one accepts the Tatars' own figure of a mortality of 46 per cent or approximately 110,000 as a result of deportation, then some 130,000 would have survived, and it seems unlikely that they would have more than doubled their number in the intervening 25 years.

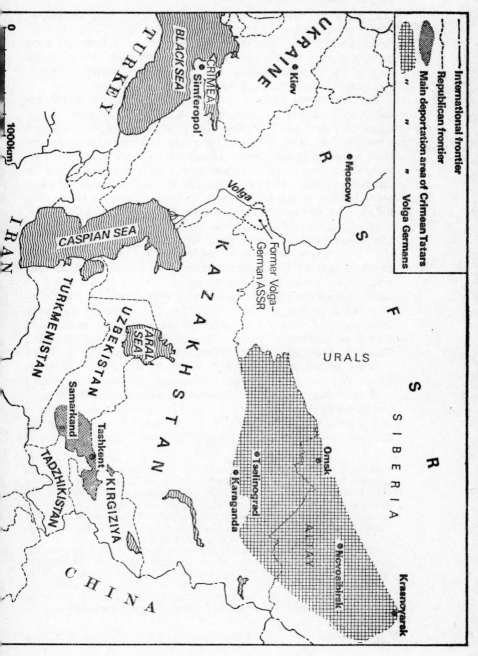

obtained their rehabilitation only as the result of a decade of campaigning. Their campaign has been paralleled in the Soviet Union only by that of the Meskhetians (a heterogeneous group deported on strategic grounds in November 1944 from the area of the Georgian S.S.R. adjacent to the Turkish frontier)* and possibly by that of the Baptists.†

The documents have also shown that the failure of the rehabilitation decree to restore the national autonomy of the Crimean Tatars and to provide for their repatriation (combined with the fact that although on paper they now enjoyed the right to reside in the Crimea thousands of them were forced to leave when they returned following the decree) merely led to an intensification of their campaign for equality of rights with the other nations of the U.S.S.R. – a campaign which is continuing today. The Crimean Tatars accuse the Soviet authorities not only of discrimination but also of genocide, maintaining that the manner in which they were deported and the conditions in the deportation areas were such that 46 per cent of their numbers died on the journey or during the first eighteen months after deportation. They also allege that the present policy of denying them their national autonomy (and hence the possibility of developing as a nation) – and moreover, of denying their very existence as a nation by describing them in the rehabilitation decree as 'citizens of Tatar nationality formerly resident in the Crimea' – is aimed at their destruction as a nation.

Much of the report on the Crimean Tatars which follows is necessarily based on *samizdat* documents, for the simple reason that no description of their deportation has appeared in material published in the Soviet Union, nor has there been any mention in the Soviet press to date of their campaign for the restitution of their national rights.‡ Where available, however, material

---

* Like the Crimean Tatars the Meskhetians were deported mainly to Uzbekistan and suffered heavy loss of life. Their deportation only became known when a decree was published in 1968 which theoretically permitted them to reside once again in Meskhetia, but in spite of an energetic campaign dating back to 1956 they have still not been allowed to return. Details of this campaign are given in *Chronicle of Current Events*, Nos. 7 and 9. Their case has also been described by Robert Conquest in *The Nation Killers* (London, 1970) and in an article in *The Times* of 5 August 1970.

† See Michael Bourdeaux, *Religious Ferment in Russia* (London, 1968) and the same author's *Religious Minorities in the Soviet Union* (1960-70) (Minority Rights Group, London, 1970) and *Faith on Trial in Russia* (London, 1971).

‡ The Soviet Embassy in London, asked in 1971 for information and comments on the Crimean Tatars and their allegations, replied: 'We are very sorry but information you are asking for in your letter is not available at the Embassy.'

published in the Soviet Union has been used to corroborate, supplement, or set against the extensive *samizdat* material. The latter includes some fifty documents, totalling 250,000 words, concerned exclusively with the Crimean Tatar question. Among them are bulletins from the Crimean Tatar lobby in Moscow to their constituents in Central Asia, protests and appeals addressed to the Soviet Party and government as well as to the outside world, and the summary transcript of the five-week trial of ten leading members of the movement in Tashkent in 1969 ('Case No. 109'), as well as frequent items in the unofficial Moscow *Chronicle of Current Events*, together with references in a number of other documents.*

The present report starts with a short history of the Crimean Tatars up to the time of their deportation. Then follows an account of their deportation, the events leading up to their political rehabilitation, and their present situation. The second part deals more briefly with the Volga Germans, whose situation has much in common with that of the Crimean Tatars.

PART ONE

THE CRIMEAN TATARS

HISTORY UP TO 1941

The confrontation between Russia and the Crimean Tatars dates back to the Mongol Tatar invasion of Europe and the subsequent emergence of the Crimean Tatars as a distinct entity in the early 15th century. The Crimean Tatars are a Moslem Turkic people. They are descended from the Mongol Tatars of the Golden Horde who established themselves in the northern and central steppe hinterland of the Crimean peninsula in the first half of the 13th century, and also from Turkic tribes who arrived before the Mongols and later assimilated Goths as well as Greeks and Genoese who occupied the southern littoral at different periods. With the disintegration of the Golden Horde

---

* Only a small portion of this material has so far been published and that mostly in Russian in the emigré press ('*Posev, Novoye russkoye slovo, Novyy zhurnal* and *Russkaya mysl'*'). Two of the documents are published in English in *In Quest of Justice*, edited by Abraham Brumberg (Praeger, 1970), and an annotated English translation of the first eleven issues of the *Chronicle of Current Events* appears in *Uncensored Russia*, edited by Peter Reddaway, published in London and New York in 1972. A few of the documents have also been published in Turkish in *Dergi*, No. 62 of 1970 and No. 63 of 1971.

in the first half of the 15th century, a separate Crimean khanate, extending into the adjacent Black Sea steppes, came into being under the Girey dynasty.* In 1478, three years after the Turks had occupied the coast of the Crimea, the Crimean khanate acknowledged the suzerainty of the Turkish sultan, and it remained a loyal vassal of the Ottoman empire until its extinction by the Russians in the late 18th century.

In the 16th and 17th centuries the Crimean khanate, with its ability to put many thousands of horsemen into the field, represented a formidable force, and in the confrontation between the khanate and the rising power of Muscovy it was the Tatars who at first had the upper hand. They exacted the old Mongol tribute from the Moscow princes and in addition constantly raided Russian and other lands to the north, carrying off thousands of their inhabitants to sell into slavery. More than once they advanced to the walls of Moscow itself, and in 1571 they besieged the city and burned down its suburbs. But from the second half of the 17th century Russia began to gain the ascendancy, and although the Turks and the Crimean Tatars defeated Peter the Great on the Pruth in 1711, Russian troops invaded and ravaged the Crimea during the Russo-Turkish wars of 1735–9 and 1768–74. At the end of the latter war Turkey was forced to give up its suzerainty over the northern shores of the Black Sea, and the Crimean khanate was declared independent. Crimean Tatar fears that this was merely a prelude to annexation by Russia were realized when Catherine the Great proclaimed the Crimea Russian in 1783.

By this date several thousand Crimean Tatars had already taken refuge in the Ottoman empire, and Tsarist rule was marked by a further series of tragic migrations to Turkey in the course of which many thousands died, as well as by the growing impoverishment of those who remained behind. It is true that Catherine adopted a relatively liberal policy towards Islam and granted the Tatar nobility the same privileges as the Russian aristocracy; but at the same time, as if to obliterate the memory of the khanate, the newly acquired territory was almost immediately renamed Tavrida and Tatar place names were replaced by Greek ones.

---

* Other successor states of the Golden Horde were the Tatar khanates of Kazan' and Astrakhan' on the Volga, which were conquered by Ivan the Terrible in 1552 and 1556 respectively. Of the Tatars in the Soviet Union (5,931,000 in 1970) the vast majority are Volga or Kazan' Tatars, whose language and culture are distinct from those of the Crimean Tatars. They have their own Tatar Autonomous Soviet Socialist Republic on the Volga, of which Kazan' is the capital, but are fairly widely dispersed throughout the Soviet Union.

From 1784 the most valuable Tatar lands were confiscated and distributed first to high officials and later to a variety of settlers who were invited to move there in large numbers after 1789. But it was Turkey's final recognition of Russia's annexation of the Crimea, in 1792, which deprived the Crimean Tatars of their last hope of regaining their independence and this sparked off the first major migration, to be followed by others in the 1860s, 1870s and 1891–1902. Over the whole period several hundred thousands Tatars abandoned their native Crimea. According to a Russian official writing a decade later, the 1792 exodus 'conformed with the wishes of the Russian authorities', and the Tsar, when he was informed in 1856 soon after the Crimean War that the Tatars were leaving the Crimea, is reported to have commented that the territory would be well rid of them. The Tatars had taken no part in the war, but they had been unable to conceal their sympathy for Turkey, and fear of reprisals (apparently fed by reports of a plan to deport the whole Tatar population to the Semipalatinsk province of what is today Kazakhstan) led to such large-scale migration in 1860–63 that hundreds of villages were completely abandoned. By the time of the 1897 census the Crimean Tatars, numbering 188,000, comprised only just over a third of the population, while the Russians and Ukrainians together accounted for some 45 per cent. The overwhelming majority of the Tatar population were peasants, 40 per cent of whom were landless on the eve of the Russian revolution. The fortunes of most of the former Tatar nobility had also declined disastrously.

It was from this impoverished and backward community that the outstanding liberal reformist Ismail Bey Gasprinskiy (Gaspirali) emerged in the latter half of the nineteenth century. Gasprinskiy aimed at a renaissance of his own as well as of all the Turkic peoples through the modernization of Islam, the practical embodiment of which was his 'New Method' education. He also preached Pan-Turk unity, and through his newspaper *Terjüman*, published in Bakhchisaray from 1883 onwards, exerted an influence that extended throughout the whole Islamic world. Among some of the younger Crimean Tatar intelligentsia, however, narrower and more radical ideas, aimed at improving the immediate lot of the Crimean Tatars, prevailed; and when the first Tatar political party, the *Milli Firqa* (National Party), was set up in July 1917 its programme demanded the federalization of Russia, cultural autonomy for the minorities, and a solution of the land question.

The *Milli Firqa* dominated the political life of the Crimean

Tatars during the upheavals of the Revolution and civil war, but as a relatively powerless minority the Tatars had little chance of achieving their aims. An autonomous government set up by the *Milli Firqa* in Simferopol' in December 1917 was disbanded in January 1918 by Bolshevik sailors from Sevastopol'. Although the left wing of the *Milli Firqa* and – under the extremely hostile White regime of General Denikin in 1919–20 – the *Milli Firqa* Central Committee collaborated with the Bolsheviks, when Soviet rule was finally established for good in November 1920, the *Milli Firqa* was declared a counter-revolutionary organization.

The Bolshevik regime in the Crimea, like those in other minority areas, was loth to share any of its power with the indigenous inhabitants, and its policy antagonized rather than won over the Tatars. Lenin had realized very soon after the Revolution, however, that some concessions to the feelings of the national minorities were necessary if he was to keep intact the old Russian empire. He had settled on the formula of 'self-determination' in the shape of nominally independent or autonomous national republics, in which national sentiments would be placated by promoting national culture, the use of the national language, and native participation in the conduct of affairs.*

Accordingly when Moscow became aware of the alienation of the Tatars in the Crimea, it decided that the solution was an autonomous republic. The objections of the local Bolsheviks that the Tatars formed a minority of the population and that they were not proletarian – as well as their argument that the Crimea was too important to the whole country as a health resort to be under the jurisdiction of an autonomous republic – were over-ruled, and the Crimean Autonomous Soviet Socialist Republic (Crimean A.S.S.R.) was formally set up on 18 October 1921 as part of the R.S.F.S.R. An editorial in *Zhizn' natsional'nostey* (the organ of the People's Commissariat of Nationality Affairs) of 25 October 1921, which announced its formation, declared that the republic was

> due compensation for all the wrongs . . . of the Tsarist regime. But chiefly the proclamation of the republic means a series of social transformations directed towards the satisfaction of all the crying needs of the toiling elements of the native population.

---

* Republics, autonomous republics, autonomous provinces and national districts, in descending order of importance, were established according to the size and compact settlement of the various nationalities. They do not enjoy independence or autonomy in any meaningful sense of the word, but are rather administrative units which take national attributes into account.

The creation of the republic would ensure

> the maximum of autonomous rights and initiative for the broad toiling masses of the native population in their cultural and economic rebirth.

The editorial also pointed out the importance of the Crimea in international policy in view of the long-standing links between the Crimean Tatars and the neighbouring Eastern peoples, and asserted that the republic would be

> yet one more brilliantly flashing beacon destined to attract all the best yearnings and aspirations of the multi-million East now under the slave yoke of the international imperialists.

The early years of the Crimean A.S.S.R. have been described as the 'Golden Age' of the Crimean Tatars under Soviet rule. Veli Ibragimov, formerly leader of the left wing of the *Milli Firqa*, was made President of the Executive Committee, and with many other Tatars in senior posts the Tatars enjoyed a more dominant political position in the republic than their numbers warranted (they comprised only 25 per cent of the population of 714,000 at the time of the 1926 census). Tatar was made an official language along with Russian; Tatar schools and theatres were opened, and Tatar literature and art encouraged; and archaeological excavations revealed the high standard of culture which had been achieved by the Crimean khanate.

This relatively happy interlude came to an end in late 1927 when a long purge of 'bourgeois nationalists' began in the Moslem republics. In the Crimea, where it was particularly drastic, the purge started with the arrest and execution of Veli Ibragimov and resulted in the disappearance of practically all the pre-Revolutionary Tatar intelligentsia. During the country-wide collectivization drive of the late 1920s and early 1930s it was the turn of the peasants: some 30,000 to 40,000 were deported to the Urals and Siberia, while a violent anti-religious campaign being conducted at the same time led to the death or deportation of the majority of the Moslem clergy. Finally came the mass terror of 1936–8 which took its toll indiscriminately on all sections of the population.

DEPORTATION

With the approach of the Second World War it is not surprising that Stalin's fears about the loyalty of some of his non-Russian subjects became intense. There is evidence that the question of deporting the peoples of the North Caucasus and the Crimean

Tatars was mooted at this time, but any such plans which existed for the Crimean Tatars were forestalled by the rapid German advance. During the war some hundreds of thousands of Soviet citizens of various nationalities – including Russians – served in the German armed forces for one reason or another; and it is true that several thousand Crimean Tatars enrolled in six German-officered Tatar battalions which fought against Soviet partisan detachments in the Crimea and were evacuated with the German forces in 1944.* Nominally they were volunteers, but many of them were prisoners-of-war seeking to escape from starvation or death in German camps. German reports also make it clear that the partisans did not always enjoy the support of the local population. The partisans' mountain operations meant that the predominantly Tatar villages there bore the brunt of both the partisans' attacks and the German reprisals. On the other hand large numbers of Crimean Tatars served loyally in the Red Army throughout the war, and others fought with the local partisans – some having a high price put on their heads by the German High Command. The Soviet press at the time carried reports of Crimean Tatar heroism, and according to the Crimean Tatars themselves, thirteen or fourteen of their number were given the highest award for bravery, the title of Hero of the Soviet Union.

The Red Army offensive in the Crimea began on 8 April 1944 and by 18 April only Sevastopol' remained in German hands. Tatars who had collaborated with the Germans were immediately sentenced to death by military tribunals (reports speak of mass executions in the streets); and then before dawn on 18 May 1944, six days after the last Germans had been cleared from Crimean soil, all the remaining Tatars were roused from their beds by N.K.V.D. troops equipped with bayonets and sub-machine guns and were deported. The deportation and the reason for it were only made known two years later with the publication in

* Over 300 families of those who left the Soviet Union during the Second World War went to the U.S.A., but the bulk of them made their way to Turkey. Back in 1918 there were estimated to be about two million Crimean Tatars in Turkey as a result of emigration from the Crimea in the preceding century and a half. There were then also roughly 80,000 in Romania and somewhat fewer in Bulgaria. At present there are about 35,000 in Romania, the remainder having moved to Turkey. Many of those in Bulgaria have also gone to Turkey. As for those in Turkey itself, they are all regarded as Turks by the Turkish government and have undergone various degrees of assimilation with the Turks. A considerable number still speak Crimean Tatar as well as some form of Turkish, and many more remain conscious of their Tatar origins. In the opinion of Dr Edige Kirimal, a Crimean Tatar emigré scholar, a number of the Crimean Tatars abroad would return to the Crimea if it became Tatar again.

Izvestiya of a decree issued on 25 June 1946 which confirmed the abolition of the Crimean and also the Chechen-Ingush A.S.S.R. The decree ran in part:

> During the Great Patriotic War . . . many Chechens and Crimean Tatars, at the instigation of German agents, joined volunteer units organized by the Germans and, together with German troops, engaged in armed struggle against units of the Red Army; also at the bidding of the Germans they formed diversionary bands for the struggle against Soviet authority in the rear; meanwhile the bulk of the population of the Chechen-Ingush and Crimean A.S.S.R.s took no counter-action against these traitors to the Fatherland. In connection with this, the Chechens and Crimean Tatars were resettled in other regions of the U.S.S.R., where they were given land together with the necessary government assistance to set themselves up.

The grim reality of the Crimean Tatars' 'resettlement' is described in some of the recent *samizdat* documents. According to an 'Open Letter from the Russian Friends of the Crimean Tartars' written in 1968 or early 1969, some of the Crimean Tatars were given only fifteen minutes to collect such belongings and provisions as they could carry. Others had no more than five minutes to assemble and, as they were forbidden to take anything at all, thought that they were being taken away to be shot. The 'Open Letter' continues:

> But it was not to be shot. It was a journey of lingering death in cattle trucks, crammed with people, like mobile gas chambers. The journey lasted three to four weeks and took them across the scorching summer steppes of Kazakhstan. They took the Red partisans of the Crimea, the fighters of the Bolshevik underground, and Soviet and Party activists. Also invalids and old men. The remaining men were fighting the Fascists at the front, but deportation awaited them at the end of the war. And in the meantime they crammed their women and children into the trucks, where they constituted the vast majority. Death mowed down the old, the young and the weak. They died of thirst, suffocation and the stench.
> On the long stages the corpses decomposed in the huddle of the trucks, and at the short halts, where water and food were handed out, the people were not allowed to bury their dead and had to leave them beside the railway track.

The Crimean Tatars were transported several thousand miles to the Urals, Siberia, Kazakhstan and Central Asia. The majority of the estimated 200,000 to 250,000 of them were taken to Uzbekistan where, according to official Soviet records produced at recent trials, the first ones arrived eleven days later and most of the remainder by 8 June 1944. By 1 July 1944 35,750 families totalling 151,424 persons had arrived in Uzbekistan. They were followed by a further 818 families before the end of the year. Another 2,000 or so Crimean Tatar men appear to have arrived in Uzbekistan in 1945, presumably on demobilization from the army.

On their arrival in Uzbekistan the deportees met with sullen hostility from the local population, who had been set against them by the authorities, and in some cases they even had stones thrown at them. They were dumped in barracks or dug-outs; in their half-starved and weak state, malaria, intestinal diseases contracted from the ditch water, and a lack of food – which persisted until they were able to harvest their own produce in 1945 – soon started to take their toll. At the trial of ten Crimean Tatars in Tashkent in July and August 1969 an elderly Crimean Tatar, Yusuf Suleymenov, testified as follows:

> They took us and unloaded us in Urta-Aul like cattle for slaughter. Nobody paid any attention to us. We were hungry, dirty and ill. People became even more ill, and started to swell from hunger and began to die in families. I want to say that from our village, where there were 206 people, 100 died. I myself buried eighteen. Out of seven households of my relatives not one remained.

Many other Crimean Tatars have described the appalling mortality in their own families. A young Crimean Tatar physicist, Yuriy Osmanov, is said to have commented: 'Yes, the Crimean Tatars were indeed given land – one and a half metres in the cemetery.'

As mentioned above, the Crimean Tatars claim, on the basis of a census they carried out in 1966, that 46 per cent or some 110,000 of their number died during deportation and the following eighteen months. This is disputed by the Soviet authorities, who have produced figures from old files indicating that a mere 22 per cent or approximately 33,000 of those who arrived in Uzbekistan died prior to 1 January 1946. But even if these figures are accurate, they take no account of those who died during the actual deportation. Moreover the Crimean Tatars claim that the mortality was higher in some other deportation areas – for example in the Urals, where in some villages up to 100 per cent of the newly arrived Crimean Tatars died.*

The years up to 1956, when they had to live under the conditions of 'special settlement', are recalled with particular bitterness by those who survived. Their freedom of movement was restricted to the immediate area to which they had been deported, the penalty for unauthorized departure being up to twenty-five years hard labour, and their lives were at the mercy of the often sadistic local M.V.D. commandants to whom they had to report once a month. Ex-Major General Pëtr Grigorenko, the leading civil rights protestor and a strong supporter of the Crimean Tatars, has compared their situation at this time to that of serfs; while according to Riza Umerov, one of the Tatars sentenced in 1969, 'up till 1956 we were used like draught animals, deprived, moreover, of the most elementary rights.' The 5,000 rouble advances they were given 'to set themselves up' turned into millstones round their necks when, in an act of gratuitous cruelty, they were made to pay back the advance with 5,000 new roubles after the 1947 monetary reform had substituted one new rouble for ten old. Their poverty made it necessary for them to forego higher education – which in any case, because of the restrictions on movement, was a possibility only for those few who happened to have been deported to areas with higher educational institutions, and even then most of the Tatars were excluded because of their nationality.

Back in the Crimea the confiscated property of the Crimean Tatars was given to settlers from the Ukraine, and in the words of the 'Open Letter of the Russian Friends of the Crimean Tatars':

Everything was done to destroy all traces of the national life of the Tatars and the very memory of their existence. Houses were demolished, and orchards and vineyards were allowed to become wild and overgrown. The cemeteries of the Tatars

* On the other hand, if Soviet official figures of 120,129 Crimean Tatar deportees in Uzbekistan on 1 January 1946 are correct, it suggests either that there were no more than about 10,000 Crimean Tatars in other republics or that the Crimean Tatar figure of a 46 per cent mortality is too high. In the 1959 (as in the 1970) Soviet census results the Crimean Tatars were not distinguished from the other Tatars. But the figures for some of the other deported peoples, which show that between 1939 and 1959 their numbers either failed to increase as fast as the Soviet average (and their normal rate of natural increase was above average) or even decreased, give some idea of their mortality rates as a result of their deportation. Thus, while the Soviet population as a whole rose by 22 per cent over the period, the number of Ingush rose by only 15, Karachay by eight and Chechens by 2½ per cent, the number of Balkars marginally declined, and the number of Kalmyks dropped by as much as 21 per cent.

were ploughed up, and the remains of their ancestors torn from the earth ... Everything written and printed in Crimean Tatar was burnt – from ancient manuscripts to the classics of Marxism-Leninism inclusive.

Many of the old Tatar place names in the Crimea were also replaced by Russian ones.

At the same time the history of the Crimea was rewritten. While the relevant volume of the first edition of the *Large Soviet Encyclopaedia* published in 1937 had dwelt on the cultural achievements of the Crimean khanate and the Crimean Tatars' sufferings under the Tsars, the second edition published in 1953 omitted all reference to both these topics and declared that the occupation of the Crimean Tatars had been war and plundering raids. It even suggsted that the Crimea had been Russian from time immemorial and that it had been 'torn away from the Russian people for many centuries' when it had become a province of the Golden Horde in the 13th century. There was no mention of the former Crimean A.S.S.R. Accounts of the Second World War in the Crimea spoke only of the treachery of the Crimean Tatars; regarding their current whereabouts and plight there was total silence.

POLITICAL REHABILITATION

This silence lasted for several more years, even after the death of Stalin, but the latter event did lead to a significant improvement in the position of the Crimean Tatars. In 1954 the 'special settle-ment' restrictions were lifted from those who had fought in the Red Army or with the partisans, and this relief was extended to the whole Crimean Tatar community by an unpublished decree of 28 April 1956. But the same decree also said that property of the Crimean Tatars confiscated at the time of their deportation would not be returned and that they did not have the right to return to the Crimea. At least, however, they could now reside freely elsewhere in the Soviet Union and even visit the Crimea, and certain cultural concessions followed. In 1957 a newspaper in Crimean Tatar called *Lenin bayragy* (Lenin's Banner) started publication in Tashkent and a Crimean Tatar song and dance ensemble was set up; and from the same year a small number of books in Crimean Tatar began to be printed.* But in the Crimea

* The conspiracy of silence surrounding the Crimean Tatars is well illustrat-ed by the fact that nine years later scholars in the U.S.S.R. Academy of Sciences' Institute of Linguistics were apparently unaware that a newspaper and books were being published in Crimean Tatar in Tashkent. At all events the introduction to Volume II (Turkic Languages) of the major five-volume *Languages of the Peoples of the U.S.S.R.* published by the Institute in 1966 put Crimean Tatar in the category of languages 'without a written form'.

itself (which had been transferred from the R.S.F.S.R. to the Ukraine on 19 February 1954 during celebrations marking the 300th anniversary of the Ukraine's 'reunion' with Russia, presumably as a friendly gesture on Kruschev's part to his erstwhile fief) the old Tatar place names continued to be changed and more Crimean Tatar monuments were destroyed. Moreover, when compared with the situation of the Kalmyks and the four Caucasian peoples (who had been publicly absolved of the charge of mass treachery and had their autonomous territories reconstituted in January 1957) the improvement in the situation of the Crimean Tatars was marginal. In 1957 they began their campaign for political rehabilitation, repatriation and the restoration of the Crimean A.S.S.R. It was only after ten years of intensive efforts that they achieved even the first, and then only after suffering numerous arrests, prison sentences, expulsions from the Party and others forms of persecution, despite the fact that they made a point of always acting within the law and their constitutional rights.

At first the Crimean Tatars concentrated on despatching petitions to the authorities in Moscow, and then later started to hold 'mass gatherings and meetings'. Between July 1957 and March 1961 five major appeals with between 6,000 and 18,000 signatures were sent to the leading Party and government bodies, and in October 1961 another petition, this one signed by 25,000 people, was submitted to the XXII Party Congress. The arrest of those most active in the movement began in 1959; but the first available details of a trial relate to October 1961, when two Crimean Tatars were sentenced in Tashkent to seven and five years respectively in 'strict regime' labour camps for having composed and distributed documents protesting against the treatment of the Crimean Tatars to compatriots in Chirchik, Namangan, Fergana, Leninabad and Sukhumi. This activity was classed as spreading anti-Soviet propaganda and stirring up racial discord (articles 60 part 1 and 64 of the Uzbek Criminal Code). Another trial in August 1962 involved Marat Omerov, a young factory foreman, and Seit Amza Umerov, a student of Tashkent University. Early in 1962 they had been among some twenty-five young Crimean Tatar students and workers from the Tashkent area who had decided to form 'The Union of Crimean Tatar Youth for the Return to the Homeland'. This organization was to be 'truly Leninist', but in the event it was not actually set up, since an older member of the group warned of the dangers and persuaded the others to think again. Nonetheless Omerov and Umerov were sentenced to four and three years respectively in 'strict regime' labour camps on a charge of making anti-Soviet propaganda and setting up and heading an anti-Soviet organization (articles 60 and 62 of the Uzbek Criminal Code). A number of the others were dismissed from their jobs or expelled from the university. But neither these measures nor the sentences imposed on their companions deterred most of them from subsequently taking a very active part in the movement.

The Crimean Tatars' campaign entered a more intensive phase in 1964, when they started to maintain a permanent lobby in Moscow. The members of this lobby replaced one another constantly and each held a mandate signed by the residents of the town or village which sent him to Moscow. These mandates were handed in to the Central Committee on arrival. Up to about September 1968 over 4,000 representatives had been sent to the capital, where they tried to obtain hearings with government and Party leaders, handed in letters and petitions, informed the Soviet public about the Crimean Tatar question, and issued a bulletin twice a month reporting to their constituents on their activity and general developments.

In 1965 complementary 'Action Groups to Assist the Party and Government in Solving the National Question of the Crimean Tatar People' were set up in all the settlements where Crimean Tatars lived. These groups had no formal organization. Their members were chosen by the local Crimean Tatar communities and their names – over 5,000 in all – were handed in to the Central Committee. In the words of a 1969 protest addressed to the Central Committee and other bodies,

> without in any way exceeding the bounds of the law, the Action Groups organized various measures, whose purpose was to bring to the knowledge of the Party and government the true aims and aspirations of the Crimean Tatar people. They engaged in the collection of signatures to petitions addressed to the government and the collection of funds by way of donations from the people for the despatch of delegates to Moscow, for assistance to the families of participants of the national movement sent to prison and so on.

The Action Groups regularly organized meetings, sometimes attended by several hundred or more Crimean Tatars, at which bulletins from the representatives in Moscow were read and current problems discussed. There were also Action Group meetings on provincial, republican and even inter-republican levels.

In 1965 and 1966 some of the representatives in Moscow were received by members of the Presidium of the Supreme Soviet, but – as when Mikoyan had seen a Crimean Tatar delegation in 1957 – with no result. The events connected with the 1966 meeting, which took place on the eve of the XXIII Party Congress, give some idea of the scale of the movement at this time. As the Congress approached, the number of Crimean Tatar representatives in Moscow rose to 125. 14,284 letters as well as numerous telegrams were sent to various Party and government bodies. A petition to the Congress, signed by more than 120,000 Crimean Tatars (i.e. virtually the whole adult population), together with seven volumes of data supporting their claim of a 46 per cent mortality rate in 1944–5, was handed in to the Central Committee. Finally on 28 March 1966 ten of the representatives were received by Georgadze, Secretary of the U.S.S.R. Supreme Soviet Presidium, who promised that their case would be reviewed in a month or so. When nothing happened a new petition with 115,000 signatures was drawn up, 17,000 more letters were sent, and the number of representatives in Moscow began to increase again. But this time they found the Moscow hotels barred to them, and on 25 June they were seized at the Central Committee building and forcibly expelled from the city. A wave of protest meetings followed in Uzbekistan and elsewhere; more representatives arrived and distributed accounts of what had happened to various public organizations and to the press. Eventually four of the representatives were arrested and after nine months in custody they were tried. Each was given a three years' suspended sentence on a charge of inflaming racial discord.

In September 1966 three new articles were added to the R.S.F.S.R., Uzbek and other republican Criminal Codes in order to provide the authorities with a new weapon for countering the meetings and demonstrations and the circulation of *samizdat*. The two important new articles in the Uzbek Criminal Code were 191-4 ('the dissemination of deliberate fabrications defaming the Soviet State and social system') and 191-6 ('the organization of or active participation in group actions violating public order'), both carrying a maximum penalty of three years' imprisonment. It was made plain to the Crimean Tatars that these measures were directed mainly against their activities. Many of the most active campaigners were summoned to the local police and K.G.B. offices and asked to sign a statement affirming that they had familiarized themselves with the new articles. The relevant decree of 27 September 1966 was hurriedly brought into force on 9 October, the day after the Crimean Tatars had begun to hold

285

meetings in many parts of Uzbekistan to mark the 45th anniversary of the Crimean A.S.S.R. Although entirely law-abiding and peaceable, a number of these meetings were forcibly broken up by the police. Hundreds of Crimean Tatars were given up to "15 days' imprisonment for 'petty hooliganism'", and seventeen, including three Party members, were sentenced for up to two years under the new article 191-6 and article 192 ('resisting the authorities').

Some of the leading Crimean Tatar campaigners were subjected to continual harassment and persecution in an effort to make them desist. Mustafa Dzhemilev, for instance, who as a boy of eighteen had been dismissed from his job in a Tashkent aircraft factory in connection with the Union of Crimean Tatar Youth episode, was in March 1965 reduced from his status as a full-time student to that of correspondence student at the Tashkent Irrigation Engineers Institute because of his political activities and also because in 1963 he had written an historical outline of Turkic culture in the Crimea in the 13th to 18th centuries. In September 1965 he was expelled altogether and at about the same time was beaten up in the street. At the very end of the year, when he returned from Moscow where he had managed to get his expulsion declared illegal, a trumped-up charge of evading military service was brought against him. Shortly afterwards an unsuccessful attempt was made to plant a watch in his pocket on a Tashkent bus. Sentenced to eighteen months on the charge of evading military service in May 1966, Dzhemilev had great difficulty in getting a job after his release and the Institute refused to reinstate him. A K.G.B. major, speaking frankly, told Reshat Dzhemilev, another Crimean Tatar leader, on 22 January 1968:

> It's easier for us if people like Mustafa and Server don't get higher education. It's more difficult for us to combat the intelligentsia than manual workers. So let them be manual workers.

Another young Crimean Tatar leader subjected to a long period of intimidation was Yuriy (Yusuf) Osmanov, a physicist at the Institute of High Energy Physics in Serpukhov near Moscow. He had antagonized the authorities by writing numerous letters to official and public figures and submitting articles on Gasprinskiy and the history of the Crimean Tatars to leading historical journals and institutes. Together with two other young scientists and a welder he was eventually sentenced to a labour camp in May 1968 on charges of composing and distributing documents defaming the Soviet state and inflaming racial discord.

In July 1967 the number of Crimean Tatar representatives in

Moscow rose to over 400. This time they had resolved to stage a demonstration in Red Square if their demands for rehabilitation and repatriation were not met; but on 21 July twenty of them were received in the Kremlin by Andropov, Chairman of the K.G.B., as well as by Georgadze, Rudenko, the U.S.S.R. Procurator General, and Shchelokov, the Minister for the Preservation of Public Order. Andropov announced that within the next few days the Central Committee would 'loudly and publicly' politically rehabilitate the Crimean Tatars, but that the question of their return to the Crimea required further study. He also promised to arrange with Rashidov, the Uzbek First Secretary, to make premises available where the representatives could tell the people about their forthcoming rehabilitation. But back in Uzbekistan no premises were made available; and five weeks later, on Sunday 27 August, after notifying the Uzbek Central Committee in writing of their intention, over 2,000 Tatars gathered in Tashkent to meet their representatives, only to be dispersed by force. The following Saturday Crimean Tatars who came to Tashkent from other parts of the republic to protest were again dispersed. In all, over 130 people were arrested during the two days, twelve of whom were later sentenced to up to three years' imprisonment on charges of organizing mass disorders and resisting the authorities.

It was only on 9 September 1967 that the decree rehabilitating the Crimean Tartars (dated 5 September 1967) was finally published in newspapers in Uzbekistan, Kazakhstan, Kirgiziya and Tadzhikistan. The decree began as follows:

After the liberation of the Crimea from Fascist occupation in 1944 instances of active collaboration with the German invaders by a certain section of the Tatars formerly resident in the Crimea were attributed without foundation to the whole Tatar population of the Crimea. These indiscriminate accusations against all citizens of Tatar nationality resident in the Crimea ought to be lifted, the more so since a new generation of people has embarked on its working and political life.

Later it went on to note that 'the Tatars formerly resident in the Crimea' had 'taken root' in the Uzbek and other republics, that they enjoyed all the rights of Soviet citizens and had a newspaper and radio broadcasts in Tatar, and it enjoined the republican governments concerned to continue to look after the Tatars' interests. The decree was accompanied by an order of the same date varying the decree of 28 April 1956 and explaining that 'citizens of Tatar nationality formerly resident in the Crimea' and members of their families were entitled to reside anywhere

287

in the Soviet Union 'in accordance with the existing legislation on employment and the passport regulations'. (Under the passport regulations a citizen has to be registered, i.e. obtain a residence permit, which is normally granted automatically if evidence of accommodation is produced.)

The publications of the decree absolving them of the charge of mass treachery was naturally a matter of great satisfaction to the Tatars, but any initial euphoria soon wore off as the unsatisfactory aspects of the rehabilitation became clear. Firstly, the decree had been published only in certain Central Asian papers (apart from the little-read *U.S.S.R. Supreme Soviet Gazette*) and therefore only a small part of the Soviet population had learnt of the rehabilitation. Secondly, and more importantly, in the words of a 1969 protest, the decree

> contained several features aimed at keeping the Crimean Tatars permanently rooted in the deportation areas. The very fact that the decree spoke not of Crimean Tatars but of 'Tatars formerly resident in the Crimea' (i.e. arbitrarily gave the Crimean Tatars a new 'ethnic' designation) was an indication that the government did not recognize the right of the Crimean Tatars to their own national territory and was even trying to deny the existence of the Crimean Tatar nation as such.

That the authorities were well aware of the limitations of the decree is evidenced by the despatch of a high-powered C.P.S.U. Central Committee commission to 'explain' it. But the 'explanation' was not always such as to reassure the Tatars, Vishnevskiy, a C.P.S.U. Central Committee representative who answered questions at a meeting in Samarkand University on the day the decree was published, merely repeated the accusations of treachery against the Crimean Tatars made by a Stalinist writer and denied that they had ever enjoyed autonomy. The brilliant young Crimean Tatar theoretical physicist Rollan Kadyyev, a lecturer at the University, objected and was later threatened with dismissal if he did not change his views, and subsequently all trips in connection with his work were refused. Nonetheless the authorites were evidently anxious to have Crimean Tatar approval of the decree, since, immediately after it was published, in every workplace the Tatars were summoned and asked to express their gratitude to the Party and government.*

* In the Uzbekistan newspaper *Pravda Vostoka* of 16 September 1967 a Crimean Tatar foreman at the Tashkent Textile Machinery Plant wrote of his 'profound joy and gratitude to our Party and government' for the decrees and went on to say that his Tatar colleagues at the works had expressed similar feelings at a recent meeting.

THE POST-REHABILITATION SITUATION

The three main features of the Crimean Tatar movement since rehabilitation have been persistent and largely unsuccessful efforts to take up residence in the Crimea, a link-up with the general democratic movement in the Soviet Union, and a continuation of their campaign for repatriation and the restoration of the Crimean A.S.S.R. in both Uzbekistan and Moscow.

Whatever the shortcomings of the decree, the Crimean Tatars interpreted the accompanying order as giving them the right to live in the Crimea. Hundreds of families immediately left for their homeland, only to be expelled by the police – sometimes with considerable violence – in spite of the fact that jobs and accommodation were readily available. A little later, for appearance's sake, the Tatars were told that they could be registered in the Crimea if they could find an average of 13·65 square metres' accommodation per capita – a much higher figure than the norm; but simultaneously the inhabitants of the Crimea were warned that they would be severely punished if they offered accommodation or sold their houses to Crimean Tatars. Contracts for the sale of houses concluded by residents who refused to be intimidated were declared invalid, and the sellers fined. In the period up to December 1967, out of the 6,000 or so Crimean Tatars who arrived only three single men and two families succeeded in obtaining registration. The remainder were either forcibly deported or, their funds exhausted after months of vain efforts to be registered, were eventually compelled to leave of their own accord.

The Tatars refused to be deterred, however, and in March 1968 the authorities took two steps in Uzbekistan to avert a mass departure for the Crimea planned for the summer. First they announced that officials of the Crimean provincial administration would come to Uzbekistan to conclude labour contracts with those wishing to return to the Crimea. But resettlement permits were issued only with the approval of the K.G.B. and then solely to those who had taken no part whatsoever in the national movement. By the end of 1970 only a token number of families had been returned to the Crimea under this scheme, although at the same time Crimean authorities had been recruiting settlers in large numbers from other parts of the Ukraine as well as using economic pressures to prevent Ukrainians and Russians from leaving the peninsula. Secondly, the Uzbek authorities tried to persuade the Crimea Tatars to renounce their aim of returning to the Crimea by circulating letters among them saying that they were being stirred up by a handful of nationalists and anti-

Soviet elements. They also threatened the leading participants in the national movement. The letters were allegedly written by members of the Crimean Tatar intelligentsia, but, although the authorities resorted to blackmail, deception and intimidation, they managed to collect only 262 signatures and a considerable number of these were later repudiated.

Undaunted, large numbers of Crimean Tatars continued to leave for the Crimea, in some cases for the second or third time. But the authorities refused to relent. Tatars who managed to get jobs there were dismissed as soon as their nationality was discovered; registration was invariably refused, and there were periodic round-ups by the police. For example, in mid-May 1968 some sixty Tatars encamped at Simferopol' reservoir were forcibly deported to Uzbekistan. On 27 May about 250 K.G.B. men, police and volunteer police tore down the tents of ninety-eight Tatars near Simferopol' and sent thirty-eight of them on a four-day bus journey without food or water to Baku, where they were embarked with considerable brutality on the ferry for Central Asia. On 26 June, eleven of the twenty-one Tatars who came to register a complaint about their treatment with the chairman of the provincial executive committee (Chemodurov) were sentenced to fifteen days' imprisonment and subsequently expelled, and ten were sent by plane at their own expense to Dushanbe, where none of them had ever lived. On 15 July eleven families, who had been told five days previously by a local official to occupy empty houses on a state farm, were literally dragged from those houses in the middle of the night, and were put, together with four families from another farm, on a train leaving the Crimea. In the latter instance Russians and Ukrainians on the farm refused to work the next day in protest; seventeen families left the farm, and four newly recruited families declined to settle there. During the first year or so after rehabilitation only eighteen families and thirteen single people in all eventually managed to become registered – while about 12,000 Tatars were expelled from the Crimea and seventeen sentenced to various terms of imprisonment.

The harassment in the Crimea continued in 1969. The experiences of eleven families who bought houses in the Belogorsk district in early 1969 are recounted in the individual protests they addressed to the U.N. Human Rights Commission after failing to obtain any redress from the Soviet authorities. All eleven were refused registration, and the majority (if not all) of their house contracts were declared invalid. At the end of June eight of the eleven families were brutally seized in the middle of the night, put on trains leaving the peninsula, and dumped at railway stations, destitute except for a handful of possessions. They were given no compensation for their houses and when, thanks to the generosity of local people, they returned to the Crimea some found their houses boarded up or occupied and their stores looted. they were all reduced to begging in order to keep alive. A protest made by 456 Crimean Tatars to the Party and government against brutal expulsions from the Crimea which is listed under 'Samizdat News' in *Chronicle of Current Events*, No. 14 of 30 June 1970, suggests that the expulsions were still continuing in the first half of 1970.

The link-up between the Tatars and the general democratic movement, whose constitutional approach they shared, occurred in early 1968. It seems to have been established primarily through the writer Aleksey Kosterin, a Communist of long-standing who had regularly championed the rights of the smaller nations. Kosterin had already requested that the Crimean Tatar and Volga German questions be discussed at two Party congresses (presumably those of 1961 and 1966), and it was probably through him that Grigorenko, with whom he became acquainted in late 1965 or early 1966, also became a staunch supporter of the Crimean Tartar cause. Both Kosterin and Grigorenko as well as Dr Zampira Asanova, a Crimean Tatar leader, were among twelve Soviet intellectuals who addressed an open letter to the Consultative Conference of Communist Parties meeting in Budapest in February–March 1968, which mentioned *inter alia* the persecution of the Crimean Tatars. On 17 March 1968 the sixty Crimean Tatar representatives in Moscow held a party in honour of Kosterin's seventy-second birthday to express their gratitude for his efforts on their behalf. The writer himself was seriously ill, and his place was taken by Grigorenko who delivered a rousing speech in which he emphasized the short-comings of the Tatars' political rehabilitation and looked forward to the rebirth of the Crimean A.S.S.R.

Kosterin's death on 10 November 1968, a month after he had been expelled from the Party for his efforts on their behalf, was a major loss for the Crimean Tatars. At his funeral, which twenty-three of them attended, Grigorenko revealed that Kosterin had bequeathed his remains to the Tatars and said that they would be taken to the Crimea as soon as Crimean Tatar autonomy was restored.

Grigorenko's speech at the banquet in March 1968 and his subsequent close association with the Crimean Tatars were clearly a matter of considerable concern to the authorities, and sometime after Kosterin's funeral the Tatars were warned against him in a letter which appeared to be the work of the same group of intelligentsia that had been party to the letters attacking the leaders of the movement in March 1968. Then at the beginning of May 1969 Grigorenko, who had accepted an invitation from about 2,000 Tatars to appear for the defence in the forthcoming trial of ten Tatars in Tashkent, was lured to Tashkent by a message, supposedly from Mustafa Dzhemilev, saying that the trial was shortly to start, only to be arrested before he could return to Moscow. Later, in a travesty of justice, he was confined to a psychiatric institution. At about the same time the 137 volumes of the Tatar campaign archives were confiscated from the Moscow flat of Il'ya Gabay, another leader of the democratic movement, and Gabay himself was arrested and sent to Tashkent for trial. The authorities appear to have used Grigorenko's and Gabay's links with the Tatars largely as a pretext for putting them on trial away from the capital, but the confinement of Grigorenko was a particularly severe blow for the Tatars. However the links between the Crimean Tatars and the civil rights movement remained. In May 1969 Mustafa Dzhemilev, described as a worker, became one of the fifteen founder members of the Action Group for the Defence of Civil Rights in the Soviet Union, and the supporters of this group included Zampira Asanova, Reshat Dzhemilev and other Crimean Tatars.

In Uzbekistan the Crimean Tatars continued to hold their Action Group meetings and to send petitions and protests to Moscow, and the authorities continued their attempts to prevent or break up any public manifestations. Thus on 21 April 1968, when the Crimean Tatars of Chirchik persisted in holding their national spring festival of 'Derviza' – at which it was apparently feared that Grigorenko's March 1968 speech would be read – police and soldiers suddenly set upon them as they were singing and dancing, and following a clash which lasted until nightfall some 300 were arrested. In both 1968 and 1969 extraordinary measures were taken to prevent the Tatars from holding their customary meetings and religious rites in the cemeteries on 18 May (the anniversary of the deportation); and at a funeral in Bekabad on 19 May 1969 the local Tatar leaders had great difficulty in restraining the anger of the mourners when the police felt the corpse to make sure the man was dead. The authorities also tried to stop the Tatars laying wreaths at the statue of Lenin on his birthday, and immediately removed any that were laid.

Not unnaturally the Crimean Tatars usually link their major petitions and protests to Party and government bodies in Moscow with important dates or events such as the anniversary of their deportation or Party congresses. Thus as the anniversary of the deportation approached in 1968 after the events in the Crimea and the clash in Chirchik, the number of representatives in Moscow rose to 800. First they found themselves barred from the hotels because of their nationality, and then they were all rounded up on 16 and 17 May and sent under escort to Tashkent – even if they lived in other parts of the country. As a result of their inhuman treatment some had heart attacks, while one man, Rustem Il'yasov, went out of his mind. But there was no interruption in the work of the representatives in Moscow since already on 18 May those who had managed to escape from the train started to return. In the period up to the end of May they visited various prominent personalities and handed in 22,984 appeals and letters with over 50,000 signatures. By this time the total number of signatures under various collective and individual protests and petitions delivered since the beginning of the campaign exceeded three million.

In July 1969 a petition, signed by 12,000, was addressed to the International Conference of Communist and Workers' Parties in Moscow. On the second day of the conference five Crimean Tatars, including Zampira Asanova and Reshat Dzhemilev, unfurled banners at midday on Mayakovskiy Square in the centre of Moscow. Probably because the conference was being held they escaped arrest, but they were interrogated and despatched home. Most of them were subsequently deprived of their registration in Krasnodar region (adjacent to the Crimea) where a number of Crimean Tatars, unable to obtain registration in the Crimea, have settled temporarily.

A number of appeals, including one from 3,000 Crimean Tatar Second World War veterans and another from 350 Crimean Tatar Communists, were addressed to the Party and government at the time of the Lenin Centenary in April 1970. At the same time 147 representatives from Uzbekistan, Kirgiziya and the southern Ukraine, who had come to Moscow to register a complaint with the Supreme Soviet that the 1967 rehabilitation decree was not being implemented and that the local authorities were doing everything in their power to prevent the Crimean Tatars from returning to the Crimea, were forcibly expelled from Moscow. The latest appeal from 60,000 Crimean Tatars to delegates to the XXIV Party Congress, which opened in Moscow on 30 March 1971, vividly describes the suffering of the Tatars in the Crimea since their rehabilitation. It ends by naming a number of police, Party and other officials in the Crimea who are accused of murder, driving people to suicide, carrying out illegal arrests and stealing property.

The trials of leading Crimean Tatars have also continued since rehabilitation, mainly on charges of organizing or participating in mass disorders or distributing deliberate fabrications defaming the state. The most important trial was 'Case No. 109' in July–August 1969, which involved ten Tatars arrested the previous autumn and was the one at which Grigorenko was going to appear. The defendants represented a typical cross-section of the leading campaigners in that they were predominantly from the younger generation who could only just remember the deportation and included workers and members of the intelligentsia. The three older accused had fought against the Germans during the war and one, Yazydzhiyev, a poet and former teacher working as a bricklayer, had been recommended for the decoration of Hero of the Soviet Union in 1942. Among the younger defendants were Rollan Kadyyev, the brilliant physicist mentioned earlier, and Izzet Khairov, engineer and Party member. All had excellent, even outstanding, work records and character references. Some had been active in the movement for several years, others only for a matter of months. They were all charged under Article 191-4 of the Uzbek Criminal Code and/or the equivalent articles of the R.S.F.S.R. and Ukrainian Codes. The allegedly incriminating documents included bulletins from the Moscow representatives and republican Action Group meetings; six articles or letters from Kosterin; Grigorenko's speech of 17 March 1968; a document written by one of the defendants, Reshat Bayramov, a young electrical fitter, entitled 'Genocide in the Policy of the Soviet Government'; and also entries in the visitors' book of Simferopol' Musuem by Khairov and others, complaining that it contained nothing about the Crimean Tatars, and in particular about the Tatar heroes of the Revolution and Second World War.

Most of the defendants had been representatives in Moscow in May–June 1968, and during this time four of them had been particularly assiduous in distributing copies of a number of the documents either in person or through the post to various organizations and individuals, some of whose names had been culled from the press. It was a copy of a bulletin sent to the Uzbek Union of Writers and passed by them to the K.G.B. in June 1968 which had initiated the case. In spite of repeated requests the defendants were not supplied with the literature necessary to the preparation of their defence. Demands that they should be removed from cells holding as many as twenty-six people (many of whom were violent criminals including murderers) were rejected by the court when the trial finally opened on 1 July, as were demands that the trial should be reported in the press and shown live on television and that an expert commission for solving the Crimean Tatar question be called.

As is the normal Soviet practice in such cases, many of the seats in the small courtroom were occupied by the K.G.B., and – as in other similar trials – the prosecutor, who seemed most concerned with the fact that one document had already been published abroad, took it for granted that the documents were slanderous and concentrated on establishing that they had been composed or disseminated by the defendants. This in most instances the defendants admitted. At the same time the defendants argued that the documents were not defamatory since the facts set out in them were true. Kadyyev was particularly eloquent in substantiating his allegations of genocide and racial discrimination, adducing in support Soviet press reports on such phenomena in other countries. Some of the prosecution witnesses unwittingly played into the hands of the accused. For example, the testimony of a Russian woman, Rozaliya Zorina, was a complete vindication of the arguments of Khairov and others that much more needed to be done to remove the stigma of the Stalinist accusations. On 5 August 1969 Bayramov and Kadyyev were sentenced to three years each in 'ordinary regime' camps, and the rest were given one or one and a half years, or sentences which entailed their immediate release. During the entire five weeks of the trial Crimean Tatars from many parts of the country stood outside the court in broiling sun in order to express their solidarity with the accused. Police handling of the large crowds on the last two days led to protests and a demonstration outside the prosecutor's office.

Other trials have included that of Mustafa Dzhemilev, who was arrested for the second time in September 1969, and Il'ya Gabay, who were each given three years' imprisonment in Tashkent in January 1970 on the usual charge of deliberate fabrications defaming the Soviet state and social system. A girl of eighteen was sentenced to three years in a labour camp in September 1970 for having hung black flags on the local police and executive council buildings on the 1970 anniversary of the deportation. This case brought the number of trials on which details are available up to thirty, involving a total of eighty-six defendants, four of whom have been sentenced twice. The Crimean Tatars claimed in 1968 that more than 200 had been sentenced since 1959, excluding the hundreds who by administrative action were given sentences of up to fifteen days' imprisonment for 'petty hooliganism'. In addition, according to 'incomplete' figures of April 1969, forty Crimean Tatars have been expelled from the Party or Komsomol for their part in the national movement, twelve have been expelled from higher or further education institutions in Tashkent and the Crimea, and sixty have been subjected to searches on suspicion of possessing documents slandering the Soviet state.

There is some evidence of a diminution in Crimean Tatar activity recently – for instance, apparently only fifteen bulletins were issued by the Moscow representatives between April 1969 and February 1971. Indeed it would hardly be surprising if the Tatars felt discouraged, since they have little to show for all their efforts since their rehabilitation. They have not been granted an interview by any leading member of the government or Party, and all their appeals and protests have been ignored. The only apparent gains have been the token organized labour recruitment scheme; the introduction of classes in Crimean Tatar for Crimean Tatar children in some primary schools from the 1968/9 school year; an increase in the number of books published in Crimean Tatar to approximately eight in 1970; and accounts in *Lenin bayragy* of the exploits of Crimean Tatars at the time of the Revolution and during the last war. But *Lenin bayragy* is read only by Crimean Tatars and the treatment of Crimean Tatar history in books accessible to the general Soviet public remains essentially that found in the second edition of the *Large Soviet Encyclopaedia*, i.e. it consists of extremely hostile and one-sided accounts of the Crimean khanate and there is no mention of the Crimean Tatars' subsequent fate. As for the organized labour recruitment scheme, only farm labour is recruited, and the circumstances of the few families who have returned to the Crimea in this way are described as being worse than those of 'special settlement' in that they must either stay permanently on the farm for which they were recruited or face expulsion from the Crimea. Moreover their children are denied higher or further education in the Crimea.

The Crimean Tatar accusation of genocide rests not only on the appalling mortality they suffered as a direct result of the mass deportation but also on the denial of the conditions necessary to preserve their national identity and in particular their national language and culture. In the context of preserving their language, therefore, Crimean Tatar lessons in some primary schools fall far short of their demand for the Crimean Tatar schools they had in the Crimea and to which they are entitled under Article 121 of the Soviet Constitution. But this demand goes very much against the current trend in the Soviet Union in that, since the 1950s at least, there has been a growing tendency for the nationalities of the autonomous republics and districts, reportedly at their own request, to have their secondary and even primary schooling in Russian. Indeed this has obvious practical advantages since not only is Russian the *lingua franca* in the Soviet Union, but some of the national minorities are too small for provision of higher education in their native tongue to be a feasible proposition, and a good knowledge of Russian is therefore vital.

However there would seem to be no good reason why Crimean Tatar children, like those of some of the other small minorities, should not be taught their native language and literature in the secondary school as a special subject. In the cultural sphere too the Crimean Tatars clearly do not have the facilities they did before their deportation (or as other nationalities of comparable size enjoy today): for example their own theatre. Although the assimilation pressures on all the smaller nationalities are great, conditions probably would be more favourable for preserving the Crimean Tatars' distinctive culture if the Tatars' national autonomy were restored. However some of their complaints in the cultural sphere, e.g. about *Lenin bayragy* not expressing their national interests, go beyond the issue of discrimination to the wider question of cultural regimentation in the Soviet Union. There is no doubt that such cultural facilities as they do enjoy today are considerably better than nothing: thus, a whole new generation of Crimean Tatar writers has been able to exercise its talents in the pages of *Lenin bayragy*.

The prosecutor in 'Case No. 109' argued that talk of genocide and discrimination against the Crimean Tatars was slander since there was a Crimean Tatar Deputy to the U.S.S.R. Supreme Soviet; many Crimean Tatars were Party members and had been elected to local soviets and held good jobs; the Crimean Tatars had their own newspaper; and from the material point of view were as well off and in many cases better off than other peoples. The Crimean Tatars do not dispute any of this. Indeed they are proud that thanks to their intelligence, industry and superior agricultural skills they are more prosperous than their neighbours (it is this prosperity which has enabled them to meet the enormous costs of their campaign). They also appear to suffer no discrimination with regard to housing or higher education in Uzbekistan, although they have complained that jobs in certain fields such as public order and state security, the courts and communications are closed to them. But Yazydzhiyev voiced their feelings when he said in his final speech at his trial:

> Let no one think that the Crimean Tatar people is a flock of sheep to whom it is a matter of no importance where it grazes as long as it has its fill.

Confirmation that the majority of Crimean Tatars share Yazydzhiyev's opinion can be seen in a report which appeared in the *Chronicle* at the end of 1969; this revealed that the Tatars had handed in to the Central Committee the first results of a referendum they were conducting to establish beyond any doubt whether the Crimean Tatars really considered that they had 'taken root' where they now live. Every adult Crimean Tatar was being asked (a) if he wanted to return to the Crimea and (b) if he wanted the restoration of the Crimean A.S.S.R. The results so far had shown that all but a handful wanted both.

One reason given unofficially for not repatriating the Crimean Tatars is the possible economic damage that it might cause to Uzbekistan. Thus G. Ya. Denisov, a high Party official, told Altunyan, a leading dissident, on 30 June 1969:

> The Crimean Tatars do not want to go anywhere. And if they did, it would undermine the economy of Uzbekistan and new problems would arise in the Crimea.

Given the industry and skills of the Crimean Tatars and the shortage of skilled labour in Uzbekistan, there is probably some truth in this; but the Tatars are agreeable to a phased repatriation which would minimize any disruption, and they also recognize that measures would be necessary to reassure the Russian and Ukrainian population in the Crimea. They themselves have repeatedly made it plain that rumours spread by the authorities that the Tatars want to turn the Russians and others out of the Crimea are completely unfounded. They would in any case be a minority, as they were before, since the population of the province in 1970 was over 1,800,000. As for accommodating them in the Crimea: according to two Ukrainian scholars who appeaed to the Ukrainian Supreme Soviet Presidium to celebrate the centenary of Lenin's birth in April 1970 by restoring the Crimean A.S.S.R., the Crimea is planning to take 500,000 settlers in order to overcome its acute shortage of labour and therefore could easily absorb all the Crimean Tatars.

What is it then that makes the Soviet authorities so intransigent? Fears about the loyalty of the Crimean Tatars in what they regard as a strategic area – fears that have their roots in history –

were probably the sole reason for not reconstituting the Crimean A.S.S.R. in 1956 and no doubt still play a large part. But an additional reason today is almost certainly an unwillingness to give in to any pressure group, and more particularly a national, pressure group. At a press conference on the national question held in April 1969 for Soviet and foreign journalists the then Chairman of the U.S.S.R. Supreme Soviet Council of Nationalities, Paleckis (whom the Crimean Tatars have on the whole found less unsympathetic to their cause than some other leading figures), is reported to have stated that the Crimean Tatars could return to the Crimea but so few wanted to that the Crimean A.S.S.R. would apparently not be restored. This seems to be a tacit admission that if large numbers of Crimean Tatars returned to the Crimea, as there is every evidence they would like to do, it would be only logical for the Crimean A.S.S.R. to be restored. The fact that a people is a minority in its own national territory was not in the past, and still is, no reason for it to be deprived of national autonomy. At a time when the question of national distinctions in the Soviet Union is becoming more rather than less acute, and when the Party may well be regretting that it ever set up the national republics in the first place, the authorities must fear that such a concession to national sentiments would merely encourage the other nationalities to step up their own demands for translation of the illusion of national statehood into the reality. In present circumstances, therefore, it is difficult to be sanguine about the prospects for a change of heart by the Soviet government, and the Crimean Tatars are clearly destined to mark 18 October 1971 – the fiftieth anniversary of the establishment of the Crimean A.S.S.R. – in exile. There would probably be a greater chance of gaining some concessions from the Soviet Government if the Crimean Tatars had as vocal and well-organized a lobby in the West as the Soviet Jews. But understandably the Turkish government is most anxious not to become involved in any nationalist movements outside Turkey.

PART TWO

THE VOLGA GERMANS

In discussing the deportations it is usual to speak of the Volga Germans, who were not only the largest and most compact group of Germans in the Soviet Union but also the only ones to have an autonomous republic. But in fact the whole German population of European Russia was deported, and strictly speaking this chapter should be called 'The Soviet Germans' since the whole Soviet German population suffered the same disabilities and it is not possible to distinguish between the various groups today.

Most of the Germans living in Russia before the Revolution were peasant farmers descended from Germans who had come to the country when Catherine the Great invited foreigners to settle on the Volga in 1762 and 1763, and in the Black Sea area and the Crimea in the 1870s. German settlements were also set up in Siberia, Kazakhstan and Central Asia. Thanks to the generous help they were given and the fact that, unlike the other peasants, they were not serfs, the Germans prospered. In 1914 there were more than 200 German villages on the Volga with a total population of over 500,000. During the First World War some anti-German measures were adopted, but a 1916 decree ordering the Germans to be expelled from the Volga area in April 1917 was suspended after the February revolution and finally rescinded by the Bolsheviks.

Lenin (whose own mother had German blood) had high hopes of revolution in Germany at this time, and it is likely that the possible propaganda benefits were to the forefront of his mind when the Volga Germans – despite their lack of a large proletarian element – were one of the first peoples to be granted some degree of autonomy in the shape of an Autonomous Workers' Commune on 19 October 1918. This became the Volga German A.S.S.R. on 20 February 1924. A total of seventeen German National Districts were also set up in other parts of the country where there were concentrations of Germans. Six were in the R.S.F.S.R., including one in the Crimea and another in the Altay, one each in Georgia and Azerbaydzhan, and nine in the Ukraine. In 1926 there were 1,238,549 Germans in the Soviet Union, of whom 14·9 per cent lived in towns and 94·9 per cent considered German to be their mother tongue. Approximately a quarter (380,000) lived in the Volga German A.S.S.R. By 1939 the number of Germans in the Soviet Union had risen to 1,423,000. Like all the other peoples in the country the German population suffered during collectivization and the various purges of the late 1920s and 1930s, but probably to no greater extent than the rest.

The deportation of the Volga Germans took place in August 1941. The decree of 28 August 1941 (which announced their 'transfer' to Novosibirsk and Omsk provinces, the Altay, Kazakhstan, and other neighbouring localities) said that it was a precautionary measure in view of the fact that none of the Germans in the Volga area had reported on the presence in their midst of tens of thousands of diversionists and spies ready to engage in sabotage at a signal from Germany. The German population of the Crimea, Ukraine and Caucasus was also deported in the latter half of 1941, except from those areas of the Ukraine which had already been overrun by the Nazis, and all the German National Districts were abolished. Those deported from the Volga republic were promised land and assistance in their new areas of settlement and theoretically each family was allowed to take a ton of luggage with them. They were also well treated by the local population at their destination, in spite of the latter's own poverty, but they nonetheless had to endure considerable privations. All the Germans were put under the same 'special settlement' restrictions and disabilities as the other deported peoples had to endure; and the Germans in occupied territory, whom the Nazis evacuated to Germany on their withdrawal, were subsequently repatriated to the Soviet Union and likewise placed in 'special settlement' conditions, mainly in Siberia and the Komi area. As with the Crimean Tatars, all mention of the existence of Soviet Germans disappeared from Soviet published material.

The Soviet Germans were released from the 'special settlement' restrictions by a decree of 13 December 1955 in what was thought to be a gesture marking the establishment of diplomatic relations between Moscow and Bonn. But the decree, like that concerning the Crimean Tatars, forbade them to return to the regions from which they had been deported. The political rehabilitation of the Soviet Germans is also thought to have been linked with Khrushchev's efforts to improve relations with West Germany. The decree, dated 29 August 1964, was very much less grudging than the one rehabilitating the Tatars. Thus it not only said that the sweeping accusations of actively assisting the German invaders were unfounded, but went on:

> In reality in the years of the Great Patriotic War the vast majority of the German population, together with the entire Soviet people, assisted the victory of the Soviet Union over Fascist Germany by their labour and in the post-war years have been actively taking part in Communist construction.

Otherwise the decree closely resembled that relating to the Tatars in noting that the Soviet Germans had 'taken firm root in their new places of residence', were taking an active part in public and political life, and enjoyed certain cultural facilities.

From 1955 there was a gradual reintroduction on a limited scale of cultural facilities for the German population. In that year

301

U

a local paper in German began to appear in the Altay, and in 1957 *Neues Leben*, now a weekly with a circulation of 300,000, started publication in Moscow. Moscow Radio started putting out programmes for Soviet Germans in 1956, Kazakh Radio in 1957 and Kirgiz Radio in 1962. In 1957 and 1958 directives were issued in a number of republics that instruction in German as the mother tongue was to be introduced where parents requested it, provided there were at least eight to ten German children in the school and qualified teachers were available. In 1960 a symposium of the works of thirty-one Soviet German writers was published by the 'Progress' publishing house.

There was a further increase in cultural provisions, except in the field of education, following rehabilitation. A third newspaper, *Freundschaft*, began to publish in Tselinograd for the Kazakhstan Germans; there were more radio programmes and an occasional TV programme; and a resolution concerning literature for the Soviet Germans, which was issued on 23 July 1965 by the U.S.S.R. State Committee for the Press, led to a substantial improvement in the literary field. More books were published, a German section was set up in the 'Kazakhstan' publishing house, and there are now German sections in a number of writers' unions. All-Union seminars of German writers were held in Moscow in January 1968 and December 1970. A professional German variety ensemble, based on Karaganda in Kazakhstan, was also founded in 1968.

Since 1964 books and articles have appeared in the German press extolling the exploits of Soviet Germans during the Revolution and Second World War, and a number of scholarly articles on the Soviet Germans, albeit concentrating on relatively innocuous topics such as linguistic studies, have been published. German representation in the local soviets has also increased sixfold since their rehabilitation and now approximates their proportion in the total population. A German holds the post of U.S.S.R. Minister of Food Industries, and another holds the same office in Kazakhstan. The Germans also appear to be at least as prosperous as the local population and, to judge by the number of outstanding farms where a high proportion of the workers have German names, they have not lost their farming skills. Their work records in industry also appear to be astonishingly good.

But from the cultural point of view the facilities enjoyed by the Soviet Germans today do not approach what they had before their deportation or what other comparable' nationalities in the Soviet Union enjoy today. Book publication has proved to be disappointing – consisting of thin brochures and translations from the Russian instead of full-length original works – and there is no school in which instruction is conducted entirely in German. Even the number of German children receiving instruction in German as the mother tongue as a special subject appears to have declined during the 1960s and is now estimated to be in the region of a quarter of the total. In part this is due to a shortage of teachers, together with organizational and other problems, but the authorities could surely have overcome these by now if they had really wanted to. On the other hand, the Soviet Germans do benefit from the fact that German is one of the most widely taught foreign languages in Soviet schools and many German children learn it in this guise.

There is no evidence of any movement among the Soviet Germans to compare with that of the Crimean Tatars; but that their position is not as rosy as would appear from the Soviet German press and that they would like the restoration of their national autonomy is clear from very occasional references in *samizdat* material. Kosterin, for instance, agitated for restoration of the Volga Germans' national autonomy and Grigorenko, in listing the papers confiscated from his flat in November 1968, refers to 'documents concerning the popular movement of the Volga Germans campaigning for the restoration of their national equality'. In the foreword to his compilation on Kosterin's funeral Grigorenko also writes:

> There were very few Volga Germans (at the funeral). But their conditions are even worse than those of the Crimean Tatars. Realizing this, we express our admiration of the courage of those who came to the funeral, but we are not giving either their names or the speech of their representative.

It appears that the Germans may be seeking either repatriation to the territory of the former Volga German A.S.S.R. (to which their historical claim is probably not very strong), or else some form of autonomy. It has been suggested that when the 1959 Soviet census results, showing a total population of 1,620,000 Germans in the U.S.S.R., were published, the exact location of the Germans was deliberately omitted so as not to reveal that in certain areas they formed a sufficiently high percentage of the population to warrant the institution of some form of autonomy. Indeed in six of the existing autonomous territories of the Soviet Union the titular nationalities make up only between 8·8 and 15·1 per cent of the population. From piecemeal figures which subsequently became available it emerged that the vast majority of the Germans remained in the Asiatic part of the Soviet Union and in particular in the areas of Siberia and Kazakhstan to which they had been deported. Of the 648,000 Germans in Kazakhstan, 334,000 were in the five northern provinces where they made up 12·1 per cent of the total population, and a large number of the 820,000 Germans in the R.S.F.S.R. were in the adjacent Altay region and Omsk and Novosibirsk provinces. Other big concentrations were in Krasnoyarsk region and the Karaganda province of Kazakhstan.

The recent improvement in Moscow's relations with Bonn does not seem to have led to any improvement in the situation of the Soviet Germans, and a continuing reluctance to treat them in the same way as the other nationalities was evident with publication in *Pravda* on 17 April 1971 of the preliminary nationality breakdown figures taken from the 1970 Soviet census results. The total number of Germans in the Soviet Union was given as 1,846,000, making them the fourteenth most numerous nationality, but they were not listed among the leading nationalities in the two republics where they mainly reside, namely the R.S.F.S.R. and Kazakhstan, although many numerically smaller peoples were included. However the republican results published in the local papers did disclose the number of Germans in the R.S.F.S.R. (only 762,000 compared with 820,000 in 1959), in Kazakhstan (839,649) and some other republics. During the last fifteen years some 22,000 Germans are reported to have left the Soviet Union (this figure may have included many former P.o.W.s), which probably accounts for the relatively small increase (12 per cent) in the size of the German population since 1959 in spite of its known high birth rate. But the drop in the number of Germans in the R.S.F.S.R. may also be due partly to assimilation and partly to a drift to southern Kazakhstan and Kirgiziya, where the German population has grown disproportionately fast in the last few years. Evidence of further linguistic assimilation can be seen in the same census results. By 1959 only 75 per cent of Soviet Germans regarded German as their mother tongue, and by 1970 this figure had dropped still further to 66·8 per cent.

In the case of the Soviet Germans there would appear to have been no strategic consideration involved in the decision not to restore their national autonomy. One can only assume that the Soviet government was motivated by anti-German feelings and by their perennial fear of dual allegiances – which does not speak much for their faith in Communism since they plainly feared identification not with the D.D.R. but with West Germany.

It is also true that a restoration of some form of autonomy – besides going against the general trend of the nationalities policy – might also meet opposition from the local population, as indeed restoration of Crimean Tatar autonomy might be bitterly resented by the Ukrainians.

SELECT BIBLIOGRAPHY

Crimean Tatars
> Alexandre Bennigsen and Chantal Lemercier-Quelquejay, *Islam in the Soviet Union*, London, 1967.
> Robert Conquest, *The Nation Killers*, London, 1970.
> Edige Kirimal, *Der Nationale Kampf der Krimtürken*, Emsdetten, 1952.
> 'The Crimean Tatars', *Studies on the Soviet Union*, New Series, Vol. X, No. 1, 1970, pp. 70–97.
> Walter Kolarz, *Russia and Her Colonies*, London, 1952.
> Chantal Lemercier-Quelquejay, 'The Tatars of the Crimea: a Retrospective Summary', *Central Asian Review*, Vol. XVI, 1968, No. 1, pp. 15–25.
> Richard Pipes, *The Formation of the Soviet Union: Communism and Nationalism 1917–1923*, Cambridge, Mass., 1964.
> *Dergi* (Turkish-language quarterly published in Munich) from 1968 on.

Soviet Germans
> In addition to Conquest and Kolarz (above):
> *Osteuropa* (particularly articles by H. Roemmich in 9/1959, 2/1964 and 4/1965, and by Dieter Jahn in 9/1964, 5/6/69, 5/70 and 3/71).
> C. C. Aronsfeld, 'National Cultural Facilities for Germans in the U.S.S.R.', *Bulletin on Soviet and East European Jewish Affairs*, No. 6, December 1970, pp. 46–7.

8 JAPAN'S OUTCASTES:

THE PROBLEM OF THE BURAKUMIN

by George A. DeVos

George A. DeVos is Professor of Anthropology at the University of California, Berkeley, U.S.A. He is the editor, with Professor Hiroshi Wagatsuma, of the book, Japan's Invisible Race—Caste in Culture and Personality, *published by the University of California Press in 1967.*

JAPAN'S OUTCASTES

INTRODUCTION

The Western world has come to recognize that Japan has now taken its place not only among the leading industrial nations but among those in the forefront of world society. The great aesthetic heritage of Japanese culture has become an enrichment for us all. The Western industrial and commercial community has realized that the Japanese have much to teach it about group co-operation and competition in the field of economic enterprise. Some have even begun to ask whether there are not other lessons to be learned from Japan, as regards, for instance, the nature of their social life, and such religious philosophies as Zen Buddhism. In short, members of Western society no longer regard Japanese culture as a distant, romanticized enigma, but rather as a distinctive pattern of human thought and behaviour that it is necessary to comprehend.

It is generally believed that Japan's traditional society was hierarchial, placing emphasis on the unequal status of the sexes. While this is true, closer examination of the intimate nature of primary family life in Japan shows it to be very different from the kinds of inequality practised in Mediterranean or South American family systems which also endorse primacy of the husband. While Japanese society does remain highly hierarchical and is therefore in conflict with modern Western ideals concerning equality, attention to formal patterns alone obscures the underlying similarities between Western and Japanese traditions in this regard. And as these formal patterns themselves are in the process of disappearing, the similarities are becoming more apparent.

The Japanese resemble Western Europeans and Americans in one particular respect to which scarce attention has been given – namely, the Japanese practise forms of 'racial' discrimination within their country, not only in respect of foreigners, including fellow Asians, but against an indigenous segment of their own population.

Japanese racialism, as manifested towards outsiders, was a

disquieting discovery to the peoples of South-East Asia during the brief military ascendancy of the Japanese during the Second World War. What is less known in the West is the secret shame felt by many Japanese about the discrimination directed against two million of their own local population who are segregated in supposedly 'different' or 'special' communities (Tokushu Buraku). The inhabitants of these 'special communities' – 'Burakumin' as they are neutrally termed today both by themselves and others – exhibit all the psychological marks of oppression that characterize so many black citizens of France, Britain and the United States. The irony of the Japanese situation is that the 'racialism' practised there derives from a form of caste feeling based on a mythology of different 'racial' origins which has no basis in fact.

Various forms of discrimination exist in Japan today which continue to handicap a particular segment of the indigenous population in the social, economic and educational spheres. Since such discriminatory practices are now illegal in Japan, and theoretically do not exist, the barriers against occupational advancement and social participation erected against the Burakumin resemble to a large extent the subtle features of exclusion that Jews in Western communities have encountered for so long.

Behaviour towards the Burakumin – or 'Eta' as they were once but are now only secretly called, as this term literally means 'full of filth' – can also be said to stem from the kind of psychological attitudes observable in India in respect of the Untouchables. Indeed, because of the historic function of the Burakumin in pre-modern Japan, they were considered as ritually polluting as any of the lowly outcaste groups in India.

The fact that there is such a large group of outcastes in Japan, most of whom still live in definable rural and urban ghettoes, tends to cause incredulity on the part of Westerners. This reaction is true even of those who have spent some time in Japan, for they have remained unaware of this hidden aspect of Japanese life. The phenomenon is often denied by Japanese questioned by interested foreigners who have heard vaguely of this situation. Indeed it has been possible for people to live their lives out in Tokyo (the capital, which is free of the problem) innocent of the fact that outcastes existed elsewhere, especially in the south-western parts of Japan. My colleague, Professor Hiroshi Wagatsuma of the University of Pittsburgh, who organized and supervised our joint investigations of outcaste life, was himself, until the age of eighteen, entirely unaware of the existence of this social problem.

To understand the present situation one must first know something about the origins of caste behaviour and feeling in Japan.

ORIGINS OF CASTE

Elementary histories describe Japan's pre-modern four-tier class system, with the samurai, the warrior administrators, acting as the political elite and governing a large peasant population of agriculturalists who formed the productive backbone of the country. Ranked beneath the farmers were the artisans, or specialists with various technical skills, and in fourth-status level (officially at least) were the merchants.

This is not an entirely true picture, however, since, with the increasing development of a money economy, merchants had, in effect, taken control of economic power in the country shortly before the revolution that led to Japanese modernization.

What is usually discussed only very briefly, if mentioned at all, in these histories is that ranked below these four 'human' classes were groups of lowly 'sub-humans'. Included in the latter category were the 'Hinin', literally 'non-people', a heterogeneous group comprised of beggars, prostitutes, fugitives from justice, itinerant entertainers, mediums, diviners and religious wanderers.

Even lower than the Hinin were the 'genetically impure' Eta whose occupations were considered ritually polluting. Some worked with leather and killed animals, eating their meat. They handled the dead and acted as executioners of criminals. Others worked in hereditary crafts such as basketry which, for forgotten reasons, had become the monopoly of hereditary outcastes.

The reasons why these occupations had acquired the stigma of impurity are shrouded in history. The most acceptable theory is that the concepts of pollution already existing in indigenous Shinto beliefs were reinforced and modified by Buddhist concepts regarding killing and eating meat.

Native beliefs, probably extending back before written records, already emphasized ritual pollution and various practices had developed designed to avoid contamination by blood and death. Animal slaughters were associated with some rituals practised by hereditary specialists. Those performing such tasks, as well as others, related to childbirth, disease, death or working with the products of slain animals, were probably subjected to some form of social segregation.

The taboo on meat eating arose only after A.D. 700 when Shinto beliefs and those concerning death found in Buddhism had fused.

In the Nara period, shortly after writing was introduced, bans are recorded in the Yōrō and Taihō codes (*circa* A.D. 702) forbidding intermarriage between free men and slaves in specified occupational categories. Although slavery *per se* was later nominally abolished, attitudes concerning the contaminating nature of certain lowly occupations persisted and reinforced these marital proscriptions, thus maintaining endogamy within given groups.

Records of the Heian period describe the 'kakibe', a category of peasants and artisans, one of whose segments was engaged in 'degrading occupations' such as tomb-watching (which involved contact with the dead) and caring for and feeding birds. It is thought by some that the term Eta is derived from Etori, the name for the keepers of falcons used by the hunting nobility. Kiyome, a somewhat less common term, is interchangeable with Eta in a 13th-century document when referring to street-sweepers, well-diggers, and craftsmen enjoined to given temples. Previous to the Tokugawa period the term Eta was also loosely interchanged with Hinin, or non-people, to describe a general category of Senmin or lowly people.

The castle towns which developed in the late feudal period saw the establishment of specific areas for the outcastes who worked as armourers and engaged in basketry as well as making musical instruments for the samurai. These settlements in the castle towns did not, however, comprise the majority of outcaste settlements. According to a careful map constructed by the geographer Hall,* the majority of outcaste settlements were scattered through the major population areas of Japan.

Pollution occupations of various kinds were recognized throughout recorded Japanese history, but it is only with the total systematizing of society under the Tokugawa military *shogunate* government from 1600 onwards that they were given their fixed official classification.

These outcaste sections of the population were forced to wear special costumes by government edict. They were not allowed, for example, to use cloth for sashes. To point up a disturbing parallel with Nazi Germany, some Eta were required to wear a patch of leather sewn on their kimono sleeves to indicate their despised occupation. Japanese Senmin, the encompassing term applied to all groups of outcastes, were strictly forbidden to intermarry with members of the ordinary population. Pains were taken by the 'proper' Japanese to avoid any direct physical

* Robert B. Hall, Sr., 'A Map of Buraku Settlements in Japan', *Papers of the Michigan Academy of Science, Arts and Letters*, Vol. 47, 1962, pp. 521–7.

contact with Eta lest they had to undergo some form of cleansing to rid themselves of the resulting pollution.

In 1871, as part of a deliberate programme of modernization, the new re-established government passed an edict officially abolishing all outcaste status positions. The former outcastes were made 'new citizens' (Shin-heimin). It is noteworthy that only a few years previously a commoner had been brought to trial for killing an outcaste without provocation. The judge ruled that this commoner could be executed in punishment only if six other outcastes were also killed, since the approximate worth of one outcaste was one-seventh that of an ordinary human.

In the cause of arguments for modernization and for abolishing the outcaste status, one of the proponents drew attention to the fact that maps of the Japanese countryside omitted to indicate the presence of outcaste settlements so that the distances between the regular settlements were inaccurate. Hence, if accurate – and up-to-date – maps were to be drawn, it would be necessary to admit the existence of outcaste settlements.

Needless to say, the emancipation edict did not radically change social attitudes. Even today, in south-western Japan where one finds 80 per cent of the outcastes, there has been only a slight weakening of basic attitudes concerning the 'biological inferiority' and 'un-Japanese' nature of the outcaste people although overt behaviour towards them is noticeably more circumspect than before. It is commonly believed that the outcastes are in some way derived from non-Japanese sources. Thus the 'scientifically' oriented consider them to be Korean in origin, but this supposition is false. Any studies attempting such physical anthropological measurements as blood typing and so on have found no appreciable differences between outcastes and majority Japanese.

Today systematic studies conducted by Japanese social scientists such as Suzuki* reveal that a marginal amount of intermarriage does occur. Socially however, attitudes toward intermarriage are no less rigid in the case of majority Japanese marrying Burakumin than those of whites in the United States towards intermarriage between whites and blacks.

DISCRIMINATION

In Japan today the rural outcaste communities, on the surface at least, participate in regional rural activities, but relationships with

* Jiro Suzuki, "Burakumin no Chikisei Sokugyōkekkon: Buraku-mondai Shirō Sono Ni" in Nihon Jinbun Gakkai, Tokyo: Shakaitekai Kinkō no Kenkyū, 1953, pp. 381–391.

other communities remain very formal and careful.* It is in the cities especially that many covert forms of social and economic discrimination are practised. We documented in our volume the impoverishment to be witnessed in the urban communities. The negative stereotype persists: the outcastes are considered by the majority of the Japanese to be intellectually dull, disorderly, sexually loose, rude, violently aggressive and physically unclean.

One striking parallel between the group situation of the American Negro and that of the Burakumin is that both American and Japanese cultures strongly encourage and reward occupational and educational achievement. Yet, while a minority member is aware that he 'should' apply himself to his own training and education, he also knows he will be faced with a highly problematical situation when he applies for work in his chosen profession or skill. He must be prepared to face rejection and self-deflation.

Both cultures offer career inducements, while at the same time denying minority group members equal access to the goal. For instance, Mahara reports that in March, 1959, 166 non-Buraku children and eighty-three Buraku children graduated from a junior high school in Kyoto.† Those who were hired by small-scale enterprises employing fewer than ten workers numbered 29·8 per cent of the Buraku and 13·1 per cent of non-Buraku children. On the other hand, 15·1 per cent of non-Buraku children could obtain employment in large-scale industries with more than 1,000 workers, while only 1·5 per cent of Buraku children could do so. Working conditions in large-scale industries are generally much better than those in small-scale enterprises. The average starting salary was 5,196 yen for non-Buraku children, 4,808 yen for Buraku children.

At another junior high school near Kyoto almost all the non-Buraku graduates found jobs in April following their March graduation, or in May at the latest, while only 39 per cent of Buraku graduates could find jobs by April and May.‡ In

---

* See the descriptions of rural outcastes by Cornell, Donoghue and Norbeck in George DeVos and Hiroshi Wagatsuma, *Japan's Invisible Race*, (Berkeley: University of California Press, 1967) and the description of outcaste farmer villages in Theodore Brameld, *Japan: Culture, Education, and Change in Two Communities*, (New York: Holt, Rinehart and Winston, 1968).

† Mahara, 'Buraku no Shakai' (*Buraku Society*), 1960, pp. 131–80. Also 'Buraku no Sangyō to Shigoto' (*Industry and Work in Buraku*), in Buraku Mondai Kenkyujō (ed.), 'Buraku no Genjō' (*Present Situations in Buraku*), Tokyo and Kyoto: San-itsu Shobō, 1960, pp. 93–130.

‡ Ishida, 'Shinro Shidō to Kōkō Zennyūgaku Mondai' (*Guidance and the Problem of an Entire Class Entering High School*), Buraku, No. 9, 1961, pp. 51–55.

many cases Buraku children are actually unqualified for jobs. But it is also true that many employers are unwilling to hire them even when they are well qualified: several of the largest companies in the Osaka region are said to exclude all Burakumin as a matter of policy.

TABLE 1

Percentage of Applicants After Graduation from School Who Are Hired by Large-Scale Industries Compared with Levels Obtained in an Objective Achievement Test

OBJECTIVE ACHIEVEMENT	NON-BURAKU	BURAKU
Poor results (10–29 points)	25%	19%
Average results (30–49 points)	41%	36%
High results (50–69 points)	53%	50%

This table, compiled from Mahara's results, illustrates this tendency. There is a consistent pattern for children of Buraku background to be hired less often. The higher the achievement results, however, the less discrimination seems operative.

In the face of discrimination the easiest solution is not to try for or to discredit the goal. A protective self-identity within a submerged group may discourage effort. Although some minority individuals have the strength to survive in spite of discrimination, many react with general apathy and lack of involvement with the educational process.

There is scattered empirical support for the general impression that the Buraku children do relatively poorly in school, compared with majority group children. Their truancy rate is often high. We see an immediate parallel with the situation observed in California in respect of Negro and Mexican-American groups.

Recent reports by Japanese psychologists demonstrate that there is a systematic difference between the scores achieved on I.Q. and achievement tests by majority and outcaste children attending the same public schools. The results of a Tanaka-Binet Group I.Q. Test, administered to 351 fifth and sixth grade children including seventy-seven Buraku children at a school in Takatsuki City near Osaka, show that the scores of the Buraku children are much lower than those of the non-Buraku children (Table 2).* Recently reported test results from a small school in Fukuchiyama City show the same differences between Buraku and non-Buraku children (Table 3).† Also, the Buraku children in

---

* Tojo, 'Sengo no Dōwa Kyōiku' (*Post-war Education for Assimilation*), in Buraku Modai Kenkyūjo (ed.), 'Dōwa Kyoiku' (*Assimilation Education*), Tokyo and Kyoto: San-itsu Shobō, 1960, pp. 49–98. 'Dōwa Kyōiku Ron' (*Debate on Assimilation*), Tokyo: Shin Hyōron Sha.

† Nishimoto, 'Buraku Mondai to Dōwa Kyōiku' (*Buraku Problems and Assimilation Education*), Tokyo: Sōbunsha, 1960, p. 71.

Fukuchiyama City are shown as doing less well than their non-Buraku classmates at both primary and junior high school levels (Table 4).*

Standard achievement tests devised by the Ministry of Education were given to a group of 247 students, eighty-three of them Buraku children, at a junior high school in Kyoto.

TABLE 2

*Comparison of Buraku and Majority Group Children
on the Tanaka-Binet Test in a City near Osaka*

I.Q.	NON-BURAKU CHILDREN (N = 274)	BURAKU CHILDREN (N = 77)
Above 125	*23·3%*	*2·6%*
124–109	*31·8%*	*19·5%*
108–93	*23·3%*	*22·1%*
92–77	*11·7%*	*18·2%*
Below 76	*9·9%*	*37·6%*

TABLE 3

*Comparison of Tanaka-Binet Tests of Primary
School Children in Fukuchiyama City*

	N	AVERAGE I.Q.
Buraku boys	*10*	*89*
Buraku girls	*9*	*87*
Non-Buraku boys	*10*	*105*
Non-Buraku girls	*12*	*103*

TABLE 4

Comparison of Grade Point Averages Obtained in Fukuchiyama City

		N	GRADE POINT AVERAGE
Primary school	*Buraku boys*	*12*	*2·29*
	Buraku girls	*10*	*2·59*
	Non-Buraku boys	*10*	*3·29*
	Non-Buraku girls	*15*	*3·16*
Junior high	*Buraku students*	*8*	*2·2*
	Non-Buraku students	*11*	*3·3*

TABLE 5

*Comparison of Standard Achievement Test Scores
in a Kyoto Junior High School*

	NON-BURAKU CHILDREN (N = 164)	BURAKU CHILDREN (N = 83)
Japanese	*55·5%*	*46·5%*
Humanities	*61·8%*	*46·6%*
Mathematics	*49·9%*	*36·4%*
Science	*51·1%*	*41·0%*

Averages in four subjects showed consistently higher achievement by the non-Buraku than by Buraku students (Table 5).*

* Nishimoto.

315

The more numerous studies undertaken in the United States similarly attest to the substandard functioning of children from culturally underprivileged ethnic backgrounds. Racialists would argue that this reflects innate differences in ability. We would argue that in both cases, in Japan were there is no racial difference, and in the United States, the results, partly at least, reflect early damage to social self-identity and self-respect vis-à-vis cultural expectations held towards a traditionally disparaged group.

SOCIAL DEVIANCY

It is apparent that in the case of the Japanese outcastes continued social discrimination towards them as a subordinate minority induces the continuance of a separate social self-identity and, in many instances, causes a self-hatred that is both personally and socially debilitating to the individual.

Such minority self-identities may involve social retreat into ghetto enclaves or, if contact with the majority is necessary or expedient, the assumption of deviant social roles vis-à-vis the majority group. These deviant roles often involve a great deal of covert hostility towards any form of authority exercised by members of the majority group. Such feelings are a consequence of one generation after another experiencing exploitation.

In effect, the socialization of minority group members such as the Burakumin becomes part of life within the group itself. Indeed, the urban Buraku create special experiences for growing children rarely experienced by members of the majority culture. Looser sexual practices, experiences of violence and aggression within urban ghettos *do* create what can be identified as patterns of differential socialization. One finds that outcaste children *are* more prone to aggressiveness and in a sense they do actualize the stereotypes attributed to them, at least in some measure and in some numbers of their population.

For example, in a fairly large-scale testing conducted in a school where children were identified by caste background, outcaste children in over 30 per cent of the cases produced I.Q. scores on individual Binet-type intelligence tests below 75. This kind of poor showing on intelligence tests is due to forms of social debilitation rather than any biological differentiation between groups.

When one examines actual social practices in cities today there appears to be a studied avoidance of overt discrimination on the part of government officials, teachers and police. Nevertheless there is a continued transmission of attitudes which can readily be sensed by children. The lessening of the more conspicuous forms of social discrimination do not lessen the effects of self-perpetuating pejorative self-images apparent within the outcaste group. Children brought up in the urban outcaste communities are still exposed to conditions that help perpetuate through such internalization their debilitated social status. A counterforce like Buraku 'pride' is not sufficiently strong to overcome the situation. Early disadvantages are compounded with the years so that by adulthood many have already acquired an irreversible sense of their inferior social destiny.*

Understandably various types of social deviancy are more prevalent in urban outcaste communities. According to our research, rates of delinquency are three and a half times those found in ordinary populations. Health authorities encounter resistance and apathy in trying to treat trichoma and other diseases endemic in some Buraku communities. A number of outcastes eventually follow deviant careers as members of outlaw gangs or as prostitutes, occupations in which family affiliations are not as closely scrutinized as in regular jobs.

It must be emphasized that deviant courses of action occur only among a minority of the outcastes, although it is a significantly high proportion compared with the main body of the population. The great majority of outcastes are apathetically resigned to their economically depressed lot in life although a growing number of them are advancing occupationally. There are notable cases of achievement and accomplishment as well as failure. Today in Japan, government careers are no longer closed to the Burakumin. Many of the educated do in fact obtain bureaucratic positions, or become active in politics. Some manage to succeed on the basis of their professional merit.

In such cases, however, the problem of whether or not to deny an outcaste background in order to 'pass' becomes a source of serious inner conflict for the outcaste individual who has already surmounted the difficulties involved in overcoming apathy and psychological retreat.

The roles which Japanese outcastes are expected to play in society, paralleling those of other disparaged minority groups such as the American Negroes or Indians, are negatively defined. To counter such negative role expectations in itself demands a great

---

* A social study made in the early 1960s showed that approximately 60 per cent of the total unemployed in Japan were Burakumin. More recent estimates put the figure at perhaps 30 per cent despite a severe shortage of labour resulting from the nation's economic boom. The Burakumin account for only 3 per cent of the population at most (their estimate), or a mere 1 per cent according to government statistics.

deal of determination and energy; the outcaste must in a sense prove that he can play an unexpected role in his society. Such extra effort is not required of members of the majority group who have similar aspirations.

Experiencing a succession of rebuffs or failures in seeking an occupational career is likely to produce acceptance of failure more readily in a minority group member who has already learned to expect failure than in a member of a majority group who interprets such setbacks as merely temporary, and likely to be overcome by persistence.

Some of the most poignant material obtained in our interviews relates to how members of the outcaste group become aware of their outcaste status at a fairly early age, finding themselves to be hated, feared and despised by members of the wider society. They in turn develop strong hatreds towards this wider society. But mutual hatred and self-hatred also abound within the group.

PROCESS OF PASSING

Today the only way one can identify an outcaste with any degree of certainty is to know his place of residence. If he manages to live in an area outside one of the outcaste settlements he may attempt to hide his identity. For example, some outcaste school-children hide their outcaste identity from their fellow pupils by getting off at bus or streetcar stops some distance from their homes. White-collar workers may also use such means of avoiding identification by their colleagues with whom they ride home.

An individual who seeks to hide his outcaste background more systematically must take more serious precautions. Passing requires the kind of deliberate foresight and planning which drastically limits the numbers of those seeking this avenue of escape. It is only among a very small minority of occupationally middle-class outcastes that the elaborate precautions necessary for complete passing are practised. Parenthetically it must be noted that, as in all situations of this kind where caste exists, one can in a sense be outcasted by contact with outcastes.

The number of outcastes is much higher today in proportion to the population than it was when the number of Eta-Hinin was estimated at the time of the emancipation. Whereas those termed Hinin did disappear, the Eta, who were branded as heredit-arily defective humans, multiplied eight-fold their proportionate population. Obviously a differential birth-rate by itself could not have contributed to so large an increase in their proportion of the population.

Every Japanese is required to have an identification certificate, which is issued in his place of registry. It states not only his current but also his previous place of residence. The procedure for disguising one's origin within an outcaste community is quite complicated as it requires changing one's place of registry several times so that the original place of residence is finally removed from the registration form. A number of white-collar outcastes have gone through this cumbersome process in order to disguise their origins. In one study of four different communities reported on by Suzuki, only 70 per cent of the households investigated were found to be maintaining their registry within obviously outcaste areas. Nevertheless, in most instances, these individuals had not completely severed their social relationships with other outcastes, a step necessary to ensure successful passing.

Passing requires a fair amount of both financial independence and psychological freedom. If a person is financially well off, he can afford to educate his children so as to equip them for a white-collar or professional occupation. With such education and with some parental financial backing, the children can move out of the outcaste community and attempt to overcome both the external sanctions and the inner psychic barriers against passing. Those who, through personal enterprise, have become successful in one of the occupations that are defined as outcaste, such as shoe-making or meat processing, have to change those occupations if they wish to join the majority community.

Attempts to pass are not easy, since the person must cut himself off from his primary ties and from the friendships of childhood. If he maintains contact with members of his family or community or visits them often, he risks discovery. It must be noted, too, that in Japanese culture family relationships have a much deeper emotional meaning than is the case in the West, since Japanese culture does not encourage the individual in the same degree to adopt an independent, individualistic life pattern.

Finally, the problem of passing becomes most excruciating in the circumstances of marriage. In middle-class circles of Japanese society go-betweens are used to insure the appropriateness of marriage bonds between families. In effect, for passing outcastes, the only safe marriage arrangement is one with someone else who is also passing. In such a social network there is continual tension over possible exposure. The revelation that one family is of outcaste origin may work like a falling domino spreading disclosure to others with whom they are affiliated.

Added to these social difficulties which make passing difficult are the internal psychological difficulties concerning personal integrity which confront thoughtful members of the outcaste group. For example, one informant, a university student who is successfully passing, explained that he frequently felt a strong impulse to declare himself to those with whom he was talking or working; he felt an urge to shout loudly that he was a Burakumin. Trying to analyse the reasons behind this impulse, he said that his attitude towards passing was extremely complicated and ambivalent.

This man is presently successful but feels that in some way it is not quite morally right to hide his background. He considers that doing so is to admit and in a way to accept the prejudice and discrimination directed towards his people by the majority society. What he really wants of the majority society is for it to know all about him and accept him fully. He knows too well, however, that if he discloses his background he will jeopardize his chances for career advancement and lose the friendship of at least some of the individuals who presently accept him on his own merits. He feels very guilty about passing. He knows he is being unfair to his relatives and friends because he is being treated as an ordinary person while they are still suffering the disadvantages of outcaste status. This informant also admits that at heart he really hates everyone who does not have an outcaste background. Sudden feelings of hostility well up within him towards outsiders. At such times particularly he feels the temptation to declare his background openly and to frighten people away as he used to do when he was a child and found that he could scare other children by announcing his background.

POLITICAL ACTIVITY

In Japan today there are political movements which emphasize the necessity of maintaining one's integrity by facing one's outcaste origins. Outcastes are constrained to join in attempts to initiate political and social change which would help overcome the discrimination suffered by the whole outcaste group.

The idea that the outcastes and their problems would simply be absorbed into regular Japanese society has been abandoned by most observers as a realistic possibility. Passing, in effect, is an impossible solution. The outcastes must be accepted for themselves before they can be assimilated or no longer feel that their identity is a source of external discrimination and internal debilitation.

There is a long history of political militancy among the Japanese outcastes which has in the course of time tended to assume a fixed leftist, Marxist orientation. The militant movement, carried on by Burakumin leaders with the assistance of some sympathetic majority citizens, began soon after the emancipation edict in 1872. These early efforts were local and unorganized. But by 1903 a large-scale organization, the Dai Nippon Dōhō Yūwa Kai (The Greater Japan Fraternal Conciliation Society), was established. It aimed to help the outcastes by promoting self-improvement in morals, manners and sanitation. After the First World War a more militant liberation movement known as the 'Levellers Association' (Suiheisha) was inaugurated. It adopted for its banner a symbol representing social martyrdom which was described as 'a crown of thorns the colour of blood against a black background of darkness'. It is interesting to note that the first militant members of the Suiheisha were influenced by Christian socialism as well as by Buddhist concepts.

Soon, however, with the increasing influence of Marxism in Japan, the movement began to diverge in three ideological directions: anarchism, communism, and what might be broadly termed 'revisionism'. By 1930 the movement took a clear leftist turn and established close ties with the more radical union movements supported by labourers as well as farmers. In theory and strategy the fight against caste discrimination was incorporated into the broader context of class struggle and the espousal of a proletarian revolution. For nearly ten years the communist red flag and the flag with the crown of thorns were flown side by side at Suiheisha meetings.

In the early thirties the militarists took power and moved Japan into war. Leftist activities were severely curtailed by government pressure. Special police were called in, forcing known leftist movements underground. At a final meeting in 1940 the Suiheisha movement capitulated, vowed loyalty to the emperor and in effect was dissolved for the duration of the war.

After the Second World War, outcastes united and formed a committee on Buraku liberation which evolved into the presently functioning Buraku Liberation League, known as the Kaihō Dōmei. It is this Marxist-oriented organization which at present spearheads militant political activity in outcaste communities.

There is also the active rival organization, the Dōwakai (Integrationist League), which is composed of more moderate and conservative members and operates in a number of rural communities as well as in some of the urban centres. This organization tends to fight for political control over particular Buraku with the Kaihō Dōmei. In general it advocates more moderate forms of pressure on the majority community. Its objectives are generally similar, however, although socially and politically its members tend to be upper-status outcastes who are in sympathy with the more conservative Liberal Democratic party. More recently some have moved over to the Kōmeitō party, the somewhat rightist reform party which is a political offshoot of the Sokagakkai, a new religious organization affiliated with Nichiren Buddhism.

Basically the Dōwakai incorporates the attitudes of the earlier Yūwa or 'peaceful meeting together' movements of the pre-war period. These movements emphasized self-improvement and internal development within the Buraku community rather than a more aggressive pressure on outside society. The Dōwakai is somewhat opposed to producing the tensions associated with open confrontation, as it is to any Marxist ideology with its seeming potential for violence.

In 1947 an outstanding Buraku leader, Jiichirō Matsumoto, considered one of the founders of the Kaihō Dōmei, ran on a socialist party ticket and was elected to the reorganized Japanese Diet. It is noteworthy that he received over 400,000 votes. Nine other Burakumin were elected either to the House of Councillors or the House of Representatives for the first time in Japanese history. In the revolutionary, innovative atmosphere of the times, Matsumoto was elected Vice-President of the House of Councillors, shattering all precedent. He was the first outcaste to enter the imperial palace and be granted audience with the emperor.

The following year Matsumoto shocked many by his refusal to bow in the traditional kow-tow to the emperor at the formal opening session of the second post-war Diet. The conservatives in the Diet vowed to purge him and, through clever manipulation of the American military authorities, had his name introduced on a purge list which included those leaders whom war crimes trials had judged responsible for the Japanese war effort.

It is questionable whether the American military authorities themselves understood why Premier Yoshida was insistent on holding back Matsumoto's name when the policy of purging began to wane. Finally, in August of 1951, Matsumoto was reinstated along with 13,000 others. Ever since, however, the outcastes have taken a decidedly anti-American as well as pro-Marxist line in their political programmes.

The American post-war land tenure reforms were of particular benefit to many of the outcastes. They were given ownership of land on which they had been tenant farmers for generations. Many of these formerly impoverished villages are at present doing very well economically.

In the rural areas at present a careful politeness is observed between members of outcaste communities and residents of majority villages. It is generally true that rural outcaste communities suffer less today from the effects of outcaste status – except for difficulties in inter-marriage – than do the urban outcaste communities. The pressure of the Kaihō Dōmei has been much more successful in upgrading the status of the outcaste farmers than of the city labourers.

In some areas the Dōwakai's activities have paralleled those of the Kaihō Dōmei, but its leaders sometimes lack the persistence shown by the Kaihō Dōmei leadership.

In the cities it has been principally the Kaihō Dōmei that has pressed strongly for slum clearance, welfare legislation, extension and improvement of sewage disposal facilities and water supplies, the expansion of nursery clinics and work centres, and the granting of loans to small-scale Buraku industries.

During the past few years pressure groups working at the local level in some of the larger cities have brought about notable improvements. Public housing has begun to progress in some of the worst city slums. Nevertheless, a trip today through the cities of Kobe, Osaka or Kyoto reveals large areas with totally inadequate sanitation and housing. In some of these areas one sees side by side the most abysmal hovels and new concrete five-storey apartment houses. The rentals charged in the hovels are higher than those in the government housing, and pressure to get into the better housing is severe. The extent of government housing is still inadequate to meet the needs of a good proportion of the urban outcastes.

The Kaihō Dōmei has generally supported union worker activities but has been relatively unsuccessful in gaining reciprocal support from the unions in its efforts to secure improved conditions for the outcastes. The situation is roughly comparable to what one finds in the United States; that is to say, most unions deliberately avoid, or are actively biased against, coming out in support of black workers. In Japan many union workers in the larger factories harbour prejudices and are opposed to outcastes being given access to the better jobs in industry.

AMELIORATIVE MEASURES

In 1966 a special committee was set up in the Diet to investigate outcaste problems. By 1968 it had prepared a report, composed mainly of already dated material. It was very imprecise in the matter of how many outcastes there actually were in Japan and made a conservative estimate of their numbers. The committee produced no new evidence regarding social conditions and its findings were quietly put aside, having had no noticeable effect on national legislation.

A 'Dōwa Affairs' research office was established by the Prime Minister and given the task of gathering and publishing statistics on Buraku problems from time to time. Buraku leaders are sceptical about this recent move, however, and do not believe it will cause the national government to pay greater attention to Buraku problems.

In fairness it should be noted that there has been some local government activity in certain areas. As mentioned, the cities of Kyoto, Osaka and Kobe, which have large populations of Burakumin, have made sporadic attempts at slum clearance. Kobe has staged educational campaigns, including the intro-duction of grade school textbooks stressing the neighbourly relationships and friendships which are possible between children of Korean as well as outcaste background and the majority children.

Recent surveys of teachers show that they are aware that special educational programmes are necessary to help eliminate discrimi-nation. In a questionnaire administered in 1966, close to 75 per cent of the teachers said they believed such measures were necessary.

One of the problems involved in conducting anti-discrimination programmes in the schools is the uncertainty about whether it is advisable to acknowledge openly that children are of outcaste origin. At times children who have been passing are exposed by such school programmes and are thereby put into categories which they themselves have attempted to avoid. Education has al-ready had some effect in one respect: people are beginning to accept the fact that feudal caste segregation was the origin of the outcaste's differentiation rather than any true racial difference from other Japanese.

It is hard as yet to say what the long-range result of school programmes against discrimination will be. It is my impression, as well as that of others with whom I have talked, that there is much less overt contact between outcastes in the student popula-tion in Japan than there is between black and white students in the United States. The peculiar nature of the problem makes for difficulties in acknowledging one's origin openly. Relatively few outcastes who enter major institutions of higher learning are willing to make a self-conscious cause out of their social status.

It is noteworthy that relatively little action is taken by either Christian or Buddhist churches in Japan to alleviate the outcaste situation. There is a large Catholic settlement house in Kyoto and Protestant missionaries have a settlement in the city of Hiroshima. The Buddhist churches, however, generally avoid any direct involvement with the outcaste problem. The Kōmeitō, the political party related to the Sōkagakkai new religion movement, also avoids any too clear reference to the fact that numbers of former outcastes in local areas have joined their organization. These organizations seem to feel that open discussion of the outcaste problem would be compromising to them. Members of religious organizations, when approached on the matter, indicate sympathy with the outcaste cause but they have put little or nothing in print except rather vague statements expressing disapproval of any form of social discrimination.

In practice the Kaihō Dōmei is the one group that addresses itself with any vigour to anti-discrimination activities. This poses a dilemma for more conservative members of the outcaste group who are seeking allies in the majority society. These people do not approve of the Marxist attitudes held by the Kaihō Dōmei but they find no other organization which is as effective in combating discrimination.

As a final word it should be said that the prejudice directed towards Japanese outcastes resembles in many respects the prejudice felt today in Japan about Japanese citizens of Korean origin.

It is only an impression, which I cannot substantiate factually, but it seems to be much simpler in Japan to cross the marriage barrier in marrying a Korean than in marrying someone from a so-called 'special community'. This is in spite of the fact that many of the negative stereotypes associated with outcastes are also attributed to Koreans. For a Japanese to cross that terrible barrier created by his caste feelings is a much greater task psychologically than establishing relationships with Chinese or Koreans or other Asians. Certainly it is much more acceptable to marry a Caucasian than a member of Japan's Invisible Race.

APPENDIX ONE

THE AINU MINORITY GROUP

The Ainu are not a present-day social problem for two reasons. First, they have almost entirely disappeared through intermarriage, and second, most of the others have deliberately followed a self-imposed policy of assimilation. Only several hundred are to be found in the special Ainu communities located on the northern island of Hokkaido. Until A.D. 700 the Ainu were in possession of a considerable portion of the northern part of Honshu and all of Hokkaido. They were fierce warriors and it took approximately 800 years for the Japanese to bring about their submission. For a great period of prehistory and part of the historical period the territory above Tokyo was a frontier region.

The basic attitudes held toward the Ainu are not as pejorative as towards the outcastes. They are not considered unclean. To draw an analogy, the Ainu have been treated ambivalently very much as the American Indians have been, in contrast to the caste distinctions which underlie the treatment of American blacks. At the present time the Japanese tend to regard the Ainu as quaint; a number of Japanese tourists visit Ainu 'reservations' to see professionals perform the bear dance, etc. According to some estimates there are fewer than 200 to 300 pure-blood Ainu left.

APPENDIX TWO

Comparison of Absences in Buraku and Non-Buraku Children (1960)

	NON-BURAKU CHILDREN	BURAKU CHILDREN
Primary School	0·49%	6·26%
Junior High School	1·38%	32·9%

The above table is based on an investigation carried out by the Welfare Department of the Kochi Prefectural Government in Sholoku Island, showing that long-term absenteeism is much more prevalent among Buraku children than non-Buraku children. Research in Nara Prefecture shows the same general prevalence of long-term absenteeism among Buraku children throughout the schools of the prefecture.

Comparison of Absentee Rates in Schools with and without Buraku Children (1963)

		NUMBER OF SCHOOLS	NUMBER OF ENROLLED CHILDREN	NUMBER OF ABSENT CHILDREN
Primary Schools	*With Buraku Children*	63	34,254	419 (1·2%)
	Without Buraku Children	254	59,516	480 (0·81%)
Junior High Schools	*With Buraku Children*	49	24,811	1,556 (6·2%)
	Without Buraku Children	76	20,381	520 (2·06%)

APPENDIX THREE

It was once believed in certain parts of Japan that the Burakumin bore upon their persons an inherited physical stigma – a bluish birth-mark (aza) under each arm. The following poem, written by a Buraku poet, Maruoka Tadao, conveys the torment of living with this symbolic brand of the outcaste.

LET COME THE DAY TO SAY 'ONCE IT WAS SO'

I heard whispering
Like the flow of wind from mouth to mouth
That under each armpit I am marked,
The size of an open hand.

Was it inherited from an ancient time?
My parents, so too I've heard
Were also bruised by nature's brand.

Yet of them no memory affords
Sight or feel of such a spot.

But in childhood I learned,
Through cruel heavy winks, how instinctively to hide.

What was it I so naively wrapped with rags,
And, hidden, dragged through dark months and years?

In these concealing rags, I had hid my heart,
When refound, it was sorely bruised
Shrivelled red from stigma I sought to lose.

Without some fresh exposure, my songs would end in lies;
Tightly bound bruises but increase the inner plight.

Who marked my sides? For what unknown cause?
Why such a brand upon my very self and soul?
Even today, my ebbing thoughts,
So pale and cold, transparent as glass,
Hold me awake.

AFTERWORD:

WHO'S TO BLAME?

by Richard and Hephzibah Hauser

*Richard Hauser is a social psychologist who was born
in Vienna and served with the British army. He is
Senior Research Fellow in Social Planning at
Nottingham University. He and his wife Hephzibah
Menuhin have worked with prisoners and homosexuals
and on disarmament problems in many countries,
and together have written* The Fraternal Society.

AFTERWORD

WHO'S TO BLAME?

A scapegoat is a person, a group of people, a sector of society, or sometimes even a nation, which has the misfortune to be used as a lightning conductor for the dissatisfaction of a more powerful group. Very often, there may be no real reason for the majority to be hostile to the scapegoat, but what always appears to be the case is that the true reasons for the majority's dissatisfaction vis-à-vis its own ruling élite are either not known to the majority itself (i.e. unconscious), or not allowed to be expressed. Therefore, repressed, negative and hostile feelings are transferred on to the scapegoat. Scapegoats occur in situations where there is an imbalance between power and citizens' rights. They are often an élite's safeguard in its dealings with a dissatisfied and potentially dangerous majority.

Scapegoats may be:

(a) The despised 'outsider' group, the most obvious of scapegoat groups – some 'foreigners', a minority which has different attitudes, values and habits. A likely scapegoat group should be easily recognizable, that is, distinguishable by colour, language or other characteristics: these are assets 'helpful' to persecutors. But if there is no such obvious group, the persecutors will pick on any other sub-group which can be made to qualify and turn them into scapegoats. These groups are easy targets and outlets for the wrath of the population who often feel that their status is 'degraded' by having to live or work next to them.

(b) Despised members at the bottom level of their own majority or subculture, who can be singled out easily as scapegoats owing to their poverty, dirtiness, poor education and negative attitudes to law and morality. These conditions are mainly a direct result of starvation by the élite of opportunities for social progress, yet it is for these very conditions (which they themselves are not responsible for) that the scapegoat groups are blamed and persecuted.

(c) Those who were yesterday's fallen leaders and who have to be humiliated and demoralized so that nobody will want to identify with them and help them to stage a comeback. By proving their powerlessness, not only they, but also any allies they might have had, are frightened off. This is a very popular way of getting rid of competing forces.

(d) Young people or any other group who subscribe to different value patterns and towards whom the majority feels hostility. These may be students or intellectuals, or simply people who are insufficiently identified with the élite, could be critical of it, and therefore qualify as scapegoats.

(e) Any member of the élite itself (in the majority in power), who can conveniently be blamed for a situation endangering the élite, and declared guilty in order to appease the majority and thereby save the rest of the élitist establishment.

Where there is as much élitism as there is today – linguistic, bureaucratic, political, industrial, international – easing the tension, removing the symptom or patching up the wounds will not prevent the scapegoat syndrome from expanding. The victim's punishment, meted out by an aggressor in the hope of mitigating his own anxiety, will only produce further and further regression into patterns of childish helplessness on the part of the one, and childish rage on the part of the other.

Who can direct the battleground of forces which seem to lie outside ourselves, and reverse the nightmarish cycle to produce, if not immediate happiness, at least a sense of hope? What stands between *us* and making the dream come true?

In any family, community, hospital, school or nation, the evaluation of scapegoatism is a measurement of the social health of that particular group. The temptation to gloss over potential or real scapegoat situations by superficial improvements should be avoided at all costs. It merely postpones issues which will explode at a later time, without warning, and probably in some highly inconvenient manner. Recent events in Northern Ireland are, unfortunately, an excellent illustration of this.

What should be done about scapegoatism? Considering that it exists in all economic categories, it should be evaluated in the first place within the total social situation from the point of view of: (1) the majority, (2) the minority, (3) the conflict between majority and minority or subculture, and (4) the framework, i.e. the legal structure which limits hostile behaviour, and within which citizens may feel safe from harm, as long as it is respected and accepted by all. The framework itself should be examined from the standpoint of the stress to which it is being subjected (a) from prejudices and stereotypes within the majority/minority; and (b) from the felt or real disparity or injustice in treatment meted out to minority members, especially minority children. If a majority is allowed to crush all legitimate opposition and to take over the framework for its own purposes, scapegoatism will flourish with disastrous results. It should also be determined who are the provokers of incidents and what mythology surrounds the scapegoat group.

To maintain a high level of community health, there is hardly anything that is more important than to develop an awareness of the scapegoat syndrome from the earliest school years onward. Furthermore, this awareness needs to be extended throughout the entire community by means of every possible teaching aid, sketches, sociodrama, exhibitions and action surveys. The 'scapegoat kit' must include every possible reference to the problem which can be tied in with personal or group experience, such as, when does a joke go sour? When does physical threat turn into physical violence? When are some children humiliated in front of others? When is self-defence considered an act of aggression by the other side? When are rationalized arguments used to justify explosive outlets on both sides in order to relieve unbearable pressure?

Scapegoat watchers or catalysts should be trained to be continually on the watch for hated groups – permitted, despised, or semi-suppressed. The watchers could prepare maps (national and international) with particular scapegoat areas to be filled in by those who know best. As the apparent helplessness of a group lacking organized defence seems to be the single greatest provocation to brutality, it is possible that the very fact that such a watch is being kept could serve to restrain the lawlessness of potentially aggressive groups.

Trained teams should be sent into areas to evaluate sociopathological forces and to prevent the escalation of violence in particularly dangerous situations – by taking pre-emptive action if necessary, such as isolating the social disease-carriers. If this attempt at organized defence is carried out in a deliberately constructive spirit, not in revenge, it may help to rally those forces in the community which might create a healthy polarization.

Organizations interested in social development could help by setting up seminars and mobile exhibitions illustrating past and present scapegoat situations, showing how these may be measured, and suggesting how they may be prevented in future.

For instance, is the battered baby a 'normal' concomitant of present-day family life, or is it the result of parents' unpreparedness to carry frustrations and responsibility? Is there a parallel between baby battering and 'overkill'? For every person on earth today there are 35,000 lbs of TNT but not 5 lbs of rice. This is not likely to improve personal, community, national or international relations. Indeed, one may continue to expect psychopathic crises on the personal level, and riots, civil war and national war in society, until a new approach to value-questions in human society creates alternative systems which will bypass the need to seek relief from hopeless anxiety by searching for 'Who's to blame?'

A scapegoat mood is highly contagious, and if not taken in hand with determination will spread like wildfire. It is always a threat to democracy and, because the demagogue fears more than anything else the people's ability to think and to act for themselves, democracy is usually the first victim of scapegoatism. Yet if the minimal, unanimously accepted, standards of social behaviour were to be kept at a high enough level, so that people felt ashamed of themselves before their disapproving peers for acting anti-socially, they would automatically refrain from indulging in behaviour which would cause them to lose status.

No one can expect to love or to be loved by (nor even to like or to be liked by) everyone else. However, each person may, no matter who they are, recognize in others their own innate will to live and to do so significantly, outstandingly, originally; to be appreciated; and to be creative by asserting to the fullest extent their gift of personality. If we are not aware of our potential value as human beings, we will seek to establish it in a negative way, perhaps by becoming outstandingly anti-social. One may be someone at the expense of others as well as in the service of others. The problem is hardly a complicated one. It merely requires that we should not be satisfied with others suffering what we consider unacceptable for ourselves.

INDEX

Abboud, Gen. Ibrahim: rules Sudan, 87–9

Adelgeim, Pavel, 235–6

Africa: nationalist parties, 149–53; Brazilian influences, 162–3

Africa, East and Central: anti-Asian speeches, 30; land policy, 30; Africans felt exploited by Asians, 33–4; non-citizen statistics, 43; restrictions on non-citizens, 44; politics, 65–7; pluralism, 67–9; statistics of Asians, 72; *see also* Asians and individual countries

African National Congress: policy, 152–3

African National Council: formed, 153

Aga Khan, 69

Ainu minority: *see* Japan

Alier, Abel, 98

Amado, Jorge, 180

American Jewish Congress, 253

Amin, Idi, 115

Amnesty International, 10

Anya Nya; S. Sudan guerrillas, 89, 91, 94–5, 98

Ardrey, Robert: quoted, 193

Arusha Declaration (1967), 59, 61

Asians (East and Central Africa): definition, 24; historical background, 25–6; indentured and 'free' immigrants, 26–7; opposition to, 27–8; growth, 29; British policy, 30–1; employment, 31–2; education, 32–3 and African independence, 35–6; position at independence, 36–8; citizenship schemes, 38–41; citizenship statistics, 42; trade licensing, 45–7; in industry, 47; emigration: to Britain, 48–53; to Canada, 53; financial and family factors in emigration, 55–6; official policy towards Asians, 57–8; economic factors, 58–62; effect of educational reforms, 63–5; participation in politics, 65–7; social relations, 67–71; Ismailis, 69–70

Azevedo, Thales de, 173n, 174

Baptists in Russia: origins, 243–4; closure of churches, 243; the Brest case, 244–5; schism of Council of Churches, 245; Council leaders persecuted, 245; reform Baptists, 245–6; state recognition, 246–7; educational discrimination against, 247; prison sentences and conditions, 247–9

Bastide, Roger, 172

Beshir, Mohamed Omer: quoted, 86

Bourdeaux, Michael, 217; *Patriarch and Prophets*, 222, 234;

335

ence (1965), 90; elections (1966-8), 90–1; Anzanu Liberation Front formed 91; military coup (1969), 91; 'Peoples ... charter', 93; South gets quasi-autonomy, 92–3; southerners in office, 94; religious and education reforms, 94; Anya-Nya activity, 95–6; refugees in neighbouring countries, 96–7; Abbis Ababa agreement (1972), 98; Southern government established, 98; Eritrean refugees, 110; relations with Uganda, 115; relations with Ethiopia, 116

Sunday Times, The: on Rhodesia, 122

Tadao, Maruoka (Buraku poet): poem, 'Let come the day . . ', 327

Tagor, Rabindranath: quoted, 12

Talantov, Boris, 233, 235

Tanganyika: *see* Tanzania

Tanzania: Asian association, 35; Tanzania African National Union, 35; policy towards Asians, 40–1; five-year plan (1964), 59; trading, 60; education reforms, 63–4; national service, 70; statistics of Asians, 72

Tatars, Crimean: deported by Stalin, 270; Crimean independent Khanate, 274; annexed by Russia, 275; demand for federation, 275; National Party declared revolutionary, 276; Lenin's policy, 276; Crimean Autonomous Soviet Socialist Republic set up (1921), 276; purge of 'bourgeois', 277; abolition of C.A.S.S.R.; deportations, 279–82; campaign for return, 283–6; absolved of treachery 287–8; efforts to return to Crimea, 289; arrest of leaders, 292; 'Case 109' trial, 294–5; other trials, 295–6; Russian attitude, 297; Tatar referendum, 298; desire for repatriation, 298; Russian fears of pressure groups, 299

Thaku, Harry, 35

Tikhon, Patriarch, 218

Toynbee, Arnold: quoted, 118, 121

Tredgold, Sir Robert, 133n

Trubnikova, Alla, 221

Turkey and Crimean Tatars, 273–5, 278

Uganda: India and Muslim support, 35; Action Group, 35; Asian citizenship, 41; work permits, 45; Trade Licensing Act, 45–6; Asian citizenship applications, 50; Asian monopoly in cotton, 58; nationalization, 61; education reform, 63; statistics of Asians, 72; Sudanese refugees, 96; relations with Sudan, 115

Uniates: *see* Roman Catholics

Union of Soviet Socialist Republics: *see* Russia

United Nations charter, 12

United Nations Human Rights, 21

United States: and Ethiopia, 114–15; racial similarities with Brazil, 168

University College, Salisbury (Rhodesia), 128n

Velchkovsky, Vasili, 243

Verona Fathers: in Sudan, 94

Volga Germans: *see* Germans, Volga